THE

DEFINITIVE HISTORY

OF THE

HEART OF MIDLOTHIAN

FOOTBALL CLUB

Produced by

Heart of Midlothian plc

Written by

Alex H. Knight - Club Archivist

ISBN 978-0-9564143-0-4

Published in Great Britain in 2009

Published and Written
by Alex H Knight

Produced by MD Print and Design, Edinburgh

INTRODUCTION

In 2001 when asked to check "The Official Illustrated History of Edinburgh's Oldest League Club", I found several differences to my own records and proceeded to check thirteen other books written about the Heart of Midlothian Football Club.

As a result a list of over 300 'differences' amongst them and my own records, was produced. The intention was to research all available sources to confirm which information was correct. Thus was born the idea of a book on "The Definitive History".

While the research was progressing the offer was made in July 2005, for me to become the Club Archivist to trace all archival material held by the club and to produce an inventory of memorabilia, souvenirs and trophies. Julia Goncaruk suggested that we open a mini museum and proposed a longer term plan to have a larger museum within the latest development of the stadium. The idea of a mini museum was dropped in 2006 to await the development of the Main Stand.

Nine Hearts supporters known to me, as collectors, recorders, general historians and statisticians were invited to make up the membership of an Archive Group. The only provision was that the club had to be provided with a copy of all information found and recorded. Commencing in September 2005 the Group confirmed every result of matches played by Hearts in the Scottish Cup – from 1875, the League – from 1890, the League Cup – from 1947 and European competitions – from 1958. The next check was of all Hearts players who had made Full International appearances, for their country, while playing for the club, Scottish League International appearances, followed by a record of all Hearts Club Captains.

The largest and longest piece of research was to compile a record of every player who had played for Hearts in the recognised major competitions. Following the completion of that list a "Hall of Fame" based on several criterion which would allow for the changes in competitions and number of matches played – each season – over the past 135 years.

In the meantime a register of all archival material and an inventory of all the memorabilia, souvenirs and trophies held by the club was completed..

A request to produce "a decade-by-decade history" for the Official Hearts website was accepted on the understanding that the material was protected. The Decennia History came from the draft of this book and to reach as many supporters as possible the website material was re-produced in the home match programmes as a 'taster' of what was to come.

FOREWORD

The book is not a criticism of previous writers but an attempt to have a full, accurate and comprehensive record for the Heart of Midlothian Football Club. In researching material for the book to check differences unearthed from other publications about the club it was decided that preferably, an item should be confirmed from three separate sources including original documents, Hearts own records, SFA, SFL and SPL records, where possible.

Where an original document or a club record was the only or main source it was accepted as bona fide.

I had access to the Heart of Midlothian records which is amongst the most comprehensive for football clubs in Scotland dating back to the 1880's. Making it possible to present material never previously published.

The facts and figures relate to the Scottish Cup, League Championship, League Cup and European Competitions. Individual records for any players relate to these competitions only and have been keenly researched to avoid further disagreement.

The club, however, continues to hold the appearance records of all players for all First Team matches.

An attempt has been made not to idolise any individual player as each generation of supporters have their own hero. Many of them will appear in a " Hall of Fame" later.

ACKNOWLEDGEMENTS

To Vladimir Romanov for raising the question of a brief history of Hearts and a mini museum;

To Julija Goncaruk for activating the search for a mini museum and the collection of archives;

To Roman Romanov for the appointment of a Club Archivist and approval for a Hearts Archive Group;

To the Executive management at Tynecastle and to several members of staff at Riccarton and Tynecastle.

To the Hearts Archive Group: Graham Blackwood (deceased), John Kerr (deceased), Bill Smith and David Speed.

Working with David on the decade by decade, Decennia History for the Official Hearts website and match programme turned out to be a bonus when compiling the book. We were able to compare each others records then to check them to Hearts own records. His encyclopaedic knowledge of the Heart of Midlothian Football Club and players could well be unmatched as is, I expect, his collection of press cuttings and programmes. If he ever writes a book make it 'a must buy'.

Thanks is due to Scotsman Publications for some photographs.

CONTENTS

In the Beginning ...... Page 9
1874 to 1919

A Managerial Shock ...... Page 71
1919 to 1964

Heartache at Tynecastle ...... Page 135
1964 to 2009

Facts and Figures ...... Page 199
1874 to 2009

ILLUSTRATIONS

1	The Old Tolbooth	8
2	The Heart of Midlothian c1890 & c1990	10
3	White Shirts – Red Hearts – 18/5/1878	12
4	Hooped Shirts – MFBC – 1876/1877	14
5	Edinburgh FA Cup – Winners – 1878	16
6	President's Cup – Winners – 1879	18
7	Uncovered Stand	21
8	Tynecastle Tollhouse	21
9	Rosebery Charity Cup Winners – 1882/1883	24
10	Tynecastle Map	28
11	Scottish Cup Winners – 1890/1891	33
12	League Champions – 1894/1895	38
13	Scottish Cup Winners – 1895/1896	40
14	League Champions – 1896/1897	42
15	Scottish Cup Winners – 1900/1901	46
16	New North Stand	50
17	Tynecastle – 1904	50
18	First Eleven – 1905/1906	53
19	Light Blue Change Strip – 1907	54
20	"Iron Stand"	59
21	Main Stand – 1914	63
22	Hearts 'Wartime Song' Soldiers	66/67
23	Tynecastle – 1920	72
24	War Memorial Invitation	76
25	War Memorial	77
26	War Memorial Order of Service	78/79
27	First Eleven – 1923/1924	82
28	Five Scottish Internationals – 1935	95
29	League Cup Winners – 1954/1955	114
30	Scottish Cup Winners – 1955/1956	117
31	League Champions – 1957/1958	121
32	Blazer Badges – 1958 & 1998	122
33	League Cup Winners – 1958/1959	124
34	L-shaped Enclosure – 1959	126
35	League Cup Winners – 1959/1960	128
36	League Champions – 1959/1960	129
37	League Cup Winners – 1962/1963	133
38	The Tommy Walker Collection	138
39	Tynecastle – 1984	159
40	First Team Squad – 1985/1986	161
41	Tynecastle Park – Tynecastle Terrace-1988	164
42	Seven Internationals – 1990	167
43	Eight Scottish Internationals – 1992	171
44	Model of Proposed Development – 1993	176
45	First Team Squad – 1998/1999	181
46	Scottish Cup Winners – 2005/2006	192
47	Model of Proposed Development – 2008	195

The Old Tolbooth

IN THE BEGINNING

In the late 1870's leading football clubs started to grow from their humble beginnings in local public parks. Heart of Midlothian was one of these clubs that shaped the game in Great Britain where it spread throughout the world.

A statement is often quoted:– "Heart of Mid-Lothian Football Club was formed in 1874 and took its name from a dance hall off the Royal Mile". This is partly true, and note, the hyphen in Mid-Lothian - not changed until 1900.

But let's go back to the beginning and the name "HEART OF MIDLOTHIAN".

THE OLD TOLBOOTH OF EDINBURGH

The Heart of Midlothian Football Club takes its name from the old Tolbooth -Tax House- of Edinburgh that stood in the Royal Mile, adjacent to St. Giles Cathedral. This was an ancient building which was used as a meeting place for the Parliament and Court of Justice; the Town Council; the Privy Council; and the High Court.

It was rebuilt in 1610 and by 1640 it housed the city prison with the hangman's scaffold standing on a two-storey annex. The Tolbooth pikes displayed the severed heads of criminals.

This sinister building was referred to as the "Heart of Midlothian" by the people of Edinburgh and today, the west entrance of the prison is marked by a heart formation of causeway stones, close to the door of St. Giles. Originally, these stones were painted to identify the spot.

The Tolbooth began to be demolished on 18 September 1817 but the prison was such a notable landmark that it was remembered in a famous romantic novel about Jeanie Deans, "Heart of Midlothian", written by Sir Walter Scott, one of Edinburgh's most famous sons.

Sir Walter was one of the first popular writers and the names of his books and characters were regularly adopted for a number of diverse purposes, such as The Heart of Midlothian Dancing Club from where our football team emerged. Use of this name was appropriate, because much of the story takes place in the area of the city where the original players lived and worked.

A Masonic Lodge and Foresters Lodge would also use this name, as would several sporting clubs. "The Scotsman" newspaper of 20 July 1864 actually mentions a cricket match between the Scotsman and the Heart of Midlothian. It was common, at the time, for men to play other sports in the summer, but there is no evidence to suggest a link between the cricket and football club.

Heart of Midlothian c1890 (Photo courtesy of Margeorie Meikie - The Heart of Old Edinburgh)

Heart of Midlothian c1990

FROM WASHING GREEN COURT TO THE MEADOWS

We know the origins from the writings of George Robertson who first watched Hearts in 1878 and eventually became the club secretary; a director; the match programme editor and first historian. George documented the early years and his lecture notes are held in the club's archives. He was certainly close to the original players. Robertson's parents lived in Washing Green Court, situated off the South Back Canongate (now Holyrood Road) at its junction with Dumbiedykes Road. This was the site of the neighbourhood refreshment rooms that catered for all-manner of functions and activities including the Heart of Midlothian Dancing Club.

The pals from the dance club decided to play football and 'tradition' has it that as they were known to frequent the nearby Tron Kirk area. A policeman directed the lads from there to the Meadows where he thought their energies could be put to better use kicking a ball rather than hanging around the streets. It was said that the youngsters purchased a ball from Percival King's shop in Lothian Street and proceeded to the East Meadows. There the seeds of the Heart of Midlothian Football Club were sown although they first played under local rules which were a mixture of rugby and soccer codes.

Many different styles of football were played in the nineteenth century, and in order to bring all the exponents together, on 26 October 1863 the Football Association was formed in London and uniform rules drawn up. There was not total agreement among the 12 attendees and one club walked out, refusing to accept the non-inclusion of hacking (kicking below the knee) among the rules.

Queen's Park formed in 1867 is recognised as the oldest Association Football Club in Scotland, and they, in fact, provided the team that played England, in the world's first International fixture at Partick, in Glasgow on Saturday 30 November 1872 in front of a 4,000 crowd. Scotland wore blue shirts, white shorts and blue-and-white hooped socks. "A tape was used to close the goal".

FOOTBALL ASSOCIATION RULES REACH EDINBURGH

In December 1873 the best players of Queen's Park FC and Clydesdale FC played an exhibition match at Raimes Park, Bonnington (the then new home of the Royal High School Rugby Club) to introduce Football Association Rules to Edinburgh. Among the 200 spectators were a number of the dance hall footballers, including secretary, Jake Reid, who then decided to adopt Association Rules during the early months of 1874. Their restructured side was called Heart of Midlothian Football Club after their favourite dance club.

As a matter of interest, these two sides met in the first Scottish Cup Final, on 23 March 1874 at the original Hampden Park, in Glasgow. There was no scoring at half-time but the crowd of 2,000 saw Queen's Park score twice to win 2-0.

The precise date of the club's formation was never recorded, but as it was during 1874 that the players and members adopted Football Association Rules, this has become the accepted date that the Hearts, as they are popularly known, was established. When reporting on football in October of that year, the "Edinburgh Courant" newspaper refers to four clubs playing under Association Rules. Third Edinburgh Rifle Volunteers, Thistle and Swifts were known and Hearts most probably were the fourth.

White Shirts – Red Hearts – 1875/1876

HEARTS JOIN THE SCOTTISH FOOTBALL ASSOCIATION

There was no mention of Hearts in the newspapers during season 1874-1875 but the team was clearly playing as the club immediately appears as a well-established organisation at the commencement of season 1875-1876.

In fact, in August 1875 Heart of Midlothian FC had 45 members and was strong enough to join both the Scottish Football Association and become a founder member of the Edinburgh Football Association (now the East of Scotland Football Association). The club registered its colours as 'marone' which is the old Edinburgh spelling of maroon, although the earliest known team picture shows the players in white with a heart on the left breast.

Tom Purdie was the first captain and home matches were played on the East Meadows Public Park. The main pitch ran east to west alongside the Boroughloch Brewery (now in Boroughloch Square off Buccleuch Street). It was used by many teams including Hearts greatest rivals, the Hibernians. At that time, there were no pitch markings and teams staked their claim to an area of ground by setting out their flags and portable goals – with a tape rather than a crossbar.

The club was based in Anderson's Tavern, West Crosscauseway and that establishment was recorded as Hearts' headquarters by the SFA. The players changed in an upstairs room in the tavern until 1876 when a stripping box was erected in the Meadows Schoolhouse.

THE PRESS

The crossbar was introduced in 1875

At the end of August 1875 The Scotsman reported a challenge match on the East Meadows between Hearts and the Third Edinburgh Rifle Volunteers. This was the first occasion we can find of the club being mentioned in the press, but the 'volunteers' ran out 2-0 winners.

On 16 October 1875 the team also played its first Scottish FA Cup-tie, against the same opponents. At Craigmount Park in the Grange, Hearts held the 'volunteers' to a 0-0 draw with this team:- Jake Reid; J. Kennedy and James Templeton; Peter McBeath, John Wylie and John McBeath; Tom Purdie-captain, George Mitchell, W. Johnson, J. Donnachie and P. Donnachie.

The teams met again in the East Meadows before several hundred spectators and once more drew 0-0. In accordance with the rules of the time, both sides moved on to the next round where Hearts lost 2-0 to Drumpellier FC in Coatbridge on 13 November. When the Scottish Cup began the early round ties were played on a geographical district basis.

On Christmas Day 1875 Hearts challenged Hibernians for the first time and despite playing without three men for the first twenty minutes, Hearts won 1-0 at the East Meadows. This was the first recorded match against the 'greens'.

It is believed that as many as twelve other challenge matches were played that season against such clubs as Third Edinburgh Rifle Volunteers, Dunfermline FC, Hanover, St.Andrews, Swifts and Thistle.

Hooped Shirts – 1876/1877 Note the initials MFBC (Mid-lothian Foot-ball Club)

OUR FIRST HONOUR

The team did not compete for several months in the autumn of 1876 due to a shortage of players. However, Hearts were still members of the SFA and were included in the Scottish Cup for season 1876-1877 although the player situation forced the club to withdraw after being drawn against Dunfermline FC.

Many of the remaining men turned out for St. Andrew's Football Club, such as Tom Purdie and the Barbour brothers, and by January 1877 Heart of Midlothian had re-emerged, having absorbed St.Andrew's and its players, and having adopted a new strip of red, white and blue hoops.

For season 1877-1878 the shirts were dyed to the much loved maroon, although the hoops could still be seen in contemporary photographs.

On 29 September Hearts and Hibernians were brought together for the first time in a Scottish Cup tie. It took two matches to decide the matter, but sadly, it was Hibernians who progressed into the next round, winning 2-1 in a Replay following a 0-0 draw.

Hearts then made a little bit of history by entertaining a Glasgow club – John Elder FC – for the first time, being defeated 2-1. That season, Tom Purdie and Andrew Lees became the first Hearts' players to gain representative honours when they played for the Edinburgh Football Association against Queen's Park.

Hearts played its first ever match in the Edinburgh FA Cup on 17 November at Newington, where Brunswick FC lost 3-1. In the Semi-Final, the "maroons" defeated Dunfermline FC 2-1 and as Hibernians had beaten Thistle, the stage was set for the first Cup Final clash of the two teams destined to dominate football in the East of Scotland.

In February 1878 there began a five match marathon between these two great rivals with the first four being drawn, 0-0, 1-1, 1-1 and 1-1. The club subsequently gained its first honour when, on 20 April they defeated Hibernians 3-2 at Powburn, and Hearts became the champion club in the capital. John Alexander scored his second and the winning goal late in the match while George Mitchell was the other marksman.

The winning team was:- Jake Reid; Tom Purdie-captain and George Barbour; James Whitson, John Sweeney and Andrew Lees; J. Burns, Hugh Wylie, John Alexander, George Mitchell and Bob Winton.

Captain Tom Purdie long remembered the occasion not only due to the result, but because he was attacked by a mob of Hibernians supporters on his way home. These matches brought the first recorded incidents of hooliganism and sectarian bitterness into Edinburgh football.

At this time, the game consisted of cup competitions and challenge matches, with the most important events being the Scottish Cup and the Edinburgh FA Cup, both of which were sources of great excitement. That epic Final against the Hibernians was just the boost the game needed in the east and the local and national press was now much more aware of Association Football.

Edinburgh FA Cup Winners 1878 Back Row: George Barbour, James Whitson, Jake Reid, John, Sweeney, John Alexander. Middle Row: Hugh Wyllie, Bob Winton, J. Burns, George Mitchell. Seated: Tom Purdie, Andrew Lees.

HEARTS SEARCH FOR A HOME

At the start of season 1878-1879 Hearts were still playing on the East Meadows and the club's headquarters was now Mackenzie's shop in nearby Chapel Street. This became a meeting place for footballers and club committees, and in the years before Saturday evening sports newspapers were published, results were displayed in the shop window over the week-end.

However, the Meadows were now overcrowded with spectators milling around and interfering with matches. Hearts, therefore, played important fixtures at the Edinburgh Football Association ground at Powburn, above where Saville Terrace now stands. Here the club was able to charge admission money. The reserves would continue to use the Meadows for some time.

In September, Hearts began its best run to date in the Scottish Cup, reaching the Fourth Round, only to be eliminated without actually losing a match. Wearing its new strip design of maroon jerseys with a red heart, the team met Swifts in the First Round, and had a 3-1 victory. In October a Second Round tie saw them paired with Thistle who were defeated 1-0 and then the following month, in the Third Round, the "maroons" were at home again when Arbroath paid its first visit to the capital. Hearts had a 2-1 win and earned a Fourth Round tie with Helensburgh.

The team travelled through to the west on St.Andrew's Day but there was a problem over the neutral referee and Helensburgh insisted that their own man be used. Hearts scored first but the home side hit back to win 2-1 although the second goal was disputed. In any event, the Edinburgh club protested over the refereeing situation and the SFA backed them but ordered a Replay at Helensburgh. Hearts refused to travel and were deemed to have scratched from the competition.

The club had high hopes of retaining the Edinburgh FA Cup and enjoyed a 5-1 win over Dunfermline FC in the First Round. In the Semi-Final, Hanover was disposed of by 4-0, and the stage was set for yet another Final clash with Hibernians. Edinburgh's largest attendance to date – 4,000 – crowded into the ground at Powburn to witness a 1-1 draw. The match was marred by crowd trouble and it was noted that Tom Purdie was kicked by a man called O'Reilly. The Replay took place at Union Park, Corstorphine where a large crowd travelled out on special trains to see the Hibernians win 2-0.

There was still the Presidents Cup, a competition designed to allow some of the newest clubs in the district to play the more established sides. After defeating Dunfermline FC 4-2 in the First Round, Hearts took some revenge, for the Cup defeat, beating Hibernians 1-0 in the Semi-Final on the "greens" home ground at Powderhall. The Final was again at the Hibernians' ground in May 1879 against Hanover and it took extra time to settle things before Hearts ran out winners by 5-4.

This one-off competition was won by:- Jake Reid; Tom Purdie-captain and Tom Masterton; George Ovens, Bob Barbour and Andrew Lees; James Whitson, George Mitchell, George Barbour, John Alexander and William Pullen. The Cup is one of the main trophies displayed by the club.

Hibernians won the more prestigious Edinburgh FA Cup and began a period of dominance in that competition, that lasted for nearly ten years. This did not stop the growth of Hearts who now had 120 members, and was strong enough to secure its own private park at Powderhall Grounds prior to the start of the season. This was not the well known dog track but an athletics facility next to the railway line, standing on what is now the city refuse works.

President's Cup Winners 1879

The club arranged another attractive series of challenge matches for the new season, but strangely, turned down the famous Old Etonians FC, the FA Challenge Cup holders. Hearts enjoyed an 8-2 victory over Fettes College, a 4-1 win against Edinburgh University and from further afield, Our Boys and John Elder FC were both beaten 5-0.

On 24 January Third Lanark Rifle Volunteers paid their initial visit and Hearts won 4-2. February brought the first match with Dumbarton, another leading club of the day, and a small crowd saw Hearts win easily by 4 0. The team then travelled west to Alexandria where they held the powerful Vale of Leven side to a narrow 1-2 score line. In a return match, the Dunbartonshire club defeated Hearts 2-1.

In the Scottish Cup First Round, Hearts were drawn against their old Edinburgh combatants, Third Edinburgh Rifle Volunteers, but the "volunteers" did not turn up and the club was awarded a 'walkover'. For the Second Round for season 1879-1880, Hearts had a home tie against Brunswick and progressed after a 4-2 victory. Once again there was a Hearts versus Hibernians clash in the Scottish Cup.

The teams were due to meet at Powderhall on 1 November but due to a dispute over the ground lease, the officials were ejected from the pay boxes by the owners prior to the opening of the gates. The match was re-arranged at Hibernians' Mayfield ground but again there were problems, this time over the kick-off time. Hearts arrived at 1p.m. and, as there were no opponents, claimed victory. Hibernians arrived at 3 p.m. and did the same. The SFA then stepped in and ordered the match to be played at Mayfield on 15 November.

But again there were problems, this time among the spectators. Some fans broke onto the field of play shortly after John McNeil had reduced Hibernians lead to 2-1. However, order was restored and Hearts were out of the Cup as there were no more goals. Afterwards, the club committee lodged a protest claiming one of the crossbars was three inches too high but this was rejected by the SFA.

In the Edinburgh Cup First Round, Hearts 13-1 win over Lancefield was the club's biggest victory to date and subsequent wins over Bathgate 3-1 away, and Edinburgh University 4-2 at home, took the "maroons" through to a Semi-Final contest with Hibernians. This match took place in January at Powderhall before an excited crowd of 3,500. Unfortunately, it was Hibernians fans who were excited at the end due to their teams 5-2 victory this, despite Hearts having a 2-0 lead at half-time.

Among the visitors to Powderhall late in the season was a strong Scotch-Canadian X1 that was full of International players who defeated Hearts by 5-1. Due to serious flooding at Powderhall, the season was to end with Hearts using Hibernians new ground at Easter Road, not the present stadium, but one situated below Bothwell Street. It was there at the end of April that the club first played Rangers and a hard fought 0-0 draw was the result.

The club was certainly gaining in stature and had recruited from Brunswick Alex McNeill and John McNeill, the first twins to play in maroon. In the early years of football many brothers played in the same team and Hearts was no exception with brothers being listed well into the 1930's.

Some of the local relationships were not harmonious and prior to season 1880-1881 Hearts tried to have Hibernians banned from the Edinburgh FA due to their continually rough play. The motion was later withdrawn, more than likely because of the financial implications of losing the "derby" fixtures. Income was vital as the club now ran a third team known as the Valleyfield X1 who played at Stockbridge Park and other venues within the city.

In the First Round of the Scottish Cup, Brunswick lost easily by 3-1 at home, and after receiving a bye, Hearts faced Hibernians in the Third Round. A then record attendance of 5,000 crowded into Powderhall to see the "maroons" win a thrilling contest, 5-3, against all the odds, with the goals coming from Alex McNeill 2, James Edwards, John McNeill and John Alexander. In the Fourth Round, Hearts defeated Cambuslang 3-0 at home but hopes of a lengthy cup run were then dashed by a 4-0 reverse at Arthurlie's ground in Barrhead.

The club's players were now involved in most of the representative matches played by the Edinburgh Football Association and in 9 October 1880 Hearts were the first Edinburgh side thought capable of challenging Queen's Park. Unfortunately, this was not the case and they lost 8-1 before 3,000 fans at the Powderhall Grounds, Broughton Road. Nevertheless, at local level Hearts were a major force along with Hibernians, St. Bernards and Leith Athletic.

This position was underlined in the Edinburgh FA Cup, when Hearts defeated West Calder 8-1 in the First Round. Then on 30 October they beat Anchor FC 21-0 in the Second Round, a result that remains the club's record confirmed victory. The match was so one-sided that the newspaper reporters were too bored to report the goal scorers. Later claims of 27-0 and 23-0 over Lancefield and Royal Oak respectively, cannot be substantiated.

The Third Round brought another clash with Hibernians and more than 7,000 packed into Powderhall for the match. Hearts scored first but Hibernians came back to win 2-1, although after the game, Hearts protested about crowd interference and the eligibility of a Hibernians player. This was dismissed and our great rivals went on to win the cup which they were then allowed to keep.

The bulk of the season consisted of 18 challenge matches. In one of these, against Hamilton Academical, Dunn of Hamilton Acadedmical suffered a broken leg which was the first such incident in a Hearts match. The players showed they had learned some valuable lessons from the Queen's Park match in October and on 6 November Hearts beat the strong Vale of Leven 3-2. Three weeks later they defeated Petershill FC 8-2.

WE MOVE TO GORGIE-DALRY

In January 1881 Hearts became the first city club to play in England although the team lost 4-2 against Aston Villa and 2-1 against Blackburn Rovers. Another major step forward came in February when the club took over a private field in the flourishing industrial suburb of Gorgie where it has long been associated. This was not the present ground, the pitch being laid out on the site of what are now Wardlaw Street and Wardlaw Place.

Initially the players stripped in a local public house but facilities were quickly erected including a pavilion and an uncovered stand, and the original Tynecastle was officially opened on 9 April 1881 with a match against Hanover. Hearts won 8-0 and admission was 6d (2.5p) with ladies admitted free. The name for the ground was taken from the Tynecastle Tollhouse in Gorgie Road, which was at the entrance to the grounds of Merchiston about 50 yards from McLeod Street.

For some time, the club found it difficult to attract its regular supporters out to Gorgie. As a result, Hearts often put on two and sometimes three matches for the admission price for one – in order to stimulate interest. Those fans who did take the trouble to attend were at least able to admire the skills of Nick Ross, the club's first exceptionally gifted player, whose most famous days were, alas to be, with Preston North End.

At representative level, several other Hearts players were in demand and John Alexander, Bob Barbour, Andrew Lees, John McNeill, Jake Reid and John Sweeney all played in the International trials although none were ultimately capped.

It was just as well that Hearts supporters had Nick Ross to watch because season 1881-1882 was not one of the club's better campaigns, with the team being eliminated in the First Round of the Scottish Cup and the Second Round of the Edinburgh Cup. The rest of the fixtures were challenge matches of various standards.

After hosting the Edinburgh FA Sports at Tynecastle, Hearts began their programme with a 13-0 win over the Black Watch. After winning 4-2 at Rugby Park, Kilmarnock, the team looked in good shape for the First

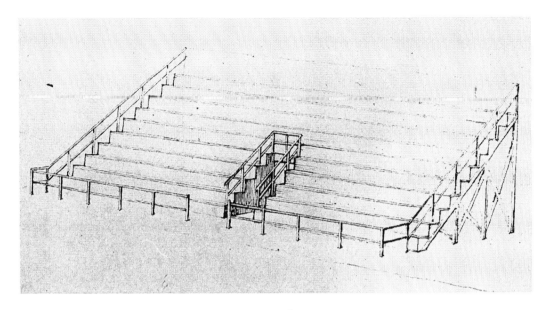

Uncovered Stand

Tynecastle Tollhouse - photo courtesy of 'Malcolm Cant Collection'

Round of the Scottish Cup against St.Bernards but lost 2-1 on the "saints" ground at the Royal Gymnasium, Canonmills.

Hearts bounced back to record a 6-0 win over Edina FC in the First Round of the Edinburgh FA Cup and on 1 October the "maroons" met Hibernians in the Second Round of the competition. There was a new trophy this season the present East of Scotland Shield, but Hibernians proved too strong winning the match 4-2. The team look a long time to recover from this defeat and suffered a couple of heavy reverses – 4-1 against Third Lanark on 8 October and 6-0 to Vale of Leven on 22 October.

November saw Hearts and Edinburgh University play a match in aid of the Eyemouth fishing disaster fund following many local deaths in heavy storms. It was a pity that poor weather badly affected the crowd for a game which Hearts won 3-1. A series of other challenge matches followed in which Ross began to catch the eye and largely due to his genius, Hearts were confident of avenging their Shield defeat when they visited Easter Road on 31 December – not so – Hibernians won 3-2.

Hearts began experimenting with the team and the supporters enjoyed some good results from December, such as 5-0 and 8-0 versus Alexandra Athletic and 6-0 against Hanover, ending the season in April with a 4-0 defeat of Airdrieonians.

Generally, the supporters received value for their admission money which had now been fixed at 6d. They sometimes had to be patient, however, because the only methods of transport were the railway and horse drawn carriages, and games often started up to an hour after the advertised kick-off time.

Hearts made their second visit to England on 21 February 1882 to play Nottingham Forest at their Trent Bridge ground but lost an exciting contest 2-1. Then in April, Hearts had another go at Hibernians but were overwhelmed 6-2 at Tynecastle. That month Aston Villa became the first English club to play in Edinburgh and their splendid running with the ball earned them a 6-2 win over Hearts.

The Reserves had a better season and won their first trophy when they defeated St. Bernards Reserves 2-0 in the Edinburgh FA Second X1 Cup Final at Easter Road.

Another interesting feature of the season occurred on 17 December 1881 when a match against Brunswick was called off as there was no ball available – football was still in its infancy in the capital.

For season 1882-1883 Nick Ross was appointed captain and at 20 he was the club's youngest skipper to date. He led the team in the Scottish Cup which commenced on 9 September with a First Round tie against St.Bernards, a repeat of the previous season. A large crowd at Tynecastle witnessed a 1-1 draw and for the Replay at Powderhall a good turnout of 3,000 saw a 4-3 victory for Hearts.

In the Second Round, the team travelled to West Calder to play Addiewell and this proved to be a stroll for the capital side who won 14-0, a result which remains the club's best away victory. The Third Round also produced a record score, but this time Hearts were on the receiving end of their biggest Scottish Cup disaster, an 8-1 reverse against Vale of Leven. It was played on a rain-sodden pitch at Alexandria on 21 October and the result stood as Hearts record defeat for almost a hundred years. Hearts were 3-1 down at half time then were 'swamped' in the second period.

In the East of Scotland Shield, Hearts overwhelmed Holyrood 20-2 in the First Round, the biggest ever victory at the original Tynecastle. This took place a week before the Addiewell Cup match and the 34 goals scored in these matches is the best that the club has ever achieved consecutively.

In the Second Round, Hearts were drawn to play Norton Park, but they scratched, and the team went to West Calder FC in the Third Round to win 1-0. The Semi-Finals saw Hearts play Edinburgh University at Powderhall, a game in which the students pulled off a shock 5-2 victory.

The team picked up near the end of a season that brought into the Edinburgh football scene a new tournament, the Rosebery Charity Cup, a handsome Monteith Sterling Silver Rose Bowl which is now kept in perpetuity by the club. It was gifted by Lord Rosebery for competition among the leading clubs in the district with the majority of the gate receipts going to local charities.

In the Semi-Final, Hearts played Hibernians at Powderhall and having already beaten and drawn with them in challenge matches the "maroons" were confident of victory. Their confidence was justified and they won 3-1. The result delighted most of the 5,000 fans, but the Easter Road club was so upset that it began to import men of Irish extraction from the west to strengthen its side. In the Final, Hearts had an easy win over St.Bernards at Powderhall goals, from Andrew Lees and Bob Waugh earning a 2-0 victory.

The winning team was:- Jake Reid; J.McLennan and Johnny Gair; James Fraser-captain, Bob Barbour and John Ferguson; Nick Ross, Andrew Lees, Bob Waugh, Jimmy Wood and Will Ronaldson.

Following the Charity Cup win the club's fine team was ravaged by English sides who lured Scotsmen down south to play professionally. This included Hearts' captain, Nick Ross, who starred for Preston North End, the first English Champions. Hearts were not averse to paying players but could not match the wealthy Lancashire clubs. Indeed it was said that if only the Tynecastle club had been able to pay the recently married Ross 10/- (50p) more each week, then he might have stayed.

Within two years at least ten of the finest Tynecastle players had followed him. Not surprisingly, Hearts began to struggle although the club's best players were still in demand for local representative matches including the Edinburgh FA's first fixture against London. Bob Barbour, Andrew Lees, Jake Reid, Jim Renwick, Nick Ross and Jimmy Wood took part, but lost 9-2.

In season 1883-1884 Hibernians beat Hearts in both the Scottish Cup and the East of Scotland Shield. Our city rivals did not have the same recruitment problems, as in those days, Catholic and Irish lads from all over Scotland wanted to play in a green shirt.

The first match of the season was a 3-3 draw with Dumbarton. Then the Hearts met Brunswick in the First Round of the Scottish Cup and ran out 8-0 winners, with six goals from Jimmy Wood. The reward was a 160-mile round-trip to play Newcastleton FC, in the Second Round, the home club refusing all attempts to switch the tie to Tynecastle. Hearts left at 6 a.m. for the long journey, but at least a victory of 4-1 was recorded.

The Third Round brought the revitalised Hibernians to Gorgie. Before a record Scottish Cup crowd of 6,500 they won easily by 4-1 with McGhee, later to manage Hearts, scoring a hat-trick. James Brogan who scored Hibernians other goal joined Hearts later in the season after being asked to leave Easter Road when it was discovered he was not a Roman Catholic.

Hibernians put paid to any hopes of revenge in a Semi-Final of the Shield after Hearts had disposed of Rose FC 7-0, Leith Thistle 5-2, Kirkcaldy Wanderers 3-0 and Edinburgh University 5-1 in the first four rounds. The team was severely weakened by the loss of John Ferguson, Johnny Gair and Will Ronaldson to England and lost 4-1 to their city rivals.

The Rosebery Charity Cup brought little joy to Tynecastle as, despite the return of Johnny Gair and Nick Ross as guests, St.Bernards won 4-2 in a Semi-Final tie at Powderhall.

Rosebery Charity Cup Winners 1882–1883 Standing: John Gai; Bob Barbour, Jake Reid, James Fraser, J. McLennan. Sitting: Andrew Lees, Bob Waugh, Nick Ross (captain), J. Ferguson, Will Ronalcson, Jimmy Wood. On Floor: George Barbour – who did not play.

The bulk of the season was made up of challenge matches with at least 29 matches played including a 12-1 victory over West Calder in which guest player Nick Ross, scored five goals. Hearts also received their first Irish visitors on 26 December when they defeated Ulster FC of Belfast 4-0.

In addition, three matches were played on a New Year tour of England, with Hearts losing 5-0 to Blackburn Rovers and 4-0 to Bolton Wanderers. The team did manage a creditable 1-1 draw with Preston North End. Then in April, Hearts defeated Queen's Park for the first time with a 2-1 win at Tynecastle over the 'Champions of Scotland'.

HEARTS SUSPENDED

Season 1884-1885 was dominated by one major issue – the question of professionalism which was not recognised by the football authorities until 1885 in England and 1893 in Scotland. Despite all the clubs being ostensibly amateur, many offered financial inducements, but it was Hearts who were 'to be the patsies' for the SFA. This was ironic considering the number of players who had been enticed from Tynecastle to play in England for money.

With Hibernians dominating the local scene, Hearts were forced to make underhand payments in order to attract and retain quality players. The club began to import players to Edinburgh, including three men from Cartvale – John Calderwood, Chris McNee and Jimmy Maxwell. While this policy was not unique to Hearts, in October 1884 the club became the first to be suspended by the SFA following a protest by Dunfermline FC. Hearts beat the Fifers 11-1 in the Scottish Cup Second Round at Lady's Mill.

However, the home side acting on information believed to have come from the Cartvale club lodged a complaint on the grounds that Hearts were paying players. The SFA investigated the matter and on 21 October Hearts were found guilty of giving James Maxwell and Chris McNee 26/- per week (£1.30) and expelled from the competition.

In November 1884 the Heart of Midlothian Committee admitted the irregularities, and after a new Committee was elected, the club was quickly re-admitted to the national association.

Many people had sympathy for the club, including the Edinburgh FA who allowed Hearts to play on, and consequently no fixtures were missed.

That season, the SFA produced a list of 57 players who had gone to play for money in England and were, therefore, banned in Scotland. Ten were Hearts men:- James Brogan, G. Douglas, T. Douglas, John Ferguson, Chris McNee, Jim Renwick, Will Ronaldson, Jim Ross, Nick Ross and John Scotland but for some reason Johnny Gair was not listed.

During the brief suspension, Hearts staged a challenge match with the F.A. Cup holders Blackburn Rovers who won 1-0 at Tynecastle and 6-0 at Blackburn in December. Then in January Hibernians won 7-2 at Tynecastle but on the positive side there was an 11-2 defeat of the Fifth Kirkcudbright Rifle Volunteers in which Tommy Jenkinson and Jimmy Wood both scored four goals.

Jenkinson was an interesting signing because he had been destined for Easter Road until they realised he was not a Roman Catholic, and another fine player was rejected by Hibernians for that reason. Their loss was Hearts gain as he became a prolific goal scorer throughout the 1880's and was the first Hearts player to be capped for Scotland.

In the Shield that season, the Edinburgh FA would not allow Hearts to cancel a First Round match with Royal Oak of Leith in order to play a game against the mighty Queen's Park. The Hearts therefore, played an 80 minute match against the Glasgow side which ended 0-0 and virtually the same team was asked to stay on the pitch to play and crush Royal Oak 7-1. Hearts coasted to a 5-0 win over Easter in the Second Round.

When the Third Round tie came along against St.Bernards, the club was then under the SFA suspension but Hearts played the match and defeated "saints" 4-2. In the Fourth Round, 4,000 spectators saw Hearts play Hibernians at Easter Road, but sadly, the "greens" continued their local domination with a 3-1 victory.

After a 2-1 win over Edinburgh University in the penultimate round, the Rosebery Charity Cup Final was lost 3-0 to Hibernians.

A MOVE ACROSS GORGIE ROAD

1885-1886 was the last season at the original Tynecastle. As in April 1886 Hearts moved across the road to its present home. Unfortunately, it was not a successful one as the club required time to regroup after suspension. This severely impacted on the campaign when the Hibernians defeated Hearts in the Scottish Cup and the East of Scotland Shield.

Under new captain James Fraser, Hearts began with a couple of challenge matches before taking on St.Bernards at home in the First Round of the Scottish Cup. Tommy Jenkinson starred for Hearts in a 5-2 victory but the 'saints' protested and a Replay was ordered. A huge crowd packed Powderhall for the match and an exciting tie ended in a 1-0 win for the Tynecastle team. The Second Round took Hearts down to a packed Easter Road where the home side won 2-1.

The Shield also ended in disappointment in Leith, because after beating Easter FC, Leith Harp and Bo'ness, Hearts went down 4-3 to Hibernians in the Fourth Round.

Hearts had a measure of revenge in the Rosebery Charity Cup Final which they reached with a 4-1 victory over St.Bernards. The Final took place at Tynecastle on 15 May before 4,500 spectators and Hibernians took a commanding 2-0 lead. However, the match was abandoned with 15 minutes left to play after large numbers of spectators invaded the field of play when James McGhee of Hibernians, broke the leg of Hearts left winger Peter Bell, in a tackle.

The Replayed Final took place at Powderhall on 1 June and this time Hearts were leading 2-0 when the crowd again invaded the pitch in protest over the second goal. James McGhee was the hero this time, saving the referee from a severe beating from the Hibernians' fans. A Second Replay was ordered on 24 June at Powderhall and Hearts won at last through a Willie Mackay goal.

The club's overall progress could not be stopped and that season Hearts even entered the FA Cup, along with Queen's Park, Partick Thistle, Rangers and Third Lanark. When drawn against the Lancashire professional side Padiham FC. Hearts scratched rather than risk upsetting the SFA which had previously disapproved of this practice. Despite this Hearts would enter the following season in the hope of drawing one of the major English clubs to Edinburgh.

Incidentally, Queen's Park FC played in the FA Cup and reached the Final in 1884 and 1885 losing on both occasions to Blackbutrn Rovers 2-1 & 2-0 respectively. The Semi-Final for 1885 was played in Edinburgh against Nottingham Forest. They had drawn 1-1 at Derby on 14 March and "Queens" refused to play an extra half-hour and applied for the Replay to be played on neutral ground at Edinburgh.

After much debate the grounds of Merchiston Castle School – now occupied by George Watson's School – was made available. A grand stand was erected capable of holding 600 spectators and a strong wire rope was run round the ground. Kick-off 3.30, Admission 1s, Schoolboys 6d, Ladies Free, Grand Stand 2s per person. On 20 March Queen's Park were victors by 3-0.

Hearts played 30 challenge matches during the season, winning 18 and losing seven. One of these was the final match to be played at the original Tynecastle on 27 February 1886 against Sunderland. Davie Aitken and Rab Henderson scored the goals in Hearts 2-1 farewell victory.

The club had secured the tenancy of part of a vast meadow that Edinburgh Corporation was letting for housing and industry. £200 was spent to lay out Tynecastle Park and the new ground had two pitches which ran side-by-side in an east-west direction. These were fully utilised as Hearts still ran three teams. Spectators stood on three sides of each pitch behind a stout rope and an unroofed wooden trestle stand ran alongside the South pitch, holding some 250 spectators.

The ground stretched from Gorgie Road in the south to the railway line in the north, and the stadium was opened on 10 April with a 4-1 victory over Bolton Wanderers. A crowd of 5,500 saw Tommy Jenkinson score the first goal at Hearts' new home, with the others coming from Rab Henderson (2) and Bobby McNeill. The kick-off was at 4 p.m. and ground admission was 6d, with the Stand 1/- and ladies free. Another leading side Preston North End, also visited Tynecastle in May and proved too strong for Hearts, winning 4-1.

The first meeting of the International Football Association Board (IFAB) – the English – formed 1863, Scottish – 1873, Welsh – 1876 and Irish – 1880 Associations. Two representatives from each of the four associations met on 2 June 1886 to guard the Laws of the Game.

The 1886-1887 season was one to forget as Hearts suffered a heavy reverse in the club's only appearance in the FA Cup. The team was routed 7-1 by the Lancashire professionals, Darwen FC, and the SFA quickly banned its members from taking part in the English competition. With Cowlairs and Renton added to the previous five participants Scottish clubs were well represented.

Hearts did record a 7-1 win over Edina in the First Round of the Scottish Cup and then defeated Broxburn 2-1 in the Second Round. However, Hibernians still dominated the local scene and defeated Hearts 5-1 on their way to become the first Edinburgh club to win the Scottish Cup.

On a much brighter note, Tommy Jenkinson became the first Heart of Midlothian player to represent his country when he played for Scotland against Ireland on 19 February 1887 and scored in a 4-1 win at the new Hampden Park, Glasgow.

Hearts made confident progress in the East of Scotland Shield, defeating Glencairn 6-0 and Royal Oak 2-1 in the first two rounds at Tynecastle. The team then travelled in the Third Round to play Dunfermline Athletic for the first time, winning 5-2. Leith Thistle lost 7-0 in a Quarter-Final match at home then in a Semi-Final tie Broxburn Shamrock lost 3-1. The Final at Powderhall against Hibernians attracted 4,000 spectators but was a major disappointment, when Hearts meekly went down 3-0.

There was a chance of revenge in the Rosebery Charity Cup, but after beating Edinburgh University 1-0 in a Semi-Final, a barren season ended with a 7-1 defeat from the Easter Road side in the Final.

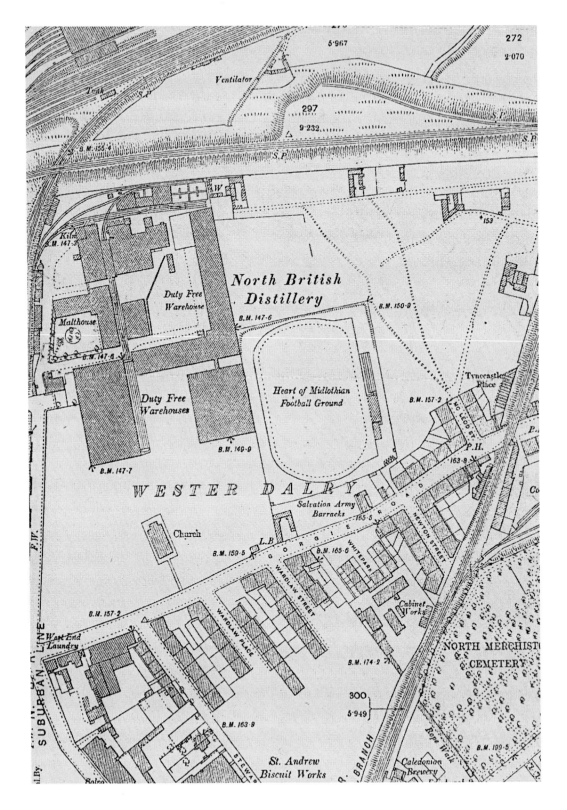

Hearts played 28 challenge matches winning 10 and losing 14 including some bad defeats such as 9-3 and 6-1 against St.Bernards. Matches against English clubs at the annual New Year tour saw defeats from Halliwell FC, Bolton Wanderers and Sheffield Wednesday. There was a further reverse from an English team when Preston North End won 5-1 at Tynecastle in April.

HEARTS ECLIPSE HIBERNIANS

For the start of season 1887-1888 new markings were added to pitch regulations; a centre circle and two six-yard semi-circles in front of each goal to assist in bye kicks.

This campaign was significantly better and Hearts ended the long period of Hibernians' supremacy by eliminating the holders from the Scottish Cup. Hibernians were claiming to be "World Champions" following a victory over Preston North End but, after meeting Hearts, they would never again be regarded as the leading club in the capital. The formation of Celtic further drained their traditional source of players and they eventually stopped playing in 1891.

A challenge match against Stoke FC on 12 August saw Hearts win by 4-2 and was just the boost required prior to the start of the Scottish Cup competition in September. Hearts defeated Norton Park FC 4-1 in the First Round, and then received a bye.

In the Third Round the team was drawn against Hibernians at Tynecastle on 15 October and this was a hard fought 1-1 draw before a new record attendance of 7,500. The Replay attracted 8,500 to Easter Road where Hearts gained a 3-1 victory amid wild excitement. Common and Lindsay scored two of the goals but the third was referred to in the press as a scrimmage. This is 'a rugby term' used when a group of players forced the ball over the line.

Hopes of winning the cup were dashed in the Fourth Round when the "maroons" went down 4-2 after a third Replay against St.Mirren at Cathkin Park, Glasgow after a 1-1 and two 2-2 draws.

But that victory over the Hibernians was much more significant even though they beat Hearts in the Shield and Rosebery Charity Cup. To keep our feet firmly on the ground, Preston North End won 7-1 at Tynecastle, although they were the "Real World Champions" and won the English double the following year.

Another notable match took place on 17 September 1887 in the Shield, and saw Hearts defeat Vale of Midlothian 18-0 with Tommy Brackenridge scoring seven goals. This remains the club's biggest win on our current ground. After this remarkable victory, Hearts reached the Semi-Finals defeating Bonnyrigg Rose Athletic 6-0, St.Bernards losing 5-2, and Bo'ness 6-1. Unfortunately, at that stage Hibernians proved to be too strong and won the match 5-2. Hearts did not fare any better in the Rosebery Charity Cup and went down 6-0 to Hibernians in the Semi-Finals at Powderhall.

On the usual annual New Year tour Hearts lost 5-3 to Blackburn Rovers, 4-1 to Preston North End and 3-1 to Bolton Wanderers which demonstrated that professionalism had taken the game in England well ahead of Scotland.

Tommy Brackenridge made his first appearance for Scotland in a Full International on 24 March 1888 against Ireland and he scored, in a 10-2 win at the Solitude Ground, Cliftonville, Belfast.

THE CHAMPIONSHIP OF THE EAST IS REGAINED

There was a new look at Tynecastle Park for season 1888-1889 with the two pitches being reduced to one, running in a north-south direction and surrounded by a wide athletics track. Two open stands and a pavilion were erected on the east side – McLeod Street – separated by an entrance tunnel and holding approximately 1,500 spectators with the overall capacity being 10,000.

The new campaign saw the introduction of several men who would make Hearts famous:- Davie Baird, Isaac Begbie, Johnny Hill and John Macpherson. It would be some time before their influence spread throughout the team and this season, they witnessed an embarrassing exit in the Scottish Cup.

At the outset, Hearts travelled to play Bo'ness on 1 September in the First Round and a capacity crowd at Newtown Park saw the "maroons" win by the only goal. In the Second Round, Hearts met Erin Rovers of Bathgate at Tynecastle and won 4-0. The next stage paired Hearts with Broxburn FC at the Public Park in the West Lothian town. A tight 2-2 draw led to a Replay at Tynecastle and an eventual 2-0 win for Hearts. Hopes that the team could go all the way to the Final ended with a shock defeat at Alum Works Park, in Lennoxtown, where on the 3 November, Campsie won 3-1 before a crowd of only 800.

Despite this shock result, in March 1889 for the first time since 1878 Hearts won the "Championship of the East" when they defeated Leith Athletic 5-2 in the Shield Final at Easter Road. St.Bernards lost in the First Round by 2-1 after a 1-1 draw then Norton Park lost 4-0 in the Second Round. Hearts received a bye and in the Fourth Round Mossend Swifts forced a 1-1 draw at Tynecastle before losing the replay 4-0 at Powderhall. Polton Vale were the Semi-Final lambs to the slaughter and lost 11-0 at Tynecastle.

Mossend Swifts had a measure of revenge when they defeated Hearts 2-0 in the Semi-Finals of the Rosebery Charity Cup.

During the season Hearts played 33 challenge matches, winning 20. The New Year games were against Blackburn Rovers, Newton Heath and Sheffield Wednesday. While Hearts lost two out of three, the team managed to beat Newton Heath (now Manchester United) by 2-1.

There was another big match against English opposition in April when Everton came to Tynecastle, and lost 3-0. In addition, on 15 September the first foreign team to play at Tynecastle was a Canadian FA Touring X1 who managed to defeat Hearts 3-0.

Jimmy Adams made his first appearance for Scotland in a Full International on 9 March 1889 against Ireland in a 7-0 win at the first Ibrox Park, Glasgow.

Season 1889-1890 was the last when the fixture list would comprise mainly of challenge matches. The coming of League football saw the leading clubs band together to ensure a guaranteed fixture list and a regular income.

This was probably the best campaign since the club's formation with Hearts reaching the Fifth Round of the Scottish Cup before losing to the eventual finalists, Vale of Leven. The team also dominated local soccer and won both the Shield and the Rosebery Charity Cup with Leith Athletic beaten in the Final of both competitions.

The first competitive match was a Scottish Cup tie against St.Bernards on 7 September at Powderhall which was won by 3-0. The Second Round was against Bellstane Birds at South Queensferry and Hearts were victorious by 4-1. Then another new name appeared on the fixture list when Champfleure FC from Kingscavil, in West Lothian was drawn at home to face Hearts and lost 5-0 to the city side. The Fourth Round brought a home tie and Alloa Athletic were thrashed 9-1 by a rampant Tynecastle side.

A match against Vale of Leven beckoned for Hearts in the Fifth Round but the week before, Third Lanark inflicted Hearts first defeat of the season, after the opening 14 matches had been won. Whether this affected the morale of the team we do not know but they lost easily at Alexandria by 3-1.

In the Shield, Hearts had a fairly straight forward run to the final apart from the usual tussle with Mossend Swifts. The two initial rounds saw Norton Park FC defeated 6-1 and St.Bernards lost 3-0, both at Tynecastle. Hearts reward was a bye and then Muirhouse Rovers were unfortunate to be sent to Gorgie in the Fourth Round and were soundly beaten 11-0.

Mossend Swifts held Hearts 0-0 at home in a Semi-Final tie but in the Replay at Tynecastle, the "maroons" won 6-2. The Final was at Logie Green against Leith Athletic and Hearts claimed the Shield for a third time, winning 2-0 with Rab Henderson and Willie Taylor scoring the goals.

The Rosebery Charity Cup was added when Hearts won that trophy also, for the third time. St.Bernards lost 6-1 in the First Round and Hibernians lost 3-2 in a Semi-Final tie before Hearts met Leith Athletic in the Final, at Logie Green, and won by 4-2.

In the challenge matches the only Scottish sides to beat Hearts were Celtic and Third Lanark although the defeat by Celtic was a resounding 7-0.

During the season 43 matches were played and 170 goals scored.

Davie Baird and Isaac Begbie made their first appearance for Scotland in a Full International on 29 March 1890 against Ireland in a 4-1 win at the Ulster FC Ground, Ballynafeigh, Belfast.

FOUNDER MEMBERS OF THE LEAGUE

In season 1890-1891 as the leading club in the east of Scotland, Hearts became one of the eleven founder members of the Scottish Football League. However, only ten teams completed the first season as Renton, one of the founder clubs, was suspended after five matches for playing against a professional team called Edinburgh Saints.

The club's initial League campaign got off to a disastrous start with defeats in the first three matches, 2-5 away to Rangers; 0-5 at home to Celtic and 1-3 at Dumbarton. The joint Champions, Rangers and Dumbarton both defeated Hearts home and away, and after that poor start the Tynecastle team was never in contention for the title and finished sixth in the League.

The historic opening League match was played on Saturday 16 August at the original Ibrox Park, when Isaac Begbie scored Hearts first Championship goal. The initial home match was played the following Saturday, when Celtic beat the "maroons". Hearts first League win eventually came against Cowlairs at Tynecastle on 13 September when Willie Taylor scored the first home goal in the Championship in a 4-0 victory. Hearts also beat Cowlairs at Springvale Park, Glasgow to record the club's first League double.

The largest home attendance in the League was 5,500 against Dumbarton in April.

Hearts may have finished higher in the League but they had to play the last nine matches without four important players, Davie Baird, Isaac Begbie, Johnny Hill and John Macpherson. These men had taken part in an International Trial against the wishes of the Scottish League and as a result, they were suspended from the competition. At least all four had the satisfaction of playing against England, the first Hearts players to do so.

SUCCESS IN THE SCOTTISH CUP

The team reserved its best form for the Scottish Cup, and thankfully, the ban did not apply to this tournament and Hearts gained national fame for the first time. The successful run started with an easy 7-2 home win over Raith Rovers in the First Round and then Burntisland Thistle scratched in the Second. In the Third Round Methlan Park had the advantage of a home tie but for financial reasons they agreed to switch the match to Meggetland and lost 3-0. This was the one and only Scottish Cup-tie played inside the grounds of an exhibition, the sports enclosure where it took place being part of the Edinburgh Electrical Exhibition of that time – Electric Power was in its infancy!

The Fourth Round saw a 4-3 win over Ayr FC and Greenock Morton lost 5-1 in the Fifth Round. In the Quarter-Finals, East Stirlingshire lost 3-1 – that victory over the "Shire" at Bainsford was controversial with Hearts' defender Jimmy Adams punching a goal bound shot off the line. This was one of several high profile incidents that led to the introduction of the penalty kick in June 1891.

On the day of the Semi-Final match storms and a rail strike led to the Hearts supporter's train not arriving in Glasgow until half-time. Hearts were 3-1 up at that stage and eventually defeated Third Lanark 4-1 at Cathkin Park. As a result, on 7 February 1891 the club made its first appearance in a Scottish Cup Final.

Isaac Begbie then captained the team to victory over Dumbarton at Hampden Park. The only goal of the match came after fifteen minutes when George Scott sent through a perfect pass for Willie Mason to run on to and strike a low shot past the "sons" keeper. Tragically, he went into hospital shortly after the Final due to injuries and never played for Hearts again. There were 5,000 Hearts supporters in the crowd, which numbered about 12,000.

The historic winning team was:- Jock Fairbairn; Jimmy Adams and George Goodfellow; Isaac Begbie-captain, John Macpherson and Johnny Hill; Willie Taylor, Willie Mason, Davie Russell, George Scott and Davie Baird.

They received a heroic welcome at Edinburgh's Caledonian Station. Supporters uncoupled the horses from the waiting carriage and led by two silver bands they pulled the vehicle up Lothian Road for a celebration at Kays Union Hotel – at the corner of Lothian Road and Morrison Street.

That season, Hearts also won the Shield for the fourth time, with a 3-0 win over Armadale but lost out on the Rosebery Charity Cup against Leith Athletic in the Final at Logie Green.

James Robertson & Son 101 Princes Street, presented the International Exhibition Edinburgh 1890 trophy to be played at Meggetland, between Heart of Midlothian FC and Hibernian FC. On 6 August Hearts defeated Hibernians 2-0 to win the cup and a gold medal for each winning player. No doubt that succes encouraged them to later play that Scottish Cup tie there.

SCOTTISH CUP WINNERS 1890/1891 Standing: Joe Newton (trainer), Jock Fairbairn, Jimmy Adams, John Macpherson, Seated: Davie Russell, Isaac Begbie, Johnny Hill, George Goodfellow, On Ground: Willie Taylor, Willie Mason, George Scott, Davie Baird

Johnny Hill and John Macpherson made their first appearance for Scotland in a Full International on 4 April 1891 against England in a 2-1 defeat at Ewood Park in Blackburn.

This was the first International match in which goal nets were used. Four Hearts players appeared for the first time in a Scotland team. The debutants, being joined by Davie Baird and Isaac Begbie.

The club subsequently invested in a handsome new clubhouse incorporating committee rooms, gymnasium and stripping facilities for the players. A press box was also situated over the tunnel between the two open stands. At this time the committee selected the team with an input from the trainer Joe Newton, the captain and senior players.

A NEW SQUAD

For season 1891-1892 there were important changes to the Laws of the Game including a centre circle on the pitch, to prevent players encroaching at the kick-off. In addition, nets were now required to complete the make-up of the goal after the introduction of the crossbar 16 years previously.

More significantly the IFAB – ratified the penalty kick instigated by the Irish FA and it was introduced this season. The kick could be taken from any point along a line drawn across the pitch 12 yards from goal.

Up until this time there were two umpires, one per team, with the referee standing on the touchline keeping time and being 'referred' to if the umpires could not agree. That all changed this season and from now, a single person with powers to send players off as well as give penalties and free kicks without listening to appeals, became a permanent fixture in the game. The two umpires were made linesmen or 'assistant referees' as they are called today.

Hearts suffered a major blow with the departure of John Macpherson to Nottingham Forest and they tried to lure Davie Baird down south but, thankfully, to no avail.

The team made a strong challenge in the 12-club League this season being unbeaten at home with ten wins from eleven matches. Only St.Mirren took a point in a 2-2 draw. A 3-1 victory was recorded over the eventual Champions, Dumbarton, a major club at that time, before a new record League crowd of 7,000. The western club won 5-1 in the return match at Boghead and this proved decisive with Hearts finishing third, three points behind the title winners.

During that campaign, Davie Russell became the first Hearts' man to score a League hat trick when he hit a treble in the 4-2 win against Renton at Tynecastle on 12 September. In October the team also had a remarkable 10-3 win against Clyde at Barrowfield Park, with James Fairbairn becoming the first Hearts' player to score four goals in a League match.

This season saw the first Edinburgh League derby, but not Hearts v Hibernians. The matches were against Leith Athletic and resulted in a 3-1 home win for Hearts and a 2-2 draw at Bank Park in Leith. The "maroons" also recorded a first League double over Rangers, winning 1-0 in Glasgow and 3-2 in Edinburgh.

After defeating Clyde 8-0 and Broxburn Shamrock 5-4, Hearts hold on the Scottish Cup ended against Renton in the Third Round. The teams drew 4-4 at Renton and 2-2 at Tynecastle before a record equalling crowd of 7,500 in the ground, with thousands more watching from the two nearby railway embankments. A third match was lost 3-2 at neutral Hampden Park, Glasgow where the majority of the crowd was backing the popular west of Scotland side.

Winning both the Shield and the Rosebery Charity Cup against St.Bernards and Leith Athletic respectively brought some consolation.

The status of the club was recognised by the SFA when Tynecastle was chosen to host the International match against Wales on 26 March 1892. Unfortunately, a snowstorm limited the crowd to 1,200 but they saw Scotland win 6-1 with a team that included Jimmy Adams, Davie Baird, Isaac Begbie and Johnny Hill who captained the side. He was the first Hearts' player to achieve this honour.

The club certainly needed to improve the spectator facilities and in the summer of 1892 the South Stand was given a roof. This was the first covered accommodation for the public and was known as the 'Covered Stand' with supporters entering from McLeod Street for the first time.

Willie Taylor made his first appearance for Scotland in a Full International on 2 April 1892 against England in a 4-1 defeat at Ibrox Park Glasgow.

Hearts needed to expand the squad to make any impression in the League. In season 1892-1893 several players were secured who would bring great success to the club. Tom Chambers, George Hogg, Bob McLaren, Harry Marshall, and John Walker all came into the team.

Hearts made an impressive start to the League campaign dropping only one point during the first six matches. This run included a 3-1 win over Celtic at Tynecastle on 27 August and drew a new record crowd of 8,000. Only three matches were won out of the next ten fixtures and Hearts ended the campaign in fifth place, largely due to the unsettling effect of so many new players coming in at the same time.

In the Scottish Cup, Hearts travelled to Stenhousemuir in the First Round and salvaged a 1-1 draw before winning the Replay at Tynecastle by 8-0. The team then went to Motherwell where they won 4-2 and earned a Third Round tie against Queen's Park at Tynecastle. They had refused to join the Scottish League but were still a formidable force.

A new attendance record of 13,500 packed the ground to overflowing on the day of the match which ended in a 1-1 draw. Hearts lost the replay 5-2 at Hampden Park before 16,000 spectators and Queen's Park went on to win the Cup.

In February 1893 – after a lapse of two years – a new Hibernian Football Club emerged from the ashes of the old club, but they were not strong enough to stop Hearts winning both the Shield 3-1 and the Rosebery Charity Cup – St.Bernards provided the opposition in both finals. The Charity Cup actually ended in a 3-3 draw but as St.Bernards disputed a goal and refused to replay, Hearts were awarded the trophy.

Among the 18 challenge matches was a meeting with the new Hibernian team and the Leith men gave a good account of themselves losing only 2-1.

HEARTS ADOPT PROFESSIONALISM

In May 1893 the shape of Scottish football changed forever when, in order to combat the drain of talent to England, the Scottish Football Association authorised its clubs to use professional players. The Heart of Midlothian Football Club immediately grasped the opportunity and began to pay its leading men the sum of £2 per week plus bonuses.

Hearts were now able to further strengthen the squad and at the start of season 1893-1894. Tom Chambers, Davie Russell and Willie Taylor all returned from England and Willie Michael – Wishaw Thistle was recruited.

As a result, Hearts made a late assault on the Championship on the back of an unbeaten away record. The "maroons" finished in second place, being just unable to catch Celtic after losing the first two home matches against Leith Athletic and the Glasgow side. That match against Celtic in September 1893 created a new attendance record of 14,000 but they saw Hearts go down 4-2.

Shortly after the match, the club ordered a pair of proper goal nets – fixed to the posts – to replace the free standing pair that had been used for the best part of a year.

Hearts had doubles over Rangers, Renton and Dundee, but stumbled to weaker clubs particularly at home. As a result, a 3-2 victory in the return match at Celtic Park was not enough to overhaul their lead.

Even though Hearts lost 1-0 to St.Mirren at Paisley in the First Round of the Scottish Cup, the supporters had been comforted by a particularly resounding victory over the Second Division Champions, Hibernian. On 12 August 1893 the "greens" were destroyed 10-2 at Easter Road, the biggest result between the clubs. Davie Baird and John Walker both scored hat-tricks that day.

In a return match on 28 October Hibernian lost 7-3. However, at the end of the season the Leith team did manage to defeat Hearts 4-2 in the Rosebery Charity Cup Final.

During yet another eventful campaign, Hearts won the Shield for the sixth time in a row with a 4-2 victory over Leith Athletic. In addition, in March 1894 Hearts Reserve Team won the Scottish Second XI Cup for the first time beating St.Mirren in the Final.

That same month the club made its first visit to Ireland and drew 1-1 with Linfield FC. But unfortunately, the season ended with some animosity and Hearts, Hibernian and St.Bernards all resigned from the East of Scotland FA after a dispute over match dates.

Tom Chambers made his first appearance for Scotland in a Full International on 24 March 1894 against Wales scoring twice in a 5-2 win at Rugby Park, Kilmarnock.

CHAMPIONS OF SCOTLAND

Professional clubs began to flourish and Hearts now had 1,000 members and were able to attract the best players. In 1894-1895 Hearts' Committee assembled a squad that became Scottish Champions for the first time. Isaac Begbie was the captain, ably supported by George Hogg, Bob McLaren, Willie Michael and Jock Walker, while the new full back partnership of Barney Battles and James Mirk turned a good side into a great one.

Trainer Joe Newton had the players in excellent condition and playing a wide passing game Hearts left all the challengers in their wake, winning the first eleven League fixtures. A remarkable start which remains a Club record but Clyde put a stop to the run with a 4-2 victory on a day of miserable weather in December.

With the 'Old Firm' failing to make any impression, the title was all but secured on 16 February in the fourth last match when Celtic were destroyed at Tynecastle by the razor sharp Jock Walker, who scored twice in a 4-0 win.

It was actually clinched on 30 March in the second last fixture when Dundee lost 4-0 in Gorgie. The final match of the campaign drew a capacity crowd of 15,000 to Logie Green where, the now Champions of Scotland gained revenge over St. Bernards for the Scottish Cup defeat that season. The players received a £5 bonus as Hearts finished with 31 points from 18 matches, five ahead of Celtic, scoring 50 goals and conceding only 18.

The men who would go down in Hearts folklore were:- Bill Cox 15 appearances and 6 shut-outs, John Fairbairn 3/2, Bob McLaren 18 appearances and 8 goals, Willie Michael 17/10, Barney Battles 16/-, James Mirk 16/-, George Scott 16/5, Tom Chambers 15/8, George Hogg 15/-, Jock Walker 15/8, Davie Russell 14/3, Alex Hall 13/1, Isaac Begbie-captain 8/-, Davie Baird 6/3, Tom Wilkie 3/-, George Macdonald 2/-, David Black 1/-, Willie Nicol 1/-, Willie Maxwell 1/1, Willie Phillips 1/1, Richardson 1/-, Willie Taylor 1/1.

Hearts should have added the Scottish Cup but unaccountably lost in a Semi-Final Replay against the eventual winners, St.Bernards. Rangers lost 2-1 in the First Round at Ibrox Park and Abercorn FC went down 6-1 to Hearts in Paisley in the Second Round. The Third Round saw Hearts win 4-2 against Kings Park at Tynecastle.

St.Bernards awaited them in the Semi-Finals but nerves affected the players in the 0-0 draw at Tynecastle because a new record crowd of 14,500 had broken down fences and spilled onto the track. In the replay at Logie Green, Hearts surprisingly lost by the only goal in the match.

Having temporarily left the East of Scotland FA, the region's senior clubs – Hearts, Hibernian, Leith Athletic and St.Bernards – formed the Edinburgh League and Hearts were the first Champions, winning five out of the six matches. The team was also successful in the Rosebery Charity Cup defeating Leith Athletic 3-1 in the Final at Easter Road, while the reserves retained the Second X1 Cup.

This superb campaign included a "World Championship" match against the English Champions, Sunderland, but Hearts went down 5-3 at Tynecastle before a crowd of 12,000.

Davie Russell and Jock Walker made their first appearance for Scotland in a Full International on 30 March 1895 against Ireland and Walker scored in a 3-1 win at Celtic Park, Glasgow.

On the administrative front, in March, the lease of Tynecastle was extended by five years by the Town Council – by the Casting Vote of the Treasurer of Edinburgh – at an annual rent of £150. The popularity of the game continued to grow and the Edinburgh Evening News installed the first telephone in a football ground for reporting purposes.

LEAGUE CHAMPIONS 1894/1895 Standing – R. Waugh–Trainer, R. Cheyne, B. Battles, J. Stir ing, R. Smith, W. Cox, W. Lorimer, J. Mirk, J.R. Cairns, W. Amos, G. Hogg, J. Adams. Seated – R. McLaren, W. Michael, I. Begbie–Captain, A. Hall G. Scott. On Ground – T. Chambers, J. Walker.

A CAPITAL CUP FINAL

On the playing side, there were some major changes in 1895-1896 with Alex King – Dykehead FC, George Scott and Bob McCartney – Leith Athletic coming in and Barney Battles' departing to Celtic.

However, Hearts failed to retain the Championship, finishing in fourth place. This was due to a leaky defence that conceded 36 goals, twice as many as last season, and clearly missed Barney Battles. With 68 goals Hearts were actually the top scorers in the League, and there were no draws. The team was either brilliant or poor.

On a good day in September, Hearts beat Celtic 5-0 in Glasgow and Alex King became our first man to score a hat-trick against either of the Old Firm. That same month, Hearts won the initial League "Derby" against Hibernian by 4-3. A new Tynecastle League record attendance of 17,500 cheered a late winner from Davie Baird.

In October, Hearts crushed Clyde by 9-1 and then in the next match, went down 5-0 to Dundee at Dens Park. Such inconsistency ruined the League campaign, and Celtic, the eventual title winners, even won the return League match at Tynecastle by 4-1.

The season will be remembered for Hearts Scottish Cup Final, victory over Hibernian, which silenced the Easter Road's claim to be the East of Scotland's premier club. This spurious statement was made due to the fact that they had finished ahead of Hearts in this, their initial season in Division One.

The players reserved their best form for the Scottish Cup, starting with away victories over Blantyre 12-1, Ayr FC 5-1 and Arbroath 4-0. The Semi-Finals brought St.Bernards to Gorgie and Willie Michael forced home the only goal. Hibernian won against Renton and for the first, and to date, only time, two Edinburgh clubs met in the Final.

As a result, the SFA chose St.Bernards' ground at Logie Green as the venue, the only time the Final has been played outside of Glasgow. This ground has disappeared under Logie Green Road but on 14 March 1896 it was packed, with a crowd of fully 17,000.

The players were fit, due to the preparation of trainer James Chapman, and Hearts started brilliantly with Davie Baird scoring from a penalty after a handball incident. Shortly after half time, Alex King made it 2-0 with a shot from a tight angle and Willie Michael headed a third goal. O'Neill scored a consolation for Hibernian to make the final score 3-1.

Hearts winning team was:- Jock Fairbairn; Bob McCartney and James Mirk; Isaac Begbie, Davie Russell and George Hogg-captain; Bob McLaren, Davie Baird, Willie Michael, Alex King and John Walker.

Despite the fact that an Edinburgh club had to win the Cup, the trophy was not at Logie Green on the day. It was not presented to Hearts until Tuesday 24 March at the Royal Restaurant in Glasgow.

Hearts clearly benefited from the player judgement of Committee man Tom Purdie, and the talent spotting of Robert Cheyne. This was evident in April 1896 when 17-year old Bobby Walker of Dalry Primrose was given a trial against Sunderland and was immediately signed. Even then, he showed touches that indicated that he would play for Scotland.

Hearts beat Hibernian 7-1 on the way to retaining the Edinburgh League – five wins and a draw. In addition, the team won the Rosebery Charity Cup Final with an 8-2 thrashing of Leith Athletic. Sunderland visited Gorgie twice winning once and drawing the other then Sheffield Wednesday lost 3-0 at Tynecastle on 29 April

SCOTTISH CUP WINNERS 1895/1896 Standing – R. McLaren, R. McCartney, J. Fairbairn, J. Mirk, A. King, J. Chapman-Trainer. Seated – D. Baird, W. Michael, J. Walker, G. Hogg-Captain, I. Begbie, D. Russell.

in a Cup Winners Challenge, and the reserves added their Championship. All this meant that resources were available to expand the stadium banking and construct a track and cycle raceway.

Alex King made his first appearance for Scotland in a Full International on 21 March 1896 against Wales in a 4-0 win at Carolina Park, Dundee.

George Hogg made his first appearance for Scotland in a Full International on 28 March 1896 against Ireland in a 3-3 draw at the Solitude Ground, Cliftonville, Belfast.

CHAMPIONS AGAIN

This was a glorious period and in 1896-1897 Hearts became Scottish Champions for a second time, finishing two points ahead of Hibernian, despite the loss of Alex King and Davie Russell to Celtic and Willie Michael to Liverpool. However, the club had several players at their peak including Davie Baird, Isaac Begbie, Jock Fairbairn, George Hogg, Bob McLaren and Willie Taylor. There had also been some shrewd recruitment in Albert Buick, George Livingston, Harry Marshall, Tom Robertson and, of course, Bobby Walker.

Hearts captain was John Walker, a creative inside forward, and the Championship began well with a 5-0 win over Dundee at Dena Park, followed by a 6-1 victory against Abercorn. Then after 3-1 defeat of St.Mirren at Tynecastle things started to go wrong and three of the next five matches were lost. Hearts looked far from champions after a 2-0 defeat at Easter Road but it was to be their last League reverse of the season.

The team was certainly ready for a crucial match against Hibernian at home on 5 December 1896. Our neighbours were four points clear and would probably have secured the title with a win, but a Tom Robertson goal defeated the "greens" and brought Hearts and Celtic within two points of the Leith side. By mid-January, the three teams were on 24 points with two games to play.

Hibernian went to 26 points after beating St.Mirren and Hearts moved to 26 after defeating Clyde away from home. Hibernian lost their last match at Paisley to finish on 26 and Hearts could finish on 28 if their final fixture was won. However, Celtic had two matches to play and could also reach 28. On 20 February thanks to a brilliant four goals from Tom Robertson, Clyde were hammered 5-0 and there was jubilation when news reached Tynecastle that Celtic had lost at home to Dundee and could no longer match Hearts total of points

Hearts successful squad was:- Jock Fairbairn 18 appearances and 5 shut-outs, Bob McCartney 17 appearances and 0 goals, John Walker 18/7, George Hogg-captain 16/0, Bob McLaren 16/3, Willie Taylor 16/10, Davie Baird 15/2, Isaac Begbie 13/0, James Mirk 12/1, Harry Marshal 10/0, James Sharp 10/5, Tom Robertson 8/9, Alex Gillies 6/2, Jimmy Adams 4/1, Robert Gray 3/1, George Livingston 3/2, Bobby Walker 3/2, William White 3/0, Albert Buick 2/0, David Alexander 1/0, Harry Allan 1/0, Tom Keir 1/0, H.Paterson 1/0, George Scott 1/0.

Nine of the players now had two Championship medals:- Davie Baird, Isaac Begbie, Jock Fairbairn, George Hogg, Bob McLaren, James Mirk, George Scott, Willie Taylor and John Walker. A feat not repeated until 1960.

In the Scottish Cup First Round, Hearts beat Clyde at Tynecastle but the holders went out against Third Lanark losing 5-2 at Cathkin Park, although the team did win the East of Scotland League (formerly the Edinburgh League). This was not the most attractive competition, but the inferior make up of the teams allowed players such as Bobby Walker to quickly develop. The Rosebery Charity Cup Final was lost 3-0 to Hibernian but the reserves again won the Second XI Cup.

LEAGUE CHAMPIONS 1896/1897 Standing – D. Baird, W. Taylor, J. Sharp, J. Walker, J. Chapman-Trainer, J. Fairbairn, J. Mirk, H. Marshall. Seated – G. Hogg, R McCartney, R McLaren, I. Begbie.

HEARTS COME BACK TO EARTH

At the start of season 1897-1898 Hearts suffered injuries to key men and failed to retain the title. Even though consistency was never achieved, the artistry of Bobby Walker and George Livingston was often thrilling, but just not enough to deliver even the Scottish Cup with Hearts crashing out against Dundee.

This led to strained finances and the sale of Tom Robertson and John Walker to Liverpool for £350. In addition, after winning a friendly at Anfield Road, Bobby Walker, who scored the only goal, became another target for English clubs.

Hearts failed to win any of the first six League matches and were never in contention for the Championship which was eventually won by Celtic without losing a match. However, when Hearts were able to field their strongest side they were a match for any team, and won their last four fixtures scoring 23 goals to pull themselves up to fourth position.

In the Scottish Cup First Round, Hearts defeated Lochee United 8-0 in Dundee and then beat Greenock Morton 4-1 at Tynecastle. In the Third Round, Hearts returned to Tayside but went down 3-0 at Dens Park against Dundee.

The team was successful at local level and won the East of Scotland League – six wins a draw and a loss – and the Rosebery Charity Cup Final when George Livingston scored a hat-trick in a 6-1 win over Hibernian. The club also retained the Shield winning the Final 2-0 against Leith Athletic after a Replay.

Tom Robertson made his first appearance for Scotland in a Full International on 26 March 1898 against Ireland and he scored in a 3-0 win at the Solitude Ground, Cliftonville, Belfast.

This increased the players' confidence for season 1898-1899 and an extra boost was the recruitment of Scotland's best goalkeeper, Harry Rennie – Greenock Morton (£50), and Johnny Walker – Leith Athletic (£50), the club's first coloured player.

Hearts did perform well, but finished second in the League, ten points behind Rangers, who won all their matches. The men in maroon did provide some great entertainment and beat Hibernian 4-0 at home and 5-1 away. In the latter match, Bobby Walker scored the first League hat trick against our city rivals.

The First Round of the Scottish Cup saw Hearts at Ibrox Park where Rangers won a stormy encounter 4-1. The Tynecastle players claimed that the ball did not cross the line for Rangers first goal and disputed the penalty that made it 2-0. In the second half, with the score 4-0, Isaac Begbie and George Hogg were sent off for rough play. The other players then wanted to walk off and only the intervention of Hearts' officials enabled the game to proceed. Isaac Begbie was later suspended for two months.

This early exit had other ramifications. Centre-half Harry Marshall missed the match through injury and was not Cup-tied. This led to Celtic requesting to have him on loan for their Scottish Cup matches. He was eventually persuaded to join them permanently for (£200) and the Glasgow side won the trophy with an ex-Hearts half-back line of Battles, Marshall and King.

Despite a poorer season Hearts support was growing strongly and brake-clubs were emerging throughout Edinburgh and district. The well known Southside Brake Club – which held 15 supporters – left for Tynecastle from Causewayside in one of these large horse drawn wagons draped by a banner depicting Cocky Taylor and Davie Baird.

As the season drew to a conclusion, Hearts again won the East of Scotland League plus the Shield, defeating Hibernian 1-0 at Logie Green. The Rosebery Charity Cup Final was held at the same venue but Hearts slipped up and lost by the only goal to Leith Athletic.

A NEW CENTURY

Hearts defence was now reputed to be the best in Scotland but the team lacked a cutting edge and finished fourth in the League in 1899-1900. To get there they completed the 'double' over Celtic, Clyde and St.Bernards. In addition, by holding Rangers to a 1-1 draw, in September they broke the Glasgow club's run of 22 consecutive League victories.

The supporters' expectations that the first season of the new Century would see honours come to Tynecastle again were not realised. Harry Rennie the goalkeeper was the finest custodian in Scotland and George Hogg at half-back was at his peak. Bobby Walker was regarded as Europe's leading player who brought out the best in Davie Baird, Isaac Begbie, George Livingston and Willie Michael.

The Scottish Cup was now the main target and Hearts were drawn against St.Mirren at Tynecastle in the First Round but could only achieve a 0-0 draw but in the Replay at Love Street, they won 3-0. The Second Round brought the Edinburgh city rivals together and again Hearts could only draw at home but true to their colours they won 2-1 in the Replay at Easter Road.

Third Lanark stood in their way for a Semi-Final place when they met at Cathkin Park in the Third Round and hopes were raised for another trophy when they won 2-1. However on 10 March Queen's Park, the stalwarts of the Scottish Cup, defeated Hearts at Hampden Park 2-1 to reach the final.

A new Inter City League was introduced comprising Hearts, Hibernian and the four Glasgow clubs – Celtic, Queen's Park, Rangers and Third Lanark. When the team played Rangers on 30 December 1899 the present Ibrox Park was opened, but the rest of the competition was uneventful and Hearts were fourth.

The Tynecastle side did win the East of Scotland League and defeated Hibernian 3-0 to win the Rosebery Charity Cup, making up for losing by the same score to Hibernian in the Shield Final 18 days previously.

Harry Rennie and Bobby Walker made their first appearance for Scotland in a Full International on 3 March 1900 against Ireland in a 3-0 win at Solitude Ground, Cliftonville, Belfast.

They were in the Scottish team that crushed England 4-1 in April 1900 but soon afterwards, Harry Rennie made a shock move to Hibernian for £50 as he had a 'sell on clause' in his contract. In addition, George Livingston, went to Sunderland for £175 while Isaac Begbie and Willie Taylor retired. The same clause was in his Hibs contract but later a new by-law in the Scottish League constitution and rules forbid such a clause.

The squad that had been playing for ten years was finished and it was time to invest in quality players, as Hearts were the only club that could challenge the "Old Firm". It was also necessary to introduce sign-on fees and the club paid £39 to keep the illustrious Bobby Walker at home.

To finance the need to pay and retain top players Hearts began to concentrate on a number of commercial ventures including an Annual Concert, advertising within the ground, running, cycle and athletics meetings, operation of refreshment stalls and the sale of picture post cards and fixture cards.

ENIGMATIC HEARTS

For 1900-1901 Bob Waugh replaced John Dalziel as trainer and he had his work cut out due to the departure of so many players. Hearts made a woeful start failing to win any of the first seven League matches and only won one home match out of ten. The away form was better with four wins, one of which was a surprising 3-1 victory over Celtic in Glasgow and the only 'double' was against Kilmarnock.

Accordingly, with no automatic relegation, Hearts had to apply for re-election to Division One after finishing tenth in the eleven-club League. Only 22 goals were scored which is the club's poorest ever figure, but nevertheless, Hearts were unanimously re-elected.

The club Members felt that at 31, far too many players had been used in the various competitions leading to a lack of cohesion in their play. They also encouraged the Committee to enter the transfer market as the club could not challenge the 'Old Firm' by playing youngsters. In their view, Hearts were the only club who could consistently challenge Celtic and Rangers and we owed it to Scottish football to make every effort do so.

Astonishingly, the team was good enough to win the Scottish Cup. This was in no small measure due to the fact that in October 1900 the club signed the influential Mark Bell and Bob Houston – St.Bernards (£270). Goals started to flow and Hearts scored 21 in the competition, defeating Mossend Swifts 7-0, Queens Park 2-1 and Port Glasgow Athletic 5-1, before drawing Hibernian in the Semi-Finals at Tynecastle.

A record Scottish Cup crowd of 22,500 gave a tumultuous roar when Mark Bell scored for Hearts and although Hibernian equalised in the second half, the boys in maroon comfortably won the replay 2-1 with Bill Porteous and Bobby Walker scoring either side of the interval. Hearts savoured the Bobby Walker goal because it embarrassed goalkeeper Rennie, who had walked out on Hearts. His clearance landed at the feet of the Hearts captain who volleyed the ball into the net catching him well off his line.

In one of the best Finals ever played on 6 April it was Bobby Walker who inspired Hearts to victory against Celtic at Ibrox Park. In fact the game was known for many years as the "Walker Final" due to the brilliant dribbling and passing of the Hearts captain. The youth and pace of the capital side upset Celtic, as did the team's direct, long passing game. Sadly, only 16,000 watched a magnificent contest, due to wet conditions and high admission costs.

Some newspapers credit Bobby Walker with the opening goal in Hearts 4-3 victory but although he was involved, it came from a blistering shot from Bill Porteous. Celtic equalised and then Mark Bell made it 2-1. Bobby Walker set up the chance for Charlie Thomson to make it 3-1, but following an injury to George Key, Celtic fought back to equalise. With ten minutes left, Bobby Walker dribbled through and struck a shot that the keeper could only block. This caused a scramble and after the Celtic keeper could not hold Bob Houston's shot, Mark Bell raced in to hit the dramatic winner.

The heroes were:- George Philip; Harry Allan and Davie Baird; George Key, Albert Buick and George Hogg; Bill Porteous, Bobby Walker-captain, Charlie Thomson, Bob Houston and Mark Bell.

A mighty procession with two bands led the team to the University Hotel in Chambers Street where the players held a celebration.

The rest of the season was forgettable although the Reserves won the Second X1 Cup. Defeats were suffered in the Final of the Shield – 3-2 to Leith Athletic and the Rosebery Charity Cup – 4-0 to Hibernian. In addition,

Scottish Cup Winners 1900/1901 Standing: Bob Waugh (trainer), Davie Baird, Albert Buick, George Hogg, George Philip, Harry Allan. Seated: George Key, Bobby Walker (captain), Charlie Thomsor, Bob Houston. On Ground: Bill Porteous, Markie Bell.

they failed to win the East of Scotland League after winning it six times in succession. The Inter-City League was disappointing with only three wins.

Mark Bell made his first appearance for Scotland in a Full International on 2 March 1901 against Wales in 1-1 draw at The Racecourse, Wrexham.

WORLD CLASS HEARTS

In May 1901 the former Renton secretary, Peter Fairley, became the first Hearts manager responsible for the instruction of the players and trainers, and a number of administrative tasks. He soon became heavily involved in ground developments because the uncovered North Stand was replaced during the summer by a covered structure with a standing enclosure in front. Wooden beams were also laid in the banking to provide the first terracing. The stand was opened in September 1901 when Rangers beat Hearts 2-0 in the League.

Form during season 1901-1902 showed a vast improvement with Hearts finishing third behind Rangers and the runners-up, Celtic. Other significant League results included three 'doubles' – Hibernian were defeated twice by 2-1, Greenock Morton twice by 3-1 and St.Mirren by 2-1 and 2-0.

The Scottish Cup was a struggle, with Cowdenbeath drawing 0-0 in Fife in the First Round and Hearts having to take them to Tynecastle in the Replay to win 3-0. The Second Round saw Third Lanark travel to Edinburgh and end up losing 4-1. In February Celtic prevented Hearts from retaining the Cup winning a Third Round Replay by 2-1 after drawing 1-1 in Gorgie before a record equalling attendance of 22,500.

Inconsistency against mediocre teams let the supporters down, but Hearts certainly played well against the FA Cup winners, Tottenham Hotspur, in an unofficial 'World Championship' event. The first leg in London, in September ended 0-0 with the return match in January being a 3-1 victory for Hearts. The club was clearly an attraction and Hearts were invited to take part in the Glasgow Exhibition Cup and the Glasgow Charity Cup, but lost in both competitions to Celtic.

The supporters had to be content with winning the Inter City League and defeating Hibernian 2-1 in the Final of the Shield, but Hibernian won by 1-0 in the Rosebery Charity Cup Final.

The season was overshadowed by the tragedy at Ibrox Park in April 1902 when parts of the terracing collapsed during the Scotland versus England match killing 25 people.

Albert Buick-Captain- and George Key made their first appearance for Scotland in a Full International on 1 March 1902 against Ireland and Albert Buick scored in the 5-1 win at Grosvenor Park, Belfast.

Harry Allan made his first appearance for Scotland in a Full International Cap on 15 March 1902 against Wales in a 5-1 win at Cappielow Park, Greenock.

THE FINAL DISAPPOINTMENT

From the start of season 1902-1903 new pitch markings were confirmed. The kick-off required a centre spot; keeping players ten yards from a kick-off brought the centre circle; a game of two halves meant a centre line. Throw-ins, two-handed from 1882 were taken from behind the sidelines. The 1902 decision to award penalties for fouls committed in an area 18 yards from the goal line and 44 yards wide, created both the penalty box and penalty spot. Another box "goal area", commonly called the "six-yard-box", six yards long and 20 wide replaced a semi circle in the goalmouth.

Hearts had to replace the departing Mark Bell and Bob Houston, and paid Liverpool £200 to re-sign Tom Robertson together with John Hunter. In addition, in January 1903 Andrew Orr – Greenock Morton was signed.

Despite expensive team building, Hearts lost their two opening League fixtures against Greenock Morton 2-3 and Dundee 0-2 but there were 'doubles' over Queen's Park, Port Glasgow Athletic and Third Lanark. The team's key player Bobby Walker had an indifferent season and this affected the team. Bill Porteous came on strongly this term and Hearts had an astonishing finish to the League race, taking 13 out of 14 points in the final seven matches, helping them to finish fourth in the Championship.

Hearts were ready to make an impact in the Scottish Cup. Clyde 2-1, Ayr FC 4-2 and Third Lanark 2-1 were defeated before the team met Dundee at Dens Park in the Semi-Finals. After a 0-0 draw, Hearts won the replay 1-0 thanks to a blockbuster goal from Bill Porteous. The new record Gorgie crowd of 30,000 was the largest to watch a Scottish match outside of Glasgow.

In April 1903 it required three games at Celtic Park to separate Hearts and Rangers in the Cup Final, but eventually the Glasgow team won 2-0 before 32,000 spectators. The first match ended 1-1 with Bobby Walker scoring and the replay finished 0-0. Hearts felt aggrieved at being denied a clear penalty in the first game and in the second encounter, the Edinburgh side was again unlucky when a George Key shot appeared to cross the line before being cleared. Even in the third match Hunter had a goal disallowed at a crucial time, although the loss of Albert Buick through injury was the main reason that Hearts did not secure the Cup.

The team in the first two matches was:- George McWattie; Andrew Orr and Charlie Thomson; George Key, Albert Buick-captain and George Hogg; Bob Dalrymple, Bobby Walker, Bill Porteous, John Hunter and Davie Baird, who was playing his fourth Cup Final for the club. In that third game, Albert Buick had been injured and was replaced by John Anderson.

The team was poor in the minor competitions, losing to Leith Athletic in both the Shield and the Rosebery Charity Cup Semi-Finals, but they did win the Inter City League by shrewd use of reserve strength.

Over the campaign there had been discipline problems for the manager and indeed, William Waugh eventually took over from Peter Fairley then in May James Chapman replaced Bob Waugh as trainer.

Bill Porteous made his first appearance for Scotland in a Full International on 21 March 1903 against Ireland in a 2-0 defeat at Celtic Park, Glasgow.

UNDER NEW MANAGEMENT

The club had been criticised for crushing that occurred at the Cup game against Dundee and took action, joining the two grandstands to make a continuous structure with a new pavilion at the Gorgie Road end. The new facilities were opened in August 1903.

There were changes off the field and on 14 August 1903 The Heart of Midlothian Football Club was incorporated as a Limited Company and included in the Register of joint Stock Companies, with an authorised share capital of £5,000 divided into 5,000 ordinary shares of £1 each. . Surprisingly, the Committee found that the sale of shares was not an immediate success. A story repeated on at least three future occasions.

The First Statutory Meeting of the Shareholders was held in the Central Halls, Edinburgh on 6 November. With the obvious implications of Members losing their voting powers, there was some resistance, and it would be 28 March 1904 before the Articles of Association were unanimously confirmed.

The League was expanded to 14 clubs for the 1903-1904 season and Hearts finished second, four points behind Third Lanark. Early in the campaign, Hearts lost 2-1 to the Glasgow club and this success gave them an edge, even though Hearts won the return game at Tynecastle 4-1. In fact, Hearts won all thirteen home matches but did not recover from early inconsistency on the road.

This was a fair performance as Mr. Waugh introduced young players and had to cope with the loss of Albert Buick to Portsmouth and Alex Menzies to Motherwell In came Mark Bell, Tom Collins and David Wilson, who joined his brother. He also made the astute decision that Charlie Thomson's best position was centre half.

In the Scottish Cup First Round, Hearts were unlucky to lose 3-2 against Rangers, missing several chances to equalise in the closing quarter of an hour.

An experimental team did win the Inter City League, even though the fixtures were not completed, but Hearts were regarded as winners with eleven points from seven matches placing them top of the table when the season ended.

Hearts dominated the local competitions winning the East of Scotland League and defeating Hibernian in the Shield Final 7-2, the Rosebery Charity Cup Final 3-0, and the City Cup Final 5-1. Including a benefit and a friendly, Hearts played the Easter Road side nine times that season, winning seven and drawing two.

Unfortunately the campaign ended with an unexpected player exodus, including Bill Porteous and John Hunter who went to Arsenal.

George Wilson made his first appearance for Scotland in a Full International on 12 March 1904 against Wales in a 1-1 draw at Dens Park, Dundee.

Charlie Thomson made his first appearance for Scotland in a Full International on 26 March 1904 against Ireland in a 1-1 draw at Dalymount Park, Dublin.

Although Hearts would not venture abroad for another eight years, the game in other countries was rapidly developing. As a result The Federation of International Football Associations was founded in May 1904 in Paris, with seven original members:- Belgium, Denmark, France, Netherlands, Spain, Sweden and Switzerland.

There was some initial disquiet in the home countries – as they had formed the International Football Association Board, in 1886 – to the idea of a world body governing the sport for which they had created rules.

New North Stand

Tynecastle 1904

FINANCIAL CRISIS

In 1904 the Limited Company formed in 1903 ran into financial difficulties. On 13 February 1905 the Directors were advised of "debts" amounting to about £1,400 and decided that the Club's agents consider matters and form an opinion as to what action to take.

On 15 February they advised the directors of two options:- 1) to appeal to the generosity of the present shareholders to come forward with financial assistance, 2) to lay the position of the Club before members to consent to voluntary liquidation when the assets would be taken up by a new body at a reasonable valuation and the debts and obligations undertaken by the restructured company.

On 2 March at a Quarterly General Meeting a resolution "Proposed the Temporary Loans from present Shareholders" it was defeated, 94 votes to 72. On the 20 March the Board decided at an Extraordinary General Meeting that the old Company was wound up voluntarily.

The new Company picked up the old concern's debts of £1,600 and on 29 April 1905 was incorporated on the Register of Companies number SC005863 and despite a problem selling all the shares it cleared most of the debts quickly.

Due to the financial uncertainty, the club was unable to invest in fresh talent for season 1904-1905 and Hearts finished seventh equal in the League.

Despite being captained by Scotland's best defender, Charlie Thomson, performances ranged between brilliant and mediocre. For example, Hearts won three out of four points against eventual champions, Celtic. It is worth noting that these two matches were played within 16 days of each other. The team suffered heavy reverses against poorer teams including 7-1 against Third Lanark, the club's record League defeat at that time. Typically, Hearts bounced back, the following Saturday, to beat Airdrieonians 6-0 when Bobby Walker became the first Tynecastle player to score five goals in a League fixture and ended the season with 14 goals.

In the Scottish Cup First Round, Hearts defeated Dundee 3-1 at Dens Park and immediately signed their David Wilson who scored in the Second Round. However, Hearts lost 2-1 to St.Mirren at Love Street, largely due to playing 87 minutes without injured full back, Andrew Orr.

The Inter City League was abandoned and the East of Scotland League was unfinished, although Hearts won the title after playing off against Dundee during the following season. With the expansion of the Scottish League these lengthy affairs had had their day, but knock-out competitions survived, with Hearts winning the East of Scotland/ City Cup and the Rosebery Charity Cup, defeating Leith Athletic in both Finals. That season Hibernian won the Final of the Shield 1-0 after two draws.

A FOURTH SCOTTISH CUP SUCCESS

The new Board brought fresh ideas and there was a large turnover of players during the summer of 1905. Those coming to Tynecastle - Alex Menzies – Motherwell, David Lindsay – St.Mirren and George Couper – Kings Park. Among the departures were George Key, Robert Mackie and Martin Moran who were all signed by a new club, Chelsea. The feel good factor was reflected in one of the club's best ever campaigns in which Hearts did well in the League and won the Scottish Cup.

Credit was due to the team building skills of manager, William Waugh, and the majestic form of the country's two best players, Charlie Thomson and Bobby Walker. Alex Menzies became the first Hearts man to score 20 League goals in a season.

The team was unbeaten in the first sixteen League matches of the 1905-1906 season. That included a 5-0 away victory over Rangers at Ibrox Park and a 3-0 win at Easter Road, in which Bobby Walker scored a hat-trick. Significantly, Celtic became the first side to take a point from Hearts in a 1-1 draw at Tynecastle. The team actually never lost at home, but on the road, only 6 games were won from 15 with the players faltering in December to allow Celtic to build up an invincible lead and Hearts ended up in second place.

This may have been linked to a new playing contract that caused disharmony around the festive period. The team threatened not to play for the club in the Scottish Cup.

Contract issues were resolved before the run that began with comfortable wins over Nithsdale Wanderers 4-1 and Beith 3-0. Then there was the famous 2-1 Quarter Final victory away to Celtic before 52,000, the largest crowd to have watched Hearts up to that time.

In a Semi-Final tie at Clune Park against Port Glasgow Athletic lost 2-0 and this took Hearts into the Final against Third Lanark at Ibrox Park on 28 April 1906. On a day of snow, hail and rain, Tynecastle fans made up the bulk of the 25,000 crowd many wearing blue – Hearts colours for the day. After constant pressure, the only goal came in the 81st minute. Bobby Walker tried to convert a George Couper cross, but after he was blocked, the ball broke to George Wilson who rolled it into an empty net.

The team was:- George Philip; Harry McNaught and David Philip; Frank McLaren, Charlie Thomson-captain and Jimmy Dickson; George Couper, Bobby Walker, Alex Menzies, David Wilson and George Wilson.

Over 30,000 supporters later accompanied the victorious team from the Caledonian Station to the Imperial Hotel in Leith Street for a celebration

Hearts won the East of Scotland Cup Final 4-1 against Leith Athletic and the Shield Final 2-1 against Hibernian. They lost out on the Rosebery Charity Cup Final 2-0 to Hibernian and East of Scotland League.

As Hibernian wanted to play Hearts during the festive period, Hearts director, Robert Wilson, presented the Wilson New Year Cup for annual competition between the two major city clubs – Hibernian won the initial match.

There was another notable match at Tynecastle on 3 March when Scotland lost 2-0 to Wales before a crowd of 25,000 – who paid for admission, but after a break-in the actual crowd was nearer 30,000. Subsequently the ground was enlarged.

Alex Menzies made his first appearance for Scotland in a Full International on 7 April 1906 against England in a 2-1 win at Hampden Park, Glasgow.

On 18 April the SFA decided that players playing in English International matches each receive £5 for wages and other Internationals £3 each.

The Hearts directors did not agree. On 25 April they were informed their letter of disagreement would be placed before the International Committee and that Charlie Thomson and Alex Menzies had each been paid the extra for the English International on 1 April. Hearts withdrew their complaint to a £4 limit.

FIRST ELEVEN 1905/1906 Standing – G. Goodfe low-Assistant Trainer, G. Philip. D. Bain, F. McLaren, H. McNaught, Wm. Lindsay Waugh–Manager, J. Chapman–Trainer.
Seated – D. Lirdsay, R. Walker, A, Menzies, C. Thomson–Captain, J. Dickson, D. Wilson, G. Wilson.

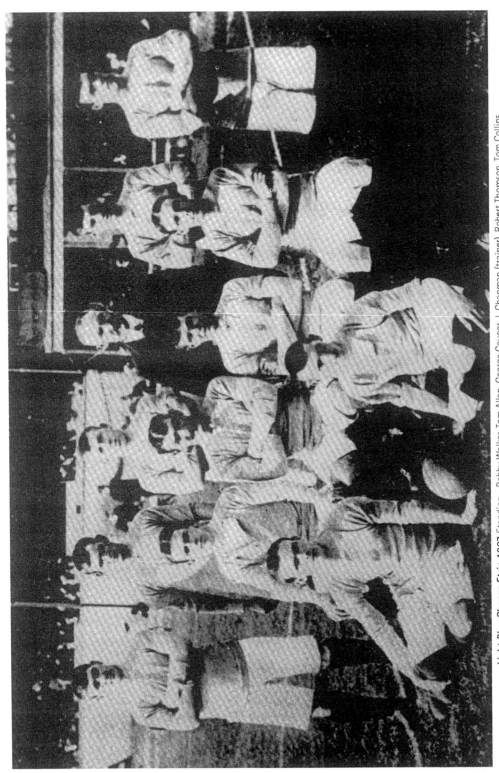

Light Blue Change Strip 1907 Standing – Bobby Walker, Tom Allan, George Couper, J. Chapman (trainer), Robert Thomson, Tom Collins. Seated – David Philip, Charlie Thomson, Jimmy Dickson, Alex Merzies. Lying – William Williamson, Tommy Pearson.

A SECOND SUCCESSIVE SCOTTISH CUP FINAL

The Cup winning team quickly broke up with the Wilson brothers joining Everton for £725. George Philip, David Lindsay and Harry McNaught also went to England and even Alex Menzies was lured to Manchester United for £500. The manager was told to find replacements and among others, he recruited Tom Allan – Rutherglen Glencairn, and Tom Collins – East Fife.

However, 1906-1907 was a disappointing season with Hearts unable to field a settled side and falling to ninth place in the League. The players denied bad behavior, even though the trainer said that they were in poor physical shape. Charlie Thomson also asked to give up the captaincy and Tom Collins was appointed. A month later, this decision was reversed and with George Couper moving to Everton after being suspended, there were clearly problems behind the scenes.

The constant changes affected the team's form and following a 3-0 defeat from Celtic at Celtic Park in late September, even that early, Hearts League challenge was over and the Glasgow side easily retained the Championship. There were no 'doubles' and the best League result was a resounding 4-1 over Hibernian at Tynecastle and a "last match of the season" 3-3 draw with Celtic.

The directors knew the team could not retain the Scottish Cup and £600 was paid to Manchester United for John Peddie, Richard Wombwell and William Yates – players who never quite made the grade – although their appearance attracted a large crowd. Hearts consistency this season was that Replays were required to dispose of Airdrieonians, Kilmarnock and Raith Rovers before Queen's Park came to Tynecastle in a Semi-Final.

The attendance of 35,000 was a record for the ground, that had been expanded prior to the match with the cycle track being removed and the banking sunk below the pitch level.

A brick wall was built around three sides of the park and Tynecastle was measured to hold 61,784 of which 4,000 were in the stand. On the day, Hearts won 1-0 but the estimated capacity was greatly exaggerated.

Hearts had reached a second successive Cup Final a feat they had not managed before or since. On the eve of the match at Hampden Park, Hearts suffered a mortal blow when Charlie Thomson, joined Jimmy Dickson and John Peddie on the injured list. They were sadly missed as Hearts went down 3-0 to Celtic before 50,000 spectators.

The team was:- Tom Allan; Robert Reid and Tom Collins; David Philip, Frank McLaren and William Henderson; William Bauchop, Bobby Walker-captain, David Axford, William Yates and Richard Wombwell.

Before the season finished Hearts won the Shield and Rosebery Charity Cup and won both the East of Scotland City Cup and the Wilson Cup but failed to win the East of Scotland League.

Hearts had entered a period of decline, not helped by several senior players whose life style was the talk of the town.

HEARTS SLUMP

William Waugh took close control of scouting and instructing the players and trainers, but season 1907-1908 was bitterly disappointing as Hearts fell to eleventh equal in the League and made no impact in the Scottish Cup or the local competitions.

There were promising League results, including a 7-2 win over Queen's Park, in August and Hearts won 3-2 at Easter Road in November after being 2-0 down. The following week a Tynecastle record League crowd of 22,500 saw Hearts beat Celtic by a single goal, but it was a false dawn. Action was taken by the Club with the signing of big bustling, Basil Colombo – Clydebank – his father was a Corsican – in October.

The signing of promising Juniors could not stop Hearts slide and the team lost five matches in succession halted by a 5-0 defeat of Port Glasgow at Tynecastle in January. On 20 April Hearts even lost 6-0 to Celtic in Glasgow, a record League defeat that stood for many years.

The manager's plans were also hit by a severe injury crisis when ten first team men were sidelined. This included Bobby Walker although when he later played against Ireland, he became the first Scot to make 21 appearances for his country.

The Scottish Cup brought temporary relief with four goals being scored against both St.Johnstone 4-1 and Port Glasgow Athletic 4-0. However, Hearts lost 3-1 away to St.Mirren at St.Mirren Park, in the Third Round.

William Waugh decided to make an exit and received an interview for the manager's job at Arsenal, before retiring in March 1908.

The local competitions reflected the whole season as Hearts failed in the East of Scotland League and lost in the Shield Final 1-0 to Hibernian and the Rosebery Charity Cup Final 3-2 to St.Bernards.

MCGHEE'S TURBULENT SPELL

The directors appointed James McGhee, one of the original Hibernans, in April 1908. Not for the first time, nor the last time, directors of Hearts made a monumental error of judgement. The man was not respected by the players and was disliked by the supporters. He walked into problems, as a wage dispute resulted in Charlie Thomson and Tom Allan being sold to Sunderland for a combined fee of £700.

Things became tougher, because Mr. McGhee was a strict disciplinarian and this brought conflict with several players whose lifestyle was not as the manager desired. However, he was an astute judge of a player and recruited several men who would become very influential such as Peter Nellies, George Sinclair and Roddy Walker.

The big question for 1908-1909 was how would Hearts perform without Thomson? The answer was poorly and the team spent most of the campaign in the lower half of the League, again finishing eleventh equal.

In September 1908 Hearts won 6-1 at Motherwell and seemed to be making progress but later that month, they lost 6-2 at home to Airdrieonians and the supporters became restless. Crowds drifted away to the extent that on 28 April only 1,000 witnessed the 1-0 home victory over Partick Thistle.

In the Scottish Cup, after beating Kilmarnock 2-1, Hearts were knocked out at Broomfield, losing 2-0 to Airdrieonians.

The Hearts had a miserable time locally, winning only the East of Scotland/City Cup Final against St.Bernards 2-1, which had been held over from the previous season. That was the end of that competition and the East of Scotland League was reduced to a Cup competition – The North Eastern Cup – but Hearts went out against Aberdeen and lost in the Final of the Shield 1-0 to Hibernian after 2-2 and 1-1 draws and they also defeated Hearts 1-0 in the Final of the Wilson Cup.

Tom Collins made his first appearance for Scotland in a Full International on 1 March 1909 against Wales in 3-2 defeat, at The Racecourse, Wrexham.

On a more pleasant note, William Lorimer was elected President of the SFA the first Heart of Midlothian man to receive this honour.

ANOTHER ROUGH RIDE

The Club sold the lease of the hay field behind the North embankment to the School Board and Tynecastle School was subsequently built on the site and opened in 1912.

Season 1909-1910 was dominated by off the field events and James McGhee had issues from the start which led to a managerial change.

He suspended Tom Collins, for misconduct and fined Bobby Walker for missing the first match. The two players were eventually suspended for the rest of the season and this caused consternation among the fans. In October both players were reinstated when pressure was brought to bear on the directors, but the manager felt he had been undermined by the lack of support from Chairman Elias Furst, and resigned in December.

This situation masked good business, signing – Bob Mercer – Leith Athletic and Richard Harker – Hibernian. However, disharmony off the field certainly affected the players' form although the new half-back line of Frank McLaren, Bob Mercer and Peter Nellies looked promising.

After a slow start, Hearts were inconsistent, but the die-hards among the supporters enjoyed another Edinburgh derby double over Hibernian, 4-1 at Easter Road and 1-0 in Gorgie, even though their team finished twelfth equal in the League. George Buchanan was the leading scorer with 12 goals, the first player to reach double figures since Alex Menzies and Bobby Walker in 1905-1906.

The club needed a strong manager and in January 1910 the St.Mirren boss, John McCartney, signed a two-year contract at £5 per week.

Hearts had defeated Bathgate FC 4-0 in the Scottish Cup First Round and were due to meet St.Mirren in the Second Round. Diplomatically, he started after Hearts played St.Mirren, in a tie that required a third game at Ibrox Park which Hearts won 4-0 after 2-2 and 0-0 draws. In the Third Round, Hearts visited Easter Road where the match was abandoned after many of the 24,000 crowd spilled onto the pitch with Hearts leading 1-0. The game was replayed at Tynecastle where Hibernian won by the only goal.

Hearts did claim the lion's share of the local honours with success in the Wilson Cup v Hibernian, the Shield v St.Bernards and the North Eastern Cup v Leith Athletic.

George Sinclair made his first appearance for Scotland in a Full International on 19 March 1910 against Ireland in a 1-0 defeat at Windsor Park, Belfast.

LITTLE SIGN OF GREATNESS

There was little sign of progress in Mr. McCartney's first full season 1910-1911 when his side contained many players from the south and Hearts were often referred to as the "Englishmen". Players came and went at regular intervals, most notably Tom Collins who was again suspended and then transferred to Tottenham Hotspur for £825. At the turn of the year players were brought in, Lawrence Abrams and Fred Burden – Stockport County (£695) and Percy Dawson – North Shields Athletic, a player who became a scoring machine after his first goal within two minutes of his debut.

Hearts could never field a settled side and there was little team spirit. In addition, as the players were in poor shape, Tom Brandon became trainer.

There were clearly issues that John McCartney had to address and as a result, Hearts suffered 18 Championship defeats including a run of 16 matches with only two wins, and finished fourteenth equal in the League, the worst position since we had to seek re-election in 1901. Surprisingly Hearts had a 'double' over Hamilton Academical 2-1 away and 2-0 at home.

Discontent among the fans was possibly the reason behind bad language at Tynecastle which resulted in the SFA ordering warning notices to be posted around the ground as to future behaviour.

The Scottish Cup added to the frustration as Clyde scrambled a draw at Tynecastle in the First Round and Hearts loyal fans swelled the crowd at Shawfield Stadium to a generous 25,000, but the Replay was lost 1-0.

As team building continued, the reserves won both the Second X1 Cup and the League Championship giving an indication of better times ahead. In the local competitions Hearts only won the Dunedin Cup – 5-1 v Falkirk and the East of Scotland/City Cup 4-1 v Broxburn.

A milestone was reached when Bobby Walker scored Hearts 1,000th League goal in their 477th. match, on 19 November 1910 in a 2-2 draw against Airdrie at Tynecastle.

HEARTS ABROAD

Tynecastle had a new look in August 1911 with the introduction of crush barriers and the building of the "Iron Stand" a 120 yard, covered enclosure for 4,500 standing spectators on the distillery side, who paid extra for the privilege.

Changes on the playing front saw, youngsters, Tom Allan – Sunderland, Paddy Crossan and Willie Wilson – Arniston Rangers and Willie Macpherson – Rangers, Tommy Murray – Aberdeen and David Taylor – Darlington were signed.

Performances significantly improved and Hearts finished fourth equal in the League in season 1911-1912.

They defeated the eventual champions, Rangers, at home in April 1912 and enjoyed a fine 'double' over Hibernian, 4-0 at Easter Road and 3-0 at Tynecastle on New Year's Day. Interestingly, there were only two other 'doubles' Clyde 1-0 and 2-1 and Motherwell 3-0 and 2-1. In addition, a brilliant 2-1 win over Celtic in September proved one of the season's highlights with a record League attendance of 23,000 in the ground. Percy Dawson was the leading marksman with 14 goals.

Hibernian came to Tynecastle in the Scottish Cup First Round, and a crowd of 32,000 witnessed a 0-0 draw. The Replay, due to bad weather, was declared a friendly by the clubs but they were subsequently fined £25 by the SFA for having done so, then after a 1-1 draw, Hearts won the third match 3-1 at Ibrox Park before 24,500 fans. Hearts beat Dundee 1-0 and then defeated Greenock Morton 1-0 in the Quarter-Finals. Film of the latter game was shown in the evening at the Olympia Picture Palace in Annandale Street.

This was the first time that the Semi-Finals were held on neutral grounds but, due to the miners' strike, Hearts fans had trouble getting to the match against Celtic at Ibrox Park. Many did so, swelling the gate to 45,000, but Hearts went down rather easily by 3-0.

Hearts had to settle for local cup wins with success in the Dunedin Cup 1-0 v Raith Rovers and the Wilson Cup 2-0 v Hibernian. The team had to scratch from the Rosebery Charity Cup Final due to the club's first overseas tour, four games being played in Scandinavia. In a 9-0 win over Kristiania Kredslag, Percy Dawson scored four goals and King Haakon of Norway became the only reigning monarch to have attended a Hearts match.

Bob Mercer made his first appearance for Scotland in a Full International on 2 March 1912 against Wales in a 1-0 win at Tynecastle Park, Edinburgh.

That afternoon he was joined by George Sinclair and Bobby Walker which no doubt helped to swell the attendance to 31,000, which was then a record for the fixture.

During the summer, the Club obtained a 19 year lease from Edinburgh Corporation. With tenancy secure the Tynecastle and McLeod Street entrances were given modern pay-boxes and the banking was built up and strengthened with fresh ashes.

Iron Stand

BOBBY WALKER'S FAREWELL

It was announced that season 1912-1913 would be Bobby Walker's last campaign and Sir Harry Lauder launched a national testimonial. He received 250 gold sovereigns and an inscribed pocket watch, but sadly, Walker missed much of the season due to a back problem while Tom Hegarty also suffered a terrible eye injury that forced him to retire.

"Goalkeepers, in their own half, could handle the ball both inside and outside penalty area before 1912".

Hearts finished third equal in the League, the best performance in seven years. The team made a promising start with some notable results, including a 10-3 victory over Queen's Park at Tynecastle, which remains the only occasion that Hearts have hit double figures in the League. They also defeated the eventual champions, Rangers, at Ibrox Park before hitting a poor spell at the end of the year and dropping out of the title race.

'Doubles' over Hibernian 1-0 and 3-0, Aberdeen 1-0 and 4-1 and Partick Thistle 4-0 and 3-1 helped in Hearts improved League position and aided by Percy Dawson's 24 goals. Injuries disrupted the team for, in addition to Bobby Walker and Tom Hegarty, Willie Wilson dislocated his shoulder and Willie Macpherson was out for a long spells.

In the Scottish Cup, after disposing of Dunfermline Athletic 3-1 and Kilmarnock 2-0 in the Second and Third Rounds, a crowd of 65,000 watched the 1-0 victory over Celtic in a Quarter-Final tie in Glasgow. This was the largest crowd to have watched Hearts up to that time and the club organized twelve trains and earned substantial commission from the 8,064 fans who took advantage. For the second successive season Hearts reached the Semi-Finals, but this time the team lost 1-0 to Falkirk at Ibrox Park.

On the local scene, Hearts won the Dunedin Cup 1-0 v Hibernian and the North Eastern Cup 3-0 v Falkirk but lost in the Rosebery Charity Cup 2-0 and the Wilson Cup 3-2 to Hibernian.

A decision to erect a new stand to replace the present structure was proposed. On 10 February 1913 the directors instructed the "Secretary to get into communication with Mr.Leitch, Stand and Ground specialist". A week later Archibald Leitch met the board, and a week after that two members of his staff measured up Tynecastle.

Peter Nellies made his first appearance for Scotland in a Full International on 15 March 1913 against Ireland in a 2-1 win at Dalymount Park, Dublin.

THE CLUB REACHES A PEAK

Hearts had already made their first trip overseas to promote the game and many more European associations joined the FIFA ranks before South Africa (1909/1910), Argentina and Chile (1912), and the USA (1913) became the first non-European members. "As a consequence of the evolution of the game and the expanding number of associations (20 by the end of the WW1).

FIFA was welcomed onto the IFAB and given the same voting powers as the four U.K. associations put together. There remained eight votes and the same 75% majority needed for a proposal to be passed, but instead of two each, England, Scotland, Wales and Ireland now had one, while FIFA was given four. Balanced so football's world governing body needed the support of half the original associations to approve a change, while being able to block a proposal alone, "it was felt the Board would retain its necessary conservatism while maintaining a progressive attitude to the game".

"Before 1913 when a corner was taken, instead of deciding on an in-swinger, or out-swinger or taking a short one, there was nothing to stop a player dribbling the ball by himself. The rules were changed after several players teed themselves up before scoring.

Many supporters feared life without Bobby Walker but in fact, the team played very well, as John McCartney, was assembling one of the club's finest squads and Harry Graham proved a fine replacement. As a result, in season 1913-1914, Hearts again finished third equal in the League with a new club record of 54 points.

The Hearts were unbeaten in the first twelve League fixtures, playing all out attack at home, with four forwards in away games. Harry Wattie, had formed an exciting partnership with Percy Dawson and in September, Rangers 2-1 and Celtic 2-0 were beaten in the space of three days. It was unlucky 13 for Hearts, as the run was halted on 1 November by a 1-0 loss to St. Mirren, but two weeks later on 15 November the team bounced back and defeated St.Mirren 6-0 at Tynecastle.

In the early weeks of 1914, they stumbled again and lost ground. Progress was affected by Willie Wilson's dislocated shoulder and rumours that Percy Dawson was to be transferred. Then in January, a shock 2-1 defeat at Dumbarton ended any lingering hopes of the title and even though Hearts took three out of four points from the champions, Celtic, they were ultimately let down by inconsistency against lesser teams.

Hearts went out in the First Round of the Scottish Cup, losing 2-0 to Raith Rovers before a record crowd of 25,000 in Kirkcaldy.

This early exit and the need to fund the construction of the new stand led to the sale of Percy Dawson. He had scored 71 goals in 92 League and Scottish Cup matches including 24 in 28 matches this season, and was top scorer for three seasons. Blackburn Rovers paid a huge fee of £2,500 for his transfer in February and this allowed investment in the stadium with the final League fixture, against Raith Rovers, being played at Easter Road due to the demolition of the old Main Stand.

The Company announced a profit of £1,371 for the financial year 1912-13 which allowed them to agree plans for the new stand. At the time Hearts planned to rent a house at 8 McLeod Street as a store during the building of the new stand and retained a quantity of fittings, all doors and corridors, baths, closets, piping, radiators etc., as a cost saving.

The season ended with victories over Hibernian in the Shield 1-0, Rosebery Charity Cup 3-2 and the Wilson Cup 1-0 but a defeat 1-0 from Aberdeen in the North Eastern Cup.

In June 1914 Hearts travelled to Denmark for two exhibition matches. A Copenhagen Select was beaten 2-1 and Mr.McCartney had clearly built a fine team around pivot, Bob Mercer. It peaked when Hearts defeated the Danish National team 2-1 with 12,000 spectators witnessing a famous victory.

The press reported that Hearts had never looked back under John McCartney and had become the best team in Scotland without paying huge transfer fees. The manager even said that Hearts were better without Walker as no other player could match his vision. The fans were certainly supportive and attendances hit a new peak with a League average of 13,000. As a result, the directors produced a new five-year contract for the manager.

HEARTS, HEARTS, GLORIOUS HEARTS

It was agreed on 19 October that as long as the War lasted, soldiers in uniform, or on production of a pass, would be admitted to League matches at half price to the ground only, via Tynecastle Terrace turnstile three.

The Hearts squad in 1914 was one of its finest, although the players' exploits off the field would eventually earn more fame. On 4 August Britain entered what would become known as the Great War and immediately on 5 August the Club lost Geordie Sinclair and Neil Moreland, who were Army Reservists, to the forces, before a ball was kicked.

Accordingly, when the season commenced against Celtic, there was a low-key opening of the new Main Stand – the present structure. At the outset the stand's cost was estimated at £6,000. To put this in perspective, Heart's gate receipts for that entire season, after match expenses, totalled £7,723. In February 1914 the stand's estimated costs had risen to £8.000 hence the transfer of Dawson. There were several months of strongly worded correspondence, blame and counter by Leitch or the contractors but the impressive 4,000-seat structure was completed in October, at a cost of £12,780, twice the original estimate. This sum severely strained the club's finances when income crashed during the War.

Hearts opened the campaign with eight successive League wins, starting with a 2-0 home victory over the defending Champions, Celtic. The run was broken against Dumbarton, but the team bounced back and by late November only one defeat had been suffered from sixteen League matches, despite the loss of the imperious Bob Mercer who required knee surgery.

At that time, the British Army was suffering great loss of life in holding the German advance in northern France and Belgium and Jimmy Speedie decided to volunteer. But general recruitment was slowing and public opinion was firmly moving against the playing of football while men suffered and died on the battlefields.

When legislation had been passed for enlistment, "professionals" were not included and that covered professional football players. Ultimately, that situation led to questions in Parliament and many complaints in the newspapers about young athletes being exempt while sons and brothers were wounded and dying. The players were treated well although in December, the Scottish Football League requested that players be asked to accept reduced wages to enable clubs to carry out the season's engagements. The Secretary read the letter to the players and intimated that the Directors had no intention of reducing wages and hoped they would never be required to do so.

However, a letter from the League Secretary made it compulsory and there was a 25% reduction from all wages of £2:10/- and upwards, and 20% under £2:10/- with a minimum wage of £1:10/- per week. Each club was to retain its own reductions from the players' wages, and if at the end of the season, if the ordinary trading accounts showed a profit, said profit to be divided pro rata amongst players who had borne the reduction. The players were informed of the League Committee findings but were assured that any profit would be divided and they unanimously agreed to abide by the order of the League.

The League Committee requested the names of all players who had joined his Majesty's Forces and of those engaged in Government work. They proposed no summer wages to be paid, nor any sums of money in lieu of wages. They also proposed a maximum of £4:10/- instead of £6. Players had to be made an offer as hitherto in April for purposes of retained and transfer lists. "Soldiers, to be made an offer in conformity with the Clubs pledge at time of enlistment and said offer to be made by registered letter to the last known address, thus enabling clubs to place them on the retained list".

Main Stand – 1914

Sir George McCrae obtained permission to raise and command a new battalion in Edinburgh, the 16th.Royal Scots. His recruitment drive was soon to be given special impetus when in late November, with the allied forces on the retreat, thirteen Hearts players joined up and the club now had sixteen men in service.

What actually happened was that on 23 November Sir James Leishman and Sir George McCrae met the Hearts Chairman and Secretary to discuss the question of players joining the new Edinburgh Battalion for active service. After fully debating the subject "It was ultimately the unanimous finding of the Directors that no obstacle be placed in the way of any player desiring to join the colours. Should any of the players enlist, he would be paid half wages when unable to play and full wages if he played during the currency of agreement. That should any or all of them return fit and well they be re-engaged on old terms".

Sir James Leishman and Sir George McCrae were advised of this decision and invited to meet the players to explain matters etc., with Mr. Furst present to state the club's view. The "Scotsman" reported on Thursday 26 November that "a flutter of excitement was created in Edinburgh football circles yesterday afternoon when it became known that no fewer than eleven players of the Heart of Midlothian Football Club had joined the Army. They have enlisted in Sir George McCrae's Edinburgh Battalion for active service." The eleven were added to the three players already in the Army then the number rose to sixteen when two further players volunteered a few days later.

The following Monday, 30 November after an interview with Sir James Leishman, the Directors also pledged to raise for the 16th.Royal Scots an entire Hearts Company from the club's supporters. Those joining the Hearts Company would each receive a special memento of the occasion in the shape of a season ticket admitting them free to Ground and Stand for one season. They authorised special bills and leaflets for publication of an appeal for recruits, signed by the Chairman and Secretary.

The Report by the Directors for the Tenth Annual General Meeting of Shareholders, on 6 July 1915 read "at the call of patriotism, fourteen of the players enlisted for active service. The lead established by these gallant youths reverberated through the length of the land, drawing forth eulogiums from all quarters", the good name of football was restored.

In the East of Scotland Hearts had been popular as a Club who played attractive football but now it became known as "Edina's Darlings" following their high example.

THE TITLE SLIPS AWAY

In season 1914-1915 enlistment had no great effect on the team's performance at first and although there were three draws in January 1915 this included a 1-1 result at Celtic Park, after which Hearts looked good for the Championship. However, the team's flair and energy began to fade due to intensive military training, inoculations and non-availability of regular players.

Hearts' trainer, James Duckworth, suffered a nervous breakdown and the players subsequently cracked under the strain with some vital points being lost, most notably in a 4-3 home defeat against Rangers in February. Celtic then overhauled Hearts in the title race as the "maroons" drew with Aberdeen 0-0 then lost to Greenock Morton 0-2 and St.Mirren 0-1 in the final three matches. Hearts had led the League for 35 weeks out of 37, but ended four points behind Celtic in second place, when they would have been popular Champions.

The Scottish Cup was cancelled during the Great War and Hearts had to rest content this season, with defeating Hibernian to win, the Shield 1-0, the Wilson Cup 2-1 and the Dunedin Cup 6-0. The supporters were particularly delighted by the prowess of Tom Gracie who was the top scorer with a new club record of 29 League goals.

Hearts players, staff and supporters served with distinction during the Great War and right from the start, the club was also active on the home front, a recruitment station being established in the ground. The club supplied relief parcels to servicemen and women, and raised funds to assist distressed areas. In this regard, Bobby Walker appeared in the Belgian Relief Fund Match in April 1915 when 18,000 supporters saw his International XI beat an Edinburgh & Leith Select by 2-0.

At the end of the season lists of players to be retained as in former years was required. The Scottish League who resolved "that no club shall make any offer of engagement for season 1915/1916 to any professional player before the 26 July and that all professional players be placed on the Open to transfer list as at 30 April 1915".

"That no amateur player presently serving with the Colours can be signed by any club other than the club he was last registered for, until the expiry of one month from the date of his discharge from the army". The Directors duly placed all 29 Hearts players on the transfer list and put a value against each one. Interestingly, Bob Mercer and Peter Nellies, valued at £5,000, the ten other regular first team players, valued at £3,000 with the total value set at £58,500.

In 1914 an issue of the "Peoples Journal" contained within their newspaper the sheet music for a song about Hearts, 'Hearts Lead The Way'. The copy handed into the Club some years ago was already in a very bad condition with part of the music and relevant words missing. Stuart Montgomery, organist at St.Michael's Parish Church, managed to interpret the notes missing and a copy of The Scotsman in 1915 provided the missing words.

Words by T.M. Davidson and the Music is by David Stephen.
The words are:-
"When the Empire is in danger, and we hear our country's call,
"The Mother-land may count on us to leave the leather ball.
"We've hacked our way in many a fray, we've passed and gone for goal,
"But a bigger field awaits us, and we we're keen to join the roll.
Chorus
       "So it's right wing, left wing, front line and goal;
       "Half back, full back, every living soul;
       "Sound o' wind, strong of limb, eager for the fray,
       "Every soul for the goal "Hearts!" Hearts!" "Hearts" lead the way.

"We thank the Lord Almighty He has made us strong and fit,
"Our muscles are like iron and we don't know when we're hit.
"We take a lot of mauling, we can give as good's we get,
"And we wish to show the Germans we are not decadent yet.
Chorus

"Grand stand, pavilion, friend or foe, we bid you all adieu,
"We know your thoughts are with us when we go to fight for you.
"You've seen us win, you've seen us lose, but now we join the fray
"Where brute and bully must go down, And honour win the day.
Chorus

'HEARTS, LEAD THE WAY

Dedicated to the Heart of Midlothian Football Club.

Words by T. M. DAVIDSON, M.A.   **Music by DAVID S**

A GROUP OF BRAVE 'HEARTS'

Names from left to right—Back row—Currie, Crossan, Gracie, Preston,
Front row—Ness, Wattie, Low, Wilson, and Findlay

Reprinted from the "PEOPL

THE FAMOUS HEART OF MIDLOTHIAN FOOTBALL TEAM.

—("Newspaper Illust

ated for the first time by the Glasgow Rangers, but they are at the top of the League, and are all in Kitchener's Army (Royal Scot
they are training hard.

From Melbourne Argus,
April 16th, 1915.

As an old Hibs, foll
I take off my hat
the good Old Hear
their splendid example

HEARTS STRUGGLE THROUGH

When season 1915-1916 commenced, the War was biting into every day life and attendances began to decline. The club was severely hurt in September 1915 when Jimmy Speedie was killed in action at Loos in France. The following month, while in military service, Tom Gracie died of leukaemia in Stobhill Army Hospital. In addition, "McCrae's Battalion" left for France in January 1916 and the Tynecastle team would thereafter be made up from guest players, servicemen on leave, youngsters and players engaged in vital war work, with everyone earning a reduced minimum wage of £1/10/- (£1.50p) per week.

With a constantly changing team, Hearts form fluctuated, but they were occasionally superb and the Champions, Celtic, were beaten 2-0 in November. At this point, top scorer, Willie Wilson – 12 goals in 15 matches – left for the Army and in early 1916 Hearts began to slip down the League. However a measure of the team's new confidence was shown by their 'League Doubles' over Partick Thistle, Clyde, Motherwell, Queens's Park Raith Rovers and Third Lanark.

Availability of players became a real problem and in April – the first and only time – Hearts could not fulfill a League fixture. This was due to both travel problems and not being able to raise a side, "worthy of the club", to face Greenock Morton. Both sides ended with 37 matches played as against 38 for the other clubs. All things considered, Hearts did well to finish fifth equal and to win the Rosebery Charity Cup by 4-0 over Hibernian – although the "greens" won the Wilson Cup.

A TRAGIC SUMMER

The summer brought terrible news to Tynecastle, particularly after the great allied offensive on the River Somme started on 1 July 1916. This was the blackest day in the history of the British Army when nearly 20,000 men were killed and 40,000 wounded. Three Hearts players were lost in the carnage, Duncan Currie, Ernie Ellis and Harry Wattie. Bullets or shrapnel wounded several others and Hearts also lost James Boyd who was killed in August 1916.

The general depression caused by these tragic events was reflected in the team's performance in 1916-1917 and Hearts struggled through the campaign using 46 players and eventually finishing fourteenth in the League.

Hearts never recovered from a dreadful start that saw the team lose nine of the first twelve matches, including a 6-1 reverse at home to Falkirk. Although not at their best the players managed 'doubles' over Hibernian 2-1 and 2-0, Raith Rovers 2-1 and 4-1 and Dundee 1-0 and 3-2. Despite this, Hearts' reputation was at its highest ever level due to the club's War effort.

After recovering from his knee injury, Bob Mercer, was called into the Army, as was schemer Harry Graham. The manager never knew who was available until match day and his side was regularly completed with guests and juniors drafted in at the last minute. A highlight was the guest appearances of Chelsea's England International striker, George Hilsden. A likeness of the famous forward acts as a weather vane on the top of the grand stand at Stamford Bridge.

The season ended with Hearts winning the Rosebery Charity Cup following a 5-3 victory over Armadale FC at Tynecastle, but now a seventh player, John Allan, had been killed in action on the Western Front.

HEARTS HOLD ON

Season 1917-1918 was another difficult one, but the club's War effort was recognized and among many appreciative letters was one from the King of the Belgians. The club was indebted to guest players, including ace goal scorer, Andy Wilson – Middlesbrough but it was difficult to fully appreciate their displays with continuing bad news from the battlefields, where several more players were wounded or gassed.

Bob Mercer, "the mastermind of modern soccer", was now in action in France and deprived of his leadership, Hearts made little progress finishing a disappointing tenth in the League. The first eight away matches were lost and after a home defeat by Celtic on 29 September, the team's form at Tynecastle also declined. At the end of November, Hearts were second from the bottom of the League and with falling crowds, the club was heavily in debt. Only Hibernian were below them at that time and the team recorded a tenth League double over them in 23 seasons.

Quality of performance was just impossible to achieve due to the unavailability of players. An example was that on 12 January in the match against Rangers at Ibrox Park, Hearts finished with ten men when Fred Gibson left early to go to work. Hearts were even omitted from a War fund-raising tournament and there were genuine fears that the club would be excluded from the League due to travel restrictions.

Form in the local competitions was poor with defeats by Hibernian in the Final of the Rosebery Charity Cup 2-0 and Wilson Cup 3-1.

VICTORY CUP FINALISTS

At the start of season 1918-1919 the War was going well for Britain, but casualties were still high and Tynecastle stars, Paddy Crossan and Neil Moreland were again wounded.

On the playing field there were genuine fears that Hearts would be excluded from the League due to the travelling difficulties faced by the clubs from the West of Scotland. Sanity prevailed and Hearts took their place in the Championship with renewed hope for a successful campaign.

The team had a poor start in which they lost the first three matches then drew two before winning the next three. This took Hearts right out of the League race by October. Everyone was in buoyant mood when the Great War ended in November 1918 and Hearts celebrated with a 5-0 win over Falkirk on 16 November This was Andy Wilson's season and he scored 29 League goals, including a hat-trick in that Falkirk match.

He was a guest player from the Middlesbrough club and had returned to Scotland after being severely wounded on the battlefields of Arras. But his withered left arm was not a hindrance to his goal scoring exploits.Then with players returning from the War, it was hoped that the team would quickly improve, but it actually took some time before these men gained full fitness and Hearts finished seventh in the League.

In the spring of 1919 the SFA staged a Victory Cup competition and in view of their sacrifices, Hearts would have been popular winners.

After a 'bye' in the First Round Hearts defeated Third Lanark and Partick Thistle and with George Sinclair, Paddy Crossan, Willie Wilson and Bob Mercer back, Hearts were looking good. In a Semi-Final tie at Tynecastle a record attendance of 42,500 saw Hearts crush Airdrieonians by 7-1 with Andy Wilson scoring four goals. Ideally, Hearts were where everyone wanted them to be in the Final but there was no fairy tale ending as St.Mirren won 3-0, with all the goals coming in extra time. The majority of the crowd of 60,000 at Celtic Park did their best to will them on but it was not to be.

The Victory Cup Final team was:- Willie Black; Bob Birrell and John Wilson; Bob Preston, Bob Mercer-captain and John Sharp; George Sinclair, George Miller, Andy Wilson, Alex McCulloch and Willie Wilson.

Hearts ended the season defeating Hibernian in all the local competitions winning the Shield, the Rosebery Charity Cup and the Wilson Cup and Hearts were honoured by having two of their players in the Victory Internationals, George Miller and Andy Wilson.

In recognition of his efforts in keeping the football club operating during the Great War, Secretary-Manager, John McCartney, was offered and accepted, another five year contract.

Although the War was over terms were still restricted and a letter from the Scottish Football League, dated 6 January 1919 stated:- 1) No close season wages: Only 40 weeks wages to be paid at the most if signed for complete season; 2) No player to receive remuneration of any kind over £6 per week, except signing bonus; 3) Guarantee to be raised to £50; 4) Players to be signed on a uniform agreement, which permits of players being allowed to work.

THE HEART OF MIDLOTHIAN FC PLAYERS ROLL OF HONOUR

Pte. James H. Speedie, 7th Cameron Highlanders killed in action 25 September 1915.
Cpl. Thomas Gracie, 16th Royal Scots died in service 23 October 1915.
Sergt. Duncan Currie, 16th Royal Scots killed in action 1 July 1916.
Pte. Ernest E. Ellis, 16th Royal Scots killed in action 1 July 1916.
Pte. Henry Wattie, 16th Royal Scots killed in action 1 July 1916.
L-Cpl. James Boyd, 16th Royal Scots killed in action 3 August 1916.
Sergt. John Allan, 9th Royal Scots killed in action 22 April 1917.
Gunner Colin D. Blackhall, RGA.
Cpl. Alfred E. Briggs, 16th Royal Scots severely wounded.
Pte. Patrick Crossan, 16th Royal Scots thrice wounded.
Cpl. Norman Findlay, 16th Royal Scots.
Farrier Sgt. James H. Frew, RGA.
Bombardier James Gilbert, RGA.
Pte. Harry Graham, Gloucester Regiment and RAMC.
Sapper Charles Hallwood, Royal Engineers.
Pte. James Hazeldean, 16th Royal Scots severely wounded.
Lieut. James Low, 6th Seaforth Highlanders twice wounded.
L-Cpl James Macdonald, 13th Royal Scots.
Pte. Edward McGuire, 18th Royal Scots wounded.
Gunner John Mackenzie, RGA.
Pte. James Martin, 5th Royal Scots wounded.
Bombardier Robert Mercer, RGA gassed.
Sgt. George P. Miller, 9th Royal Scots.
Sgt. Neil Moreland, 8th HLI and 7th Royal Scots thrice wounded.
Lieut. Annand Ness, 16th Royal Scots and 9th Royal Scots twice wounded.
Pte. Robert Preston, 18th Royal Scots.
Driver George Sinclair, Royal Field Artillery.
Pte. Philip J. Whyte, Gloucester Regiment.
Pte. John Wilson, 9th Royal Scots twice wounded.
L-Cpl William Wilson, 18th and 16th Royal Scots wounded.

A MANAGERIAL SHOCK

Season 1919-1920 was another poor campaign, as some of the old soldiers proved to be past their best. Paddy Crossan, Harry Graham, Bob Mercer, Peter Nellies, Bob Preston, George Sinclair and Willie Wilson had all reached the veteran stage and new recruits required time to settle.

Rebuilding the squad became much more difficult in October 1919 when despite his prodigious efforts during the war John McCartney resigned as manager, due to a policy difference with the directors over player recruitment. In December 1919 his son William, who worked with the thread makers J & P Coats in Paisley and was a senior referee, surprisingly succeeded him.

With turbulence off and on the field it was hardly surprising that Hearts did not do well in the League. The team actually made a promising start with four straight wins and on 13 September a record League crowd of 40,700 came out to Gorgie for a Championship crunch match against Celtic. Hearts lost to a last minute goal by Gallagher and this started a slide down the table, principally due to a suspect defence which lost 72 goals – our worst record to date.

There were no outstanding victories that season although Clydebank and Partick Thistle were defeated home and away. But in the last home match of the year Hearts suffered a humiliating 6-3 defeat by Greenock Morton. The slide down the table after the Celtic and Greenock Morton matches saw Hearts finish a lowly fifteenth equal - two above Hibernian.

Despite this situation, the supporters were backing the team in increasing numbers with a new record average of 16,223 for League matches. With the basic price of admission rising to 1/-(5p) the club cleared the remaining debt for the new stand.

The Scottish Cup returned this season and Hearts players trained at Gullane for the matches and enjoyed wins over Nithsdale Wanderers 5-1 and Falkirk 2-0 before going down in the Third Round, 1-0 against Aberdeen in front of 21,000 at Pittodrie Park. This was Hearts first Scottish Cup match against Aberdeen and there were to be eight more before Hearts defeated their northern opponents.

The season then fell flat until the final weeks of the campaign brought success in winning the Shield, the Wilson Cup and the Rosebery Charity Cup against Hibernian.

On 22 May 1920 Celtic beat Hearts 2-0 in a Scottish War Memorial Fund-Raising Match at Tynecastle before a crowd of 15,000. Not long before this game was played wooden steps had been inserted into the ash banking at the Gorgie Road end of the ground to provide the first real terraces. Bobby Walker was also elected to the board of directors in March, this being regarded as a positive move to revive the club's fortunes.

Tynecastle - 1920

A FALSE DAWN AT TYNECASTLE

For season 1920-1921 due to Jimmy Duckworth's advanced age, William McCartney, appointed a new trainer, Charles Durning from St.Mirren who had coached the Dutch Olympic team.

Fitness and teamwork improved dramatically and after a slow start in the League – a defeat and a draw, then the first win. Hearts beat Hibernian 5-1 at Tynecastle before an encouraging early-season crowd of 27,500. Bob Mercer had returned after his long absence due to injury and stiffened up the defence. All the forwards contributed so much to the result, but Freddie Forbes scored two goals and the former Leith Benburb man was to finish as the club's top League marksman with 23 goals.

Hopes that Hearts could match the power of Rangers were dashed in late September when 34,000 watched the Glasgow side win 4-0 at Tynecastle. The team was inconsistent after this setback, partly due to Bob Mercer's retirement that forced Hearts to sign Willie Porter – Raith Rovers for a record £1,000 as a replacement. However, he was at centre-half in the memorable 5-1 defeat of Hibernian on 28 August.

Hearts had 'doubles' over Clydebank, Airdrieoians, Kilmarnock, St.Mirren and Dumbarton and eventually finished a creditable third in the League but were never in real contention for the title, being 26 points behind Rangers. Nevertheless, the supporters reckoned that if the centre-half position could be adequately filled, then honours might at long last come to the club. The average home gate for League games reached a new high of 17,928.

As always the Scottish Cup brought fresh hopes of success and Hearts had a bye in the First Round then in the Second Round, they beat Clyde 3-2 – after 1-1 and 0-0 draws. The Third Round opponents were Hamilton Academical and the "maroons" won 1-0 before travelling to Celtic Park in the Quarter-Finals.

The men in maroon earned a £10 bonus after recording a famous 2-1 victory over Celtic, with goals from Willie Wilson and Arthur Lochhead. This led to Hearts supporters dreaming of winning the Cup or at least a Cup Final appearance. Partick Thistle, the Semi-Final opponents had other ideas and three matches were played at Ibrox Park with Hearts losing out in the Second Replay by 2-0 – before a crowd of 30,000 – after two 0-0 draws.

Hearts reached the Final of all the local competitions, and won the Rosebery Charity Cup 1- 0 v St.Bernards and the Dunedin Cup 2-0 v Hibernian, but lost the Shield and Wilson Cup to Hibernian both by 1-0. The Reserves, won the Second XI Cup.

RELEGATION WORRIES

Hearts could not build upon their achievements of the previous season with several players ending their careers. Manager McCartney's rebuilding job was made even more difficult with the introduction of automatic promotion and relegation in season 1921-1922. Three clubs went down from twenty-two and unfortunately, in a transitional year, the club had one of its worst ever campaigns. Hearts avoided relegation by only two points, finishing nineteenth, the club's lowest ever ranking.

The team made a terrible start in the League failing to record their first victory until the tenth match – 4-1 v Falkirk. The following Saturday the team then had a sensational 2-0 win over Rangers at Ibrox Park but this proved an isolated success and Hearts fell quickly into the relegation zone. Hibernian even recorded a League double for the first time in twenty years.

Hearts were eventually left with the task of winning the last match of the season at Aberdeen, and definitely stay in the First Division. In a hail storm, the team duly won 1-0 thanks to a goal from Frank Stringfellow. The whole crowd cheered as Hearts were saved, although in actual fact, Dumbarton drew at Falkirk and even if defeated, the "maroons" would have stayed up on goal average.

The Scottish Cup brought little improvement despite all the matches being played at Tynecastle. After struggling to beat Arthurlie – 2-1 – in the First Round, it took three matches to dispose of Broxburn United. They were all played at Tynecastle in February 2-2, 2-2 then 3-1.The Third Round, brought Rangers to Gorgie and a new Scottish Cup record attendance of 40,000 fans witnessed an embarrassing, if not unexpected, 4-0 defeat by the Glasgow side.

A dire campaign ended with the team only reaching the Final of one local competition and lost 4-2 to Hibernian in the Wilson Cup.

There were a number of reasons for this dismal campaign, starting with poor discipline. In addition, former International Tom Miller – Manchester United was signed for a club record fee of £2,850. A more promising striker, Arthur Lochhead, went in the other direction.

The directors took immediate action and his assistant, Tom Murphy, replaced the trainer, Charles Durning. Hearts also moved decisively into the transfer market with a raft of new signings including the experienced defender, Alex Wright – Aberdeen. Shortly afterwards Hearts splashed out £2,700 to buy the country's most wanted striker, Jock White - Albion Rovers.

THE WAR MEMORIAL

On 9 April 1922 the Heart of Midlothian Football Club War Memorial was unveiled at Haymarket before a solemn crowd, estimated at 35,000. The impressive ceremony was conducted by the Rev. J. Harry Miller, CBE DD, assisted by the Rev. Alister J. Stewart, MC MA, and the Unveiling by Rt.Hon. Mr Robert Munro, KC, MP, Secretary for Scotland, who prior to the unveiling the memorial, paid an eloquent tribute to the men who had fallen.

Among the many dignitaries attending were Lord Provost Hutchison, Sir James Leishman and Sir George McCrae, present and former directors of the Club and Mr.John McCartney, the former manager. They heard tributes paid to all those who served in the 1914-191 8 war. Seven players paid the supreme sacrifice along with many shareholders and supporters.

The Secretary of State said that "they did not hesitate to serve their country in the early days of the Great War and their example was contagious". The Edinburgh Evening News recorded that, "some of those lads fell in the Battle of the Somme. They fell in the morning of their days with the dew of health upon their brows. Life was sweet to them for they were young and the easy, pleasant path lay before them. But they preferred the straight, hard rough road of duty". It was an extremely moving occasion.

As far back as May 1920 the Board of Directors decided "to ask if permission would be granted to raise our Memorial in the shape of a clock on a pillar at the site opposite the Bank of Scotland, Dalry Road Branch".

At the Annual General Meeting in June the shareholders unanimously agreed to erect the Memorial on the proposed site and that a committee of five shareholders would be appointed to act in conjunction with the Directors in raising the Memorial. By July the Convenor of the Streets and Buildings Committee had recommended to the corporation to grant the site for the Memorial and lend their assistance in erecting it with Hearts requested to produce a drawing of the memorial..

Mr.H.S.Gamley, R.S.A. was retained as sculptor to complete the design of Sir.Duncan Rhind. He was asked in October about the progress and in November he offered to produce a design and a probable cost. Sadly, he reported that the minimum cost for the erection would be £1,500. In view of the fact that £1,000 was to be about the figure to be expended, Mr.Gamley was asked to alter his design and submit a concrete offer. The target date for the unveiling of the memorial was scheduled for November 1921 but delays arose early on.

The Directors informed the sub-committee that the delay in meeting them was due to being unable to put a suitable design before them and awaiting the City Council granting the site desired. The cost of £1,500 was considerably more than at first anticipated but it was decided not to alter the design to reduce the cost as it could spoil the beauty of the structure. It was agreed that the Club find £1,000 from its own funds and by playing a match. the remaining £500 to be raised from a Concert and Boxing entertainments organised by experts who would be paid for their services..

In early January the plans submitted to the Streets and Buildings Committee were approved and would go before the Council. A Concert had been arranged for 16 March in the Usher Hall and the Waverley Market had been engaged for the 18 and 19 March for Boxing entertainments.

A letter in February was received from the Town Clerk intimating that the Magistrates and Council had granted the site asked and that the plan of the Clock had been approved and after erection the Town Council will take over and maintain it. The Memorial was to be erected to the satisfaction of the City Road Surveyor!

The following letter was received from the City Chambers, Edinburgh, dated 11 February 1921. "With reference to your letter of 27 December asking permission to erect a Public Clock at the foot of Henderson and Ardmillan Terraces as a Memorial to the Players connected with the Club who fell in the War, I have to inform you that on the recommendation of the Streets and Buildings Committee, the Magistrates and Council have granted the site asked. The Plan of the Clock was also approved of and the Town Council will take over and maintain the Clock after it is erected. You will require to communicate with the City Road Surveyor before commencing operations as the Clock will require to be erected at his sight, and his satisfaction". Signed D.Robertson, Depute Town Clerk.

At the Annual General Meeting, the shareholders were told that all arrangements had been made for the Erection of the Memorial and that the Concert and Boxing Entertainments had been organised, but had yielded only a very small profit.

On 21 September 1921 an Edinburgh X1 lost 2-1 to a Glasgow X1 in a match to raise funds – gates and stand £212:9:3d entertainment tax £62:7:9d.

There were further delays in December when the builder found difficulty in acquiring certain stones but Messrs Gamley, Rhind and the builder were told that the memorial must be completed in time for the unveiling ceremony in the early spring. By the end of January it was reported that the Memorial was ready for erection on the chosen site. It was resolved to have the unveiling ceremony take place on a Sunday in March.

Astonishingly, as late as 30 January 1922 it was reported that when Mr. Sim the City Road Surveyor was interviewed, with reference to the site for the Memorial, he intimated that the Tramways Committee desired to run rails through the site already promised by the City Council.

BLOCK A

Heart of Midlothian Football Club.

The Board of Management request the honour of your presence at the Unveiling of the War Memorial, which they have erected at Haymarket to the Memory of their Players and Members who fell in the Great War.

The Unveiling Ceremony will be performed by The Right Hon. Robert Munro, K. C., M. P., on Sunday, 9th April 1922, at 3 p.m.

Tynecastle Park,
Edinburgh.

War Memorial

Heart of Midlothian Football Club

DEDICATION OF
WAR MEMORIAL

IN MEMORY OF
THEIR PLAYERS AND MEMBERS WHO
FELL IN THE GREAT WAR, 1914-1918

Unveiling

Sunday, 9th April 1922, at 3 p.m.

BY

The Rt. Hon. ROBERT MUNRO, K.C., M.P.

Secretary for Scotland

— *CLERGY* —

Rev. J. HARRY MILLER, C.B.E., D.D.
Rev. ALISTER J. STEWART, M.C., M.A.

By Kind Permission of COL. PRENTICE, the
Band of the Highland Light Infantry
(The 71st Highlanders), under Mr M. W.
GEOGHEGAN, the Bandmaster, will play a Pro-
gramme of Sacred Music, and will lead the Praise

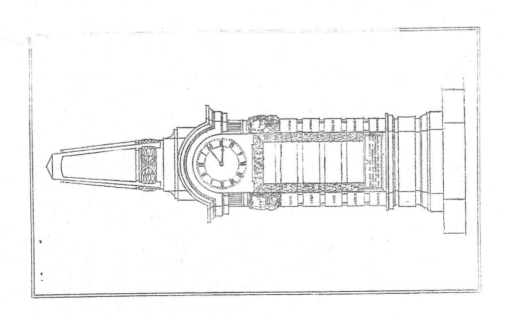

Order of Service

Praise   Hymn 477

Our God, our help in ages past,
Our hope for years to come,
Our shelter from the stormy blast,
And our eternal home!

Under the shadow of Thy throne
Thy saints have dwelt secure;
Sufficient is Thine arm alone,
And our defence is sure.

Before the hills in order stood,
Or earth received her frame,
From everlasting Thou art God,
To endless years the same.

A thousand ages in Thy sight
Are like an evening gone,
Short as the watch that ends the night
Before the rising sun.

Time, like an ever-rolling stream,
Bears all its sons away;
They fly, forgotten, as a dream
Dies at the opening day.

Our God, our help in ages past,
Our hope for years to come,
Be Thou our guard while troubles last,
And our eternal home.

Prayer   Rev. ALISTER J. STEWART, M.C., M.A.

Scripture Lesson   Psalm XLVI.
Romans VIII. 31-39

Unveiling of Memorial

BY

The Rt. Hon. ROBERT MUNRO, K.C., M.P.
Secretary for Scotland

Handing of Memorial to custody of
Edinburgh Corporation

Acceptance by the Rt. Hon. the Lord Provost

Prayer of Dedication

Rev. J. HARRY MILLER, C.B.E., D.D.

Praise   Paraphrase 66   Tune 53

How bright these glorious spirits shine!
Whence all their white array?
How came they to the blissful seats
Of everlasting day?

Lo! these are they from suff'rings great,
Who came to realms of light,
And in the blood of Christ have wash'd
These robes which shine so bright.

Now, with triumphal palms they stand
Before the throne on high,
And serve the God they love, amidst
The glories of the sky.

His presence fills each heart with joy,
Tunes ev'ry mouth to sing;
By day, by night, the sacred courts
With glad hosannas ring.

Hunger and thirst are felt no more,
Nor suns with scorching ray;
God is their sun, whose cheering beams
Diffuse eternal day.

The Lamb which dwells amidst the throne
Shall o'er them still preside;
Feed them with nourishment divine,
And all their footsteps guide.

'Mong pastures green He'll lead His flock,
Where living streams appear;
And God the Lord from ev'ry eye
Shall wipe off ev'ry tear.

Benediction

LAST POST

National Anthem

On 3 February the City Officials were met on the site promised by the Council for the Memorial. The Tramways Committee having definitely decided to connect Dalry Road and Ardmillan Terrace with car rails, further discussion as to the Erection of the Memorial at that part of the City was out of the question. The City Officials present recommended a site at Haymarket, which was viewed and proved to be an ideal position, and was agreed upon, subject to the sanction of the Council. The work to be proceeded with on the 3 March in time for the unveiling on the date arranged 20 March 1922.

A greater fifteen foot base round the Memorial would be another advantage and add to its appearance, the expense to be met by the City. The Convenor of the Streets and Buildings Committee regretted very much the change, "but that it was unavoidable and we were fortunate in having such a splendid site as that at Haymarket offered us".

Mr. W.C. Burns, senior director, present, of the Heart of Midlothian Club formally handed over the Memorial to the custody of the Edinburgh Corporation. "On behalf of the Heart of Midlothian Club he wished to express their great appreciation of the sympathetic and generous spirit in which the Corporation had seconded the efforts of the Club to perpetuate the memory of the gallant men connected with the Club who fell in the war.

In accepting custody on behalf of the Corporation, Lord Provost Hutchison said "the memorial would be preserved with all reverence for all coming times".

It had been sixteen years since Hearts had been successful on the field and many more would pass before major honours were won. However, the fame of the Heart of Midlothian had never been higher and for several seasons during the 1920s, the crowds at Tynecastle were the best in Scotland.

BUYING SUCCESS

In season 1922-1923 Hearts fans found a popular hero in the handsome, Jock White, who was Scotland's top marksman with 29 League goals – matching the previous club record – although some of the newspapers said 30. Unfortunately, his colleagues scored a combined total of only 22 and with teamwork generally poor, Hearts finished a disappointing twelfth in the table.

Jock White was a real live wire with 13 of his goals helping to spark a run of 14 unbeaten League matches from September to December. Hearts lost five of the next six matches when the run ended against Motherwell on 9 December. Home and away wins over Kilmarnock and Greenock Morton could not prevent the remainder of the season being mixed and the team finishing 18 points behind the Champions, Rangers.

Following the enormous investment in Jock White and Alex Wright, there had been further recruitment and Mr. McCartney had sixteen new men in his squad. Several required time to settle, including Colin Dand – Armadale, John Johnston – Ardeer Thistle and John's brother, Willie White –Hamilton. The manager also encountered one of those seasons when injuries and illness disrupted consistency.

Disappointment in the League was eclipsed by disaster in the Scottish Cup. Hearts met Thornhill FC in the First round at Tynecastle and won 6-0. Then they lost 3-2 to Second Division, Bo'ness FC, before 8,000 fans at Newtown Park, in the Second Round. The "maroons" were settling for a draw when the home side capitalised on a mistake by goalkeeper, Jock Gilfillan, who was beaten by a speculative shot that was caught in the high wind. With only nine minutes left, the capital side could not recover the situation.

In the local competitions, Hearts lost to the "greens" 2-1 in the Shield Final but defeated them 2-1 in both the

Rosebery Charity Cup and the Wilson Cup and in addition, beat Hibernian by the same score in a match for Lord Provost Hutchison's Rent Relief Fund. The fans were treated that day to the spectacle of the four White brothers playing in maroon, with two as guests. However, the season ended with the manager under pressure and Hearts were again forced into the transfer market.

Jock White made his first appearance for Scotland in a Full International on 3 March 1923 against Northern Ireland in a 1-0 win at Windsor Park, Belfast.

A STEP FORWARD

There was a noticeable improvement in season 1923-1924 with a good contribution from new men, Tom Green – Clapton Orient, Bob King – Dalkeith Thistle, William McLean – Dundee and Willie Murray – Middlesbrough. With his delightful wing play, Englishman, "Tiddler" Murray, became a great favourite and well worth his transfer fee. He supplied the ammunition for Jock White who had been presented with a gold medal to mark his scoring exploits of the previous campaign. He scored another 17 League goals this season but there was no other regular marksman.

The first match of the season was a home match at Tynecastle where Hearts had a resounding 6-0 victory over Clyde. In the next home match they defeated Hamilton Academical 4-0 and throughout the season they won twelve of their nineteen home fixtures. Several of these matches were filmed during the season for screening in local cinemas.

Their away form was diabolical with only two wins and the title was clearly not coming to Tynecastle and Hearts finished ninth in the League, 21 points adrift of the title winners, Rangers. Significantly, lesser sides were not their downfall this time and Hamilton Academical and Partick Thistle were defeated home and away.

League gates averaged 16,368, the best in Scotland, despite high unemployment. The team were more consistent by the time the Scottish Cup started in January. The First Round match was an away tie against Third Lanark at Cathkin Park and a 0-0 draw. The Replay at Tynecastle proved to be the first of four Cup matches there in this season's competition. Third Lanark were defeated 3-0 and Galston FC 6-0 in the Second Round. The Third Round brought Clyde to Gorgie and they left after a 3-1 loss. With a Quarter-Final tie at home Hearts were expected to see off Falkirk and before a Gorgie crowd of 34,500 the home side went down 2-1.

Hearts were unlucky, as for most of a rather rough match, they played without Jock Ramage, who broke a bone in his foot.

The main problem was a weak halfback line that could not supply decent passes. Truly great players such as Charlie Thomson and Bob Mercer had proved impossible to replace.

Hearts did win the Wilson Cup 4-1 v Hibernian but lost in the Final of the Shield and the Rosebery Charity Cup to the "greens".

On 3 December 1923 the Directors agreed to a contract with the Edinburgh Advertising, Platform and Press Agency to publish an Official Football Programme for season 1924/1925.

On the 24 December the Directors discussed an application from Geo. May Publishers, London, to write and issue the history of the Club under its auspices. It was decided to consult with Mr. William Reid, of the

FIRST ELEVEN 1923/1924 – Standing Back Row– P. Crossan–Captain, W. White, J. Wilson.
Standing Middle Row – W. McCartney–Manager, C. Dand, J. Ramage, R. King, T. Murphy–Trainer. Seated – J. Murphy, J. White, T. Green, L. McMillan, W. Murray.

Edinburgh Evening News. Geo. May of London, to submit another club's history for consideration. On 26 January it was agreed that the occasion of the 50th. Anniversary of the Club should not be allowed to pass without a book being put up for sale at a nominal charge of 1/-.

Following a survey which revealed that if every spectator was allowed a space of 14" x 24", Tynecastle's capacity was 50,068; but if 14" x 22" the capacity would be 60,018. Plans were produced to show that If the police station and the bowling green, behind the main stand, were acquired and the main stand was re-erected at the school end with the pitch swung in an east-west direction, then the capacity of the ground, with 14" x 22" per spectator, could be extended to 68,053.

Edinburgh Corporation rejected Hearts plans on the basis that a stand at the north end of the ground would block the light to the Tynecastle School.

HEARTS JUBILEE SEASON

The club celebrated its first fifty years by publishing a history and in December 1924 around 300 guests attended a Jubilee Dinner at the Freemasons' Hall in George Street. That evening a message that captured the moment was read out from former manager, John McCartney: "Heart of Midlothian! May it long continue to prosper, and it's illustrious name, traditions, and glories increase."

In that jubilee season, the SFA allocated the fixture against Wales to Tynecastle and Scotland won 3-1. The Scottish League did likewise and the home side defeated the Irish League by 3-0. Other guests were Hibernian and St.Bernards who used Tynecastle for several months due to their own ground improvement schemes.

Unfortunately, the 1924-1925 season was difficult for manager, William McCartney who was still seeking that consistent winning formula. Domestic success eluded the team and Hearts failed in the League and Cup. Lachie McMillan – Hamilton Academical was brought in as playmaker.

Perhaps the team changes accounted for the indifferent start in the League which resulted in only four wins from the opening twelve matches, including two defeats against the eventual Champions, Rangers. It proved to be unlucky 13 for Hibernian, when the run ended with a 2-0 win in October. In addition, they defeated Celtic 3-1 and St.Mirren 5-2 at Tynecastle in December. With only two away victories Hearts eventually ended up in tenth place in the table.

Hearts returned to the market in a big way, for Dave Edgar – East Fife, Alex Johnston – Rangers, George Miller – Raith Rovers, Tom Reid – Rangers and Jimmy Smith – Clydebank.

The newspapers reported that constant team changes had an adverse effect on results, as did a weak defence that conceded 68 goals against 64 scored. There was dressing room disharmony after the record-equaling 6-0 defeat at Dundee on 30 August, and a brawl among the players. They were all disciplined and told to start obeying the team captain and the trainer who both had an important coaching role at that time.

Hearts looked to the Scottish Cup as a means of reviving the campaign and Third Division, Leith Athletic, were defeated 4-1 at Tynecastle with John White scoring all four goals. However, the "maroons" failed at Rugby Park and went down 2-1 to Kilmarnock in the Second Round.

In the local competitions Hearts defeated Falkirk 2-1 in the Final of the Dunedin Cup but Hibernian had the upper hand in winning the Rosebery Charity Cup and Wilson Cup Finals.

The directors felt that buying experience to support a young squad would soon pay dividends and Jock Wilson was released along with his full back partner over many years, Paddy Crossan.

On April 1925 it was resolved that no shareholder shall hold more than 200 shares in the Company in their own right.

With League games attracting an average crowd of 17,815 they also had confidence to invest in Tynecastle and in April it was purchased for £5,000 although the city council retained a buy-back option should the club decide to move. Hearts installed a new drainage system and re-turfed the pitch, which was badly needed after the three city clubs using it for a large part of the previous season. The first few steps on the banking were also terraced in concrete.

In June 1925 the SFA successfully proposed an amendment to the off-side law which had stood since 1896 from three men between the goal and the attacker, to two men.

THE REVIVAL

The directors' optimism was justified in 1925-1926 and results dramatically improved with the team finishing third in the League, eight points behind the Champions, Celtic. John Slaven – Raith Rovers was the only major signing and this better performance came as a result of consistent selection and shrewd tactics, following the introduction of the present offside law. As the law took time to be fully understood, it was a season of high scoring with Hearts hitting 87 League goals, Jock White being the main marksman with 18.

After a slow start, the "maroons" hit some good form and at the end of September, after defeating Rangers 3-0 at home, the team was fourth in the League then lost 1-0 to Dundee at Dens Park. Following some impressive goal scoring, Hearts were top of the table at the end of February but the following month, the team lost 2-1 to Celtic in a crucial home match and the title challenge faded. The return of inconsistency was underlined when after a 6-1 win over Greenock Morton – at home, they went down 5-1 to Kilmarnock – away, a result that cost the club second place on the old goal average system.

The value of defeating the lesser sides was demonstrated this season with seven clubs being defeated home and away – Aberdeen, Clydebank, Cowdenbeath, Dundee United, Partick Thistle, Queen's Park and Raith Rovers.

Hearts looked capable of winning the Scottish Cup and in the First Round, Dundee United lost 6-0 at Tynecastle after a second replay. Jock White scored four goals that afternoon and five days later, he hit another four as Hearts put Alloa Athletic out in the Second Round with a 5-2 score line. Jock followed this with another four in a League match against Hamilton Academical and four goals in three consecutive games is a record unsurpassed in British football.

Hearts then met Celtic in the Third Round on 20 February and a new ground record attendance of 51,000 was admitted, before the gates were closed with thousands still trying to gain admission. There was serious congestion at the Gorgie Road end and mounted police restored order after spectators spilled onto the field. Sadly, the game ended in an easy 4-0 victory for Celtic, but the amazing crowd scenes led the directors to accelerate their ground expansion scheme. It was certainly required as Hearts average home gate for League games had hit a new record of 18, 473.

In the local competitions Hearts won the Rosebery Charity Cup 9-0 v Leith Athletic, the Wilson Cup 2-1 v

Hibernian and the Dunedin Cup 2-1 v Hibernian. The 'grand slam' was lost when Hibernian defeated Hearts 2-1 in the Shield Final.

However, the season had a tragic end because on 23 April 1926 reserve team trainer, 36-year old Bob Mercer, died of heart failure while playing for a Hearts XI against his home town team, Selkirk at Ettrick Park. He had never fully recovered from being injured and gassed while serving his country during the Great War.

GREATER TYNECASTLE

Massive development work started at Tynecastle during season 1926-1927 with the old "Iron Stand" on the distillery side being removed and the banking extended to the boundaries of the stadium and then terraced with wood. A crowd distribution tunnel, lit by electricity, was also built at the school end and a new entrance was started at Wheatfield Street, in addition to many minor improvements.

A double-decker stand for 9,000 supporters was to be erected at the Gorgie Road end, and the Wheatfield Street entrance and tunnels, from a strip of ground from Gerard & Co, was to be built. New gates and tunnels for the McLeod Street and White Park entrances were to be built but work was halted in October.

It was re-commenced in February, 1927, and terracing was created around the entire enclosure and an additional 2,000 spaces were added by laying 200 cubic feet of fero-concrete stepping on top of the steel standards overhanging Gerard's yard.

On the pitch, despite recruiting striker, William Henderson – Manchester United and defender, Peter Kerr – Hibernian, Hearts failed to build upon the previous season's success. It was evident early in the campaign, particularly after a 2-1 defeat at Cowdenbeath that it was going to be a hard year. In December both the local evening papers were barred from the ground due to, "unfair and abusive criticism of the players" although there was some truth in the reports.

Hearts were able to defeat Clyde and Celtic at home by scores of 5-0 and 3-0 respectively, in mid-week matches, in February and March. Despite everything the team defeated Greenock Morton, Clyde and St.Mirren home and away. Hearts fell back to a dismal thirteenth place in the League and suffered an early Scottish Cup exit.

The First Round, away to Clyde at Shawfield Stadium saw nine special trains carry Hearts supporters to swell the attendance to 18,000. After leading 2-0, Hearts collapsed and went out of the Cup by 3-2 despite the great support. It was after this match that, to the dismay of the supporters, captain, Jock White was sold to Leeds United for a record £5,700. He had scored 182 goals in 312 appearances.

In January 1927 the BBC were given permission for a broadcast commentary from Tynecastle,

The fans were not appeased by winning the Shield 2-1 the Rosebery Charity Cup 1-0 both against Hibernian and the Dunedin Cup 3-1 v Falkirk. The Wilson Cup was held over until April and won by Hibernian 2-1.

In October 1926 the Scottish League beat the Irish League 5-2 at Tynecastle before a crowd of 6,850.

A notable event was recorded when Dave Edgar scored Hearts 2,000th League goal in their 1087th. match, on 5 February 1927 in a 3-1 defeat by Motherwell at Tynecastle.

A NEW TITLE CHALLENGE

Up until 1927 a goal could not be scored direct from a free kick

Before season 1927-1928 commenced instructions from the Scottish Football League stated that visiting clubs must wear black shorts so Hearts decided to wear maroon and white hooped jerseys with them as their away strip.

There was distinct improvement this season with Hearts finishing fourth in the League, thirteen points behind the Champions, Rangers. There was a blow before the start of the campaign with full-back, Tom Reid, breaking a leg at the St.Johnstone Sports. The team soon benefited from the steadying influence of new captain, Peter Kerr and there was another experienced group of recruits including Willie Devlin – Liverpool, Andy Herd – Dunfermline Athletic and Hugh Shaw – Rangers.

Hearts lost the first two League matches but when Hugh Shaw was drafted into defence, a great run followed with seven wins in a row. This included the match at Tynecastle on 10 September when Hearts defeated Dunfermline Athletic 6-0. The visitors lost their goal keeper – due to an ankle injury – after 20 minutes. Up until then there was nothing between the sides but by half-time Hearts were ahead 3-0 and added a further three goals towards the end of the match. It was an unequal fight with Lachie McMillan, Robert Marshall, Tim Morgan -2 and Jimmy Smith -2 scoring the goals.

The fans were excited about the first real title challenge since 1914-1915, with goals galore from Lachie McMillan -19, Tim Morgan -17 and Willie Devlin -12, but when a big test came against Celtic in November, Hearts let a 2-0 lead slip into a 2-2 draw. However, after a shaky spell, Hearts went on another fine run from 31 December including, a goal scoring spree – Saturday 14 January defeated Queen's Park 4-2, Saturday 28 January hammered Dundee 7-2, Wednesday 8 February trounced Falkirk 9-3 and on Saturday 11 February Raith Rovers lost 5-0.

Throughout this spell it was not a case of a disorganized defence but more of an exhibition of football at its best and inspired forwards, deadly in front of goal. The 'hot' marksmen over that period were:- Lachie McMillan -6, Willie Devlin -5, Tom Rogers -5, George Miller -4, Willie Murray -1 and Jimmy Smith -1.

Rangers were ultimately too strong and when they drew 0-0 at Tynecastle on 7 March Hearts title hopes had gone. Following that match the team faltered during the final few weeks winning only six points from a possible 14.

In the Scottish Cup First Round, St.Johnstone held Hearts to a draw at Tynecastle, but then in gale force winds, before 11,400 spectators in Perth, the Edinburgh men won the replay 1-0 with an extra-time goal from Willie Murray. Forres Mechanics were then demolished 7-0 at Tynecastle and Motherwell came to Gorgie in the Third Round. Hearts lost 2-1 although the fans were upset at a late goal being disallowed for a foul on the visiting keeper.

At local level, Hearts did win the Rosebery Charity Cup 2-0 v Leith Athletic, the Wilson Cup 3-0 v Hibernian and the Dunedin Cup v Raith Rovers but again lost the Shield Final to Hibernian.

A NEW GROUND OR A NEW TEAM?

During the summer of 1928 building work commenced on the Gorgie Road end concrete terracing, creating an enormous standing area behind the goal at the south-east corner and turnstiles and toilets were upgraded. However, with new players also being required, the directors had to seriously consider postponing the next stage of redevelopment which was the completion of the Wheatfield Street exit and the creation of 2,000 places overhanging Gerards' Yard.

At this point some additional financial support from the ever generous chairman, William CP Brown proved crucial and this allowed the building work to continue.

The team had made a very promising start to the 1928-1929 season, unbeaten in their first five matches. Although Hearts topped the table, they failed the big challenge when Rangers visited Tynecastle on 15 September and won by the only goal in front of a then record League crowd of 48,000. After this titanic contest, the Ibrox Park men went on to easily win the Championship. Hearts lacked quality in a number of key positions, but did challenge Celtic and Motherwell for second place, and won home and away against Queen's Park, Ayr United, Cowdenbeath and Aberdeen. A poor finish without a win in eight matches, saw the capital team finish fourth.

In the First Round of the Scottish Cup, the supporters came to Tynecastle to see if this competition would restore Hearts fame. Airdrieonians had other ideas and won 2-0.

There was some compensation in the minor events where Barney Battles endeared himself to the supporters with some remarkable scoring. Within a month he netted five goals in an 8-2 win over Hibernian in the Dunedin Cup Final, two more in the 5-1 victory over the "greens" in the Wilson Cup Final Replay and another four in the 5-1 win over Hibernian in the Rosebery Charity Cup Final. He did not play in the Shield Final and that may be why Hibernian won 3-2.

While the overall playing performance was slightly disappointing, the club now had a fine stadium with an estimated capacity of 60,000. Support was once more on the increase with a new record average of 18,921 at League matches.

In the summer of 1929, the Hearts squad sailed from Harwich on a tour of Scandinavia where seven games were played in Denmark and Sweden. Hearts enjoyed wonderful hospitality and won six games, losing only in the final match to Helsingborg.

Jack Harkness, made his first appearance for Scotland in a Full International as a Hearts player, on 27 October 1928 against Wales in a 4-2 win at Ibrox Park, Glasgow.

THE PLAYERS FRUSTRATE THE FANS

In season 1929-1930 Hearts never fielded a regular side and results were erratic. New recruits included Andy Anderson – Baillieston, Stewart Chalmers – Queen's Park, Bob Johnstone – Coldstream and Willie McStay – Celtic, but they were unable to assist the "maroons" to a better finish than tenth in the League which was a massive 23 points behind the run away Champions, Rangers.

The first match in the League campaign resulted in a 2-1 defeat at Celtic Park where a new main stand was opened. Hearts then frustrated their fans with an unpredictable mixture of good and bad performances. The team did the double over Rangers with goals from Willie Murray and Andrew Miller bringing a 2-0 home victory. Hearts then won 3-1 at Ibrox which was Rangers first home defeat for over a year.

However, the team was very unsettled and only twice did the same side play consecutively. As a result, Hearts came up with some humiliating away results such as losing 6-2 to both Queen's Park in November and St.Mirren in January. In contrast they defeated Motherwell 2-0 and 3-2 and Dundee United 3-1 and 3-2.

One man not to blame was Barney Battles who hit 24 goals in his 29 League matches. His fame spread throughout the country when BBC Radio started to broadcast live football with the first game from Tynecastle coming in October 1929.

John Johnston made his first appearance for Scotland in a Full International on 26 October 1929 against Wales in a 4-2 at Ninian Park, Cardiff.

The Scottish Cup brought excitement and wins over Clydebank 1-0 and St.Bernards 5-1 after a 0-0 draw, took Hearts to Easter Road for a Third Round tie against Hibernian. A capacity crowd of 28,000 saw Hearts earn a memorable 3-1 victory. This brought a Quarter-Finals tie at Dundee where Hearts fought back from 2-0 down to force a replay which was won 4-0 in front of 32,000. At that time this was a record crowd for a midweek game outside of Glasgow.

Sadly, Hearts then froze in the Semi-Finals, losing 4-1 to Rangers at Hampden. The mighty crowd of 92,048 was the largest to have watched the Tynecastle club up to that time.

In the minor competitions, Hearts won the Shield and the Rosebery Charity Cup but lost in the Final of the Wilson Cup and Dunedin Cup. Lack of national success, led the directors to discuss the appointment of a team manager who did not have responsibility for secretarial and administrative tasks. Although no immediate action was taken, it had been many years since Hearts had won major honours and the directors at least realized that the club was falling behind.

FIFA as members of the IFAB realised a long held ambition when the first World Cup Competition was held in 1930 in Uruguay.

In 1930 the Club introduced one of Britain's first public address-systems with the Radio Recording Company playing music from a small hut at the south-west corner.

BARNEY'S RECORD SEASON

In June 1930 the club chairman, Elias Furst, was appointed President of the Scottish Football League, but a sad event then proceeded the new season when in August, Hearts most famous former player, of the period, Bobby Walker, died at the age of 51. He was buried at North Merchiston Cemetery and when his body was brought from the Royal Infirmary in Lauriston Place, many thousands lined the route to pay their respects.

On the playing field, the name Barney Battles hit the headlines week after week as Hearts burly striker powered his way to a club record of 44 League goals. During this scoring blitz he recorded three successive hat-tricks and at the end of season 1930-1931 his overall record stood at an incredible 99 League goals in 91 matches.

Hearts crashed to Hamilton Academical and Rangers in the first two League matches and Manager, William

McCartney, quickly turned to the transfer market bringing in, Alex Massie – Dolphin Club Dublin, Willie Reid – Glentoran and Jock White – Leeds United.

Hearts managed three wins then on 20 September a match at Tynecastle against Hibernian saw the players moving in something like their best style and playing sound constructive football to win 4-1 – the first defeat of their local rivals at Tynecastle since 1924/1925. The recruitment and Barney Battles' goals soon lifted performances and the year ended with a superb 3-0 win over Rangers at Tynecastle and the revival of a League title challenge.

The half-back line of Andy Herd, John Johnston and Bob Bennie outsmarted their illustrious opponents, allowing Barney Battles -2 and Lachie Mcmillan the opportunity to score. But hopes were quickly dashed after a New Year draw with Hibernian and a 1-0 defeat away to East Fife yet both these sides were relegated at the end of the season.

A late season highlight was the 9-0 defeat of Ayr United at Tynecastle, reported as being due to a fine display of Hearts forwards and the collapse of the Ayr United back division. The scorers were Battles -3, Chalmers, Johnston, Murray -2, White - 2. Queen's Park, Falkirk, Dundee and St.Mirren were all defeated home and away but Hearts generally suffered from a poor defence that conceded 63 goals in 38 matches, against 90 scored. As a result, although there was an overall improvement, the club finished fifth in the League, 16 points behind the Champions, Rangers.

At the beginning of 1931 the directors looked at improving the private entrance hallway to the Board Room. In addition to wood panelling a mosaic or terrazzo floor was considered. The "design by Clunas & Co in Mosaic" at a cost of £45 was accepted and the work was completed by 7 February 1931. Contrary to handed-down stories this was not part of the original work in 1914 and confirms that the 'logo' was a new design and not a copy of a present or previous badge or emblem.

Hearts were potential winners of the Scottish Cup and in the First Round, Stenhousemuir conceded home advantage only to be thrashed 9-1. In the next tie, Hearts went down 3-2 at Kilmarnock where good football was impossible due to gales force winds and rain.

In the local competitions, Hearts won the Shield and the Dunedin Cup, but lost out in the Final of the Rosebery Charity Cup and Wilson Cup. These fixtures and benefit matches were now choking the season and as a result, Hearts often had to field weak teams.

Due to a lack of success in the big competitions, the directors continued to debate the future role of William McCartney, and they found it necessary to publicly deny that the manager was leaving the club. To improve the level of fitness, Tom Murphy the trainer was replaced by the experienced James Stewart from Hamilton Academical.

Willie Reid made his first appearance for Northern Ireland in a Full International on 20 October 1930 against England in 5-1 defeat at Brammall Lane Ground, Sheffield.

Barney Battles made his first appearance for Scotland in a Full International on 25 October 1930 against Wales and scored in 1-1 draw at Ibrox Park, Glasgow.

HEARTS FALL BACK

In 1931-1932 Barney Battles missed many games through a knee ligament injury and without his goals Hearts fell back to eighth in the League, 27 points behind the Champions, Motherwell.

As they did two seasons previously, Queen's Park 5-2 at Hampden Park, and St.Mirren 5-1 at Paisley, humiliated Hearts, the team even lost in September to Leith Athletic who won only six matches all season. As the League campaign wore on, the press was critical of Hearts defensive weakness and lack of team spirit. The supporters were certainly unhappy at appalling results, such as a 6-2 defeat from Clyde again in January.

Despite their problems the team managed League 'doubles' over Dundee United, Hamilton Academical and Falkirk and Barney Battles scored 15 goals in 26 appearances.

Alex Massie made his first appearance for Scotland in a Full International on 19 September 1931 against Northern Ireland in a 3-1 win at Ibrox Park, Glasgow.

As always the Scottish Cup brought fresh hope and in the First Round, Lochgelly United was defeated 13-3 in Gorgie with Barney Battles scoring five times. In the Second Round an enthusiastic crowd saw Hearts defeat Cowdenbeath by 4-1 and this set up a massive tie with Rangers.

On 13 February 1932 the expanded Tynecastle held a new record attendance of 53,396 but Rangers won the match with Marshall scoring the only goal after 15 minutes. Hearts were slightly unlucky with Alex Massie missing a penalty kick and Bob King being sent off.

Hearts won the Shield 5-1 v St.Bernards, the Wilson Cup 3-1 v Hibernian the Dunedin Cup 9-3 v Falkirk, but lost in the Final of the Rosebery Charity Cup 2-1 v Leith Athletic. For some unknown reason a new competition, the Stirlingshire Charity Cup was added to the season and Hearts were the winners in that inaugural season, defeating Kings Park 3-1.

The Reserves won the 2nd.X1 Cup defeating Hibernian 1-0 at Tynecastle before a staggering 12,000 crowd. This was a play-off after the sides had drawn on aggregate in the two-leg Final.

Another positive feature was the recruitment in February 1932 of Tommy Walker who would soon commence an illustrious career. He was not yet seventeen and accordingly, he played for a spell with Linlithgow Rose Juniors.

The team had again failed to deliver with the defence letting down a potent attack. There was also a lack of spirit and proper preparation and as a result, in April James Stewart was replaced by James Kerr the Rangers and Scotland trainer.

Unfortunately, the club was not in a position to fully support the manager in the transfer market and indeed, a wage cut was introduced, causing further disharmony.

THE FANS ARE THRILLED

In 1932-1933, Hearts were again a thrilling side to watch with the players happier, fitter and sharper under the instruction of the new trainer. He had a major say in tactics and certainly had new ideas and modern methods.

Sadly, Barney Battles was sidelined for almost the entire season, following a knee operation, but Tommy Walker was introduced and it was clear that Hearts had found a real star player. Another future stalwart, Archie Miller – Royal Albert Athletic came in October and these youngsters also brought new life to the squad.

Under the captaincy of the strapping school teacher, John Johnston, Hearts had a solid League campaign finishing third, 12 points behind the Champions, Rangers.

The team profited from a fine start and was among the title contenders after only one defeat in eight matches. On 15 October the reigning Champions, Motherwell lost 2-0 at Tynecastle with Jock White scoring both goals. A week later, also at home, Rangers were defeated 1-0 with him scoring a dramatic last-minute goal – "Willie Murray tricked Dougie Gray and crossed for JW to net with the last kick of the match".

Typically, the "maroons" then lost 3-1 to Falkirk and were just too inconsistent to win the championship. At least Hearts forced a 4-4 draw at Ibrox Park in March and therefore took three points from the eventual League winners. Airdrieonians, East Stirlingshire and Greenock Morton were the clubs to suffer home and away defeats this season.

On 26 October 1932 a new record crowd for International matches at Tynecastle rose to 32,175 for Scotland v Wales.

Hearts enjoyed a run in the Scottish Cup, defeating Solway Star 3-0, Airdrieonians 6-1 and St.Johnstone 2-0 all at Tynecastle, before meeting Hibernian in the Quarter-Finals. The Second Division side held Hearts to a 0-0 draw at Easter Road before a record crowd of 33,759. The home team won the replay 2-0 with Bob Johnstone and Willie Murray scoring before a Tynecastle new midweek record attendance of 41,034.

In the Semi-Final against Celtic at Hampden, Hearts missed several chances to win but the game ended 0-0 before a massive crowd of 87,219. The "maroons" unluckily lost the replay by 2-1 at the same venue.

In the local competitions, Hearts won the Shield 4-0 v Hibernian, the Rosebery Charity Cup 3-1 v Motherwell, the Dunedin Cup 1-0 v Hibernian and the Stirlingshire Charity Cup 3-1 v Kings Park. It was fitting that skipper, John Johnston, picked up the Rosebery Charity Cup from Hearts patron, Lord Rosebery, as it was the Jubilee Final. Hearts had been the first winners of this worthy competition that had raised many thousands of pounds for good causes in Edinburgh and district.

Hearts only lost out in the Wilson Cup Final 3-2 v Hibernian and this ended one of the best campaigns for many years and the club's financial worries were now in the past.

Sadly, some tragic events occurred with the young reserve player, Robert Burns, being killed in a motor bike accident. Former manager, John McCartney also died, as did Paddy Crossan. In addition, in April 1933 a Hearts-Hibernain Select lost 3-2 against a Rangers-Celtic Select in a benefit for the dependents of the Granton Trawler Disaster in which many supporters of the club had died.

Andy Anderson made his first appearance for Scotland in a Full International on 1 April 1933 against England in a 2-1 win at Hampden Park, Glasgow.

THE TEAM FLATTER TO DECEIVE

In July 1933 manager, William McCartney, asked to be relieved of his clerical duties in order to devote more time to his work with the players. This was readily agreed because after a reasonably successful year, Hearts were hopeful that season 1933-1934 would at long last bring major honours under the captaincy of the elegant Alex Massie.

Again, however, Hearts flattered only to deceive and actually fell back to sixth place in the League, 22 points behind the Champions, Rangers. Hearts fans were at least guaranteed entertainment with Andy Anderson, Barney Battles, Alex Massie and Tommy Walker consistently shining in the gloom of mediocre results. In September, Hearts were 4-1 down to Cowdenbeath at Tynecastle, but with 20 minutes left to play, they came back to win 5-4 including a four goal romp by Barney Battles.

Hearts title hopes were effectively ended with two successive defeats in October away to Motherwell 1-2 and Rangers 1-3. Nevertheless, the festive period was eventful with Airdrieonians defeated 8-1 at Tynecastle, Hibernian routed 4-1 at Easter Road, and Dundee demolished 6-1 at Tynecastle. Cowdenbeath and Dundee were again defeated home and away then in the spring, six defeats from eight matches pushed Hearts down the table. As usual, goal scoring was fine, but the team suffered from defensive problems.

To address all the playing issues, director Alex Irvine, again promoted the idea of having a team coach in line with the major clubs in England. He was unable to gain the support of his fellow directors.

In the Scottish Cup, Montrose and Queen's Park were dispatched and in the Third Round, Hearts travelled to Ibrox Park and in a dour match forced a 0-0 draw against Rangers. The replay at Tynecastle attracted a midweek record crowd of 48,895 and the Glasgow men won 2-1 although their first goal could have been ruled out for either offside or hand ball.

In the local competitions, Hearts defeated Hibernian in the Final of the Shield 4-0, the Rosebery Charity Cup 2-1 and the Wilson Cup 2-0.

Meanwhile, at the AGM, the shareholders were told that the club would now adopt a slow build-up of players due to the residual debt arising from the recent ground developments.

HEARTS EXCITE

Due to his knee injury, Barney Battles required a year's break, but he was splendidly covered by the hard-hitting Dave McCulloch – Third Lanark who came in June. He was the League's top scorer in 1934-1935 with 38 goals in 35 appearances, including 12 in 7 consecutive matches. This marksmanship inspired Hearts to third place in the Championship.

Hearts should have finished higher. The first match in the League was against Falkirk at Brockville Park with Hearts winning 2-0 and they completed the double at Tynecastle in December. Others to suffer the double were Airdrieonians, Ayr United, Queen of the South and Clyde. In September the team started an 11-game unbeaten run, including eight wins, and reached second place. Before the festive period, there was also an outstanding 4-1 home win over the eventual Champions, Rangers, while at New Year, Hibernian lost 5-2 and Dundee were crushed 5-1 but then losing 1-0 to Dunfermline Athletic in Gorgie was just the sort of disappointing performance the supporters hoped was a thing of the past and the title challenge fizzled out.

Andy Herd made his first appearance for Scotland in a Full International on 20 October 1934, against Northern Ireland in a 2-1 defeat at Windsor Park Belfast.

Dave McCulloch and Tommy Walker made their first appearance for Scotland in a Full International on 21 November 1934 against Wales in a 3-2 win at Pittodrie Park, Aberdeen.

In December, 1934, the Board made enquiries about buying the Police Station and Bowling Green in McLeod Street with an eye, once again, towards expansion.

The Scottish Cup produced thrills, but similar disappointment. The craft of Tommy Walker and skipper, Alex Massie, engineered wins over Solway Star, Kilmarnock and Dundee United. As a result, rumours that Tommy Walker might join Arsenal for a record £12,000 caused dismay and split the directors. This interest was not pursued and he was still at Hearts when Airdrieonians lost 3-2 in a Quarter-Final tie at Broomfield, before a record attendance of 24,244.

In the Semi-Final against Rangers at Hampden Park, Hearts played before a six figure crowd for the first time, with 102,661 in the ground, including about 25,000 Tynecastle fans. Tommy Walker scored in a 1-1 draw, but the "maroons" regretted some missed chances, as Rangers won the Replay 2-0 in front of 90,428 spectators.

Hearts did win the Rosebery Charity Cup Final 2-1 v Leith Athletic, the Wilson Cup Final 4-0 v Hibernian and the Stirlingshire Charity Cup Final 3-2 v Kings Park. But Hibernian won the Shield Final 4-2.

Despite a sound campaign and a record profit, the season ended in disharmony and the resignation of Chairman, Elias Furst in March. William McCartney followed in June as new Chairman, Alex Irvine, wanted a track-suited approach to management. Mr. McCartney brought through many fine players, but his squads failed to win major honours and he paid the price.

UNDER NEW MANAGEMENT

In July 1935 a new manager, David Pratt, came from Notts County and the former Celtic and Liverpool winger, faced early problems, because the trainers' saw their position being undermined as Mr. Pratt dictated tactics. The public was confident of success, however, with a team containing many internationalists, including Andy Anderson, Jack Harkness, Andy Herd, Dave McCulloch, Alex Massie and Tommy Walker.

In season 1935-1936 Hearts' young side actually dropped back to fifth in the League, 19 points behind the Champions, Celtic. Nevertheless, some performances were special particularly the 8-3 home win over Hibernian on 21 September. This is the greatest number of goals scored in a League derby with Hearts and quoted as "a well oiled machine and hitting like a steam-hammer" the marksmen being Andy Black -2, Dave McCulloch, Alex Munro, Tommy Walker (2) and Charlie Wipfler -2.

Another outstanding result came in February when prospective title winners, Celtic, were beaten 1-0 at Tynecastle. Unfortunately, Hearts were never serious Championship contenders due to a poor away record, with only six wins from 19 matches. All of the six away wins led to home and away defeats over, Albion Rovers, Arbroath, Ayr United, Dundee, Hamilton Academical and Third Lanark.

Hearts did not miss Barney Battles goal scoring flair as much as feared as Tommy Walker 18, Dave McCulloch 17 and Andy Black 15 took over the mantle.

The new manager was not helped by the directors' decision to clear outstanding debts relating to the previous upgrading of the stadium. As a result, in December 1935, Dave McCulloch joined Brentford and within a few weeks, Alex Massie was signed by Aston Villa. Dave McCulloch's firepower and Alex Massie's midfield drive were missed while Barney Battles also gave up his struggle to regain fitness after scoring 150 goals in 162 League and Scottish Cup matches.

Hearts did sign George Robson – Brentford, William Russell – Chelsea and Charlie Wipfler – Bristol Rovers but they could not compensate for the departures.

Consequently, the "maroons" made an inglorious First Round exit in the Scottish Cup at Cathkin Park, where Third Lanark won 2-0. David Pratt was unhappy about team spirit and felt that he did not have the support of the trainers. Two weeks later, Hearts won 5-1 at the same ground in the League, sparking rumours of indiscretion by certain players before the Cup match.

Hearts cleared the board locally winning all the local competitions. The East of Scotland Shield and the Rosebery Charity Cup v St.Bernards , and the Wilson Cup v Hibernian. Even minor matches against Hibernian were still important and during the season, Willie Waugh and John Munro were loaned to the Leith club to successfully fight relegation.

Scotland beat Ireland 2-1 at Tynecastle and in view of the ever increasing attendances in March 1936 it was decided to replace all the wooden crush barriers with concrete and steel. Then the directors submitted a scheme to extend the main stand which was accepted by the Dean of Guild but the Education Committee vetoed the move.

Tommy Walker was now a fixture in the international team and that same month, the 20-year old inside-man, famously scored Scotland's equalizer in a 1-1 draw against England at Wembley, on 4 April 1936 with a penalty kick.

Mr.W.C.P.Brown, the immediate past Chairman and the present Vice-Chairman, once more demonstrated his generosity, by gifting the Club a fine gymnasium which bears his name.

Shareholders adopted a scheme to allocate to existing shareholders, holding fewer than twenty shares, new shares up to that number at 20s each. Season Ticket holders were to be allowed to buy up to ten £1 shares and the remaining shares were to be offered to the public at 30s each.

HEARTS REGROUP

After the previous season's disappointment, Hearts were active in the transfer market, signing Freddie Warren – Middlesbrough, who later became the club's first Welsh internationalist, and also Alex Ferguson – St.Johnstone. Ongoing recruitment was required, because during 1936-1937 Jack Harkness retired after a distinguished career, while stalwarts, Willie Reid and Andy Herd, moved on.

Willie Walsh, hit 22 League goals, but this was bettered by young Andy Black, who scored 30. As a result, Hearts hit a new club record of 99 League goals, but even though they were the highest scorers, the team finished fifth, being ten points behind the Champions, Rangers. Failure to take points off lesser clubs eventually damaged Hearts' League challenge, but the real reason may have been the situation behind the scenes.

Trainer, Jimmy Kerr, resigned in September as his methods were not popular with young players and his on-field instructions clashed with the manager's. As a result, in a show of player-power, most of the squad threatened to strike, if action was not taken. David Pratt, assumed total control and long term servant, George McCrae, was appointed to the downgraded role of trainer. This cleared the air and Hearts moved up to third with some splendid performances.

For example, In December, Hearts were 2-0 down to Rangers, but came back to win 5-2 at Tynecastle before 40,211 fans. As in so many matches, this magnificent recovery was inspired by Tommy Walker. Hibernian lost 3-2 at New Year and shortly afterwards, Hearts won 1-0 away to Rangers to record their first League double over them since 1929-1930.

Alex Munro made his first appearance for Scotland in a Full International on 31st.October, 1936, against Northern Ireland, and scored in a 3-1 win at Windsor Park Belfast.

The Hearts were acknowledged to be the country's finest footballing side and early in 1937, William Kean was appointed secretary, to ensure that all of the manager's time was spent with his players.

Unfortunately, the internal problems had not been resolved, because in February, David Pratt resigned. No reason was given, although Mr.Kean's appointment may have been taken as a slight to his ability. Four successive matches were lost in March and Hearts slipped down the League table.

Captain, Andy Anderson, shouldered more responsibility and Hearts defeated St. Bernards 3-1 in the Scottish Cup First Round. Hearts then faced Kings Park on 13 February. The home team won 15-0, a victory which is still a club record in a national competition. Willie Walsh scored eight goals that day which is also a club record.

Five Scottish Internationals
Mr. A. Irvine - Andy Anderson, Tommy Walker, Dave McCulloch, Andy Herd, Alex Massie.

In March, Frank Moss, the 28-year old former England and Arsenal goalkeeper, whose career had been ended by a shoulder injury, was appointed manager. The former coach of Arsenal Reserves immediately faced challenges with the departure of Alex Munro to Blackpool. Hearts were also bundled out of the Scottish Cup with a 2-1 defeat by Hamilton Academical, before a record crowd for them of 28,281.

Freddie Warren made his first appearance for Wales in a Full International on 17 March 1937 against Northern Ireland and scored in a 4-1 win at The Racecourse, Wrexham.

The new manager had quality footballers, but needed to end the absurd inconsistency. Moss was encouraged by the team sweeping the boards in winning the East of Scotland Shield, the Rosebery Charity Cup and the Wilson Cup against Hibernian and defeating Kings Park in the Stirlingshire Charity Cup

The average attendance at League matches continued to grow reaching a new record of 20,087.

As from season 1937-1938 the approved weight of the ball was changed to 14-16 ounces, and the 'D' shape drawn at the edge of the penalty area, was brought in to allow the penalty taker a clear run up.

In September, the Border Cup was donated by Hearts and Hibernian for Annual Competition to encourage football in the predominately rugby area of the Borders.

MOSS SPARKS A RECOVERY

For season 1937-1938 Frank Moss introduced modern training methods and detailed tactical talks, but more importantly, he was given a free hand to select the team. Hearts opened with a 2-1 win over St.Johnstone and four days later, at Easter Road, Hibernian lost in the Wilson Cup Final. That result became irrelevant when Alex Ferguson suffered a compound fracture of his right leg, but despite this upsetting incident, Hearts went on to have the best League campaign for over thirty years and finished second to Celtic by only three points.

Mr. Moss certainly tinkered as the campaign progressed and he sold Willie Walsh to Millwall while securing Alfie Biggs – Arsenal, Jimmy Briscoe – Preston North End, Pat Donoghue – Tranent and Alex Hyslop – Albion Rovers. Another big signing was Joe Mantle – Stockport County but he broke a leg in only his third match. However, the star of the season was Andy Black who scored 40 League goals.

After seven matches, Hearts were top of the League and travelled to play Celtic. The "maroons" lost 2-1 due to missed chances, but the players quickly recovered and were back on top after beating Rangers 3-0 at Ibrox Park in November. Andy Black scored a hat-trick that day when Hearts youth and dash made the headlines. There were reverses but Hearts were one point ahead when Celtic came for a real crunch match on 8 January 1938.

The Glasgow club deserved to win the Championship because they came out on top after a brilliant contest. Hearts led 2-1 with fifteen minutes left, but Celtic hit back in amazing style to win 4-2. Hearts never topped the League again that season and Celtic did not falter even though the Tynecastle men had a remarkable finish with nine wins in a row.

Andy Black and Willie Waugh made their first appearance for Scotland in a Full International on 8 December 1937 against Czechoslovakia while Black scored Waugh had a shut-out in a 5-0 win at Ibrox Park, Glasgow.

For a brief period, the team was shattered by the Celtic result and went down 3-1 away to Second Division, Dundee United, in the First Round of the Scottish Cup. That day, several Tynecastle men were highlighted for a lack of fight, but that never applied to Tommy Walker who was unsurpassed at skilful football and who scored Scotland's winning goal against England that season.

The season ended poorly with defeats in the Shield and the Rosebery Charity Cup. However, as one of the top eight clubs in Britain, Hearts were invited to compete in the Empire Exhibition Tournament in Glasgow. In the First Round the "maroons" defeated Brentford at Ibrox Park, but went down 1-0 to Celtic in the Semi-Finals at the same ground.

Frank Moss fielded a side that was admired for quality football and Hearts regularly provided three, or even four, players for Scotland. With League gates averaging a new record of 20,172 all the club's debts had been cleared and there was talk of a new ground on the west side of the city, as restrictions were placed on the expansion of Tynecastle.

Jimmy Dykes made his first appearance for Scotland in a Full International on 21 May 1938 against the Netherlands in a 3-1 win at the Olympisch Stadion, Amsterdam.

The white 'picket' fence in front of the main stand was replaced by a brick wall and it was felt that the Club required a new stadium and several sites for a new ground were looked at in Corstorphine, Dalkeith, Saughton Mains, Sighthill and Willowbrae Road.

Plans for a super stadium at Saughton Mains were drawn up with the Lord Provost agreeing that the Edinburgh Corporation would extend the train and bus routes to the new site and the L.M.S. Railway indicated that the adjacent Saughton Mains siding could be opened for passenger traffic. The decision was delayed when the Corporation advised the directors that they were considering the construction of a new municipal stadium for the Empire Games and it might be possible for Hearts to utilise that ground.

ERRATIC HEARTS

After finishing second the previous season, Hearts looked good for the Championship in 1938-1939. Andy Black and Tommy Walker were two of the most delightful players in the game, backed up by Andy Anderson, Jimmy Briscoe, Jimmy Dykes and Archie Miller, although the local press thought the team needed a leader of the attack. Sadly, Hearts challenge failed to materialize and the team finished fourth in the League with Rangers the runaway Champions. Hearts hit 98 goals, but the defence was too weak to support a title challenge, with 70 conceded.

The Hearts made a great start, but were put to the test on 3 September when a record League crowd of 49,905 came to Tynecastle for the match against Celtic. Hearts lost 5-1 and while the club had often been called inconsistent, this season they were erratic with good results always being spoiled by a bad one. For example, a 7-1 away victory over St.Johnstone was followed by a home draw 1-1 against Arbroath. Yet again Hearts won home and away over six clubs, a mark of their quality in the 1920s. Too many goals were lost and Hibernian even recorded their first League double since 1921/1922.

However, Hearts were always entertaining particularly when Archie Garrett came in December after a new club record of £4,000 was paid to Preston North End. At that time, there was real fear of another war.

Archie Miller made his first appearance for Scotland in a Full International on 9 November 1938 against Wales in a 3-2 win at Tynecastle Park, Edinburgh.

That afternoon he was joined by Andy Anderson-captain and Tommy Walker which no doubt helped to swell the crowd to 34,831, which was a new record for such a match at Tynecastle and a new record for the fixture.

During this campaign Tommy Brown scored Hearts 3,000th. League goal in their 1,535th. match, on 26 November 1938 in a 2-1 defeat of Raith Rovers at Starks Park, Kirkcaldy.

Goals were also a feature of the Scottish Cup run and Penicuik Athletic lost 14-2 at Tynecastle with Archie Garrett hitting six. The Second Round was even better, with Elgin City being thrashed 14-1 with Garrett and Andy Black each scoring four. This led to Tynecastle's first all ticket crowd of 50,446 which packed into the ground for the Third Round tie against Celtic – 50,709 tickets were actually sold.

Amid tremendous excitement, Hearts snatched a 2-2 draw, Garrett equalizing in the dying seconds. However, the replay ended in bitter disappointment before a massive gate of 80,840. A Freddie Warren goal had taken the tie into extra time and during that period Willie Waugh appeared to have saved a Divers' shot. Sensationally, the referee declared that the ball had crossed the line and although the whole Hearts team, except 'gentleman' Tommy Walker, protested, the goal stood and Hearts were eliminated.

Only the Wilson Cup was won this season while on the international front, apart from the usual Full and League honours, Jimmy Dykes and Archie Garrett toured North America with a Scotland XI, Archie Garret hitting 18 goals.

At a Hearts shareholders meeting, in January 1939 Mr. A. Martin, presiding, a new Shareholders Association was formed and in February, they selected William Baird, as their candidate, for the forthcoming election to the Hearts Board. But a move to increase the Board from five to seven directors failed to find sufficient support at a subsequent Extraordinary General Meeting.

In March 1939 at a meeting of shareholders in the Oddfellows Hall, Forrest Road, Mr. Alex Irvine, Chairman, met to discuss the benefits of a move from Tynecastle.

They Included:-

The Disadvantages of Tynecastle Park were:-

The ground was completely hemmed in by other buildings;

There were no training facilities;

The capacity of 53,000 was inadequate;

Fear of crushing kept many supporters from big matches;

There were only 36 turnstiles;

Extensions to the present structures would be costly;

Conversion of the enclosure to seats would prove inadequate;

There was no car park;

There was no cover for the terracing supporters;

There was no athletics track;

The Advantages of Tynecastle Park were:-

Transport to the ground by road or rail was excellent;

Crowds over 50,000 were rare and capacity was generally adequate;

The Main Stand could be re-developed to provide more seats;

£2,000 had already been spent on ground safety;

Tynecastle Park had great sentimental value to the supporters;

There was a clause in the Title Deeds allowing for 'buy-back';

The Meeting favoured the retention of the 'Club' home Tynecastle;

In May 1939 the Committee formed to look at new sites reported that the cost of a new ground would be in the region of £100,000, a sum which could ruin the club. In September 1939 the outbreak of the Second World War ended all hopes of a move.

At the Thirty-fourth Annual General Meeting of the Heart of Midlothian Football Club Limited it was noted that during season 1938/1939 Hearts had paid visiting clubs £6813 and received £5147 from away matches. The shareholders approved paying a dividend of 10% free of tax, which was equal to a rate of 13.5%. The first dividend, of the Company formed in 1905. At the same meeting the shareholders proposed that the directors receive an honorarium and the Chairman was awarded 75 guineas and the other directors 50 guineas.

WAR ONCE AGAIN

The public was weary, waiting for Hearts to mould fine players into a winning side, but more important issues overshadowed football as war was declared against Germany on 3 September 1939. Accordingly, after five matches, the Scottish League was abandoned with Hearts third on goal average.

The Government relaxed its ban on football after a month, although the game was not to interfere with work of national importance and long travelling was to be avoided.

For this season 1939-1940, from 16 October there were to be two leagues of 16 clubs each. Hearts played in the East & North Division and the ground capacity was restricted to 8,000 due to the threat of air raids. Demand for football was greatly diminished by national service, rationing and because the winter proved to be one of the most severe on record. Accordingly, the club's average League gate dropped to only 3,451. All forces in uniform were to be admitted at half price.

With the "Old Firm" in the Western League, Hearts were expected to win the East & North Division, but failed, due to constant team changes. In keeping with the tradition of the club, Hearts men had been quick to join the forces and the departure of players such as Archie Garrett and Andy Black affected performance, while others missed matches due to work commitments. To compensate, guest players were allowed and Hearts recruited internationalist, Bobby Baxter – Middlesbrough and others such as Jackie Gillies, Bob McCartney, Frank and Hugh O'Donnell.

At the end of the campaign, Hearts were second to Falkirk, despite some magnificent victories. They defeated Dundee United 9-2, Stenhousemuir 8-2, Hibernian 6-5, and Arbroath, Alloa Athletic and Kings Park all by 7-2. This was matched by Falkirk who also did the 'double' over Hearts and took the title by five points. The "bairns" won 3-2 at Tynecastle and 7-1 at Brockville and the players could have little complaint.

They scored 104 goals that season, the first time the club had scored over a century in a League competition. As the War-time matches are not recognised as relevant it is not included in the historical records. Players, however, have been credited with appearances and goals.

The SFA ran an Emergency Cup competition and Hearts defeated St.Johnstone and Raith Rovers before holding Airdrieonians to a 0-0 draw at Broomfield. The visitors won the Tynecastle replay by 4-3 and a local paper noted that, "Hearts wilted when things went against them, as they have done over the years".

Hearts won the East of Scotland Shield 3-2 v Hibernian and the Wilson Cup 2-0 v Hibernian but lost to them in the Rosebery Charity Cup Final 5-2. There were also many representative games and in April 1940 Scotland beat the Empire Army 4-1 at Tynecastle before 7,687 spectators.

Behind the scenes, the club's long serving benefactor, Mr William C.P.Brown, resigned from the board due to ill health. It was also announced that Hearts would play in the new and more lucrative Scottish Southern Football League in 1940-1941. War-time International matches were played although no caps awarded but Bobby Baxter, Tommy Brown, Duncan McClure and Tommy Walker all played in them.

HEARTS CHANGE LEAGUES

The 16-team Southern League included the Glasgow clubs, but the problem of fielding a strong side remained and Hearts offered facilities to all players working or serving in the Edinburgh area. Bobby Baxter went to Hibernian, but other guests were a feature of the season and 37 men appeared in the League matches. The most notable new faces were Tommy Dougan – Manchester United, George Hamilton – Aberdeen, Tommy Pearson – Newcastle United and Jimmy Philp – St.Bernards.

Surprisingly, the club entered the season 1940-1941 without a manager, because in July 1940 Frank Moss went home and Chairman, Alex Irvine, deputized, with the support of his fellow directors.

It soon became clear that constant changes affected performance and sure enough, the team finished tenth in the Southern League. When Hearts fielded a settled team they played well, but the opposite applied, and the control of the players by the directors' was not successful. On 19 October Clyde became the only side to hit double figures against Hearts, running up a 10-3 League victory at Shawfield. The next away game was almost as bad, with the team going down 6-2 to Hamilton Academical.

Gladly this is not included as Hearts worst defeat in League football due to the War-time results being ignored for record purposes. Hearts won only 12 matches and lost 71 goals while scoring only 64. It was obvious that some of the guest players were not Hearts standard.

Better form was shown in the Southern League Cup and Hearts progressed from a four-club Qualifying Section, including Clyde, Hibernian and Queen's Park. In the Semi-Final at Easter Road, Hearts beat Celtic 2-0 and reached a major cup final for the first time since 1919.

The Hampden Final against Rangers attracted a crowd of 68,000 and the team was:- Willie Waugh; Duncan McClure and Archie Miller; Jimmy Philip, Jimmy Dykes and Tommy Brown; Tommy Dougan, Alex Massie, George Hamilton, Tommy Walker and Robert Christie.

Tommy Walker scored after 37 minutes but Rangers forced an equalizer and a replay. The same team played in the second game and before nearly 60,000 Rangers went 2-0 ahead. George Hamilton scored twice to level the game but the "maroons" crumbled in the late stages and lost 4-2.

Hearts won the Rosebery Charity Cup 2-0 and the Wilson Cup 3-2 both against Hibernian.

The team did well in the Summer Cup where Queen's Park and St.Mirren were defeated over two legs. Hearts then went down 4-2 to Rangers in the Semi-Finals at Hampden before a crowd of 24,800.

Hearts advertised for a full time manager but no-one was suitable from seventeen applicants. In June 1941 the club approached David McLean of East Fife, a recognized talent spotter, and a man who could develop young players. He had played for Celtic, Ayr United, Cowdenbeath and East Fife, and he had also guided the Methil club to a Scottish Cup victory in 1938.

MCLEAN REBUILDS

The new manager had great plans for the future of Hearts by concentrating on young players. He inaugurated a £750 benefit for first-eleven players for every five years of service and £500 for reserves, Full-time players, top class trainers and coaches.

In August 1941 in line with the traditions of the club, Hearts played Arsenal to help pay-off the debt on the Scottish National War Memorial. Arsenal won 1-0 before 20,817 fans and including donations, an auspicious £2,000 was raised.

Davie McLean, worked hard to find promising youngsters to mix with current players and guests. Forty players were eventually used in the League with notable new guests being Harry Betmead – Grimbsy Town, Sid Bidewell – Chelsea, Jackie Gillies – Clyde, John Harvey – Kilmarnock, Bill Hughes – Birmingham and George Smith – Manchester City. Performances certainly improved and Hearts finished fifth in the Southern League scoring 85 goals in 30 matches. The defence conceded 72 and this prevented a real title challenge.

The 1941-1942 League campaign started well with Celtic defeated 3-0. Then in September, the team started a run of eight wins from nine matches. Hearts travelled to Ibrox Park on 15 November confident of victory and going on to take the League title, but despite taking an early lead, the Tynecastle men lost 5-2. They were reported as, "a delightful team, but Rangers carried heavy metal". The following Saturday Hearts were winning 4-1 at Celtic Park, but the game ended 4-4 and this sort of form took them out of the League race.

Selection problems also led to wild swings in fortune with a 6-2 defeat from Motherwell in December being followed the next week by a 7-0 win over Falkirk and an 8-2 defeat of St. Mirren at New Year.

A sign of the times was the fact that Hearts suffered a League 'double' losing 6-4 and 5-1 to Third Lanark for the first time since 1912-1913. They eventually ended up 16 points behind the Champions, Rangers.

Fine players such as Willie MacFarlane – Bathgate Thistle and Tom McKenzie – Haddington Athletic were recruited, but in the spring, Hearts crashed out of the Southern League Cup, failing to progress from a Qualifying Section including Motherwell, Third Lanark and Rangers. The Summer Cup was no better and after disposing of St.Mirren over two legs, Hearts went down 3-2 on aggregate to Albion Rovers.

The local competitions brought some cheer with victories in the East of Scotland Shield 3-2 and the Wilson Cup 1-0 against Hibernian. The Rosebery Charity Cup was also won when skipper, Tommy Walker, guessed correctly on the toss of a coin after a 1-1 draw with Hibernian.

THE WAR HITS HOME

In 1942-1943, new guests included Ted Platt – Arsenal and George Wilkins – Brentford, but Tommy Walker and Jimmy Dykes missed much of the season, with Dykes discharged from the RAF to return to his trade as a plumber. Hearts reserves now operated in the North Eastern League and the manager's recruitment drive moved into top gear, with the signing of Jimmy Brown – Bayview YC, Archie Kelly – Arthurlie, Malcolm McLure – Larkhall Thistle and Tom McSpadyen – Glencairn.

Constant changes were the order of the day, due to players' work and service commitments. Accordingly, it was a surprise to see Hearts challenging for the Southern League during the early months. This promising start ended on 31 October when Rangers won 3-0 at Tynecastle, the sides' first home defeat of the season. At that point, manager, Davie McLean, fell ill and without his influence the team hit a run of seven matches without a win at the turn of the year. Motherwell even won 6-1 at Tynecastle.

Hearts tumbled down the League but McLean returned in March and after a late rally that produced five wins from the final six matches, the Hearts finished seventh with 31 points from 30 games. Tommy Walker was majestic but he was often missing, due to military commitments and representative games. He would have been the club's most capped player but for the War.

In the Southern League Cup, Hearts failed to progress from a Qualifying Section involving Clyde, Hamilton Academical and Queen's Park. The Summer Cup also brought little joy with Hearts losing 4-1 on aggregate to Rangers. In local competitions, Hearts went down 3-2 to Hibernian in the Shield Final at Easter Road, but there was a measure of revenge in the Rosebery Charity Cup Final with Hearts again taking the trophy on the toss of a coin after a 1-1 draw.

That season, Christmas gifts were sent to twenty one players that were serving at home and overseas, but tragically, two young players were victims of the War, John Ramsey, reported missing on an air operation in Italy while Walter Smith died at home with smallpox.

PROMISING HEARTS

Although 28 players were used in the competitive matches of 1943-1944, the team was more settled and finished a promising fourth in the Southern League, 15 points behind the Champions, Rangers. The benefits of the manager's rebuilding plans were coming through and some fine men emerged such as Jimmy Brown, Alfie Conn, Charlie Cox, Archie Kelly, Alex McCrae, and Willie MacFarlane.

In August 1943, a Hearts Select beat the Royal Air Force 3-2 to commence what would become an annual Charity Match.

In October in the Southern League, the "maroons" had the satisfaction of defeating Rangers 3-1 at Ibrox Park and this was followed by a 9-0 home win over Queen's Park. But these were special events and although Hearts were usually good entertainment, they were not consistent enough to push Rangers, who won the return match 3-1 at Tynecastle in January.

Hearts were unlucky to be drawn in the same League Cup Qualifying Section as Rangers who won both matches and topped the Section which also included Airdrieonians and Motherwell. Half the stand was roofless at this time due to essential repairs, but the job was completed in June 1944.

Hearts took part in the Summer Cup which operated on a two-leg system. They disposed of Albion Rovers 8-3 on aggregate, but then crashed out against Falkirk who won 4-1 at Tynecastle and 2-0 at Brockville.

In the local competitions, Hearts won the East of Scotland Shield and the Wilson Cup, defeating Hibernian 2-1 on each occasion. The Rosebery Charity Cup went to Hibernian by a 4-1 victory. The reserves brought the Second XI Cup back to Edinburgh after a two-legged victory over St.Mirren.

However public morale was much higher following the Allied invasion of Europe and the more positive course of the War. Hearts had 53 men in the forces at that time including Tommy Walker, the club's most influential player, and guest players were still a feature. One of these was Otto Jonsson an Icelandic amateur who became the first foreign player to wear maroon.

A SEASON TO FORGET

Despite the Allied invasion of Europe, the Second World War was far from over when season 1944-1945 commenced and tragically, two more Hearts' players were killed during the year.

At home, the team made little impact in the Southern League, due to a suspect defence and a poor away record of only three wins in fifteen matches with the loss of 41 goals. As a result, and despite an eleven game unbeaten run at the turn of the year, Hearts could not make a serious challenge and eventually finished sixth.

Although away victories were few, one of these was a remarkable 10-3 win over Albion Rovers at Cliftonhill on 11 November. However, the highlight of the season was most surely the 3-0 win over Hibernian at Tynecastle during the festive period, because this ended the Easter Road club's title challenge. Rangers, the eventual Champions, were also held 1-1 at Tynecastle on 28 October.

No responsibility for a mediocre campaign could be held against Archie Kelly, because the former Arthurlie striker was the top scorer in Scotland with 33 Southern League goals. Kelly's total included seven away to Albion Rovers which is still a club record for a League match. Captained by Archie Miller, several youngsters were also breaking through, such as Alfie Conn, John Urquhart and Jimmy Walker. But with so many men in the services, guest players were still important and Jackie Oakes from Queen of the South made a particular impression.

Hearts did little in the knock-out competitions. The Southern League Cup started with the Qualifying Section matches against Dumbarton, Motherwell and St.Mirren and the team should have progressed. However, with both clubs on eight points, Motherwell beat Hearts 4-2 at Tynecastle in the last match. The home side actually led 2-1 before the defence collapsed.

Germany surrendered on 7 May 1945 and "Victory in Europe" celebrations enhanced the two-legged Summer Cup competition. After beating Airdrieonians 5-0 on aggregate, Hearts went down to Partick Thistle 4-2 on aggregate.

Lack of success in all the local competitions saw the East of Scotland Shield, Rosebery Charity Cup and Wilson Cup end up at Easter Road. This brought a rather poor season to an end but the performance of the youngsters was encouraging and Hearts won the Second XI Cup against Celtic.

PEACE RETURNS

The conflict in Europe was over when the season commenced and in August, the War in the Far East also ended. Over fifty Hearts' men had served their country and four would never return:- John Donaldson, Donald MacDonald, John Ramsey and Walter Smith.

It would be some time before football could return to normal with many players still in the forces. While the country slowly returned to peacetime conditions, it was decided that there would be no promotion or relegation between the new Scottish League "A" and "B" Divisions. The Scottish Cup was held in abeyance, although there would be a special Victory Cup competition and a new Scottish League Cup, based on the successful structure used by the Southern League.

Hearts' squad was strengthened by the return of centre-half, Bobby Baxter and he was appointed captain and coached the players.

The 1945-1946 season saw a whole clutch of 'new boys on the block' Fred Glidden and Jimmy Wardhaugh. Dave McLean's youth policy had started. On the down side, Davie McLean's attempt to reshape his team with young men was not helped by impatient supporters and questions about fitness and preparation.

Hearts eventually finished seventh in the League and with 11 wins; 11 defeats; and 8 draws, the team was unpredictable and never in serious contention for the title. There was some encouragement when Greenock Morton lost 6-0 at Tynecastle in October and young hopeful, Alfie Conn, added some much needed punch. Hearts even beat Celtic 5-3 in Glasgow in December their first League win on the Glasgow ground since 1901-1902. In addition, Hearts took three points out of four from the eventual Champions, Rangers with a 1-1 draw at Ibrox Park and a 2-0 victory at Tynecastle.

The task of rebuilding Hearts' team was an onerous one and in March 1946 the manager's job was made more difficult when his chief trainer, George McCrae, resigned. John Torbet formerly of Partick Thistle was his successor and ex-player, John Harvey, was appointed assistant trainer.

Hearts did seem happier in the knock-out competitions and in the League Cup, they progressed from a Qualifying Section involving Falkirk, Hamilton Academical and St.Mirren to set up a Quarter-Finals match against East Fife at Easter Road. After a 3-0 victory, the Semi-Final against Rangers on 27 April was again allocated to Easter Road. Nevertheless, the Hearts' officials wanted the game switched to Hampden where the team lost 2-1 before a crowd of 70,000. Jimmy Walker headed a goal after one minute, but Rangers pulled back to win in extra time

In the Victory Cup, the Tynecastle men defeated Alloa Athletic 6-3 on aggregate then played Hibernian at Easter Road on a straight knock-out basis. Tommy Walker's exultant return from the forces attracted a crowd of 39,323 but Hearts went down 3-1.

The season ended with the team losing the Wilson Cup Final and winning the Shield 3-2 v Hibernian and then flying out to Germany on 3 June and beating the British Army of the Rhine by 3-2 at Celle.

With 60 players on the books, McLean had to quickly rationalize the squad and there were many departures, including Andy Black to Manchester City.

NORMAL SERVICE RESUMED

The end of the War saw crowds streaming back to enjoy some relaxation and the Club sold their 'maximum' of 900 season tickets. After 33 people died in crushing at Bolton Wanderers ground, the major clubs in Britain had to ensure that their stadiums could cope with the huge crowds flocking back to football matches, as they sought entertainment after the grim years. The retaining wall around the track and some crush barriers were installed.

Football was nearly back to normal in season 1946-1947, but the hopes of the Hearts' fans were quickly dashed when in early September Tommy Walker was transferred to Chelsea for a club record of £6,000 just after helping to defeat the high-flying Hibernian. He was quickly followed by Archie Garrett and Jimmy Briscoe to Northampton Town and the loss of these experienced players affected the side But Willie Bauld – a future star was signed.

On 14 September, Hearts problems increased when top striker, Archie Kelly, collided with a post during a home 2-0 win over Kilmarnock, breaking his collar bone and cracking the left hand goalpost.

Davie McLean did recruit Bobby Dougan and Davie Laing and he increasingly introduced young prospects. However, the manager did not wish to push them too hard and as a result, he frequently changed the team. This had an unsettling effect and Hearts did well to finish fourth in the League, 8 points behind the Champions, Rangers. Only a lack of goals let Hearts down, as the defence, marshalled by the veterans, Bobby Baxter and Archie Miller, was very sound.

Hearts defeated Celtic in Glasgow at the start of the season and the strong rearguard was responsible for a fine 2-1 win v Rangers at Ibrox Park in April. These were the only outstanding performances of the campaign. Without a mature centre forward any hope that Hearts might actually challenge for the title ended when only one point was taken from four games over the festive period. Alex McCrae 12 and Archie Kelly 10 were the main marksmen.

In the League Cup, the players wore numbers on their shirts for the first time against Kilmarnock on 28 September. After going on to win their Qualifying Section against Clyde, Kilmarnock and Partick Thistle, they met East Fife in the two-legged Quarter-Finals. The Fifers won 1-0 at Tynecastle, but Hearts redeemed themselves at Methil with a 5-2 win. On 22 March the team went down 6-2 to Aberdeen in the Semi-Final tie at 'neutral' Easter Road, despite being 2-1 up after 37 minutes.

It was a demoralized Tynecastle side that took the field that afternoon following a shock defeat in the Scottish Cup the previous Saturday.

After beating St.Johnstone and Cowdenbeath in the Cup, Hearts were drawn away to "B" Division, Arbroath, in the Fourth Round on 15 March. Jimmy Walker failed to turn up and on a heavily sanded pitch, Hearts produced an abysmal performance, going down 2-1 with Ken Currie's goal being only a consolation.

Jimmy Walker was then exchanged for the redoubtable Bobby Parker of Partick Thistle. Alex McCrae went to Charlton Athletic for a new record fee received of £7,500 plus a friendly fixture, but Davie McLean had the magnificent Jimmy Wardhaugh ready to replace him.

Hearts lost in the Shield Final and as the SFA would not extend the season to accommodate the Rosebery Charity Cup, the life of this venerable trophy had run its course. Hearts did manage to play Chelsea in a friendly in April 1947 and Tommy Walker seemed embarrassed to score against his old club at Tynecastle as the Londoners won 4-1.

Willie Macfarlane made his first appearance for Scotland in a Full International on 24 May 1947 against Luxembourg in a 6-0 win at the Stade Municipal, Luxembourg Ville.

A RELEGATION SCARE

1947-1948 was one of Hearts poorest campaigns with the team perilously close to the relegation zone, before eventually climbing to ninth place in "A" Division. Results were so poor that the directors ignored the manager's cherished youth policy and bought the club out of trouble. This proved to be a correct short-term decision.

The season began with Tynecastle under major repair with a new drainage system, retaining wall and track being renewed and the terracing being fully concreted. As a result, the opening fixture was switched to Easter Road where Hearts had a thrilling 2-1 League Cup win over Hibernian. The other clubs in the Qualifying Section, Airdrieonians and Clyde, presented some problems, but Hearts claimed a Quarter-Finals place by recording another 2-1 win over Hibernian at home when Bobby Parker demoralized the famous Easter Road forward line with his tackling and long clearing. Hearts then met East Fife at Tynecastle and this match indicated problems ahead, with the Fifers winning 4-3 after extra time.

The League started with mixed results and concerns about a lack of experience. Alfie Conn then suffered a serious knee injury and with Jimmy Wardhaugh being called-up to the RAF, the directors decided to pay a club record £5,000 fee for the Clyde forward, Arthur Dixon. Nevertheless, after the League Cup exit, there was a serious slump with only three wins in the next eighteen League fixtures. This included six defeats in a row from 6 December against Rangers at home through to a defeat on New Years Day against Hibernian at Easter Road.

The Board made an appeal to fans to stop barracking the players even though Hearts fell to second bottom position.

The sequence ended with a winning goal in a 1-0 win over Celtic at Tynecastle on 3 January. The winner came from International striker, Bobby Flavell, who had been signed from Airdrieonians for a Scottish record fee of £10,000 in order to arrest the decline. He was joined by George Hamilton – Aberdeen for a similar fee with Archie Kelly going in part exchange.

The new men clearly lifted the team and Hearts made a much better showing in the second half of the season, indeed they were undefeated in the last ten League fixtures – five wins and five draws. On the final day, Hearts won 2-1 against Rangers at Ibrox Park, a result which gave Hibernian the Championship on points not just goal average. Hearts finished ninth but the fans came in record numbers with a League average gate of 22,694.

In the Scottish Cup, Hearts won 4-2 at Dundee in the First Round and then they took about 8,000 fans to Broomfield Park in the Second Round to swell the all ticket gate to 20,000. In heavy rain, Airdrieonian's tackling was too strong and the home side established a 2-0 lead. George Hamilton got one back, but Hearts late rally could not produce an equalizer. George Hamilton then became unsettled and went back to Aberdeen for a new record sum received of £12,000.

Davie McLean had almost resigned over the lack of faith in his youth policy and he now asked that Tommy Walker be brought back as assistant manager. This was a very far-sighted request and he received the total backing of the directors, with a deal being struck with Chelsea that Walker would return in December 1948.

During the close season the capacity of Tynecastle was agreed at 48,883 = Main Stand-3,803; Enclosure-7,080; Ground-38,000. Attendances continued to increase and all-ticket matches became commonplace.

HEARTS RECOVERY

Davie McLean had faith in his young squad but in 1948-1949 this was sorely tested when after six League games, Hearts had suffered five defeats and were two points adrift at the bottom of the table. To make matters worse, Hibernian were again on top.

At this point there was some relief when the League Cup commenced with Hearts in a Qualifying Section together with East Fife, Partick Thistle and Queen of the South. The first four matches produced only three points and forced the manager to make changes. On 9 October 1948 McLean sent out Alfie Conn, Willie Bauld and Jimmy Wardhaugh against East Fife and Hearts ripped open the visitors, winning 6-1. Willie Bauld scored a hat-trick on his senior debut and 24,374 fans witnessed the birth of the "terrible trio" whose unsurpassed firepower would lead the club to many honours.

In another inspired move, Bobby Dougan went to centre-half, where he was a class act, and Bobby Parker moved to right-back. The following week, the Hearts crushed Queen of the South by 4-0 and although Willie Bauld hit another hat-trick, the revival was too late to take them into the League Cup Quarter-Finals.

Spirits were lifted and when the League resumed on 23 October Hearts recorded a fine 2-0 victory over Rangers at Tynecastle. Alfie Conn had fully recovered from his cartilage operation and scored a brilliant goal which earned him a place in the Scottish League International team.

Towards the end of the year Hearts moved away from the relegation zone with great results, such as 4-0 against high-flying East Fife. Then in December a 5-1 defeat of Albion Rovers the following Saturday at Cliftonhill Park where Jimmy Wardhaugh scored his first hat-trick. In the return at Tynecastle Hearts completed their only double of the season with a cracking 7-1 victory.

On New Year's Day, Hearts beat Hibernian by 3-2 at Tynecastle, with Alfie Conn scoring a last minute winner. The team then lost to Celtic and Dundee, with the new assistant manager, Tommy Walker, returning in the latter match, and at the end of January Motherwell lost 5-1. Unfortunately, the loss of Bobby Parker for a cartilage operation was a major blow and mixed results followed. Eventually Hearts finished eighth, 16 points behind the Champions, Rangers with Willie Bauld top marksman with 17 goals.

In the Scottish Cup, Airdrieonians 4-1, Third Lanark 3-1 and Dumbarton 3-0 were all beaten at Tynecastle then Dundee came to Gorgie in the Quarter-Finals. After a thrilling contest in the rain, the visitors won 4-2, although Hearts were worthy of a replay and Davie Laing failed to score from a penalty with Dundee leading 3-2.

Significantly, the club's average League crowd was the highest in Hearts' history at 28,196. This was due not only to the post war boom, but also because the rewards from Mr. McLean's youth policy were clearly coming through.

The season ended with defeat in the East of Scotland Shield Final and stalwart goalkeeper, Jimmy Brown, earning a place on the SFA tour of North America. Hearts also signed Colin Liddell – Greenock Morton for a record equaling £10,000.

REAL PROGRESS AT TYNECASTLE

Despite a lack of honours since 1906, attendances at Tynecastle were still superb in season 1949-1950. The Scotsman explained that, "supporters knew that they stood a fair chance of seeing real football at Tynecastle with the key man being Willie Bauld, a player of unsurpassed skills and unselfish to a fault. Hearts play the game, a policy fostered over the years by management". "This partly explains the consistency of the faithful crowds the envy of others no matter how badly Hearts fare".

Proof, if it were needed, came when Willie Bauld opened the season in the League Cup Qualifying Section with a hat-trick as Hearts defeated Stirling Albion 5-1 at Annfield. Hearts then defeated Raith Rovers 5-1 at Tynecastle, but stumbled to a 1-1 home draw against East Fife. The team lost 5-4 in the return match against Stirling Albion and although they won away to Raith Rovers, Hearts went out of the League Cup after losing 4-3 against East Fife.

The club had East Fife in their Section for the fourth successive time and failed to progress for the second season in a row. Davie McLean had firepower, but could he find a strong defence?

Tangible progress was made in the Championship and Hearts finished third, seven points behind the title winners, Rangers. This seemed unlikely after six matches when Hearts had only three points and were bottom of the League. However, two of these points came in a 5-2 win over Hibernian at Tynecastle, a match that Hearts led 5-0 after 54 minutes. At that stage Bobby Parker even missed a penalty before Hibs grabbed two goals and respectability.

The team suddenly hit form on 29 October with a 6-2 home win over Clyde, the first of twelve consecutive League victories, and including an astonishing 9-0 romp against Falkirk at Tynecastle – everybody wanted in on the act but it was Willie Bauld, Alfie Conn, Bobby Flavell -2, Davie Laing, Tommy Sloan -2, Jimmy Wardhaugh -2, who got there. During this run, which was then a record in one season, Hearts looked like Champions, particularly when Celtic lost 4-2 at Tynecastle, in December.

Two days later, with Hearts second and Hibernian on top, the "maroons" won 2-1 at Easter Road. The attendance on 2 January 1950 was a record 65,840 the largest crowd to have watched a Scottish match outside of Glasgow and bigger than the "Old Firm" attendance that day. St.Mirren lost in Gorgie 5-0 on 3 January but the run came to an end on 7 January with a 3-1 defeat at Dundee. When Rangers won 1-0 at Tynecastle later in the month Hearts were out of the title race. Willie Bauld was the League's top scorer with 30 goals.

In the Scottish Cup First Round, a Willie Bauld goal after 82 minutes earned a replay with Dundee at Dens Park, which Hearts won 2-1 after extra time. In the Second Round at Pittodrie Park, Hearts lost 3-1 to Aberdeen when the team just did not perform. A few weeks later, Hearts won 5-0 there on League business, but it was too late. Defeating Aberdeen in the Scottish Cup appeared 'mission impossible'.

Willie Bauld made his first appearance for Scotland in a Full International on 15 April 1950 against England in a 1-0 defeat at Hampden Park, Glasgow.

Bobby Dougan made his first appearance for Scotland in a Full International on 26 April 1950 against Switzerland in a 3-1 win at Hampden Park, Glasgow,

The season ended on a strange note with Bobby Flavell running out on the club for a lucrative contract with CD Los Millonarios of Bogota, Colombia.

TOMMY WALKER TAKES CONTROL

There were high hopes for supporters, as Hearts had out-gunned the Champions, Rangers, during the previous campaign, scoring 86 League goals to their 58. However, defence was still a problem with Hearts conceding 40 goals against Rangers 37.

There was soon encouragement in that direction with the performance of centre-half, Bobby Dougan. The manager's youth policy appeared to be paying dividends and Hearts began season 1950-1951 with optimism. The 'terrible trio' was knitting together and the defence had tightened up.

Hearts were indeed destined for major honours but tragically, 67-year old manager, Davie McLean, was not to see the result of his youth policy as he passed away on 14 February 1951. The task of guiding Hearts to trophy success then fell to the illustrious Tommy Walker who nevertheless, was always quick to acknowledge the foundations laid by Davie McLean.

The League Cup Qualifying Section saw Hearts joined by Airdrieonians, Motherwell, and Partick Thistle. A 1-1 draw at Firhill Park was followed by a brilliant 4-1 victory over Motherwell. Hearts then defeated Airdrieonians and Partick Thistle before losing 3-2 at Motherwell and ending the group matches with a 3-1 home win over Airdrieonians. Only three points were dropped, but Hearts failed for the third season in a row to reach the Quarter-Finals, as Motherwell only lost two.

The League campaign started with a 1-0 defeat at Dundee, but Hearts won the next five matches to go top of the table. This included a 1-0 victory over the eventual Champions, Hibernian, at Easter Road. Hearts good form ended with an injury-hit team losing 5-2 away to Partick Thistle and a period of mixed results followed. Defensive problems continued and this took Hearts out of the title race, but the fans had the satisfaction of a double over Hibernian with the New Year game ending 2-1 on a rain swept afternoon. Other 'doubles' came against East Fife, Airdrieonians, Third Lanark and Greenock Morton.

Hearts ran up some great wins, such as 8-0 versus Greenock Morton and 4-1 versus Aberdeen, but overall, the team lacked consistency and eventually finished fourth in the League. Alfie Conn, Willie Bauld and Jimmy Wardhaugh were the top marksmen with a total of 50 goals out of 72.

In the Scottish Cup, the "maroons" had away victories over Alloa Athletic and East Stirlingshire. This set up a Third Round match against Celtic, but tragically, a week before the big event at Tynecastle, Davie McLean died. This fatherly man was succeeded by Tommy Walker, who controlled the team for the big Cup match where a crowd of 47,672 witnessed a 2-1 Celtic victory. At the end, the Glasgow fans carried their goalkeeper shoulder high off the field, a clear sign that Hearts deserved more.

Bobby Flavell, who had returned from Bogota, was sold to Dundee and John Prentice moved to Rangers. The season then ended with an invitation to visit West Germany and the tourists managed a 3-3 draw against the Champions, VfB Stuttgart. In heat wave conditions, they also beat Fortuna 1895 of Dusseldorf 2-0, but lost to FC Kickers 1901 of Offenbach 3-0 and FC Augsburg 5-1.

In the close season the club acquired the tennis courts behind the stand, which had originally been the bowling green, and asked the South of Scotland Electricity Board to provide an estimate for the installation of floodlights, but the cost was prohibitive.

TOMMY WALKER GETS TO WORK

Tommy Walker's influence was soon apparent and at the start of season 1951-1952, he brought over Paul Oswald, the coach of FC Kickers Offenbach, to assist with pre-season training. The fitness of the German players during the recent tour had made a lasting impression on the new manager, who appointed Bobby Parker as captain. In addition, Colin Liddell was exchanged for Eddie Rutherford of Rangers and both Tommy Sloan and Charlie Cox moved to Motherwell.

Hearts' overall form certainly improved, but at the start of the season, the performance in the League Cup was disappointing. For the fourth season in succession the team failed to progress from the Qualifying Section against Dundee, Raith Rovers and St.Mirren. Dundee progressed on goal average after finishing with the same seven points. The highlight was a 5-5 draw against St.Mirren at Paisley, where Willie Bauld scored all Hearts' goals.

The Hearts made a listless start in the League, but the fourth match brought a 3-1 victory at Celtic Park. A cruel run of injuries then prevented Hearts from building upon this result, particularly one to Bobby Dougan, who found his leg in plaster after playing for the Scottish League. Nevertheless, in November 1951, the team started a great run of thirteen unbeaten matches and this included a polished 5-0 victory at Motherwell, a 6-1 home win against Airdrieonians and a 3-2 win at Easter Road on New Year's Day.

This was followed by a 2-1 victory against Celtic and Hearts stood second in the League. At the end of January, Hearts lost a two goal lead and drew 2-2 with Rangers at Tynecastle. The following Saturday, the unbeaten run came to an end at Aberdeen and Hearts' Championship challenge collapsed, with only one win from the next seven League matches. The team fell back to finish fourth and with Hibernian winning the title, the pressure was on to do well in the Scottish Cup.

At a Board Meeting on 19 November 1951 it was confirmed that the Haymarket Memorial was now the property of the "Town".

Hearts entered the Scottish Cup in the Second Round against Raith Rovers at Tynecastle and a large crowd observed a minute's silence following the death of King George VI. Willie Bauld scored the only goal with four minutes left and then the Third Round took Hearts to Dumfries where a record attendance of 26,552 saw the Edinburgh men defeat Queen of the South by 3-1. Many of the fans who travelled in 200 buses and three special trains, later watched film of the match at the Lyceum Cinema.

Another record attendance, some 26,000, packed Broomfield Park for the Fourth Round tie against Airdrieonians. The match ended in a 2-2 draw and Hearts won an exciting replay at Tynecastle by 6-4.

Tommy Walker's men then faltered at the Semi-Finals stage, after a three match epic against Motherwell at Hampden Park. The first game ended 1-1 before a 98,208 crowd and goalkeeper, Jimmy Brown, earned Hearts a replay. The gate that day is still the biggest at a Hearts' match not involving the "Old Firm".

The replay was also a huge affair and 80,141 fans saw another 1-1 draw. In the third encounter, the defence had an off day and the "maroons" went down 3-1 in front of a 60,290 crowd.

The season ended with Hearts winning the Penman Cup and Jimmy Wardhaugh scoring eight goals as the team won 12-2 at the opening of Burntisland Shipyard's new ground. More significantly, in May 1952, the club trainer, John Torbet was replaced by his assistant, John Harvey.

CHASING A WINNING FORMULA

Season 1952-1953 opened with news that goalkeeper, Jimmy Brown, had again dislocated his shoulder and sadly, this would lead to his release in April 1953. His cover man, Jimmy Watters, rose to the challenge, as did centre-half, Jimmy Milne, who replaced Bobby Dougan during his long absence.

Another unsettling event concerned Jimmy Wardhaugh who asked for a transfer and only personal terms stopped him joining Newcastle United. It was just as well, because in due course, Jimmy became Hearts' all-time leading goal scorer.

Away from team matters – prior to the Remembrance Day Service – the Board added a plaque to the Cub's War Memorial at Haymarket to respect those who served in the 1939-1945 War.

Training lights were also erected along the walls of Bond Three, although many other clubs were pushing ahead with full floodlighting systems.

For the fifth season in succession Hearts failed to win their Qualifying Section in the League Cup. Their opponents were Aberdeen, Motherwell, and Rangers and with a resounding 5-0 win over Rangers in the first match at Tynecastle followed by an equally good 4-2 defeat of Aberdeen at Pittodrie Park the supporters were in good spirits but the team stumbled in the third game, when Motherwell won 1-0 at Tynecastle. They then lost the decisive game at Ibrox Park against Rangers who went on to win the Section.

League form was somewhat erratic to say the least, and nine defeats by the turn of the year took Hearts out of the title race. In fact after losing to Hibernian on New Years Day, they were in relegation trouble. Things were difficult for Tommy Walker because of injury to six first team players, while six others were on National Service.

Matters certainly improved in 1953, following the signing of Jim Souness – Hibernian and the return of Davie Laing and Bobby Dougan from injury.

Hearts lost only two of the last twelve League matches the highlight of this run was a 7-0 thrashing of Clyde at Tynecastle in March. Willie Bauld – 3, John Cumming – 2, Eddie Rutherford and Jimmy Wardhaugh. A precursor of many high scoring matches to come in, the immediate future. Hearts finished in fourth place for the third season.

Hearts entered the Scottish Cup in the Second Round, and did quite well starting with a 1-0 victory over Raith Rovers in front of a Starks Park record attendance of 31,306. Willie Bauld scored the solitary goal to earn a Third Round tie at home to Montrose. The Angus team was defeated 3-1 and Hearts next opponents, Queen of the South provided a much stiffer test.

The Quarter-Final match was at home and Hearts went through by 2-1 to set up a Semi-Finals match against Rangers at Hampden Park. A huge Tynecastle following swelled the Hampden attendance to 116,262 and that was the largest crowd to have watched Hearts up to that time. The "maroons" fans were first to cheer when Jimmy Wardhaugh scored after 12 minutes, but Rangers powered back to win 2-1. John Cumming was injured in the first half and Hearts did well with virtually ten men.

Another landmark saw Jimmy Wardhaugh score Hearts 4,000th. League goal in their 1,969th. match, on 7 March 1953 in a 3-1 defeat of Aberdeen at Tynecastle.

The season ended with a cruise to Scandinavia. Hearts beat AIK 4-1 at Solna but then went down 5-1 to Djurgaardens at the Olympic Stadium in Stockholm. Overall it seemed as if the management team of Mr. Walker, John Harvey and assistant trainer, Donald McLeod were slowly putting things right.

A CHAMPIONSHIP CHALLENGE

In season 1953-1954, the Hearts' team produced its best Championship performance since 1937/1938, but the outcome was similar with the "maroons" finishing second to Celtic who finished five points ahead.

Tynecastle had a new look this term with modern glass-fronted trainers' dug outs having been erected, and a start made to concrete the terracing. The club was still unsure about floodlighting, preferring to play a number of friendlies in England in order to inspect the systems.

On the playing front, the season opened with the usual four-club League Cup Qualifying Section. Hearts yet again failed to progress and with only two wins they lost out to Rangers in a group that also included Hamilton Academical and Raith Rovers.

In the Championship, Hearts took a while to settle but at least enjoyed an early 4-0 success over Hibernian at home, with the "terrible trio" all scoring. The team then improved rapidly and although Willie Bauld and Bobby Dougan suffered injuries, Jimmy Wardhaugh was in brilliant form and eventually hit 27 League goals. This made sure that Hearts were always in a challenging position and John Cumming was also proving to be a huge success.

On 14 November Hearts defeated Raith Rovers 5-1 at Tynecastle then the following Saturday beat Hamilton Academical 5-1 away, and subsequently lost only one of the next fourteen League fixtures. This included an incident packed 3-2 victory over Celtic in February before a capacity crowd at Tynecastle. The "maroons" dropped seven points in the last six matches, immediately after defeating Celtic at Tynecastle, but again Mr. Walker's squad suffered from an appalling injury list which partly explains why the title was lost.

At the business end of the season, no team could afford to lose defenders such as Bobby Dougan and Bobby Parker, and forwards such as Alfie Conn and Jimmy Wardhaugh.

The Championship dream was alive, but the Scottish Cup brought problems after Hearts had won away to Fraserburgh and then Queen of the South. The "maroons" faced their bogey team, Aberdeen, and a record gate of 45,061 packed Pittodrie Park to see Hearts swept aside 3-0. During the match, Bobby Parker broke his jaw, while Alfie Conn injured his back and Jimmy Wardhaugh suffered a shin injury. Not only did this affect the Cup tie, but it damaged the League challenge, bearing in mind the already serious injury to Bobby Dougan.

Hearts did win the East of Scotland Shield and Penman Cup before the season ended with a 16-player squad flying to South Africa via Rome, Cairo, Khartoum, Nairobi and Livingstone to undertake a ten match tour.

It was memorable for the players due to the hospitality, playing facilities and general environment of the country. Hearts won the First Test Match against South Africa by 2-0 in Pretoria and the Second Test in Durban was the tourist's only defeat (1-2).

All the other matches were won and produced 36 goals with only 8 lost. The players developed a superb team spirit that was soon to be of enormous benefit.

HEARTS MAKE THE BREAKTHROUGH

The capacity of the ground for the new season was restricted to 49.000. Although the team earned one more point than during the previous season, Hearts could not win the League in 1954-1955. This was of little concern because on 23 October 1954 for the first time since 1906, Hearts won a major honour – the Scottish Football League Cup.

There was a potentially damaging wage dispute, born no doubt by many weeks together to compare opinions. It was amicably resolved and wages were increased to the not inconsiderable sum of £15 per week. With the players all very fit and healthy after their South African trip the Hearts supporters were very optimistic. Confidence was high and this was further enhanced by the development of John Cumming and Dave Mackay into international-class half-backs.

Hearts were in a Qualifying Section in the League Cup with strong opponents in Celtic, Dundee and Falkirk. For the first time since 1947/1948 Hearts progressed beyond the Section matches. They won five out of the six, losing only to Dundee at Dens Park. In the two-leg Quarter-Final against 'B' Division, St.Johnstone, Hearts tied it up in the First Leg with a 5-0 win in Perth. They then won 2-0 at home and moved into the Semi-Finals where Airdrieonians lost 4-1 at 'neutral' Easter Road, and the team reached their first League Cup Final.

Steady drizzle could not spoil the occasion at Hampden Park where a crowd of 55,640 saw a match of outstanding quality. Motherwell who had defeated Hearts in the Semi-Finals of the Scottish Cup as recently as April 1952 were confident. It turned out to be a fascinating tussle between two teams renowned for their style of football and encounters. Willie Bauld scored twice before the "steelmen" reduced the deficit with a Willie Redpath penalty. The Motherwell support dreamt of victory but they were disillusioned just on half-time when Jimmy Wardhaugh ghosted in to head home a Jim Souness cross. Willie Bauld completed his hat-trick in the last minute, although a fighting Motherwell side made the final score 4-2 in the dying seconds through Bain.

Hearts players were all heroes but Willie Bauld was known ever after as 'King Willie' but Bobby Parker was a stout captain, Fred 'Steady Freddie' Glidden was a tower of strength in the centre of defence, Jim Souness was

LEAGUE CUP WINNERS 1954/1955 Standing – Mr. T. Walker (Manager), D. Mackay, T. Mackenzie, F. Glidden, W. Duff, W. Bauld, J. Cumming, J. Harvey (Trainer). Seated – J. Souness, A. Conn, R. Parker (Captain), J. Wardhaugh, J. Urquhart.

devastating down the right wing and Jimmy Wardhaugh covered every blade of grass to make sure Hearts went home rejoicing.

The final whistle brought emotional scenes on and off the park and that evening, the reception back in Edinburgh led to the victors banquet at the North British hotel which had to be held up to let celebrating supporters, outside in their thousands, to cheer each player on to the balcony with the Cup. The whole city seemed to rejoice in "Edina's Darlings" bringing home silverware to the capital for the first time in 48 years, and the celebrations continued throughout the night in Gorgie Road and Princes Street.

The winning team was:- Willie Duff; Bobby Parker-captain and Tom McKenzie; Dave Mackay, Fred Glidden and John Cumming; Jim Souness, Alfie Conn, Willie Bauld, Jimmy Wardhaugh and John Urquhart.

Shortly after in November, for the first time, the Hearts logo designed by William Wilson of Kirkwoods, Jewellers, St. James Square, was painted on the woodwork above the entrance to the playing field, by Johnny Muir of W.C. Simpson (£85:10/-). The design incorporated the original 'Heart of Midlothian' set in cobblestones just off the High Street, beside St. Giles, Cathedral, and the centrepiece was drawn from the actual ball used by Hearts in a Scottish Cup Final against Rangers in 1903.

As for the Championship, the Hearts were high scoring and entertaining, and in a challenging position by the turn of the year. The quality was underlined on New Year's Day when goals by Willie Bauld-2, Alfie Conn, Jim Souness, and Jimmy Wardhaugh earned a 5-1 victory over Hibs at Tynecastle. Injuries took their toll after that and in the run up to the final matches only six of the last sixteen matches were won. As a result the club finished fourth, despite defeating Champions-elect, Aberdeen, by 2-0 at Tynecastle during March.

John Cumming and Jimmy Wardhaugh made their first appearance for Scotland in a Full International on 8 December 1954 against Hungary in 4-2 defeat at Hampden Park, Glasgow.

In the Scottish Cup, Hearts first tie was in the Fifth Round, in which they were drawn against their local rivals at Tynecastle. This season Hibernian could not cope with Hearts. They lost the League matches – 3-2 and 5-1 and the match for the official opening of their floodlights by 2-0. In the 5-0 victory in this Cup tie the 'terrible trio' scored all the goals to prove they were the masters over the 'famous five'.

Then into the Sixth Round for the long trip north, where they defeated Buckie Thistle 6-0 at Victoria Park. In the Quarter-Finals, Hearts drew 1-1 with Aberdeen at Tynecastle thanks to an inspired display from their goalkeeper, Martin, Hearts chance had gone and they lost the Replay at Pittodrie Park by 2-0.

Honours a plenty were poured on the Hearts players and in addition to the full internationalists, Willie Duff and Dave Mackay played in the first ever, under 23 International match against England.

Hearts won the Shield defeating Hibernian 4-3 in the Final to inflict a fifth win over them during one season.

On the 25 May 1955 the directors agreed to pay Mr.W.B.Robertson, the son of George Robertson, a former director, historian and programme editor, £25 for his father's Notes, Slides and Projector of the "Story of Hearts". Eventually, on 29 August 1955 he accepted the offer. The notes are held in the club archive but the 'slides' have, sadly, not survived.

SCOTTISH CUP GLORY

Hearts were hungry for more honours and with two thirds of season 1955-1956 gone, the League and Scottish Cup double was possible. Alas only the Cup came to Gorgie after a 50-year gap, but this sparked off scenes of jubilation that are recalled to this day.

Several new faces contributed to the challenge, Ian Crawford, Johnny Hamilton, Bobby Kirk and Alex Young being the main success stories. Hearts reserves strength was certainly tested when Willie Bauld broke a bone in his foot and Bobby Parker required a cartilage operation.

In defence of the League Cup the team did well to top their Qualifying Section against, East Fife, Partick Thistle and Raith Rovers. Hearts then met Aberdeen in the Quarter-finals and in the First Leg at Pittodrie Park, came back to equalise from 3-0 down. Bobby Kirk and Jimmy Wardhaugh suffered bad injuries after which Aberdeen went on to win 5-3. Willie Bauld and Jimmy Wardhaugh missed the return match where Hearts went down 4-2 to the eventual winners.

In the Championship Hearts were brilliant at times, but dropped points after that morale damaging League Cup exit. The team eventually recovered and in November started an 18 match unbeaten run which included a superb 7-1 victory over Motherwell at Tynecastle in December. The irrepressible Jimmy Wardhaugh hit four goals that afternoon and the team soon moved up to second place, hard on the heels of Rangers.

The unbeaten run ended on 2 April against Partick Thistle at Firhill Park, and unfortunately, as progress was made in the Cup points were dropped in the League with the squad strength being overly taxed. Only two wins were recorded from the last seven matches and Rangers went on to win the title, with Hearts finishing third.

In winning 13 out of 17 home matches the supporters were treated to some fantastic goal scoring sprees – Dundee 4-0, Stirling Albion 5-0, Motherwell 7-1, Partick Thistle 5-0, Dunfermline Athletic 5-0, Falkirk 8-3 and Raith Rovers 7-2 – leading to 65 goals at home the highest since 1939-1940.

This season was to be all about the Scottish Cup which returned to Tynecastle for the first time since 1906 after a marvellous run during which only one goal was conceded. Hearts met Forfar in the Fifth Round, at Tynecastle and won 3-0. The Sixth Round brought another home tie and Stirling Albion lost 5-0. For the Seventh Round Hearts were fortunate to receive another home tie, and on a glorious afternoon in Gorgie, a crowd of 47,258 saw high-flying Rangers defeated 4-0.

The Cup run was certainly exciting the fans and when Hearts faced Raith Rovers in the Semi-Finals at Easter Road, there was a phenomenal crowd of 58,448. They witnessed a tight 0-0 draw, with Hearts winning the Replay 3-0, thanks to goals from Ian Crawford and Jimmy Wardhaugh-2, in front of another massive crowd of 54,233.

It was hardly surprising that when the Cup Final, against Celtic, took place on 21 April 1956 the attendance was 133,538 which is the largest crowd ever to watch a Hearts match and included an estimated 60,000 Tynecastle supporters. Hearts played some polished football and after 19 minutes Ian Crawford scored. Before half-time John Cumming suffered a gashed brow, and looked as if he was off for good, but he appeared shortly after the start of the second-half to bolster the team's morale. After 49 minutes Ian Crawford scored again then Celtic pulled one back, the team did not collapse, in those days, and secured the 3-1 victory after 81 minutes, when Alfie 'cannonball' Conn scored. A remarkable total of 324,119 spectators had watched Hearts six Scottish Cup matches.

SCOTTISH CUP WINNERS – 1955/1956 Standing – D. MacLeod (Asst. Trainer), R. Kirk, D. Mackay, T. Mackenzie, Mr. T. Walker (Manager), W. Duff, W. Bauld, J. Cumming, J. Harvey (Trainer). Seated – A. Young, A. Conn, F. Glidden (Captain), J. Wardhaugh, J. Crawford.

The winning side was one of the finest in the club's history- those who were to be legends :- Willie Duff; Bobby Kirk and Tom McKenzie; Dave Mackay, Fred Glidden-captain and John Cumming; Alex Young, Alfie Conn, Willie Bauld, Jimmy Wardhaugh and Ian Crawford.

Edinburgh went wild that night and the Daily Mail said "the will of the nation prevailed". Before the victory celebrations were held in Macvities Guest' Charlotte Rooms, Fred Glidden led the team around the city in a specially decorated open topped bus.

Hearts rounded off a memorable campaign by defeating Hibernian 2-1 in the East of Scotland Shield Final.

Alfie Conn made his first appearance for Scotland in a Full International on 2 May 1956 against Austria in a 1-1- draw at Hampden Park, Glasgow.

Barriers were erected at the entrance to the McLeod Street and White Park turnstiles in December, 1955.

There was a profit of £5,445 and the club paid a 20% dividend to shareholders.

BRILLIANT HEARTS GO CLOSE

After the success of the previous two seasons Hearts supporters were looking forward to more of the same in season 1956-1957. They played well and had some good results but there were no trophies.

In the League Cup, Hearts failed to win their Qualifying Section for the first time in three seasons. Their opponents were Falkirk, Hibernian and Partick Thistle and it started with a breathtaking 6-1 win over Hibernian at Tynecastle, where Bobby Kirk scored two penalties but failed with a third. In the next match they lost 3-1 to Partick Thistle at Firhill Park and they went on to win the section with Hearts form being too patchy. However, the team did manage to beat Hibernian 2-1 in the return match at Easter Road.

The team made a fine assault on the Championship and finished second, only two points behind Rangers. It was remarkable that the squad made such a spirited challenge, as there was a succession of injuries to vital players at crucial times.

The Championship started well with nine points from the first five matches, including a fine 3-2 defeat of Hibernian. Unfortunately, Alfie Conn broke his jaw in this match and was sidelined for four months. The run came to an end on 13 October against East Fife at Tynecastle, but Hearts bounced back and were soon top of the League, defeating their nearest challenger, Motherwell 3-2 at Tynecastle during another run of eight unbeaten matches. This set up a crucial match away to Rangers on 15 December. Two goals from Jimmy Wardhaugh gave Hearts an early lead, but the defence collapsed under pressure and Rangers were 5-3 winners.

Even so, Hearts were still leaders at the turn of the year and after another good run, they were seven points ahead, but with Rangers having three matches in hand. Careless points were then lost and the title hinged on Rangers visit on 13 April. A capacity crowd watched a tense match in which Rangers goalkeeper, Niven, was in fine form and Hearts could not beat him. The only goal came from Simpson of Rangers who scored on the break in 35 minutes to put his side two points behind Hearts with two matches in hand. Hearts won their final two fixtures but Rangers won their last four, to take the title.

Rangers were Hearts biggest problem this season and went on to defeat them 4-0 at Tynecastle in the Fifth

Round of the Scottish Cup. The crowd saw the match die after Rangers scored three times during four minutes in the first half.

Hearts did not even have the satisfaction of defeating Hibernian in the Shield Final.

Dave Mackay made his first appearance for Scotland in Full International on 26 May 1957 against Spain in a 4-1 defeat at the Estadia Santiago Bernabeu, Madrid.

Sadly, on 26 July 1957 the directors agreed that all correspondence may be destroyed after a period of five years. This decision has led to many interesting and even valuable correspondence being lost to future generations.

On 7 October 1957 the first floodlights were installed at Tynecastle, by Miller & Stables at a cost of £1,410:2:9, and used for the inaugural friendly match against Hibernian. The same year a new press box was installed at the rear of the Centre Stand.

CHAMPIONS OF SCOTLAND

In season 1957-1958, Hearts became Scottish Champions for the first time since 1896/1897 and this was achieved with some style, with a top division of Scotland record of 132 goals scored and a record number of points, 62 over a 34-match programme. This campaign stands out in the club's history with only Clyde managing to defeat them in the League and the runners-up, Rangers, finishing 13 points behind.

Tommy Walker's side harnessed individual brilliance with team work, and had spirit of the highest order. In addition, the players were in superb condition, thanks to trainer John Harvey and his assistant Donald McLeod and local boy Dave Mackay was a quite inspirational captain.

The season began inauspiciously with Hearts joining Dundee, Kilmarnock and Queen's Park in a League Cup Qualifying Section. The opposition was not seen as all that strong and the team ran up a brilliant 9-2 win over Queen's Park. It was Kilmarnock though who had the overall consistency, and took three points from Hearts, to progress to the Quarter-Finals.

Alfie Conn was out with a serious ankle injury, but compensation was at hand with Jimmy Murray having an outstanding League campaign that started with a stunning 6-0 win over Dundee. In successive weeks, Airdrieonians lost 7-2, Hibernian 3-1 and East Fife 9-0 before Hearts were held 0-0 by Third Lanark. The team recovered to win 4-0 against Aberdeen and with the side virtually unchanged week on week, it became unstoppable, playing an attacking style that generated great enthusiasm.

An early crunch match was the one at Ibrox Park in October where 62,000 fans saw Rangers race into a 2-0 lead only to lose 3-2. Hearts were made of sterner stuff in those days and staged a tremendous fight back, with goals from Willie Bauld, Jimmy Wardhaugh and Alex Young. After Hearts lost at Clyde in November, the team won the next five League fixtures including a 9-1 thrashing of Falkirk.

They saw off every challenger with devastating displays and Hearts were seven points ahead of second place Hibernian after the 2-0 win at Easter Road on New Years Day and each week seemed to bring a higher level of performance.

Before that run ended Hearts defeated Celtic 5-3 in Gorgie – on a Friday evening – with as slick a display as you could hope to see with goals from Bobby Blackwood, Ian Crawford-2 and Jimmy Murray-2 and as would be expected of Celtic they never gave up and although 2-0 down then 4-1 down the got back to 4-3 but could not prevent Hearts scoring a fifth goal.

In March, Dave Mackay broke a bone in his foot and missed the last five League matches, but even without their skipper, Hearts did not falter. When they beat Raith Rovers 4-1 at Tynecastle on 29 March Jimmy Murray's goal equalled the Motherwell record of 119 goals in a League season. Appropriately, it was Jimmy Wardhaugh, the most consistent goal scorer, over the successful years, should score League goal 120, setting a new record for the top level that Hearts eventually extended to 132.

On 12 April the Tynecastle men went to Paisley and clinched the Championship with a 3-2 win over St.Mirren, classy forward Alex Young scoring the winner. Hearts finished the campaign by defeating Aberdeen 4-0 at Pittodrie Park and Rangers 2-1 at Tynecastle. The Championship had rarely been won in a more convincing and entertaining fashion. Jimmy Wardhaugh with 28 and Jimmy Murray with 27 were the leading League goal scorers.

In such an outstanding performance it is worth recording the teams who were defeated home and away, Dundee 6-0 and 5-0, Airdrieonians 7-2 and 4-0, Hibernian 3-1 and 2-0, East Fife 9-0 and 3-0, Aberdeen 4-0 and 4-0, Rangers 3-2 and 2-1, Queen of the South 4-1 and 3-1, Partick Thistle 3-1 and 4-1, Queen's Park 8-0 and 4-1, Falkirk 9-1 and 4-0, Raith Rovers 3-0 and 4-1, St.Mirren 5-1 and 3-2 and Celtic 2-0 and 5-3.

The heroes of that campaign were:- Alex Young 34 appearances and 24 goals, Jimmy Murray 33/27, Gordon Marshall 31 appearances and 12 shut-outs, Bobby Kirk 30/2, Jimmy Wardhaugh 30/28, George Thomson 30/0, Dave Mackay-captain 28/12. Ian Crawford 25/10, Bobby Blackwood 23/4, Jimmy Milne 21/3, John Cumming 20/5, Andy Bowman 18/2 and Fred Glidden 13/0, Willie Bauld 9/5, Tom McKenzie 8/0, Alfie Conn 5/4, Johnny Hamilton 4/4, Bobby Parker 4/0, Wilson Brown 3 appearances and 1 shut-out, Danny Paton 3/1, Billy Higgins 1/0,Billy Lindores 1/0.

In the Scottish Cup, Hearts were drawn against East Fife in the First Round at Methil and won 2-1. In the Second Round, they had a home tie against Albion Rovers and won 4-1. In the Third round a home tie against Hibernian resulted in a surprise 4-3 defeat in which Baker scored all their goals.

In October 1957 Hibernian defeated Hearts at Tynecastle when the club's floodlighting system was inaugurated.

Among other matches played, there was a Hearts v Scotland X1 in a World Cup Trial on 3 March. The Scottish Champions were worthy of their 3-2 win, in their new candy striped jersey as Johnny Hamilton had the match of his life running riot on the right wing against Caldow of Rangers. Alex Young scored Hearts first goal from 12 yards, Johnny Hamilton then scored with a wonderful left foot drive from 30 yards for the second. The opponents neutralised the two goal lead before Captain Dave Mackay dribbled brilliantly through a maze of defenders and after two saves by Tommy Younger [Hibernian and Liverpool], scored the third to the delight of the fans.

Jimmy Murray made his first appearance for Scotland in a Full International on 19 April 1958 against England in a 4-0 defeat at Hampden Park, Glasgow.

During the summer, the squad toured North America, except for Dave Mackay and Jimmy Murray who were on World Cup duty for Scotland in Sweden. Jimmy was the first Scotland player – never mind Hearts player – to score in a World Cup match.

LEAGUE CHAMPIONS 1957/1958 Standing Back Row – A. Bowman, D. Paton, R. Parker, T. Mackenzie, G. Marshall Mr. T. Walker–Manager/Secretary, W. Brown, F. Glidden, J. Milne, W. Higgins, G. Thomson. Standing Middle Row – D. MacLeod–Asst.Trainer, J. Hamilton, R. Blackwood, J. Murray, J Crawford, A. Conn, W. Lindores, A. Young, W. Bauld, J. Harvey–Trainer. Seated – Mr. R. Tait–Director, R. Kirk, Mr. A. W. Strachan–Vice Chairman, D. Mackay–Captain, Mr. N. G. Kilgour–Chairman, J. Wardhaugh, Mr.A. Irvine JP–Director, J. Cumming, Mr.J. C. Ford–Director.

Those who travelled won eight of the nine matches played and provided outstanding entertainment. Four were against Manchester City, including a stunning 6-5 victory at the famous Ebbets Field in Brooklyn, on 25 May for the Empire State Cup donated in recognition of the 25th.Anniversary of the American Soccer League. They scored a total of 64 goals and conceded 19 and against Manchester City it was 18 and 14.

Hearts won the Shield the only local competition still in operation.

BLAZER BADGE

Contemporary photographs show the directors, manager and trainers with a badge on their blazers. The first one in 1954, was a heart shape in white piping followed by a heart shape in white piping with HMFC in the middle, in 1956.

However, Hearts moved up market and in January 1957 asked suppliers to submit a design for a new blazer badge. The outcome was a design by Mr. William Wilson in the form of a heart-shaped badge, in gold and silver wire, incorporating a football, the Saltire cross and the cobblestones of the "Heart of Midlothian". The Directors requested that the letters H M F C and figures 1874 be in 'Old English' lettering round the cross.

The badge was primarily based on the club logo painted above the players' tunnel in 1954 but the centre of the badge was originally the three castle towers which are part of the Edinburgh Coat of Arms. When the sketch was taken to the Lord Lyon for approval he took one look at it, got a pencil, and scored out the towers and said "the only castle Hearts are entitled to is Tynecastle".

The players were able to wear the badge on their blazer for the first time on their tour of North America in 1958. Originally the directors laid down that a player could only be provided with the blazer badge after playing at least ten first team competitive matches. Hence the Hearts' supporters, admiration and pride of 'their' badge.

In August 1988 when Cruzeiro Esporte Clube played Hearts they were very effusive about the badge, maintaining that it was the finest football club badge in the world. Sadly, for many Hearts supporters, in 1998 the badge had the letters changed to ordinary capitals, the Saltire made thinner and less gold and silver wire. The decision by the Directors was in complete contrast to their predecessors forty years before.

1958

1998

MORE SILVERWARE FOR TYNECASTLE

In 1958-1959, Hearts tragically lost the Championship on the final Saturday of the season, but overall, it was another successful campaign.

It started in a League Cup Qualifying Section, with Raith Rovers, Rangers and Third Lanark. Hearts won ten points from a possible twelve then cruised to an 8-2 aggregate victory against Ayr United in the Quarter-Finals. Easter Road housed the Semi-Final against Kilmarnock where goals from Willie Bauld, Ian Crawford and George Thomson without reply, took Hearts into the Final. On 25 October 1958.

Hearts won the Scottish League Cup for a second time, crushing Partick Thistle 5-1 in the Final at Hampden Park before a crowd of 59,960. They led 2-0 within ten minutes, through goals from Willie Bauld and Jimmy Murray. The same two players scored another goal each before half time and although Thistle pulled one back in the second half, Johnny Hamilton netted a fifth to spark off the usual wild celebrations when the team returned to Edinburgh.

The team was:- Gordon Marshall; Bobby Kirk and George Thomson; Dave Mackay-captain, Fred Glidden and John Cumming; Johnny Hamilton, Jimmy Murray, Willie Bauld, Jimmy Wardhaugh and Ian Crawford.

They were outstanding on the day, but had played attractive football throughout the competition scoring 32 goals in the ten matches.

During the League Cup run, the club's performance in the European Champions Cup was not so inspired and they went down 6-3 on aggregate to Royal Standard Liege. Hearts first match in Europe as Scotland's representatives, was a tactical disaster and the team was humbled 5-1 in the First Leg, in Belgium, even though Ian Crawford actually opened the scoring.

STV 'Scotsport' transmitted the second half of the Second Leg throughout Europe but an attendance of 37,500 illustrated the fans interest. Thankfully, viewers saw two goals from Willie Bauld earn a 2-1 victory that restored some of Hearts reputation. Jimmy Wardhaugh was not able to play in the home Leg due to the harsh treatment meted out to him in Belgium and Willie Bauld became their target second time round and without any protection suffered severe bruising to both legs.

Hearts should have retained the Championship, but were second, two points behind Rangers. The Tynecastle men started with nine undefeated matches, including a 6-2 defeat of Dunfermline Athletic on the opening day, then a crushing 4-0 win over Hibernian at Easter Road and an 8-3 home victory over Third Lanark on 27 September. In the latter match, Willie Bauld scored five times, while his hat-trick came in seven minutes.

Motherwell ended that run in November with a 2-0 victory at Tynecastle and even though the team was not as devastating, they still looked like Champions when they went to face Rangers at Ibrox Park on 13 December. Hearts were two points clear, but Edinburgh fans in the crowd were severely let down, when Rangers swept to a 5-0 win. Hearts were badly hit by injuries and George Robertson was forced to make his debut at centre-half in this crucial match. That was the beginning of the end of the Championship aspirations.

The defeat dented morale and only two wins came from the next seven matches, leaving Hearts six points behind Rangers by the end of January. A good win over Raith Rovers in February, sparked a revival and Hearts were back in with a chance. A further three victories were cheered by the fans, then there came the shock of Dave Mackay being transferred to Tottenham Hotspur for £32,000. With no defeats in the next six fixtures the match on 11 April at Tynecastle against Rangers had the look of a Championship decider and Hearts won 2-0 with John Cumming and Bobby Rankin the scorers.

LEAGUE CUP WINNERS 1958/1959 Standing – D. Macleod-Asst.Trainer, R.Kirk, F.Glidden, G. Marshall, Mr. T. Walker-Manager, G. Thomson, J. Cumming, W. Bauld, J. Harvey-Trainer.
Seated – J. Hamilton, J. Murray, D. Mackay-Captain, J.Wardhaugh, J. Crawford.

Bobby Rankin was one of the players signed after Dave Mackay's departure, along with Danny Ferguson. After that match Hearts defeated Aberdeen at Pittodrie Park, and on the final day of the season Rangers had 50 points and were due to play Aberdeen at home, Hearts had 48 points and were away to Celtic. Level on goal average, Hearts would retain the title if they won and Rangers lost, but the inevitable happened and both sides went down 2-1.

Perhaps if Dave Mackay had stayed on it might have been different. Injuries had caught up with Hearts and on the final day, both full backs were fringe players, John Lough and John MacKintosh.

In the Scottish Cup, Hearts defeated Queen of the South 3-1 in the First Round at Dumfries. In the Second round defensive lapses led to a 3-2 defeat by Rangers at Ibrox Park.

The "terrible trio" parted company that season, Alfie Conn joining Raith Rovers in September 1958. Willie Bauld and Jimmy Wardhaugh were plagued by injuries and with the departure of Dave Mackay one of Hearts great teams was slowly breaking up.

The season ended with another marathon trip, the players flying to Australia where they scored 109 goals in an unbeaten tour of 15 matches

At the Annual General Meeting of the Company on 30 July 1959 a heated debate about the allocation of shares took place. This had been brewing for some time with rumours that directors were looking after themselves, relatives and friends. A special committee was elected to look into all share holdings, sales and transfers.

The capacity of Tynecastle was agreed as 48,751 – Stand 3,751, Enclosure 6,000 and Ground 39,000. Plans to build a stand and enclosure on the distillery side were to cost £170,000 and during the summer an L-shaped covered enclosure was built instead, at a cost of £23,000 which interestingly enough, was also lovingly called the 'shed'. Two half-time scoreboards were erected at either end of the boundary wall.

CHAMPIONS ONCE MORE

As the fifties drew to a close, Hearts had possibly the most successful season in its history. Not only did the team retain the League Cup in 1959-1960, but they also regained the Scottish Championship, the only time that the club has won two major trophies in the same season.

Andy Bowman and Billy Higgins were now featuring in the half-back line and the team had been freshened up by the signing of International winger, Gordon Smith, who had surprisingly been freed by Hibernian. Sadly, Jimmy Wardhaugh left shortly after and both men expressed personal regret at having played only one match together with a player they rated very highly.

The defence of the League Cup started with Hearts winning their Qualifying Section against Aberdeen, Kilmarnock and Stirling Albion without losing a match. Hearts eliminated Motherwell in the Quarter-Finals, after a 1-1 draw at Fir Park and a 6-2 win at Tynecastle.

That first-leg was Jimmy Wardhaugh's last appearance for the club and shortly afterwards, that extraordinary forward, moved to Dunfermline Athletic. In all matches he is still Hearts most prolific marksman with 376 goals between 1946 and 1959.

L-shaped Enclosure – 1959

In the Semi-Finals, Cowdenbeath suffered against the Hearts attack, the men from Gorgie winning 9-3 at Easter Road

The League Cup Final against Third Lanark on 24 October 1959 attracted 57,994 to Hampden Park, Glasgow, and Hearts narrowly won 2-1. It should have been more, but the Glasgow club's goalkeeper, Jocky Robertson, a Hearts fan from Edinburgh, defied the team in their candy striped shirts. Third Lanark scored an early goal and Robertson held out until 57 minutes but he could do nothing with Johnny Hamilton's thunder bolt strike from 25 yards to equalise nor Alex Young's winner shortly after. Hearts returned in triumph once again.

The players on the day were:- Gordon Marshall; Bobby Kirk and George Thomson; Andy Bowman, John Cumming-captain and Billy Higgins; Gordon Smith, Ian Crawford, Alex Young, Bobby Blackwood and Johnny Hamilton.

In the Championship, Hearts opening spell probably earned the title with eleven wins and three draws bringing 25 points from a possible 28. During this run the squad of 16 saw off the "Old Firm" with a 4-3 victory at Celtic Park and a 2-0 win at Ibrox Park. Early in December, there were a couple of shock defeats, but the team recovered and lost only one more League match. The team certainly entered the New Year in brilliant fashion, an Alex Young hat-trick inspiring a 5-1 victory at Easter Road. The biggest cheer had to be when Gordon Smith scored his goal with a first-time volley.

In March, Rangers lost 2-0 at Tynecastle and the Glasgow club fell out of the title race. Kilmarnock on the other hand hung in there and after defeating Hearts 2-1 at Rugby Park on 19 March they were three points behind with a match in hand. Hearts pace was too hot to handle and the fans saw eight doubles including, Celtic 3-1 and 4-3 and Rangers 2-0 and 2-0. The only home defeat was from St.Mirren by 2-0 and significantly, for the second time in two years Hearts clinched a League Championship at Love Street, Paisley in the penultimate match.

St.Mirren held out for a 4-4 draw but it was the Hearts players and supporters who drew the applause. Hearts finished four points clear of Kilmarnock and scored a total of 102 goals.

The Championship heroes were – George Thomson 34 appearances and 4 goals. Bobby Kirk 34/0, Gordon Marshall 33 and 4 shut-outs, John Cumming-captain 32/5, Gordon Smith 29/11, Alex Young 28/23, Bobby Blackwood 28/12, Johnny Hamilton 27/7, Jimmy Milne 25/0, Andy Bowman 24/0, Billy Higgins 21/3, Ian Crawford 18/12, Jimmy Murray 18/11 and Willie Bauld 17/10, Jim McFadzean 5/1, Wilson Brown 1 appearance and 0 shut-outs.

For the first time since 1897 a number of Hearts players had two Championship medals:- Willie Bauld, Bobby Blackwood, Andy Bowman, Ian Crawford, John Cumming, Johnny Hamilton, Billy Higgins, Bobby Kirk, Gordon Marshall, Jimmy Milne, Jimmy Murray, George Thomson and Alex Young.

There was to be no 'treble' as Kilmarnock proved the bogey team that season knocking Hearts out of the Scottish Cup with a 2-1 win in the Replay at Rugby Park, after a 1-1 draw at Tynecastle in the First Round.

Alex Young made his first appearance for Scotland in a Full International on 9 April 1960 against England in a 1-1 draw at Hampden Park, Glasgow.

After the season ended the club undertook another extensive tour of North America which included four exhibition matches against Manchester United. Hearts won one, drew one and lost two with eight goals for and eight goals against. The victory over the English giants was an impressive margin of 4-0 at Wrigley Field in Los Angeles on 1 June.

LEAGUE CUP WINNERS 1959/1960 Standing – A. Bowman, A. Young, G. Smith, G. Marshall, Mr. T. Walker (Manager), W. Higgins, R. Kirk, G. Thomson. Seated – J. Crawford, Mr. A. W. Strachan (Vice Chairman), J. Cumming (Captain), Mr. N. G. Kilgour (Chairman), R. Blackwood, Mr. A. Irvine J. P. (Director), J., Hamilton.

LEAGUE CHAMPIONS 1959/1960 Standing Back Row – A. Bowman, R. Kirk, A. Young, J. Murray, J. Hamilton. Standing Middle Row – D. MacLeod (Asst. Trainer), G. Thomson, G. Smith, W. Brown, G. Marshall, Mr. T. Walker (Manager), W. Higgins, A. Fraser, J. McFadzean, W. Bauld, J. Harvey (Trainer). Seated – Mr. R. Tait (Director), J. Crawford, Mr. A. W. Strachan (Vice Chairman), J. Milne (Captain), Mr. N. G. Kilgour (Chairman), J. Cumming (Vice Captain), Mr. A. Irvine J. P. (Director), R. Blacwood, Mr. W. A. Eadie (Director).

Before returning to Scotland, it was announced that the achievements of Tommy Walker, had been recognised in the Queen's Birthday Honours List and the Hearts' manager was presented with his OBE at Buckingham Palace on 22 November 1960 – "for outstanding services to the game".

On 18 July 1960 the directors were made aware that George Walker – a nephew of Bobby Walker – intimated that he wished to sell his uncle's International Caps. It was agreed that the club was interested and to find out the cost. George Walker wished the club to make an offer, but was told that the club would be delighted to acquire and display the Caps bit did not wish to make an offer. George Walker did not want to say what he wanted for them and no offer was made.

HEARTS RESTRUCTURE

In season 1960-1961, Hearts made an early exit from the domestic cup competitions and finished seventh in the League. The first time the club had been out of the top four places since 1948/1949. The team was unpredictable and failed to add to their double honours season. Failure to consolidate on the previous season's title win was extremely disappointing and in no small measure, due to a large turnover of players which resulted in the team becoming unpredictable.

Hearts supporters were amazed, in November, when the directors transferred two of their star players – George Thomson and Alex Young – to Everton for £55,000. Ian Crawford, Jim McFadzean and Gordon Smith all left at the end of the season and Andy Bowman and Jimmy Milne received free transfers. Several new faces appeared to take their place but did not match the quality of those who had left. The second golden era was about to end.

Hearts played in the European Champions Cup for a second time but lost in the Preliminary Round to Benfica, 2-1 in the First Leg at Tynecastle and 3-0 in the Second Leg in Lisbon. Hearts were heavily criticized for their efforts by the media but the consolation was that, Benfica won the Cup v Barcelona, that season and won it again the following season. Despite the barbed comments by the know-alls, about Hearts failure to progress, there were no apologies.

John Cumming captained the team which began the defence of the League Cup, Hearts failed to progress from their Qualifying Section in which they played Clyde, Motherwell and St.Mirren. Hearts and Clyde finished on top with only seven points each, but as their goal average was identical, the teams met in a play-off at Celtic Park. Despite having the bulk of possession Hearts lost 2-1.

The Championship began well enough, with a 3-1 win over St.Johnstone then a 4-1 demolition versus Hibernian at Easter Road, Jimmy Murray who had come back after a poor 1959/1960 season scored two of the goals but defeat in the European Cup seemed to affect the players' confidence and points started to be dropped on a regular basis. Hearts slipped down the table after a run of ten matches without a win and Tommy Walker needed to make changes, although his hand was forced when George Thomson and Alex Young left.

A few days later the Hearts ended that bad run with a 1-0 home win over Raith Rovers but they could not find consistency to climb the table and the challenge was almost over before Christmas. The team eventually scored only 51 goals, the club's worst Championship total since 1947/1948, and many supporters had doubts about the manager's new 4-2-4 system. There was even a brief relegation threat, although the team was unbeaten in the final six matches.

The manager had used 30 players in the League matches, compared to 16 during the title winning season. He needed to replace older players with younger ones and brought in Willie Polland and Willie Wallace – Raith Rovers (£15,000).

Hearts had a slightly better Scottish Cup run having defeated Tarff Rovers 9-0 in the First Round at Tynecastle and earned a Second Round tie against Kilmarnock at Rugby Park and won 2-1. The Third Round tie was again away from home but Hearts defeated Partick Thistle 2-1 at Firhill Park. The Quarter-Finals match was at home and expectations were high having drawn a tie at Tynecastle against St.Mirren, but Hearts were too anxious and on the break, the 'buddies' scored the only goal.

SOME PROGRESS

During season 1961-1962, it was clear that Tommy Walker's restructured squad was not as skilful as those of the fifties, tactics were becoming crucial. The modern tactics were accompanied by a new and professional training facility at Colinton, but the change in direction did not bring immediate results.

The team managed to progress through a League Cup Qualifying Section against Kilmarnock, Raith Rovers and St.Mirren and won four and lost two matches to go into the Quarter-Finals. They met Hamilton and won 2-1 away and 2-0 at home. In the Semi-Finals at 'neutral' Easter Road, Stirling Albion proved to be much tougher opponents although Hearts won through 2-1 after extra time.

In the Final against Rangers at Hampden Park on 28 October, Hearts dominated the match but had to settle for a 1-1 draw before a crowd of 88,635. John Cumming scored Hearts goal from a penalty after 78 minutes and the team was:- Gordon Marshall; Bobby Kirk and Davie Holt; John Cumming-captain, Willie Polland and Billy Higgins; Danny Fergusson, Maurice Elliot, Willie Wallace, Alan Gordon and Johnny Hamilton.

In the Replay on 18 December 1961 Hearts went down rather easily, although young goal keeper Jim Cruickshank, could not be held responsible for the 3-1 defeat. Norrie Davidson scored Hearts goal before 47,552 spectators at Hampden Park.

The team was:- Jim Cruickshank; Bobby Kirk and Davie Holt; John Cumming-captain, Willie Polland and Billy Higgins; Danny Ferguson, Norrie Davidson, Willie Bauld, Bobby Blackwood and Johnny Hamilton.

Hearts were invited to play in the European Inter Cities Fairs Cup and in the Preliminary Round, First Leg, they travelled to Brussels to play Royale Union St.Gilloise and goals from Bobby Blackwood and Norrie Davidson-2 earned a 3-1 victory. In the Second Leg at Tynecastle they won 2-0 with goals from Robin Stenhouse and Willie Wallace. Hearts were then drawn against Internazionale of Milan and the First Round, First Leg at Tynecastle saw Hearts lose 1-0 after a nervous performance by the players. Inter then ran up a 4-0 victory in the Second Leg at the San Siro Stadium, despite fielding a weakened team.

European elimination followed by the League Cup Final defeat, dented the players' confidence and League results were very mixed. Hearts took only five points from the first six matches but seemed to have recovered with back to back wins over Aberdeen and Celtic in October. But in early December they lost 6-2 to Motherwell at Tynecastle and subsequently struggled to score goals, hitting only 54 in the Championship.

As a result Hearts were out of the title race by January. A double against Hibernian 4-2 at home and 4-1 away brightened a dull season and Celtic lost 2-1 at Tynecastle and could only draw at Celtic Park. A late run of seven matches without a win saw Hearts finish in sixth place, 16 points behind the Champions, Dundee.

On the 19 December 1961 Bill Lindsay a director of the club and Mr. George Forest a former reserve player, learning that the International Caps of the late Bobby Walker – offered to the cub in July 1960 - could still be acquired bought them and offered them to the club for safe keeping and to preserve them and exhibit them among the many other interesting club souvenirs.

Hearts received a bye in the Scottish Cup First Round, then an all ticket crowd of 3,716 watched a 5-0 away win over Vale of Leithen in which Alan Gordon scored his first ever hat-trick for the club. This brought Celtic to Tynecastle for a controversial Third Round match. With ten minutes left to play and with just about everyone expecting offside, Celtic went 3-2 ahead. Danny Paton equalized but worse was to follow at 3-3 when a Celtic player fell in 'the box' to earn a dubious penalty. Gordon Marshall saved Crerand's kick but the referee, Bobby Davidson, for some unknown reason ordered a re-take this time Crerand scored to win the match 4-3.

On the local level Hearts won the Shield which still managed to survive the growing fixture list.

A COMEBACK

Prompted by a new quality player, Willie Hamilton – Middlesbrough, the Hearts were outstanding in the early part of season 1962-1963. The team lost its momentum when a very severe winter descended on Scotland and incredibly from 15 December until 16 March the players made only one appearance.

The first half of the campaign really did belong to Willie Hamilton who made a huge impression with his passing and dribbling skills. As a result, even though Hearts lost the opening League Cup match against Celtic they actually recovered to win their Qualifying Section which also included Dundee and Dundee United. In the two-leg Quarter-Finals Hearts defeated Greenock Morton 3-0 at home and 3-1 away. The Semi-Final tie was played at Easter Road and St.Johnstone lost 4-0 and Hearts were into their fifth League Cup Final.

The match on 27 October 1962 at Hampden Park, Glasgow saw Hearts face Kilmarnock before a 51,280 crowd and come out victors by 1-0. Despite torrential rain, Hearts fans made up the bulk of the crowd and they cheered lustily as Willie Hamilton set up the goal with an incisive run down the right wing and a cut back that Norrie Davidson sent into the net. Kilmarnock had a late equaliser disallowed due to a foul – hotly disputed – but Hearts were worthy winners of a seventh honour under Manager, Tommy Walker. Celebrations were mute compared to the first League Cup win in 1954 but much enjoyed nevertheless.

The players on the day were:- Gordon Marshall; Willie Polland and Davie Holt; John Cumming-captain, Roy Barry and Billy Higgins; Willie Wallace, Danny Paton, Norrie Davidson, Willie Hamilton and Johnny Hamilton.

Before the great freeze, Hearts Championship challenge had been strong, with only one defeat in 16 matches. The team produced some tremendous displays including, a 4-0 victory at Easter Road where Danny Paton – relatively unknown until the previous season – rocked Hibernian with a hat-trick. Airdrieonians lost 6-1 and St.Mirren 5-0.

After Hearts drew with Dundee United on 15 December the team next took the field on 12 January at Station Park, Forfar in the Scottish Cup.

The impetus had gone from the team after the long lay-off and some shocking results were subsequently recorded in a hugely demanding schedule of 19 matches within 75 days between 6 March and 18 May. Hearts lost 5-0 at home to Rangers and 7-3 away to St.Mirren, but the match that hurt most came in May, when relegation-threatened Hibernian earned a 3-3 draw at Tynecastle, after Hearts were ahead 2-0 and coasting. At the end of a long season the club found themselves in fifth place, 14 points behind the Champions Rangers.

In the First Round of the Scottish Cup, Hearts defeated Forfar Athletic 3-1 at Station Park. The victory was missed by many Tynecastle fans due to heavy snow on the road north. The Second Round meant a trip to

LEAGUE CUP WINNERS 1962/1963 Standing – D. MacLeod (Asst. Trainer), W. Higgins, N. Davidson, W. Hamilton, G. Marshall, Mr. T. Walker Esq. O. B. E. (Manager), R. Paton, R. Barry, W. Polland, J. Harvey (Trainer), Seated – Mr. W. Lindsay W. S., N. P. (Director), W. Wallace, Mr. A. Irvine J. P. (Vice Chairman), J. Cumming (Captain), Mr. A. W. Strachan (Chairman), D. Holt, Mr. N. G. Kilgour (Director), J. Hamilton, Mr. R. N. Tait (Director).

Glasgow on 6 March but without Willie Hamilton – suspended by the manager – the team lacked inspiration and lost 3-1 to Celtic.

Davie Holt made his first appearance for Scotland in a Full International on 8 May 1963 against Austria in a 4-1 win at Hampden Park, Glasgow.

Gordon Marshall was transferred to Newcastle United for £18,000 leaving the door open for another star Hearts goalkeeper.

HEART FAILURE

Before the 1963-1964 campaign started, Hearts suffered a major setback when Willie Hamilton, twisted a knee and required a cartilage operation. In any event, his Tynecastle days were numbered due to disciplinary issues and the supporters were shocked when he moved to Hibernian in October for a derisory sum.

Under new captain, Danny Ferguson, Hearts began with a 7-0 win over Dunfermline Athletic in the annual Charity Match, but this scintillating form was not carried forward. Hearts were back to their pre-glory days when they failed to win their Qualifying Section in the League Cup against Falkirk, Motherwell and Partick Thistle and Motherwell qualified.

The team was involved in the European Inter-Cities Fairs Cup and faced Lausanne Sports in the First Round First Leg. A 2-2 draw in Switzerland was encouraging, but at Tynecastle in the Second Leg, only a last minute equaliser from Johnny Hamilton, earned another 2-2 draw. A play-off was required and on the toss of a coin, Lausanne earned the right of home advantage. Goals from Danny Ferguson and Willie Wallace took the match into extra-time, Where the Swiss side scored late on to win 3-2.

Hearts were unbeaten in the first six league matches, including an encouraging 4-2 defeat over Hibernian at home, before going down 1-0 to Queen of the South at Tynecastle in the seventh match. This indicated lean times ahead and frustration for the fans who had known great success for almost a decade. Inconsistency, the bug bear of Hearts supporters, raised its ugly head again when the team could only add two wins in the next six encounters.

Hearts were capable of a sound 3-0 victory over Rangers at Ibrox Park on 30 November, but followed this up with 1-1 draws at home to Motherwell and Celtic.. It was clear that the squad was not strong enough for a sustained Championship challenge and Tommy Walker moved into the transfer market to recruit Alan Anderson – Scunthorpe United, Jim Murphy – Alloa and Tommy White – St.Mirren. The new faces gave the team a lift and early in 1964, Hearts moved into third place.

Remarkably, four goals were scored in successive matches against East Stirlingshire – 4-0, Falkirk – 4-1, St.Johnstone – 4-1 and Queen of the South – 4-1 and the attacking partnership of Willie Wallace and Tommy White was looking good. Jim Cruickshank, Chris Shevlane and Davie Holt provided a solid defence and Hearts were still in contention for the title in mid-March. Sadly, the team's goal scoring partnership suffered a major blow earlier that month, when Tommy White was injured in a car crash.

On 14 March after losing 4-0 at home to Dundee United, the League challenge was over. Hearts eventually finished a disappointing fourth, eight points behind Champions Rangers.

The 50th.Anniversary Dinner to mark the mobilisation of Sir George McCrae's Battalion, the 16th.Royal Scots, on 15 December 1914 was held in Edinburgh on 11 December 1964. To mark this special occasion for the famous unit, which will always be associated with Hearts, a number of those attending were guests of the club at Tynecastle for the match against Aberdeen on Saturday, 12 December 1964.

In the Second Round of the Scottish Cup, Hearts easily defeated Queen of the South at Palmerston Park by 3 0. In the Third Round another away tie was their fortune and set up a titanic struggle with Motherwell. At Fir Park, Hearts came back from 3-1 down to salvage a 3-3 draw. The Replay brought 32,403 fans to Tynecastle, but substitutes were not permitted at that time and bad injuries to Roy Barry and John Cumming crippled the brave home side, allowing Motherwell to win 2-1.

The season was extended for the new Scottish Summer Cup and Hearts won their Qualifying Section against Dunfermline Athletic, Falkirk, and Hibernian but the club were forced to withdraw from the competition, as it was committed to playing in the New York Soccer League. In the USA, Hearts finished second in their Section playing against, Brazilian, English, German and Italian opponents.

Jim Cruickshank made his first appearance for Scotland in a Full International on 12 May1964 against West Germany in a 2-2 draw at Niedersachsen Stadion, Hanover.

Hearts won the Shield in the only local competition.

HEARTACHE AT TYNECASTLE

Hearts failed to win their Section of the 1964-1965 League Cup against Celtic, Kilmarnock and Partick Thistle and although strong opponents only three wins out of six matches was considered not good enough.

In the League Championship, Hearts delighted the supporters with some scintillating displays and did not lose any of their first 16 matches scoring 53 goals. An 8-1 defeat of Airdrieonians in the first match set them on their way then a sizzling see-saw match at Easter Road saw Hearts win 5-3 over Hibernian. After a 1-1 draw at Tynecastle against Dunfermline Athletic the "maroons" won 5-1 against Third Lanark away and 4-2 versus Celtic at home which raised expectations.

It was Kilmarnock who won 3-1 at Rugby Park on 19 December, to break the run – a shock, after hammering Aberdeen 6-3 the previous Saturday. Two defeats over the festive period didn't daunt the team's spirit and some good results were recorded, including a 2-1 victory over Celtic and a 1-1 draw away to Rangers. In a dramatic season it was difficult to explain how Dundee managed to win 7-1 at Tynecastle on 27 February but once again the players stood up and dropped only one point from the next seven matches.

Going into the final League match of the season, Hearts were at the top of the League Table, two points ahead of Kilmarnock who were the visitors to Tynecastle that fateful afternoon. All the players had to do was avoid a 2-0 defeat and they would be Champions, sad to say the team flopped. The day turned into an absolute disaster for the vast majority of the 37,725 crowd, who turned up to see Hearts add another League Championship to their record, Kilmarnock winning 2-0 and claiming the title by 0.04 of a goal under the old goal average system. If the present goal difference system had been in place, Hearts would have comfortably won the title having scored 90 goals to Kilmarnock's 62. Thus the most traumatic ending to a League campaign in the history of the Heart of Midlothian Football Club meant they were runners-up for the tenth time.

The unfortunate squad of players were:- Jim Cruickshank 34 appearances and 6 shut-outs, Willie Wallace 34 appearances and 21 goals, Alan Anderson 33/0, Johnny Hamilton 32/16, Billy Higgins 32/1, David Holt 32/-, Willie Polland 31/-, Alan Gordon 29/19, Chris Shevlane 25/0, Tommy White 18/13, Danny Ferguson 18/3, Tommy Traynor 17/3, Roy Barry 16/7, Roald Jensen 15/3, Donald Ford 7/2, Jimmy Murray 1/-.

Willie Wallace made his first appearance for Scotland in a Full International on 25 November 1964 against Northern Ireland in a 3-2 win at Hampden Park, Glasgow.

In the Scottish Cup, Falkirk lost 3-0 at Brockville Park in the First Round and in the Second round Hearts drew 3-3 with Greenock Morton at Cappielow Park and disposed of them 2-0 in the Replay at Tynecastle. In the Third Round the team went to Fir Park to face Motherwell but lost 1-0 to the better side on the day.

Danny Ferguson scored Hearts 5,000th.League goal in their 2,367th match, on 10 March 1965 in a 3-2 victory over Greenock Morton at Cappielow Park.

Hearts won the Shield in the only local competition.

There was little enthusiasm for the Scottish Summer Cup in which Hearts met Dunfermline, Falkirk and Hibernian. Not surprisingly, they failed to win the Section which Hibernian won.

The players were relieved, after such a season, to be able to enjoy a short tour of Norway where they played four and won four matches.

On the 19 June 1965 Hearts played Kilmarnock in an experimental match on behalf of FIFA. Offside was restricted that day and Hearts won 8-2. If only one of these goals had come against the Ayrshire club a few weeks earlier.

HEARTS HANGOVER

The 1965-1966 League Cup Section, included Aberdeen, Clyde and Rangers and despite three wins out of the six matches Hearts again failed to progress when Rangers won the Section.

The Club again took part in the Inter-Cities Fairs Cup and met Valerengens in the Second Round First Leg at Tynecastle and won 1-0. In the Second Leg in Oslo they defeated them 3-1 in the famous athletic Bislett Stadium. An early goal in just eight minutes settled Hearts and the 4 -1 aggregate was justified. In the Third round First Leg, Hearts drew 3-3 with Real Zaragoza at Tynecastle after being 2-0 down at half-time and in the Second Leg in Spain they forced a 2-2 draw.

This led to a play-off in March, again in Spain, when Hearts lost in the toss of a coin and going out by 1-0. The club made it clear in their following match programme that the standard of refereeing in the matches in Spain was not to their satisfaction.

The club and supporters were still affected by the tragic end to the previous season and attendances dropped by nearly a third.

George Miller – Wolverhampton Wanderers (£20,000) was added to the team but the League campaign started with Hearts winning only one of the first seven matches including an embarrassing 4-0 defeat by Hibernian at Tynecastle. There were no victories until Motherwell lost 5-2 at Tynecastle on 23 October then only Rangers defeated Hearts in the following 17 matches.

The 3-2 defeat of Hibernian on New Years Day at Easter Road was some consolation for the earlier defeat in Gorgie, especially as Hearts came back from 2-0 down. Far too many matches were drawn – 12 in all. Clyde 4-1 and 1-0, Greenock Morton 2-1 and 3-0 and Hamilton Academical 2-0 and 1-0 all suffered defeats home and away. Goal scoring was a real issue with only 56 netted in 34 matches and at the end of the season Hearts finished in seventh place the worst for five seasons.

In the Scottish Cup, Hearts defeated Clyde 2-1 in the First Round at Tynecastle then met Hibernian in the Second round. The match was again at home and Hibernian went out of the competition by 2-1. The Third Round tie brought Celtic to Gorgie and a crowd of 46,957 gathered hoping to see another home win. Celtic gained a 3-3 draw after some strange refereeing decisions and easily won the Replay 3-1 before an astonishing mid-week crowd of 72,100.

In the local competition Hearts won the Shield for the third time in a row.

TOMMY WALKER BOMBSHELL

Season 1966-1967 saw the first season tickets available, other than for the stands. The prices were, Ground £4, Enclosure £5 and Juveniles £2.

From now each team was permitted to substitute one player during a League match for injury only.

On the 26 September 1966 the Directors met and decided to ask Tommy Walker to resign as Manager/ Secretary "as it was felt that an irreparable breach had grown between the Manager and the dressing room". On the 3 October, Tommy Walker's written resignation was tabled for the Directors. "As he had resigned there was no obligation on the Club to pay salary but it was decided, in view of his past services, to pay him the sum of £2,000 for loss of office as Secretary".

Tommy Walker was deprived of exceeding Bobby Walker's record number of International Caps, due to the Second World War, he, however, set a record all of his own as the most successful Manager of Heart of Midlothian Football Club.

Between 23 October 1954 and 27 October 1962 he managed Hearts when they won the League Cup four times, 1954, 1958,1959, 1962, the Scottish Cup in 1956 and the League Championship twice in 1957/1958 and 1959/1960. At the time these seven trophies were just over half of all Hearts major trophy successes in their history. The failure to win the Championship in 1965 was held against him but time would show the Directors made a monumental error of judgement.

A new full time Secretary was appointed to relieve the new 'tracksuit' manager Johnny Harvey – promoted from trainer – and John Cumming took over as Trainer. It was not a job that Harvey especially wanted but he stood by the Club.

On 12 December 1966 the Directors received Bobby Walker's 'presentation watch', which was handed over by Mr. Robert Paterson, Dalkeith Road, Edinburgh to be displayed in the Board Room. It was agreed that he be given a season ticket for the season as a token of the Directors' appreciation.

In the League Cup, Hearts failed to progress from a very strong Section including Celtic, Clyde and St.Mirren, once more winning only three matches. Celtic was destined to win all the honours and easily topped the Section. On 20 August Johnny Hamilton became the first Hearts 'substitute' replacing the injured Chris Shevlane.

The new manager had a tough initial season, not helped by losing Roy Barry to Coventry City and Willie Wallace

The Tommy Walker Collection - Scottish Cup 1956 - League Championship 1957-1958 - League Championship 1959-1960
Scottish League Cup 1954 - Scottish League Cup 1958 - Scottish League Cup 1959 - Scottish League Cup 1962

to Celtic and several other players being released. Jim Townsend – St.Johnstone (£20,000) was brought in to strengthen the squad.

The League started badly, with an opening day, 3-1 defeat by Hibernian at Easter Road – Hearts first League derby defeat there since 1952. The number of players coming and going meant team selection was irregular and 31 players used at one time or another. There were few memorable matches and attendances were dreadful with only 2,500 turning up to see Hearts defeat Stirling Albion in April. Earlier from 4 March to 8 April Hearts played six successive League matches without scoring a goal.

Only Ayr United 1-0 and 1-0, Kilmarnock 2-1 and 1-0 and Stirling Albion 3-0 and 5-1 suffered double defeats. It was quite clear that the treatment meted out to Tommy Walker after his record as a player and a manager compared to the total contribution of all the Directors had been punished by the true Hearts supporters. At the end of the season, Hearts finished in eleventh place, their lowest position since 1926/1927. "This was the beginning of the end".

The Scottish Cup was a First Round 'wonder;' with Hearts losing 3-0 to Dundee United before a mere 17,139 at Tynecastle.

The Club toured Iceland at the end of the season and played three matches winning two and drawing the other. Alan Anderson, Jim Cruickshank and Jim Townsend did not travel as they took part in an overseas tour organised by the SFA.

Johnny Harvey had served Hearts well over many years but he was not up to managing a major football club. A factor he was aware from the beginning.

MIXED FORTUNES

From season 1967-1968 each team was permitted to substitute one player during a match under the auspices of the SFA, for any reason other than a sending-off.

The first recording of the Hearts song "Away up in Gorgie at Tynecastle Park" was released in July.

In the League Cup, Hearts failed to win their Section which included Falkirk, St.Johnstone and Stirling Albion. In previous seasons this would have been a foregone conclusion, but not now. Four of the six matches were won but the "saints" beat Hearts home and away and deserved to progress to the knock-out stage.

Once again the first League match was against Hibernian, this time at Tynecastle which Hearts lost 4-1. The team bounced back and lost only one of the next eleven fixtures, which included an excellent 5-2 victory over Motherwell at Fir Park and a 1-1 draw away to Rangers. The remainder of the campaign was not good and to add gloom to the story Hibernian enjoyed a League double. This was their fifth time to Hearts seventeenth. The biggest insult was a humbling 6-3 defeat by Clyde at the Shawfield Stadium in January. Then in February, a 3-2 victory over our traditional adversaries Motherwell at Tynecastle, to record the only 'double' of the season, was not greeted with much enthusiasm and Hearts finished in twelfth place.

With so much going wrong, the start of the Scottish Cup competition was seen as an opportunity for the team to do themselves justice. In many ways they did just that. In the First Round, Brechin City lost 4-1 at Tynecastle and an away tie was the challenge for the Second Round. Dundee United on their own ground proved to be difficult opponents but Hearts persevered and an exhilarating match ended 6-5. The winning goal came in the

85th.minute with new signing Rene Moller scoring twice.

For the Quarter-Finals, Hearts were drawn away to Rangers and on form were expected to lose, but the team stuck to their task and recorded a fighting 1-1 draw. The Replay in Gorgie drew a crowd of 44,094 who witnessed a remarkable result when Hearts scored the only goal in the 87th.minute. Having come this far you would have expected the hopes to be high but even a Semi-Final against Greenock Morton was faced with doubt. The match was played at Hampden Park and they held Hearts to a 1-1 draw. In the Replay a much smaller attendance suggested the supporters felt the club had blown their chance to play in a Cup Final. The truly yo-yo performances continued and the team won 2-1 after extra time.

The Final at Hampden Park, was against Dunfermline Athletic, who had never beaten Hearts in the Scottish Cup and although Manager Harvey stuck to the players who defeated Greenock Morton they failed miserably and went down easily to a 3-1 defeat.

The team was:- Jim Cruickshank; Ian Sneddon and Arthur Mann; Alan Anderson, Arthur Thomson and George Miller-captain; Roald Jensen, Jim Townsend, Donald Ford, Jim Irvine and Tommy Traynor. Rene Moller for Jensen.

The Hearts Memorial Clock was moved 34 yards to the east to accommodate a new one-way traffic system at Haymarket.

The Shield returned to Tynecastle after an absence of one year.

YOUNG HEARTS PROGRESS

For no apparent reason the club programme listed players in a 4-2-4 formation in season 1968-1969. Having finished last season in better form the new season was greeted with some confidence.

The League Cup Section opponents were Airdrieonians, Dundee and Kilmarnock and together they immediately brought the supporters down to earth with Hearts winning only two matches out of the six.

The first match of the League campaign was as usual against Hibernian, but this season Hearts won 3-1 at Easter Road after being 1-0 down at half-time. The defence had totally subdued Hibernian's forwards. A similar score against Dunfermline Athletic, at Tynecastle gained revenge for the Cup Final, and things looked promising until Hearts lost 2-1 against Airdrieonians in the next match. This proved to be the pattern for the season, with just about every good result followed by a defeat and in November Arthur Mann was transferred to Manchester City (£65,000).

Jock Wallace was appointed at the turn of the year as assistant manager and he introduced his own style of training, tactics and motivation. He helped Hearts to make a minor recovery near the end of the season but they were embarrassed by a 5-0 defeat by Celtic in Glasgow and a 5-1 defeat by Partick Thistle at Firhill Park.

With 'doubles' against Aberdeen 2-1 and 3-2, Falkirk 3-1 and 2-1 and Raith Rovers 1-0 and 3-0, an eighth place finish was at least an improvement.

The Scottish Cup, First Round tie was against Dundee at Dens Park and Hearts came home with a 2-1 victory. In the Second Round Hearts were drawn away again but lost 2-0 to Rangers.

In January 1969 Hearts three licensed premises were opened – Ace of Hearts, the Midlothian Club and the Rosebery Suite. Member subscriptions were Ace of Hearts £1-couple £1.10/-; Midlothian Club and Rosebery Suite £5-couple £7-10/-. Alas they closed in 1976.

Roald Jensen made his first appearance for Norway in a Full International, as a Hearts player, on 8 May 1969 against Mexico in a 2-0 defeat at Ullevaal Stadium, Oslo.

A STEP FORWARD

Jock Wallace having come to assist Johnny Harvey was looking a natural successor and as a result the supporters were optimistic for the 1969-1970 season.

The League Cup Section included Dundee United, Greenock Morton and St.Mirren but Hearts failed to progress after three wins only one of which was at home. It began with a 3-2 defeat of Dundee United at Tannadice Park but after that they only scored three goals in the remaining five matches. Success in this competition was now a distant memory.

In the League Championship the team struggled to put together a winning run. At home they won six out of 17 matches making it impossible to sustain a challenge for the title. One of the home wins saw Kilmarnock defeated 4-1 on 13 September but it was a further seven matches before the next victory. Although the second half of the campaign was much improved – they lost only three matches out of the last seventeen.

This included a 0-0 draw with Celtic at Tynecastle to match their 2-0 win at Celtic Park and Hearts were the only team to prevent Celtic scoring in every match.. In the end with 'doubles' only against Airdrieonians 2-1 and 5-0 and Raith Rovers 3-2 and 3-0, Hearts finished in an improved fourth place, the best for five seasons.

On the 8 December 1969 the Directors were advised of a letter from Mr.N.Robertson offering, as a gift to the Club, the primrose and pink jersey (Lord Rosebery's racing colours) worn by Bobby Walker on 30 March 1901 for the match against England. On 29 December they were told of a letter from Mr.W.B.Dow enclosing the jersey.

The Scottish Cup was the last chance the team had to offer the supporters any hope. In the First Round, Montrose proved to be a tougher nut to crack than many thought and Hearts could only draw 1-1 at Links Park but they scraped through 1-0 in the Replay. Hearts were then drawn to meet Kilmarnock at Rugby Park where two early goals from the home team sent the Tynecastle men crashing out of the Cup.

The Shield was won in the only local competition.

Hearts experimented with a new service for supporters by opening the first Hearts souvenir shop in August 1970.

Hearts needed to add a striking threat to a sound defence and Wilson Wood – Dundee United was exchanged for Tommy Traynor – what a mistake that turned out to be!

TEXACO EXCITEMENT

Sponsored football was introduced in Scotland for season 1970-1971 with the Texaco Cup, an Anglo-Scottish knock-out competition over two-legs. Hearts were invited to take part and their performances were the only highlight of a poor season. Hearts had a good run in the inaugural year and met Burnley in the First Round at Turf Moor and lost 3-1. The return match produced an exciting fight back with Hearts winning 4-1. The Second Round paired Hearts against Airdrieonians and a 5-0 rout at Broomfield. This time it was Airdrieonians who fought back and they won 3-2 at Tynecastle but lost out 7-3 on aggregate.

The Semi-Finals brought Scottish opposition in the form of Motherwell who were dispatched 3-2 on aggregate after a 1-1 draw at Tynecastle and a 2-1 win at Fir Park. The Final saw Hearts play Wolverhampton Wanderers at Tynecastle where the English side had a comfortable 3-1. In the Second Leg Hearts won 1-0 but "wolves" won the Cup 3-2 on aggregate.

The Hearts made their now traditional early exit from the League Cup, from a Section that included Celtic, Clyde and Dundee United. They won only one match out of the six when they defeated Clyde at Shawfield Stadium 5-1 in the final match.

The League campaign got off to a bad start with a defeat in the very first match 3-1 by St.Johnstone at Tynecastle. This was one of several disappointing results early in the season and only two wins were recorded in the first nine matches. The home results were slightly better than the previous season – 8 as against 6 – and the only favourable win was the 5-2 defeat of Airdrieonians in September. Away victories were limited to five, the best of which was a 4-2 win against Falkirk in March. Hearts had 'doubles' over Cowdenbeath 1-0 and 4-0, Dunfermline Athletic 3-0 and 2-1 and St.Mirren 1-0 twice and eventually finished in eleventh place in the table.

With Jock Wallace leaving in the summer to go to Rangers, John Harvey was more determined than ever to stand aside, and in December Bobby Seith was appointed as manager.

In the Scottish Cup, Hearts met Stranraer for the first ever time and had a comfortable 3-0 home victory. The next round brought Hibernian and Hearts together and although the match was played at Tynecastsle Hibernian won 2-1.

The Hearts lost to Hibernian in the Shield Final then went on tour to North America at the end of the season to take part in ten matches between 6 and 30 May 1971 in which they won 6, drew 3 and lost 1.

At a meeting of the Directors on 16 March 1971 it was agreed to sign the lease on 7/9 McLeod Street, the former Police Station, which had been used as a First Aid Station since 1952. On the 4 October 1971 work began to bring the floodlighting system up to the new UEFA standards. The Directors decided to go for ten lights per tower at 40-45 lumens per square foot.

BOBBY SEITH MAKES CHANGES

No action was taken during the close season to strengthen the team and the supporters were not optimistic about the 1971-1972 season ahead.

In the League Cup, Hearts were faced by Airdrieonians, Dunfermline Athletic and St.Johnstone in their

Section and won 4-1 at Tynecastle against St.Johnstone in the first match and defeated Airdrieonians 3-1 at Broomfield in the second match. Hearts for several seasons had fallen at this stage of the competition and this time it was no different. The two wins were followed by three defeats and the final match win of 4-0 over Dunfermline Athletic was too late.

The League campaign began with a defeat by Hibernian at Tynecastle but the team rallied and were undefeated in their next eight matches including a sound defeat of Rangers by 2-1 at Tynecastle.. Some good results followed including a 6-1 defeat of Greenock Morton at Tynecastle and a 3-2 victory over Aberdeen at Pittodrie Park, when from 2-1 down the team bounced back and scored two goals in the final ten minutes. Aberdeen also lost 1-0 at Tynecastle and along with Clyde 1-0 and 2-0 were the only 'doubles' that season. At the end of the campaign Hearts finished in sixth place.

On the 3 January 1972 the Heart of Midlothian Associates Club was formed. They took over the old billiard room in the South Stand and created a seated area for members with upholstered ex-cinema seats and their Season ticket was £50.

On the 19 February 1972 a telephone link between the main stand and the trainer's bench was installed "so that the manager could communicate directly with the trainer".

The Texaco Cup was not as successful as the previous season. In the First Round Hearts defeated Newcastle United 1-0 at home then lost 2-1 away. This took the tie into extra time without any more goals and eventually Hearts lost their first penalty shoot out.

In the Third Round of the Scottish Cup, Hearts were drawn against St.Johnstone at Tynecastle and won 2-0 then enjoyed a 4-0 home win over Clydebank to set up a Quarter-Final tie against Celtic in Glasgow. Hearts drew 1-1 but lost the Replay 1-0 at Tynecastle. This match on 27 March 1972 drew an attendance of 40,354 and is Gorgie's last crowd in excess of 40,000.

The Shield was won as the only local competition tried hard to continue.

NOT AJAX

Hearts prepared for the 1972-1973 season at Papendal Sports Centre in Holland and by coincidence wore a new jersey with a broad maroon centre-panel a la Ajax of Amsterdam.

The League Cup started the season off as usual, and as usual, Hearts failed to progress form their Section, which included Airdrieonians, Berwick Rangers and Dumbarton. In the not too distant past this Section would have been seen as a passport into the Quarter-Finals yet it was the final match of the section before they recorded a win – 3-0 against Berwick Rangers.

The Texaco Cup was also a let down because with Crystal Palace being defeated 1-0 in both legs this earned a Quarter-Finals match with Motherwell. Hearts were held to a 0-0 draw at Tynecastle in the First Leg but at Fir Park they were 2-0 ahead when Ian Sneddon was sent off and Motherwell hit back to win 4-2.

Team performances bordered on the careless, and a humiliating 7-0 defeat from Hibernian on New Years Day at Tynecastle was more than embarrassing. After a shaky start Hearts improved and were in third place by mid-December. The 1-0 defeat of Rangers in Glasgow was not remembered for the score but the way in which it was achieved. With the score at 0-0 and minutes left to play Tommy Murray was toying with the Rangers players and decided to sit on the ball. When their right back lunged in, Tommy coolly got up, passed the ball to Jim Brown on the overlap and his cross was headed home by Donald Ford.

Following that, the festive period fixtures saw a slump with defeats from Dundee, St.Johnstone and the record defeat by Hibernian. The rot had set in and points were dropped with regularity. Only Dumbarton 1-0 and 2-0 and Falkirk 3-1 and 1-0 lost home and away with Hearts finishing up in an unacceptable tenth place in the League.

This season's Scottish Cup competition was a non-event, with Hearts going out in the Third round to bottom of the League Airdrieomians 3-1 at Broomfield Park after a 0-0 draw at Tynecastle.

Hearts won the Shield again but the only local competition was now more of an inconvenience than an attraction.

In March 1973 the supporters were shocked at the transfer of Eddie Thomson to Aberdeen for £60,000. The new faces being brought in did not appear to be of the same calibre. Manager Bobby Seith would have to work hard during the close season if results were to improve.

HEARTS COME BACK

From Season 1973-1974 each team was permitted to substitute two players during a match.

Hearts had new faces in the team including – Kenny Aird – St.Johnstone, and Drew Busby – Airdrieonians (£35,000) and hopes were high that they would help revive the enthusiasm of the supporters.

The League Cup was not the answer as once more Hearts failed to progress from their Section against Dundee, Partick Thistle and St.Johnstone after two wins, two draws and two defeats.

The League campaign was a bit better and in the first fixture away to Greenock Morton the team came from 2-0 down to win 3-2 – all three goals were penalties scored by Donald Ford. When Hibernian lost 4-1 at Tynecastle in the first home match of the season the supporters expected more of the same – that home win was the first against Hibernian since 1963. Draws against Motherwell and Dundee followed before a match at Ibrox Park loomed. Rangers had not started the season well and a 3-0 defeat by a smart-looking Hearts rubbed salt in the wound.

But when Celtic played at Tynecastle in late October the tide had turned and they had a 3-1 win. Poor results at home and inconsistency spoiled a good start but with 'doubles' against Arbroath 3-2 and 4-0, Dunfermline Athletic 3-0 and 3-2, Falkirk 2-1 and 2-0 and Partick Thistle 3-1 twice, Hearts finished in an improved sixth place.

Donald Ford made his first appearance for Scotland in a Full International on 17 October 1973 against Czechoslovakia in a 1-0 defeat at Tehelne Pole, Bratislavia.

In the Texaco Cup, First Round, Hearts defeated Everton 1-0 at Goodison Park then drew 0-0 at Tynecastle to progress on aggregate. In the Second Round Hearts had no answer to the flair of Burnley and lost 3-0 at Tynecastle and 5-0 at Turf Moor.

In the Scottish Cup Third Round, Hearts met Clyde at Tynecastle and won 3-1. The Fourth Round tie was again at Tynecastle but Hearts could only draw 1-1 against Partick Thistle but in the Replay, Hearts were dominant at Firhill Park and won 4-1.

In the Quarter-Final tie at Tynecastle Ayr United held Hearts to a 1-1 draw and in the replay at Somerset Park, Hearts struggled through 2-1. In the Semi-Final match at Hampden Park, Hearts met Dundee United and for the third time in the competition drew 1-1. The Replay was again in Glasgow but there was to be no joy for Hearts as they lost 4-2.

This was Hearts Centenary Year and the Centenary Flag, presented by the Heart of Midlothian Associates, was unveiled before the match against Motherwell on 5 January 1974 by the Earl of Rosebery and four former players who were all over 80 years old, John Low-Leven, John Hanlon-Addiewell, Walter Scott-Edinburgh and Willie White-Airdrie along with 16 year-old Campbell (Cammy) Fraser who was the youngest player on the staff.

OUR CENTENARY SEASON

The Club's Centenary Season - 1974-1975 - was to be the last under the Scottish League's long-standing, two division system. A ten-club Premier Division was to commence the following year and Hearts main priority was to secure a place. The team did so finishing eighth in the 18-club League with a struggle as there were times when qualification looked anything but certain.

The season began with the Centenary Challenge match against Tottenham Hotspur which ended in a 1-1 draw. Then for the first time in eleven seasons Hearts progressed from their League Cup Section against Aberdeen, Dunfermline Athletic and Greenock Morton. In the two-leg Quarter-Finals Hearts lost out to Falkirk with a 0-0 draw in the First Leg at Tynecastle and a 1-0 defeat at Brockville Park in the Second Leg, a match marred by John Gallacher suffering a broken ankle .

In the Texaco Cup, Hearts went out in the First Round to Oldham Athletic by a 1-0 aggregate. Hearts confidently expected to overcome the 1-0 defeat at Boundary Park, but at Tynecastle the English Second Division side defended stoutly to go through to the next round..

Hearts had a poor start to this vital League campaign and failed to win any of their first seven matches including losing 4-1 against Partick Thistle and Aberdeen in successive weeks. This led to manager Bobby Seith being sacked and John Hagart became caretaker- manager. His first match in charge on 12 October, ended in a 5-0 away defeat to Dundee United. He steadied the defence adding Don Murray – Cardiff City, to an already stable part of the team. Apart from a lapse at Arbroath, the team was undefeated in 18 League matches.

Hearts moved off the bottom of the League on 9 November and Dumbarton 2-1 and 1-0 and Motherwell 3-1 and 4-1 were defeated home and away. The supporters stood by the team and a crowd of 36,750 witnessed the 0-0 draw against Hibernian on New Year's Day. This was to be the last time over 30,000 spectators watched Hearts at Tynecastle. The Hearts only took eight points from their final eight matches but Premier Division football was assured on 19 April with the home win over Motherwell.

In the Scottish Cup, Third Round, Hearts were drawn against Kilmarnock at Tynecastle and won 2-0. In the Fourth Round they defeated Queen of the South at Palmerston Park with another 2-0 win. In the Quarter-Finals their opponents were Dundee who drew 1-1 at Tynecastle then won 3-2 in the Replay at Dens Park.

The East of Scotland Shield was struggling for survival and there was no competition in 1973-1974. However, it was back in 1974-1975 and Hearts defeated Hibernian 2-1 in the Final.

Hearts now had to gear up to the increased demands of the Premier Division where rewards were high, but two from ten teams faced relegation.

THE PREMIER ERA

The attraction of the new Premier Division in 1975-1976 led to increased crowds, which of course was one of the reasons for the change. Hearts eventually finished fifth in the inaugural season and went all the way to the Scottish Cup Final.

In the League Cup, Hearts were back to their old habits and failed to progress from their Section which included Aberdeen, Celtic and Dumbarton but credit was due after they won all three home matches and had a double over Aberdeen. Four wins out of six was an improvement but Celtic had one more.

At this time Hearts were knocked out of the Anglo-Scottish Cup, a competition that had replaced the Texaco Cup. After beating Queen of the South in the First Round, they were eliminated by Fulham in the Second Round. They lost 3-2 in London and Fulham held out for a 2-2 draw at Tynecastle.

In the Premier Division, each side met four times and life in the new set-up for Hearts, was launched with a match against Hibernian at Easter Road where they lost 1-0 and that was the beginning of a sad story. Hibernian won three and drew one of the four League matches that season, and Celtic and Rangers won three and lost one. For Aberdeen they had three draws and one loss. The only teams to fare badly in all four matches with Hearts were Ayr United and St.Johnstone, both ending with one draw and three defeats.

After a poor start, Dundee were defeated 3-2 at Dens Park and only two of the following fifteen Championship matches were lost both to Celtic. In November, Hearts were second in the Division and just after Christmas the team was only four points off the top position. In 1976 there was a dramatic downturn and only one victory was recorded in the first ten matches of the year. Relegation was a real threat and Graham Shaw – Dunfermline Athletic was signed.

With only four matches remaining only one point separated Hearts and ninth placed Dundee but with two wins and a draw they then ended the season defeating Celtic 1-0 at Tynecastle. Dundee and St.Johnstone were relegated but this first Premier campaign should have served as a warning.

The Scottish Cup was all that was left to play for and the team played well with that in mind. Progress was made but it took Replays against three First Division clubs to reach the Final. The Third Round draw saw Hearts paired with Clyde at Tynecastle and they could only draw 2-2 but gained a 1-0 victory in the Replay at Shawfield Stadium. In the Fourth Round, home advantage saw Stirling Albion defeated 3-0. So on to the Quarter-Finals for a marathon of three matches against Montrose.

The first match at Links Park ended in a lucky 2-2 draw for Hearts. The Replay at Tynecastle also ended in a 2-2 draw which led to a Second Replay played at neutral Muirton Park, Perth and Hearts finally won 2-1 after extra-time. Dumbarton were waiting for Hearts in the Semi-Finals and at Hampden Park, they drew 0-0 but in the Replay again at Hampden Park, Hearts won quite easily, 3-0.

The club was safe in the Premier Division and could concentrate on defeating Rangers in the Final on 1 May 1976. Rangers famously scored within 41 seconds of the kick-off in a match started two minutes before the scheduled three o'clock. There was no way back for Hearts although they did score a consolation goal in the 3-1 defeat. The only benefit was that the Hearts would play in the European Cup Winners Cup the following season as Rangers had won the League..

The Cup Final team was:- Jim Cruickshank; Jimmy Brown-captain and Sandy Burrell; Jim Jefferies, John Gallacher and Roy Kay; Willie Gibson, Drew Busby, Graham Shaw, Ralph Callachan and Rab Prentice. Kenny

Aird came on for Sandy Burrell and Donald Park for Willie Gibson.

The campaign ended with a gruelling eight match 'world tour', being played in Norway, New Zealand, Australia and Mauritius.

Hearts did have one success when they won the Shield.

Since the implementation of the Safety at Sports Grounds Act 1975, all designated stadiums with a capacity over 10,000 were required to have a Local Authority Safety Certificate. Following an inspection of the capacity, exits, barriers, etc by the Authority, the capacity of Tynecastle was reduced to 30,000. This legislation was to have a devastating effect on the Club in the near future.

HEARTS GO DOWN

Alan Anderson retired and Donald Ford was transferred.

With Hearts in a European competition for the first time since 1965/1966 following their Cup Final appearance, season 1976-1977 started full of promise but ended in disgrace. For the first time in its history of over 100 years the club was relegated. Despite being involved with the Scottish Cup all the way to the Final the team had briefly become involved in the relegation issue but failed to learn a lesson.

The only significant recruit was Brian Wilson – Arbroath but Bert Paton came as a coach to assist John Hagart

In the European Cup Winners Cup, First Round, First Leg Hearts were drawn to play away against FC Locomotive Leipzig and lost 2-0, in the Central Stadium. The Second Leg at Tynecastle was a night to remember. Hearts had to score at least three goals without reply to advance to the next round, and in a evening of high drama won 5-1. Hearts levelled the aggregate to 2-2 early on but Leipzig scored just before half-time. Hearts would need at least another two goals to progress. The team rallied and duly obliged with three more goals. This brought jubilation to the fans but an over zealous invasion of the pitch after the final whistle cost Hearts a fine of 1000 Swiss Francs plus a warning from UEFA.

In the Second Round, First Leg, Hearts met Hamburg SV in the Volksparkstadion and lost 4-2. Oddly, the supporters were not critical, being only too pleased to see their team amongst the big guns again. In the Second Leg at Tynecastle the crowd saw Hamburg give Hearts a lesson, in an easy 4-1 win.

The League Cup Section with Dundee United, Motherwell and Partick Thistle saw Hearts progress to the Quarter-Finals after four wins and a draw. There they met Falkirk at home 4-1 then away 3-4 and went through 7-5 on aggregate after a very shaky second-leg.. The Semi-Final tie was played against Celtic at Hampden Park, Glasgow on a wet October night and Hearts lost 2-1 to a disputed penalty – surprise, surprise – and with Rab Prentice sent-off.

Defeat in these two competitions disheartened the players and much worse was to follow. This was the season of reckoning and Hearts failed miserably. In their first nine matches they drew seven and lost two but the run was halted with the 2-1 defeat of Aberdeen at Tynecastle in November. Hearts were in sixth place at the end of the year but by the end of January the team had recorded only four wins in 20 matches.

A resounding 4-0 defeat of Kilmarnock on 5 February brightened the gloom but within a week Ralph Callachan was transferred to Newcastle United for a new record fee of £90,000. Hearts failed to win any of the next twelve matches despite signing Malcolm Robertson – Ayr United. It was impossible for Hearts to survive having scored only 49 goals and conceded 66 with the only team to lose more than once to the "maroons" was Motherwell. Out of 18 home matches Hearts won five and drew six and although no-one connected with the club could believe that Hearts could actually be relegated they ended up in ninth place and dropped into the First Division.

In the Scottish Cup, Hearts entered at the Third Round to meet Dumbarton at Tynecastle and drew 1-1. Then in the Replay at Boghead Park, Hearts scraped through 1-0. The Fourth Round brought Clydebank to Gorgie and they were defeated 1-0. The Quarter-Finals saw Hearts at home once more and again the result was a draw, 0-0 against East Fife. The Replay at Methil saw Hearts win 3-2 to set them up for the Scottish Cup, Semi-Finals for the third time in four seasons. However, at Hampden Park, Glasgow in front of a crowd of only 23,652 Hearts went down rather easily by 2-0 to Rangers.

The East of Scotland Shield had again fallen behind and during the season, Hearts won the 1975/1976 Final with an 8-0 demolition of Meadowbank Thistle.

After the numbing experience of relegation, and under pressure from the directors, John Hagart resigned and was replaced by the former Hibernian player and St.Johnstone and Scotland manager, Willie Ormond. His Hibernian connections, like Mr.McGhee before him, proved to be a problem. As before the Directors were so removed from the supporters they failed to recognise he would have to be outstanding to survive.

John Cumming retired having served the Club since 1948 as a player and from 1967 as the trainer. He has his own place in Hearts history having won seven winners' medals – four League Cup, two League Championship and a Scottish Cup, between 1954 and 1962, with 503 appearances and 44 goals in major competitions.

On a positive note, the club bought for £10,000 the City's right to acquire Tynecastle for only £5,000, should football cease to be played there. Hearts now had a real property asset that might help to raise funds with which to restructure the club.

They had to spend £100,000 to ensure the Safety Certificate was continued. The terraces had to be sectioned off and fenced and additional barriers were placed around the ground with the capacity further reduced to 27,440.

WE BOUNCE BACK

In season 1977-1978 Hearts supporters were to visit pastures new when the First Division matches began and there was some concern about the reaction of the supporters to their team playing at a lower level for the first time. They remained remarkably loyal and the average home gate in the League was 10,084. Several changes to the playing staff were made and a pay dispute had to be settled by the new manager before the big 'Kick-Off'.

Restoring the club's fortunes was a hugely demanding task, because with a massive loss of income expected in the First Division, there had to be a clear out of 14 players including Jim Cruickshank and Dave Clunie. The nucleus of the team was to be younger players with Dave McNicoll – Montrose added.

The League Cup had a different format for 1977/1978 and did not start until after Hearts had played three League matches which had resulted in a win and two draws. The Second Round draw brought Stenhousemuir to Tynecastle for the First Leg in the new two-leg matches. Hearts won 1-0 at home and 5-0 at Ochilview Park.

In the Third Round, Hearts played Greenock Morton in the First Leg at Tynecastle and won 3-0 but had a scary 2-0 defeat at Cappielaw Park. Hearts progressed through to the Quarter-Finals for the third time in four seasons and played Dundee United at Tannadice In the First Leg losing 3-1 then at Tynecastle in the Second Leg Hearts won 2-0 and so it went to a penalty shoot-out which Hearts won 4-3. The Semi-Final match was not until March and when Hearts met Celtic at Hampden Park interest had waned and the 2-0 defeat was just accepted.

The first ever League match in a lower division was away to Dumbarton and ended in a 2-2 draw where Jim Cruickshank played for the home team. This was the early evidence that the Edinburgh side would be a big scalp for smaller clubs. The initial home match was against Dundee the following week and the fans witnessed a 2-1 win. The Hearts were unbeaten in the first eight matches, but the run ended at home against Hamilton Academical and led to a difficult spell, with them losing four out of the following seven matches.

This included a defeat at home by Kilmarnock on 5 November which was marred by Jimmy Brown suffering a broken leg. The team responded, and on 19 November a 1-0 victory over St.Johnstone at Muirton Park, started an excellent run that saw Hearts undefeated until the end of the season, a total of 23 matches. The contenders for promotion were soon to the fore with Dundee and Greenock Morton vying with Hearts for the coveted places.

Surprisingly, the only club to prevent the Hearts winning a match against them was Montrose but several sides lost all three matches – Airdrieonians, Arbroath, Alloa Athletic, St.Johnstone and Stirling Albion. Hearts had to win the final match at Arbroath to secure an immediate return to the Premier Division and duly obliged by winning 1-0.

Dundee defeated Greenock Morton that day and would have pipped Hearts for promotion if they had faltered. Greenock Morton became Champions and Hearts finished in second place.

The attempt to win the Scottish Cup was undistinguished. In the Third Round, Hearts had a decent 3-2 victory over Airdrieonians at Broomfield Park then in the Fourth Round Dumbarton beckoned. Hearts managed to draw 1-1 away from home but inexplicably lost the Replay 1-0. A bonus dispute may have led to the poor performance and Mr. Ormond criticized the players for lack of professionalism.

In the Shield, Hearts lost to Hibernian in the 1976/1977 Final.

NO SURVIVAL

Hearts prepared for the new season by taking part in the Tennent Caledonian Cup, against Rangers, Southampton and West Bromwich. Unfortunately, a reasonable show in this competition was not maintained.

Hearts played again in the Anglo Scottish Cup and met Partick Thistle in the home and away format but lost 2-1 away and drew 1-1 at home.

In 1978-1979 the new League Cup format saw Hearts go out of their second competition within a month losing embarrassingly 7-2 on aggregate to Greenock Morton – 3-1 at Tynecastle and 4-1 in Greenock.

Hearts return to the Premier Division was a disaster and it was clear that after the opening fixture produced a 4-1 home defeat from Aberdeen, the squad would struggle to survive. Only Frank Liddell – Alloa Athletic had been recruited and the team did not win any of the first five matches. This included a controversial 1-1 draw against Hibernian when the Leith men equalized in injury time when Hearts were down to nine men. A pitch invasion followed, similar to that against Leipzig, and this resulted in the club pushing forward their security plans.

In September a 7' high perimeter fence was erected round the ground following the pitch invasion and segregation barriers split the terracing at the Wheatfield entrance and were in place for the next home match. The omens were there from the start and the team failed to win any matches against Greenock Morton or St.Mirren and only five matches were won at home. Donald Park was exchanged for John Craig and Denis McQuade – Partick Thistle and later Derek O'Connor – St.Johnstone was signed and scored after 50 seconds of his debut in a 2-1 win at Aberdeen.

This was followed by a 2-0 home victory over Celtic and a 2-1 win at Easter Road – the first time in ten years. These three successive victories actually took Hearts to sixth place, but hope of revival was shattered in January when Eamonn Bannon was sold to Chelsea for £225,000 and there were calls for the resignation of chairman Bobby Parker. At the same time Alex Rennie replaced Bert Paton who had resigned. The tonic the supporters needed came when Rangers, who were top of the League, were brilliantly defeated 3-2 at Tynecastle in February.

A threatened boycott of the match by angered fans flopped as a 16,500 crowd – only 1,659 less than the earlier attendance – against the same opponents in October. At the start of April, two successive victories over Dundee United and Motherwell sparked hopes of a relegation reprieve, with Hearts just two points behind Partick Thistle. However, on 11 April the "jags" won 2-0 at Tynecastle. Things went from bad to worse and Hearts lost all of the remaining nine matches including the final home match against Greenock Morton which only attracted 2,400 spectators. Hearts finished in ninth place and were relegated again – the yo-yo string was being wound.

The Scottish Cup brought a little flurry of hope when in the Third Round, Hearts defeated Raith Rovers 2-0 at Starks Park. In the Fourth Round, the opponents Greenock Morton drew 1-1 at Tynecastle but in the Replay the team surpassed themselves and won 1-0 over their recent bogey team. Of all clubs to meet in the Quarter-Finals it had to be Hibernian and they won 2-1 at Easter Road.

In a season of turmoil, the team even lost to Meadowbank Thistle in the Semi-Finals of the Shield for 1977/1978.

The fans were numbed when their team was relegated for the first time in 1977 but the second time round they were riled and several actions took place. In April The Federation of Hearts Supporters Clubs advertised a "Share Option Account" in an attempt to raise £200,000 to press for a change in the club's Articles of Association, essentially to allow shares to be offered to the public.

More importantly, following a campaign of "Are you dissatisfied with Hearts' results" waged by Archie Martin and Iain Watt, during May and June, saw them decisively elected as directors at an AGM on 29 July. The wind of change was blowing and this was a very significant development.

FIRST DIVISION CHAMPIONS

At the end of the season, manager, Willie Ormond, had come under pressure and decided to instigate a major rebuilding programme, starting with the departure of eleven players. But would season 1979-1980 see an improvement? As could be expected the sale of Season Tickets were down and the new Board would have their work cut out to ensure immediate promotion to the Premier Division.

It was clear that the supporters were now disillusioned. In fact, by the end of the season, the average home gate for First Division matches had fallen to the lowest level since the Second World War – only 5,741.

On the playing side, at the start of the season, Willie Ormond, was absent through illness for several weeks and there were no major signings, apart from Bobby Robinson – Dundee United and later Jim Denny – Rangers. Nevertheless, the squad was strong enough for the First Division and the team made a fine start, winning the first five matches.

The League Cup was another example of how low Hearts had sunk in terms of quality and effort. Having drawn Ayr United away in the First Round First Leg they scrambled a 2-2 draw then unforgivably lost the Replay 1-0 at home.

Early in September, things took a turn for the worse, after Hearts had crashed out of the League Cup. A week later, Raith Rovers inflicted Hearts first League defeat of the season and only eight points were then taken from the next eight matches. Hearts brought in Crawford Boyd – Queen of the South but still struggled to end the poor run of form. This was not helped by yet another bonus dispute that saw the whole first team squad demand transfers.

A compromise was reached and Hearts put together an undefeated run of 16 League matches that started on 3 November with a 0-0 draw at Shielfield Park in Berwick.

However, the team had won only half of the fixtures and the supporters expected more dynamic performances in the First Division. As a result, crowds of over 6,000 had become very rare at Tynecastle and matters came to a head on 5 January after Hearts drew 3-3 at home to Clydebank after throwing away a 3-0 lead and the crowd of 5,172 expressed its displeasure. This result helped the Directors to make up their mind about the Manager and he was dismissed and his assistant Alex Rennie took over as caretaker-manager.

The run into the final matches was tense but as the season moved into April, Hearts gathered enough points to make promotion almost certain. Airdrieonians led the title race and along with Ayr United challenged the "maroons". On 5 April, the Tynecastle men won 1-0 against Airdrieonians and both the Lanarkshire side and Ayrshire side, then failed to take advantage of Hearts dropping five points from the following five matches. In such a successful campaign it was a surprise that only Arbroath, St.Johnstone and Stirling Albion lost all three matches to Hearts. Victories in the final two matches saw Hearts win the First Division Championship.

In the Scottish Cup, Third Round, Hearts were struggling to pull back a 1-0 deficit away to Alloa Athletic, but fog caused the match to be abandoned and when it was replayed a solitary goal was enough for the team to progress. A new Manager, Bobby Moncur, was appointed on 16 February 1980 in time for the Fourth Round which saw Hearts drawn at home to Stirling Albion and they won 2-0. In the next round, 'the bubble burst' and Rangers, at Ibrox Park, emphasised the gulf between the First and Premier Divisions winning 6-1 and sending a message for the next season.

The Articles of Association of the Company were changed at an Extraordinary General Meeting on 28 April

1980. The 5,000 shares of £1 each - £5,000 were sub-divided into 50,000 Ordinary Shares of 10p each and the authorised share capital was increased to £15,000 by the creation of 100,000 Ordinary Shares which now stood at 150,000.

The reason for the change, apart from the fact that the total number of shares had been the same since 1905, was to raise the limit of a personal holding to 1,000. In addition, it would create funds for ground improvements. This move was to lead to unexpected sweeping changes, despite all the shares not being taken up by shareholders or supporters.

SIMPLY THE WORST

Mr.Moncur was charged with changing the 'yo-yo' tag attached to Hearts over recent years and for season 1980-1981 he introduced several new players and brought in a completely unknown assistant in Tony Ford. The significance of signing Alex MacDonald at this time was to prove to be much more of a bonus to Hearts in the not too distant future. But the manager had to further enhance a squad that, from the start, struggled in the top ten and brought in Alex Hamill, Gary Liddell and Peter Shields. The fans, however, were more impressed by youngsters Davie Bowman and Gary Mackay.

In the League Cup, Second Round, Montrose lost 2-1 at Tynecastle and 3-1 at home. Then in the Third Round, Hearts faced First Division Ayr United who proved to be our bogey once more, winning 3-2 away and 4-0 at Somerset Park. Not an auspicious start for Bobby Moncur and the term crisis was now being used.

The Anglo Scottish Cup was to prove another disappointment when Hearts lost in the First Round to Airdrieonians by a 6-3 aggregate.

Despite the apparent strengthening of the team, the players failed to blend and 1980-1981 was probably the club's worst ever League campaign with only six victories in 36 matches, the fewest since 1900/1901 when only 20 matches were played. A dismal 27 goals were scored and in addition, by finishing tenth Hearts were at the bottom of the League Table for the first time.

Hearts lost the first two League matches that should have been winnable, against Partick Thistle and Airdrieonians. The team then beat St.Mirren and Kilmarnock – both away – but this was a temporary respite and Hearts failed to win any of their next eleven League fixtures. Coincidently, the run was halted at Tynecastle by a second defeat of Kilmarnock. Hearts went another ten matches without a win until they defeated Rangers 2-1 at Tynecastle on 14 March.

The team's most depressing result was on New Year's Day at Tynecastle. Hearts led Airdrieonians 2-0 with only 18 minutes left to play, but incredibly lost 3-2. This meant that the Lanarkshire team opened up a five point gap at the foot of the table and left Hearts and Kilmarnock in serious relegation trouble. After the Rangers match the team lost four in a row until they again defeated Kilmarnock at Tynecastle on 4 April in a match that produced an un-wanted record, the lowest home attendance at a League match, of 1,866.

Hearts won only two of the final nine League matches and suffered the club's worst Premier defeat, losing 6-0 against Celtic in Glasgow and in the final match of the season lost 4-0 to Rangers at Ibrox Park. Hearts were just not good enough for the Premier Division, with a massive 24 defeats and with only three wins at Tynecastle and the same on their travels.

The Scottish Cup was another major disappointment to all with interests in Hearts when they went out in the Third Round to Greenock Morton. They managed to come away from Greenock with a 0-0 draw but inexplicably lost 3-1 in the Replay.

Hearts even lost the East of Scotland Shield Final for 1978/1979 to First Division, Hibernian. Concluding a horrendous and embarrassing season for all associated with this great club.

Bobby Moncur had already decided to place his faith in young players but would have to develop their talents in the First Division.

Massive safety work requirements on the stand staircases, entrances, exits, toilets and crush barriers were to cost £100,000. The crowd dispersal tunnels at both ends of the ground had to be permanently closed and the capacity of the ground further reduced to 27,169. The income from the new Ordinary Shares earmarked for other improvements was gone. Bench seats for 3,000 spectators were bolted onto the terraces under the enclosure – the shed – opposite the main stand. The Club had intended to incorporate the safety works within a radical plan to create a modern all-seated stadium within a five year period. The overall cost would be approximately £1,000,000 with the first phase amounting to £25,000.

Clearly the Club needed a change of direction and on 21 May 1981 the Articles of Association were changed at an Extraordinary General Meeting when the authorised share capital was increased to £50,000 by the creation of 350,000 Ordinary Shares of 10p – 500,000 at £1. In addition the 1,000 ceiling on shareholding was withdrawn with a view to allowing a major investor to become involved with Hearts.

What happened next was not what Chairman, Archie Martin planned. A late evening meeting was held in the North British Hotel and then it was announced that Mr.Kenny Waugh, a city bookmaker, made an immediate offer for 250,000 shares. When this information became known many Hearts shareholders were annoyed and immediate steps were taken to prevent one major shareholder controlling the Company.

The Evening News and Radio Forth advertised that a meeting for shareholders and supporters was arranged for Monday 25 May 1981 at the Tynecastle Hearts Supporters Club on Slateford Road. The meeting was opened with a statement "If one man controlled the club that would be the end for Hearts".

A proposal was made that 3,500 supporters put in £100 each to raise the cash. More than 100 shareholders and supporters attended and over £60,000 was promised. The meeting elected a Consortium Committee with John Bell, Chairman, Alex Knight, Spokesman and Secretary, Bob Haig, Harry Smith and Alan West then a list of 'pledges' was drawn up for the Committee. The following day their bid was handed in to Hearts by their solicitor Mr. James Stewart. The Committee met that evening and received an updated list of 'pledges'.

Mr. Wallace Mercer of Pentland Securities Limited offered to match Mr. Waugh's bid but faced the same problem that the Board were anxious that no one shareholder should hold a majority of the equity.

An alliance between the Consortium and Pentland Securities was approved after a meeting between Mr.Mercer and the Consortium Committee on condition that two members of the Consortium became directors if both offers were successful.

Having formed such an amorphous group who had never worked together, it was not unexpectedly fraught with problems. Their only connection was a similar goal of saving the Heart of Midlothian Football Club. Arguments, disagreements, threats and withdrawals were all witnessed during a hectic ten days of meetings and press conferences.

Now there were two distinct factions, the Hearts Shareholders Association backed Mr Waugh and the Consortium who had allied themselves with Mr. Mercer.

The Club's records narrate that at a Board Meeting with all directors present on 2 June 1981 "The Board resolved as follows:-

1.   that 255,000 shares be provisionally allotted to Pentland Securities on terms of the application therefor but subject to undertakings being given by or on behalf of the applicant as follows:-

    (i)   "Pentland Securities Limited shall offer to sell sufficient shares as should reduce their shareholding in the company to 25.1% of the authorised share capital, such offer to be made within three months and to remain open for a further three months".

    (ii)   "that so long as Mr. A. Wallace Mercer remained associated with Pentland Securities Limited or any other company in which he might have a substantial shareholding and which might own shares in the Company he would procure that the voting rights attached to the shares to be allotted would not be exercised in favour of any Resolution or Proposal:-
            (a) to amalgamate the Heart of Midlothian Football Club with any other football club;
            (b) to change the name of the Heart of Midlothian Football Club;
            (c) to cease the playing of the game of associated football at Tynecastle Park".

2.   "To provisionally allot to the applicants whose names and addresses are set out in the annexation to this Minute the shares set opposite the name of each applicant in such annexation and aggregating 85,000 shares, each at the price of £1 per share and on the terms of the application therefor, subject to such modification of such terms as the Club's solicitors thought necessary".

        "Mr. McKim said that he hoped he had been able to make some contribution as a Director of the Company, but now that the immediate future of the Company had been secured he felt that he should afford the new major shareholder an opportunity of appointing someone else to the Board and submitted his resignation. Mr. McKim's resignation was very reluctantly at his insistence accepted".

The Club's records further narrate that at a Board Meeting on 3 June 1981 "it was agreed that Mr. Martin should step down as Chairman to be replaced by Mr. Naylor". Then at another Board Meeting on 9 June 1981 "it was noted that Mr. Martin had resigned from the Board on Friday 5 June 1981".

Clause 1 (i) of the Board's resolution of 2 June was to prove a major stumbling block over the following months having never been implemented and Pentland Securities Limited failed to offer to reduce its shareholding to 25.1%. Mr. Naylor, Mr. Haig and Mr. Watt subsequently resigned in 1982.

On 15 June 1981 a meeting of all those who had made 'pledges' met in the Tynecastle Hearts Supporters Club, to elect two nominee directors. Alan West withdrew from the election as he head previously reduced his "pledge". Only 63 members were in attendance but there was confusion as Pilmar Smith, who had not previously made himself known as an interested party until that evening, and who was not on the pledges list, stood at the behest of Mr. Mercer to replace Alan West. Bob Haig polled 23 votes, Alex Knight 21 votes and Pilmar Smith 19 votes.

Only Bob Haig's name went forward, in breach of the alliance between the Consortium and Pentland Securities Limited, to the Hearts AGM on 29 July. Manager Bobby Moncur resigned on 22 June 1981 and the new Board faced their first major challenge.

NO QUICK RETURN

The 1981-1982 season began with the Board promising to do all in their power to see Hearts were promoted to the Premier Division at the end of the campaign, but failed to bring in Jim McLean as manager. Instead, Tony Ford, who had been Bobby Moncur's assistant, was appointed Manager with Walter Borthwick as his assistant. Some astute signings, most notably Roddy MacDonald – Celtic and Henry Smith – Leeds United were made by him and great things were expected to happen.

The League Cup went back to its Qualifying Section format, played during August, but Hearts failed to progress against Aberdeen, Airdrieonians and Kilmarnock and things did not look promising for the League matches.

Hearts found the First Division was not going to be a straightforward matter. They made a stuttering start and did not produce a win until the fourth match. Action was taken and Derek Addison and Willie Pettigrew – Dundee United were recruited (£159,850). Although points were steadily accumulated, Hearts did not dominate as expected in the League. Matters took a turn for the worse on 31 October when East Stirlingshire won 1-0 at Tynecastle. Only one match was won out of the following six matches and in December, when Queen's Park stole a 1-1 draw at Tynecastle the small crowd were distinctly unhappy.

Something had to give and four days later Mr. Ford was dismissed. Hearts were only two points adrift of second place, however, the Board decided to make changes and appointed the experienced Alex MacDonald as player/coach who faced a hard task in leading the club to promotion.

Bad weather led to a shut-down for almost two months and when play resumed on 30 January the team went down 3-0 at home to Motherwell. This left Hearts sixth in the League, 11 points off the pace and five behind Clydebank in the second promotion place. But the directors promoted Alex MacDonald to player-manager in February and results improved. During the bad weather, the lack of income resulted in the club not paying the balance of the Addison/Pettigrew fee to Dundee United. Results improved and the team won 12 of the next 15 League matches but during the fine run, several players were picking up cautions and this would eventually hit hard.

With three matches left against Dumbarton, Kilmarnock and Motherwell, three points were required for promotion, but the pressure was on, due to injuries and the inevitable suspensions. Against Dumbarton at Tynecastle Hearts were leading 2-1 at half-time and stunned their fans when they collapsed in the second half and lost four goals without reply.

Hearts had to face the other two promotion challengers and at Rugby Park were without several players through suspension but forced a 0-0 draw with ten men. For the final match of the season at home to Motherwell, a win was required if the club was to go back to the Premier Division but they went down 1-0. Hearts took full points from Hamilton Academical, Queen of the South and Raith Rovers, but Motherwell and Kilmarnock were promoted when Hearts finished in third place.

An early exit from the Scottish Cup was expected but not they way it happened. In the Third Round, East Stirlingshire lost 4-1 at Firs Park. The Fourth Round brought Forfar Athletic to Tynecastle and a famous defeat by 1-0. This was one of the worst results in the club's history as Hearts had never lost to a lower level team at home in the Scottish Cup.

The only glimpse of sun on the horizon was the success in winning the Shield for the first time since 1976 in defeating Meadowbank Thistle 5-0.

The Heart of Midlothian Football Club was registered as a Public Limited Company on 8 April 1982.

Having made a substantial investment in new players over the season, failure to gain promotion was a hugely damaging blow for the club. Faced with another season in the First Division the Board had to wrestle with some difficult financial challenges, with the well publicised debt to Dundee United and Celtic. However failure to clear these debts led to an SFA ban on purchasing players.

Douglas Park bought 75,000 shares from Pentland Securities which meant they had, therefore, reduced their shareholding to 43% and Mr. Park became a director.

Alex MacDonald released a number of fringe players and turned his full attention to the development of the club's young players.

THE TIDE TURNS

Hearts had lost over £300,000 during the financial year and the debt was over £500,000. As a result the club was forced to sell Derek Addison to St.Johnstone.

For the start of the 1982-1983 season Alex MacDonald had Sandy Jardine as assistant player/manager. A unique combination in British football and Alexanders of Edinburgh – Ford Car dealers – added to the novelty as the Club's first ever shirt sponsor. Other new moves were the creation of an Executive Club with seats in an extended area next to the directors' box, and a players' lounge was created from within the offices and rooms under the main stand. This venture was mainly financed by the advance payment of three year's subscription from the Executive Club Members.

In the League Cup, the opponents in their Section were Clyde, Forfar Athletic and Motherwell and they managed to get some revenge over Forfar and Motherwell and recorded a devastating 7-1 victory over Clyde at Shawfield Stadium, where Willie Pettigrew scored four goals. Hearts won their Section and in the Quarter-Finals, put St.Mirren out of the competition after a 1-1 draw at Paisley and a 2-1 win at Tynecastle. A novelty that evening was the first ever free raffle, the draw at half-time allowed the top prizewinner to drive off in a Ford Fiesta car.

Hearts then met Rangers over two matches in the Semi-Finals and although the team fought well at Ibrox Park they went down 2-0. At Tynecastle the return match was lost 2-1 but the highlight for many in the crowd was a competition in the match programme "Win a FREE £35,000 Miller Home & Ford Sierra (supplied by Alexanders)".

The League campaign started well with a 2-1 win over Queen's Park at Hampden Park, leading to no defeats in the first six matches. Only Raith Rovers managed to beat Hearts during the next eleven fixtures and already, the Tynecastle men looked favourites for promotion, although they were second in the table, as a result of several draws. A 4-2 defeat at Tynecastle by Airdrieonians in November was followed an away 3-0 victory over Clydebank.

The team put together another fine run of nine unbeaten matches including a 1-0 defeat of St.Johnstone – the main promotion rivals – on New Year's Day. John Robertson began to show his goalscoring aptitude when he scored a hat-trick against Queen's Park at Hampden Park on 26 February and another treble as Partick Thistle lost 4-0 at Tynecastle on 19 March, finishing the season as top marksman with 21 goals. Most teams were motivated against Hearts and there were a few slip-ups that stopped Hearts from totally dominating the First Division.

Clydebank, Partick Thistle and St.Johnstone were all involved in the promotion battle but only Clydebank failed to win one match against Hearts.

The players produced a strong finish and promotion was clinched after the penultimate fixture at Boghead Park when Dumbarton lost 4-0. Full points from the three matches were taken from Airdrieonians, Clyde, Hamilton Academical and Queens Park, and Hearts finished in second place to St.Johnstone but promotion was gained. The future was brighter. Significantly, only 17 players had been used in the League, four of whom were ever present: Henry Smith, Sandy Jardine, Roddy MacDonald and Davie Bowman.

Hearts entered the Scottish Cup in the Third Round where they met Queen of the South and drew 1-1 at Dumfries but won the Replay in Gorgie by 1-0. The Fourth Round opponents were East Fife and they were defeated 2-1 at Tynecastle on a Sunday. The Quarter-Finals brought Celtic and Hearts together in Glasgow. Once again controversy marred the 4-1 Celtic victory. Peter Shields was carried off early in the match after a bad tackle then Willie Johnston was red-carded for an offence that no Edinburgh fan could fathom.

A sponsors lounge was built within the main stand taking up some of the North Stand seats plus the area beneath.

PRIDE RESTORED

As season 1983-1984 dawned there were reservations at to whether Hearts could end their 'yo-yo' form and survive on their return to the Premier Division. The players 'punched above their weight' and the club enjoyed its best season to date in the 'top ten'. Indeed, the team performed so well, that Hearts qualified for a place in the UEFA Cup.

The club was still banned from buying players and again had to work in the free transfer market bringing in Jimmy Bone, George Cowie and Donald Park.

The League Cup had yet another new format of home and away matches in the Preliminary Round and Hearts defeated Cowdenbeath on penalties after two draws 0-0 away and a 1-1 at home. The manager spotted a quality player in these matches and a few months later, Craig Levein moved to Hearts from Central Park. The League Cup then reverted to a long drawn out Section with Hearts Clydebank, Rangers and St.Mirren. In the first four fixtures, Hearts lost home and away to Rangers and could only draw with St.Mirren away and Clydebank at home – the team was effectively out of the competition.

The League campaign started brilliantly with five consecutive wins, three away from home, against St.Johnstone, Dundee and St.Mirren. The two home victories were significant with Rangers being defeated 3-1 and the other being a dazzling 3-2 win over Hibernian. John Robertson scored twice, to start his unbelievable record of goals against Hibernian, and Jimmy Bone scored the winner. The run came to an end with a 2-0 home defeat from Aberdeen – the team had laid the foundation for a successful season.

League results were mixed until the turn of the year, but the supporters recognised the improvement and attendances were at long last growing in support of the team. Through November and December, Hearts had a lean spell with only one win in nine matches and this took them close to the relegation zone. New Year brought a 1-1 draw against Hibernian at Tynecastle but they had set backs at Dens Park and Celtic Park in January. The team only lost one of the last eleven League fixtures and when Celtic were held to a 1-1 draw on 5 May at Tynecastle the Hearts were assured of a place in Europe.

Most of the matches were keenly fought and 16 were drawn but the "maroons" were undefeated against Hibernian, Motherwell, St.Johnstone and St.Mirren. Goals were hard to come by with Hearts scoring only 38 all season. and finishing in fifth place.

The Scottish Cup journey was a short one as Hearts entered at the Third Round and defeated Partick Thistle 2-0 at Tynecastle but in the Fourth Round lost 2-1 to Dundee United at Tannadice Park.

In the East of Scotland Shield, Hearts lost to Berwick Rangers in the Semi-Finals of the 1982/1983 competition and in the Semi-Finals for 1983/1984. Time was running out for this old competition as clubs preferred not to play their top team.

Playing in the Premier Division brought out the supporters in greater numbers resulting in a trading profit for the first time in ten years.

During the close season new crush barriers were erected and a new capacity of 27,093 was set and the floodlighting system was brought up to date.

WE RETURN TO EUROPE

Throughout season 1984-1985 players were released and others added to the First team squad. Jimmy Bone, Willie Johnston, Stewart McLaren and Derek O'Connor were allowed to leave. Neil Berry – Bolton Wanderers, Kenny Black – Motherwell, Sandy Clark – Rangers and Brian Whittaker – Celtic, came in as replacements. Naturally the changes unsettled the team until the blend was perfected.

The League Cup format for this season consisted of a knock-out up to the Quarter-Finals stage. Hearts entered in the Second Round and defeated East Stirlingshire 4-0 at Tynecastle. The Third round saw Hearts at home again and Ayr United lost 1-0. In the Quarter-Finals, Hearts played Dundee at Dens Park and won 1-0 then met their neighbours Dundee United in a two-legged Semi-Final. At Tynecastle Hearts lost 2-1 and in the second leg at Tannadice Park, the home side cruised to a 3-1 victory.

Hearts initial appearance in the UEFA Cup was their first venture into Europe for eight years and they were drawn against very strong opposition in Paris St.Germain. The First Round, First Leg, was played in the Parc des Princess and Hearts lost heavily 4-0 to a slick pacey team. Nevertheless, a large crowd turned up to watch the Second Leg at Tynecastle and the players salvaged some pride with an honourable 2-2 draw.

In the League Hearts lost six of the first eight matches which caused a lot of concern. Memories of relegation were never far from the minds of the faithful. But there was a smile on their faces when one of the wins was against Hibernian – 2-1 at Easter Road. After the spirited performance against Paris St.Germain in October the team went on a run of five wins and a draw. This included a splendid 1-0 win over Rangers at Tynecastle followed by a 2-0 defeat of Dundee United at Tannadice Park. The run was halted by Celtic winning 5-1 at Tynecastle on 17 November and this roller coaster season continued with a poor sequence of results. It was not helped by the transfer of Davie Bowman to Coventry City in December.

The festive period saw Hearts produce three successive wins – Greenock Morton 1-0, Hibernian 2-1 and Dumbarton 5-1 but after that form was patchy and the team won only three of the last 14 matches which included losing the final five matches. Dumbarton lost all four matches and Hibernian failed to defeat Hearts but by losing 64 goals and only scoring 47 Hearts finished in a poor seventh place.

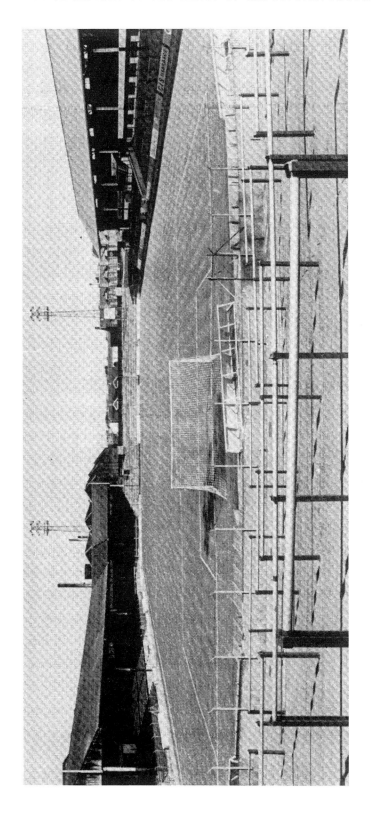

Tynecastle – 1984

Jimmy Bone scored Hearts 6,000th League goal in their 3,069th.League match, on the 15 December 1984 in a 5-2 defeat by Dundee United at Tannadice Park.

Over the week-end of 21/22 January 1985 Hearts won the Tennents' Six-a-side tournament at Ingliston by defeating Greenock Morton 4-1 in the Final.

The Scottish Cup was Hearts chance to prove their worth and in the Third Round, they defeated Caledonian FC 6-0 at Tynecastle, and Gary Mackay scored four goals that day. In the Fourth Round, Hearts travelled to Glebe Park to face Brechin City on a tricky pitch and were fortunate to snatch a 1-1 draw. The replay at Tynecastle saw another tense encounter end in a 1-0 win for Hearts. The Quarter-Finals brought together Aberdeen and Hearts who were held to a draw at Tynecastle and lost the replay 1-0 at Pittodrie Park with Hearts down to ten men.

Hundreds of Hearts supporters were locked out when Aberdeen inexplicably allowed their supporters to gain admission to the area allocated to Hearts supporters.

The East of Scotland Shield, first competed for in 1875/1876 as the Edinburgh FA Cup, had now been downgraded from a first team fixture.

The North Enclosure was seated and converted into a 1,000 seated Family Enclosure.

SO NEAR AND YET SO FAR

A successful pre-season five match tour in Germany was the pre-curser to an exciting yet dramatic season and the defining feature was the regularity of team selection with a squad of players all of whom were above average and laced with stars augmented by the signing of John Colquhoun – Celtic. Sadly, the dream of an audacious League and Cup double was snatched away during the final eight days. Hearts had won nothing but the greatest respect and the club regained its traditional place among the elite of Scottish football.

In season 1985-1986 Hearts entered the League Cup in the Third Round when they met Montrose at Links Park and won 3-1. The Fourth Round draw saw Hearts at home against Stirling Albion with a 2-1 win to their credit. The Quarter-Finals brought an away match against Aberdeen at Pittodrie Park where the home side were victors by a narrow 1-0 score.

The League campaign got off to stuttering start with the team drawing with Celtic 1-1 at Tynecastle, losing away to St.Mirren 6-2 and Rangers 3-1, before a 2-1 victory over Hibernian at Tynecastle. However, the main thrust came on 5 October when Dundee drew 1-1 at Tynecastle, after which Hearts went a further 26 matches without defeat up to the final match of the Championship. This season Hearts defeated Hibernian three times and drew once and won three matches and lost one against – Motherwell, Rangers and St.Mirren while Celtic and Dundee United failed to win any of the four matches.

Even the Glasgow based media started to take note of the "maroons" form. Advantage was taken when other clubs had to postpone matches due to International commitments and as the season came to a conclusion Hearts were nine points ahead of major challengers Celtic. They had 50 points and a goal difference of +28 – Celtic had 48 points and a goal difference of +24. The team only had to avoid defeat to be Champions but the squad was hit by a virus that week and with players out and others suffering from the after effects of the virus the team was not at full strength.

Hearts were denied a blatant penalty early in the match that might have steadied the nerves but it was not to

FIRST TEAM SQUAD 1985/1986 Standing Back Row – S. Clark, M. Murray, R. MacDonald, B. Whittaker, C. Levein, N. Berry, I. Jardine.
Standing Middle Row – I. Binnie-Coach, A. Watson, J. Sandison, H. Smith, B. McNaughtan, G. Cowie, W. Borthwick-Coach.
Seated – A. MacDonald-Manager, J. Colquhoun, G. Mackay, W. Kidd-Captain, K. Black, J. Robertson, S. Jardine-Asst. Manager.

be and anxiety eventually crept in. Dundee who had drawn twice with Hearts that season scored twice in the final seven minutes of play. The collapse of Celtic's opponents St.Mirren in their final match handed them the title and the "maroons" ended up in second place.

The gallant squad was:- Henry Smith 36 appearances 14 shut-outs, John Colquhoun 36 appearances 8 goals, John Robertson 35/20, Sandy Jardine 35/-, Sandy Clark 33/12, Craig Levein 33/2, Gary Mackay 32/4, Neil Berry 32/2, Kenny Black 29/2, Walter Kidd 28/-, Brian Whittaker 25/-, Iain Jardine 23/7, Andy Watson 12/-, Roddy MacDonald 10/2, George Cowie 8/-, Paul Cherry 5/-, Colin McAdam 5/-, Brian McNaughton 4/-, Billy Mackay 3/-, Jimmy Sandison 3/-, Alex MacDonald 1/-.

The Scottish Cup was just as exciting and disappointing as the Championship. In the Third Round, Hearts were drawn against Rangers at Tynecastle and in front of a packed house defeated them 3-2 in a thrilling match. The Fourth Round saw Hearts defeat Hamilton Academical 2-1 at Douglas Park. In the Quarter-Finals at Tynecastle Hearts won easily, 4-1 although St.Mirren had lost their goalkeeper through injury early in the match.

The Semi-Final was played at Hampden Park against Dundee United and they proved stubborn opponents, however, Hearts gained a sound 1-0 victory. The Final at Hampden Park came only seven days after that demoralising League defeat in Dundee and the odds were stacked against Hearts. Could they overcome their disappointment and defeat Aberdeen for the first time in a Scottish Cup match? Sadly, the answer was no and Aberdeen romped home 3-0. They scored after five minutes and again early in the second half and after Walter Kidd was sent off following a second yellow card they scored again.

The team was:- Henry Smith; Walter Kidd-captain, Sandy Jardine, Craig Levein and Brian Whittaker; Gary Mackay, Neil Berry and Kenny Black; John Colquhoun, Sandy Clark and John Robertson.

This was Hearts' best season for 21 years when the title was also lost on the final day. However, the team had given the fans many special moments and Alex MacDonald was deservedly voted Premier Division Manager of the Year. The squad was treated to an end-of-season tour of the West Indies, where three wins were recorded in challenge matches.

The former police station was bought for commercial offices for £33,000 plus the access roadway 7/9 McLeod Street for £500. A restaurant was created in the concourse between the North and Centre Stands with seats in a further extended area next to the director's box. In 1988 this facility was named the William Younger restaurant in recognition of their sponsorship.

ANOTHER HANGOVER

A tournament in the Isle of Man launched the 1986-1987 season and a new 12 club Premier Division. The only new face to join the first team squad was Wayne Foster – Preston North End as the whole club tried to recover from the trauma of the previous campaign.

The League Cup, Second Round match against Montrose, at Tynecastle, on 19 August 1986 was Hearts fourth of the season and after two victories and a draw they unforgivably lost 2-0. The supporters were shocked, as this defeat also ended a 15 month unbeaten home record.

As runners up in the League last season Hearts entered the UEFA Cup and in the First Round, First Leg at Tynecastle defeated Dukla Prague 3-2 in a very strenuous tight match. These two away goals by Dukla were crucial. In the Second Leg in Czechoslovakia the players fought hard and unluckily went down 1-0 to go out – yet again – on the 'away goals' rule.

The League was to be the measure of a club that had come so close to success without reward. Hearts had the players although the club needed to prove that it was not a one season wonder. A reasonable start saw Hearts win twelve – including defeating Aberdeen home and away and lost only four times in the first 22 matches – Hamilton Academical lost 7-0 – Heart's greatest Premier result – Falkirk 4-0 and Clydebank 3-0 all at Tynecastle but they lost five in the second 22.

There was not to be the same fluency in their play compared to the previous season. A serious knee injury to Craig Levein in October ruined his season and gravely reduced Hearts composure. Rangers were heading for the title and when they defeated Hearts 5-2 at Tynecastle on 7 February the race for the title was beyond the "maroons". The Tynecastle squad was too tight for this marathon season and Rangers larger squad lost only six matches over the entire 44 match programme.

Hearts did defeat Celtic in both home matches and Hamilton Academical lost all four matches. The team were undefeated against Clydebank, Hibernian, Motherwell and St. Mirren but finished fifth and failed to make the UEFA Cup place.

The Scottish Cup was all that was left to fight for, and they did. In the Third Round, Hearts met Kilmarnock at Tynecastle but drew 0-0. In the Replay at Rugby Park there was a 1-1 draw at full time and after extra time. The Second Replay was again at Kilmarnock but this time Hearts won 3-1. The Fourth Round produced an epic 1-0 victory over Celtic at Tynecastle, the winner coming from a free-kick in the 80th. minute. This earned a home tie in the Quarter-Finals against Motherwell and after a 1-1 draw the tie was settled at Fir Park by the only goal in 1-0 victory.

Hearts went into the Semi-Final against St.Mirren at Hampden Park, without six of their main players due to injury and suspensions. However, after going a goal down they equalised but the team was hit by a goal on the break and lost 2-1.

The season was finished off with a four match tour of the west coast of America with two wins and two draws.

In the close season the players' tunnel onto the pitch was moved further south and a Business Club was opened with private seating in part of the South Enclosure. New turnstiles were installed at McLeod Street and Wheatfield Street and the family enclosure increased to seat 1,500.

The Heart of Midlothian Associates Club in its present form could no longer continue and were given one months notice.

In July there was a pre-season tour to Germany and in the five matches against varied levels of opponents there were three wins, one draw and one defeat.

SECOND BEST AGAIN

During the summer Hugh Burns – and Dave McPherson – £325,000 were signed from Rangers. George Cowie, Roddy MacDonald and Andy Watson were allowed to leave and Mike Galloway – Halifax Town FC came in November.

In the 1987-1988 season the club was again respected as power in the land but Celtic proved too consistent and won the Championship.

In the League Cup, Second Round, Hearts met Kilmarnock, yet again, and at Tynecastle won easily by 6-1. The Third Round gave Hearts another home tie and they despatched Clyde 2-0. The Fourth Round was their downfall when they played poorly against Rangers at Ibrox Park and deservedly lost 4-1.

The League was anticipated with some confidence by the supporters. Without the distraction of playing in a European Competition and a good pre-season workout they felt the team were ready to perform well.

The first match was an entertaining 4-2 win against Falkirk at Tynecastle but was followed by a 1-0 defeat by Celtic in Glasgow with an 86th.minute goal. The team bounced back and recorded a 4-1 victory over Dundee United and a 1-0 defeat of Hibernian in consecutive weeks at Tynecastle and they did not lose any of the following seven matches. The fans were delighted when the team went to the top of the Division after defeating Aberdeen 2-1 at Tynecastle on 7 October. Unfortunately the run was ended at Easter Road on 17 October with a 2-1 defeat the first in 18 matches against Hibernian since March 1979.

In the match against Rangers at Tynecastle on 16 January the 1-1 draw was marred by a recurrence of Craig Levein's knee injury. Hearts only lost five matches all season but too many draws – 16 – saw them fall well behind the eventual Champions Celtic who lost only three matches over the entire 44 match campaign. Dunfermline Athletic lost all four matches and Aberdeen, Dundee United and Motherwell were the teams who failed to defeat Hearts who finished in second place.

Tynecastle Park Tynecastle Terrace 1988

The Scottish Cup began with a 3-1 win over Falkirk in the Third Round at Brockville Park. In the Fourth Round, Greenock Morton visited Gorgie and lost 2-0. The Quarter-Finals tie was at home and saw Hearts defeat Dunfermline Athletic 3-0. Hearts were in the Semi-Finals for the third season in succession and faced Celtic at Hampden Park. With a lead of 1-0 going in to the final minutes Hearts looked set for another final only to lose two quick goals in the dying minutes. Henry Smith was clearly barged at both goals. It was hard to believe that either goal was legitimate, far less both, or that the "breaks even out" against the Old Firm. These brave players seemed destined never to win trophies.

Gary Mackay made his first appearance for Scotland in a Full International, as a substitute, on 11 November 1987 against Bulgaria and scored in a 1-0 win at Vasili Levski Stadium, Sofia.

Gary was the first Hearts player to appear for Scotland in a Full International since Jim Cruickshank in December 1975 and the first to score for Scotland since Alex Young in November 1960.

John Colquhoun and Henry Smith made their first appearance for Scotland in a Full International, as substitutes, on 17 February 1988 against Saudi Arabia in a 2-2 draw at Malaz Stadium, (King Fahd) Riahd.

John Robertson was transferred to Newcastle United, at the end of the season, for £700,000.

EUROSTARS

Before season 1988-1989 was begun the Business Club was renamed the Private Members' Club.

With the departure of John Robertson a replacement was required and was filled by Iain Ferguson – Dundee United (£325,000) but he alone could not make the improvement necessary and once more Hearts started to go backwards. Eamonn Bannon – Dundee United returned to Hearts and in December John Robertson returned from Newcastle United, for a new record transfer fee (£750,000) and Tosh McKinlay arrived from Dundee.

Hearts were back in European competition and great things were expected, with several players having already experienced playing in the UEFA Cup. In the First Round, First Leg, Hearts made the short journey to Dublin where they readily disposed of St.Patrick's Athletic by 2-0. The same result came in the Second Leg in Gorgie and Hearts went in to the draw for the Second Round. In the First Leg they met FK Austria Memphis at home drawing 0-0 in a tight match with no great play on show.

Prior to the return match the Directors decided on 2 November that the Co-Managership was not functioning and agreed that Sandy Jardine's contract be cancelled.

In the Second Leg in the Wiener Stadion, Vienna, the players silenced the critics of the home draw by winning 1-0 in another close match. The Third Round saw Hearts drawn against Velez Mostar of Yugoslavia. The First Leg was at Tynecastle and the team used home advantage to good effect, winning 3-0. This gave Hearts a sound base for the Second Leg which was played in a very hostile atmosphere both on the pitch and in the town after the match. Hearts resisted the temptation to 'mix it' and came away with a 2-1 defeat and entry into the Quarter-Finals.

It was Hearts best achievement in European Competitions, and at this level, had to meet strong opponents. This they did when drawn to meet FC Bayern and once again the First Leg was at home and a narrow 1-0 victory was achieved – keeping the dream alive. The Second leg in the Olympic Stadium, was going well for

Hearts but the manager failed to use his star strikers – Ferguson and Robertson and with two goals down lesser marksmen failed to score from three golden opportunities to gain victory.

The League Cup began in the Second Round for Hearts and they had a handsome 5-0 victory over St.Johnstone with Iain Ferguson scoring a hat-trick. In the Third Round Hearts were drawn against Meadowbank Thistle and because of safety concerns, should it be played at their home ground at Meadowbank Commonwealth Stadium, the match was played at Brockville Park, Falkirk. Hearts duly won 2-0 to go forward to the Quarter-Finals for the fifth time in six seasons. Dunfermline Athletic at East End Park did not cause any problems and Hearts won 4-1.

In contrast to the mediocre performances in the League Hearts reached the Semi-Finals but played poorly and lost 3-0 to Rangers at Hampden Park.

The League had reverted to ten clubs and a 36 match championship for season 1988/1989 but Hearts were not much of a threat to the top sides.

On 1 November Hearts lost 3-0 to Rangers in Glasgow and were third bottom of the League. As a result Sandy Jardine left the club and maintained they had been deprived of cash for players and Douglas Park resigned as a director as, according to press reports, he felt the club was not run on a democratic basis and that there was no collective planning or voting.

The next match against Rangers at Tynecastle on 10 December was a 'teethy' affair which Hearts won 2-0, and was one of the few highlights of the season. The team was inconsistent and only twice were they able to win two consecutive matches. They lost all four matches against Celtic and drew all four matches against Dundee United but did win all four matches against Hamilton Academical. Nine wins all season and a pitiful scoring record of 35 goals in 36 matches meant Hearts finished in sixth place.

The Scottish Cup did nothing to ease the pain of an average season but in the Third Round, a 4-1 defeat of Ayr United at Tynecastle raised hopes. The Fourth Round draw saw Hearts against Partick Thistle at Tynecastle where the home side won 2-0. Hearts then met Celtic in the Quarter-Finals in Glasgow and were defeated 2-1 after a stormy match in which they lost Craig Levein through injury. For the umpteenth time against Celtic it seemed they were immune to being disciplined, and it was Hearts who had two players sent-off to their one, in the inevitable Celtic Park shambles, a defeat was in many ways a gallant result.

Dave McPherson made his first appearance for Scotland in a Full International on the 26 April 1989 against Cyprus in a 2-1 win at Hampden Park, Glasgow.

A Premier Suite was built using the William Younger Restaurant and part of a new office construction in the Main Stand. The former billiard room/Hearts Associates room in the South Stand was renamed the William Younger Suite.

The Office Bearers of the HMSA were invited to meet Mr. & Mrs. Mercer at their home during the evening of 5 January 1989. They discussed the names of new shareholders, the forward strategy and the fact that they were unable, as a family, to continue to invest more money to maintain Hearts. The increase in competition from other wealthier clubs saw the gap growing year on year.

SEVEN INTERNATIONALS 1990 Back Row – David McCreery (Northern Ireland), Henry Smith (Scotland), Husref Musemic (Yugoslavia).
Front Row – Eamonn Bannon (Scotland), John Colquhoun (Scotland), Gary Mackay (Scotland), Dave McPherson (Scotland).

BACK AMONG THE CHALLENGERS

For season 1989-1990 players were allowed to leave and new ones brought in to freshen up the First Team Squad. Kenny Black went to Portsmouth and Mike Galloway went to Celtic. Davie Kirkwood – Rangers, David McCreery – GIF Sundsvall, Husref Musemic – Red Star Belgrade and Nicky Walker – Rangers were the new men.

In the League Cup, Second Round Hearts met Montrose at Tynecastle and had a comfortable 3-0 win. This was followed in the Third Round at Brockville Park against Falkirk and Hearts won comfortably 4-1 in a stormy contest. The Quarter-Finals brought Celtic to Gorgie and a dramatic contest in which Hearts were losing 2-1 with only minutes left of extra-time to play. They equalised but the delight of the crowd was dashed when in the subsequent penalty shoot out Celtic won 3-1.

David McCreery made his first appearance for Northern Ireland in a Full International, as a Hearts player, on 6 September 1989 against Hungary in a 2-1 defeat at Windsor Park Belfast.

The League Championship was the goal this season, to make up for too many fallow seasons. Hearts had a poor start losing the opening fixture 3-1 to Celtic at Tynecastle, then went on a run of five matches without defeat including a 1-0 defeat of Hibernian at Tynecastle. By 11 November when they defeated Dundee 6-3 at Tynecastle Hearts were top of the League winning seven of the first 14 matches.

Inconsistency – Hearts middle name in the 1930's – raised its ugly head and despite starting off on a run of only one defeat from the remaining 15 matches, after beating Hibernian 2-0 on New Years Day, it was too late. Only eight matches were lost but with twelve drawn matches the team was out of contention for the title. They failed to beat either of the" Old Firm" and Motherwell lost all four matches. Aberdeen, Dundee and Hibernian could not record a win over the "maroons". Hearts qualified for Europe after finishing in third place, in the table.

With the team playing well the Scottish Cup was the next target and in the Third Round, Hearts met Falkirk at Tynecastle and won 2-0. In the Fourth Round they were at home again and this time defeated Motherwell 4-0. The Quarter-Finals meant Hearts had to face Aberdeen at Pittodrie Park, their bogey team in Scottish Cup matches. They unaccountably collapsed despite going in 1-1 at half time and starting the second half on top, but Aberdeen picked up and swept to a 4-1 victory.

On 22 February 1990 Hearts registered a subsidiary company, Heart of Midlothian Commercial Limited and on 2 March 1990 they registered another subsidiary company, Heart of Midlothian Publishing Limited. Both were more of a hindrance than a help and provided no value whatsoever before being discarded.

In May the Directors decided to proceed with a bid to acquire the entire issued Share Capital of Edinburgh Hibernian Plc. The bid to take over Hibernian Football Club Limited was announced by Mr.Mercer. But later, despite gaining 67% of the equity the bid was withdrawn under death threats to the Chairman, and demonstrations and acrimonious resistance against the bid by Hearts and Hibernian players and supporters. Relations between the clubs were damaged for many years.

Craig Levein made his first appearance for Scotland in a Full International on 28 March 1990 against Argentina in a 1-0 win at Hampden Park, Glasgow.

During the close season plans were announced for a 30,000 seated stadium at Millerhill in conjunction with hotels, retail and industrial outlets plus a secondary stadium. The planning application was rejected by

Lothian Regional Council in November. A revised application for a 25,000 seated stadium at Millerhill without warehousing etc was then submitted.

There were changes to the stadium with the South Enclosure being fully seated. The Main Stand now held 5,191 but the overall capacity was reduced to 25,605.

In October the Private Member's Club was converted into the Willie Bauld Restaurant. The previous Members retained their seats.

John Robertson made his first appearance for Scotland in a Full International on 12 September 1990 against Romania and scored in a 2-1 win at Hampden Park, Glasgow.

The Hillsborough Stadium Disaster Inquiry under Lord Taylor led to 76 recommendations applicable in England and Wales but applied in Scotland through the Scottish Secretary of State. All seated stadia for English 1st.and 2nd.Division Clubs and Scottish Premier Clubs and standing eliminated by August 1994 through the Football Licensing Authority.

Plans for, a stand alone, 30,000 seated stadium at Hermiston was submitted to Lothian Regional Council. The applications for Millerhill and Hermiston were rejected by the Council in December.

Derek Ferguson joined Hearts from Rangers for £750,000.

HEARTS MAKE NEWS

Strenuous and unwise pre-season tournaments, in Romania then Spain, led to health problems and it took several weeks for some players to fully recover. This was considered to be the cause of a poor 1990-1991 season of results on all fronts.

In the League Cup Hearts entered in the Second Round and met Cowdenbeath at East End Park, Dunfermline and went on to win 2-0. In the Third Round they met St.Mirren in Paisley and won 1-0. The Quarter Finals were their downfall once more and Aberdeen, their masters in Cup matches, won 3-0 at Pittodrie Park.

In the UEFA Cup, Hearts were drawn against Dnepr of the USSR and gave the Club and its supporters their first opportunity to travel to the Ukraine for the First Round, First Leg and came home with a credible 1-1 draw. In the Second Leg, Tynecastle was set alight by an unbelievable performance by all 13 players who took part in Hearts 3-1 victory. In the Second Round, First Leg, Hearts met Bologna in Edinburgh and won 3-1, they opened the scoring in six minutes and were 3-0 up at half-time. The only disappointment, being the loss, once more, of an away goal, which had been their downfall, so many times in the past. In the Second Leg it proved to be the case and they went out of the competition by losing 3-0 and 3-4 on aggregate.

A mixed start to the League campaign a 1-1 home draw against St.Mirren followed by defeats away to Dunfermline Athletic and at home to Rangers. That 3-1 reverse against Rangers on top of the League Cup failure led to Manager, Alex MacDonald being dismissed in September and Joe Jordan appointed in his place. The players lost a popular manager.

As fate would direct the next match was against Hibernian at Easter Road and stand-in boss Sandy Clark urged the disappointed players to a 3-0 victory. As relations between the two sets of supporters was still tense there were several crowd incidents and John Robertson was even attacked on the field leading to the referee taking the players off the field until order was restored.

There was no immediate improvement in the League matches after the new manager took over. In fact before going to Bologona on 7 November Hearts were bottom of the table. On returning home they defeated Celtic 1-0 three days later, at Tynecastle on 10 November – their first defeat of the "celts" since April 1988. The festive period went well with Motherwell losing 3-2 at Tyencastle, a draw against Celtic in Glasgow and crushing 4-1 defeat of Hibernian at Easter Road at New Year.

However, the supporters were satisfied in winning three and drawing one of the four matches against Hibernian, for the second season running. In addition they won three and drew one with Motherwell, but lost all four to Rangers and finished in fifth place – missing out on Europe.

On 24 January 1991 a full report about the various options open to the Club for new stadia or redevelopment of Tynecastle was discussed by the directors covering Ingliston, Hermiston, Bilston Glen, Straiton Caravan Car Park, The Drum, Newton Farm/Millerhill and Murrayfield.

Hearts entered the Scottish Cup in the Second Round and it proved to be a non-event with them losing 2-1 to Airdrieonians at Broomfield Park despite having the bulk of possession.

Over the week-end of 20/21January 1991 Hearts won the Tennents Six-a-side tournament at Ingliston defeating Motherwell 4-3.

On 26 August 1991 Pentland Securities (Holdings) Limited, reminded the Directors that since November 1988 Heart of Midlothian had been a subsidiary of theirs and proposed that the Management Fee be increased from £50,000 to £100,000 per annum. The Board agreed that the request be supported.

THE CLUB REGROUP

Season 1991-1992 saw Joe Jordan in charge for the first full season and great things were expected by the supporters. John Colquhoun, Walter Kidd, David Kirkwood, David McCreery and Brian Whittaker had gone. Ian Baird – Middlesbrough, Ian Ferguson – Raith Rovers, John Millar – Blackburn Rovers came in and later Graeme Hogg – Portsmouth and Glynn Snodin – Rotherham United were recruited.

Hearts entered the League Cup in the Second Round and met Clydebank at Tynecastle to run out 3-0 winners. They travelled in the Third Round to Douglas Park, and defeated Hamilton Academical 2-0. In the Quarter-Finals their opponents Rangers came to Tynecastle and won 1-0 in a very close match.

The Premier Division contained twelve teams yet again producing a marathon 44 match Championship. Hearts League campaign got off to a good start when they failed to lose any of their first nine matches. An early highlight was a 1-0 defeat of Rangers in a tight, tough encounter at Tynecastle on 17 August when Scott Crabbe caught Andy Goram out with a 22 yard lob come shot. The run was halted by Celtic winning 3-1 in Glasgow on 5 October then the following Wednesday 9 October Hearts won a titanic match 1-0 at Aberdeen and went top of the Premier Division.

In addition, there was a 3-1 defeat of Celtic in Gorgie on 16 November, in a scintillating match. Hearts consistent play and team selection resulted in only two away matches against Rangers and Celtic being lost from the 26 League matches played up to the end of 1991.

EIGHT SCOTTISH INTERNATIONALS Back Row - Alan McLaren, Nicky Walker, Craig Levein, Henry Smith, Eamonn Bannon. Front Row - Gary Mackay, John Robertson, Derek Ferguson.

January brought a 1-1 draw at Easter Road and a 2-1 defeat of Celtic in Glasgow. Mixed results followed but Hearts won all four matches against Dunfermline Athletic, Motherwell and St.Johnstone and continued their run of unbeaten League matches against Hibernian. Goals conceded dropped to 37 in 44 matches against last season's 55 in 36 matches. At the end of the season this helped Hearts to finish in second place, and were heading for Europe again.

Thoughts now focused on the Scottish Cup and Hearts made a brave attempt at winning it but stumbled in the Semi-Finals. In the Third Round they played against St.Mirren at Paisley, where Hearts managed a 0-0 draw. In the replay in Gorgie they had a comfortable 3-0 win. They had to travel in the Fourth Round to face Dunfermline Athletic at East End Park and progressed by a 2-1 victory. Falkirk at Tynecastle was their reward in the Quarter-Finals and they went through to the Semi-Finals defeating them 3-1.

At Hampden Park, Hearts faced Airdrieonians – laced with former Hearts staff – and drew 0-0 but in the Replay, again at Hampden Park, they lost 4-2 on penalties after a 1-1 score line after 90 minutes and extra-time.

On 18 January 1992 the Directors decided to squash any suggestion of Heart of Midlothian Football Club sharing a stadium.

On the 21 April 1992 the authorised capital of the Company was increased to £25,000 by the creation of 2,000,000 ordinary shares = 2,500,000 – a four for one bonus issue.

Alan McLaren made his first appearance for Scotland in a Full International on 17 May 1992 against the USA, in a 1-0 win at Mile High Stadium, Denver.

EXIT JOE JORDAN

In the close-season Dave McPherson was transferred to Rangers and his place was taken up by the signing of Peter Van de Ven – Aberdeen and Ally Mauchlen – Leicester City was added to the squad.

The first issue for Manager Jordan was the team's disciplinary record and the club was fined £5,000 in this regard.

In season 1992-1993 Hearts were back in the UEFA Cup for a fifth time. They met Slavia Prague in the First Round, First Leg in the Dr.Vacka Stadium and came away with a credible 1-0 defeat. In the Second Leg at Tynecastle Hearts won a pulsating match 4-2 after being shocked into action – possibly by the incompetent performance of the Swedish referee – but the decisive goal was a stunning thirty yard free kick. In the Second Round, First Leg, Hearts met their first ever European opponents from 1958 Standard Liege, and at Tynecastle lost 1-0. There were no great hopes of a win in Liege in the Second Leg but the team played above themselves and lost narrowly by 1-0.

In the League Cup, for the second year in succession, Hearts met Clydebank in the Second round, at Tynecastle, and won 1-0 in a very edgy match. Their Third Round opponents were Brechin City at Glebe Park and now that ties had to be settled in the first match, Hearts had the embarrassment of having to play extra-time and scraped through 2-1. That did not make for confidence in facing Celtic in the Quarter-Finals. The match was played at Tynecastle but home advantage did not count for anything as Celtic again proved to be Hearts 'nemesis' winning 2-1.

The League Championship was the target, after finishing second in the previous season. After Hearts lost the opening match at home to Celtic the players responded and took 12 points from the next seven matches to top the table. Defeats by Rangers and Airdrieonians away followed, but another unbeaten run of eight matches, including four successive wins against Dundee United, Motherwell, Dundee and Hibernian raised morale.

After being thrashed by Aberdeen 6-2 at Pittodrie on 28 November results became erratic with only four wins in the next 14 League fixtures. Hearts failed to win all four matches against any club for the first time, and failed to win any matches against Rangers. They won 1-0 against Hibernian in both home matches but could only draw 0-0 in both matches at Easter Road. Dundee United and Partick Thistle were the two teams not to record a win over Hearts.

Had the directors provided funds in December to strengthen the squad for the run in to the final matches, results may have been better. As it was, Hearts failed to win any of the last eight League matches including a humiliating 6-0 defeat by Falkirk, on 1 May, at Brockville Park. All hopes were dashed in a season of massive under achievement and a fifth place finish led to the sacking of Joe Jordan.

In November the Scottish Football League rejected a proposal for a Super League but indicated that a proposal for 14 clubs in a Premier League and 12 in the First and Second Divisions might find favour. Hearts were not interested in a Premier Division of 14 clubs.

Hearts formerly withdrew their application to build a stadium at Millerhill.

The Club having tried to find a new site for a stadium and been thwarted at every stage agreed on 7 December 1992 to remain at Tynecastle.

Nicky Walker made his first appearance for Scotland in a Full International on 24 March 1993 against Germany in a 1-0 defeat at Hampden Park, Glasgow.

In that match, Craig Levein became the first Hearts player to captain Scotland since Dave Mackay in 1958.

In the Scottish Cup, Third Round, Hearts met Huntly at Tynecastle and won 6-0. The Fourth Round draw saw Hearts at home again and Dundee lost 2-0. The Quarter-Finals brought Falkirk to Gorgie for the second year running and Hearts won 2-0. The Semi-Final tie was played at Celtic Park – due to the redevelopment of Hampden Park – against Rangers and Hearts failed 'to turn up' and lost 2-1.

At a Board Meeting on 7 December 1992 "it was unanimously agreed that Tynecastle Stadium Limited would be appointed to manage the project at Tynecastle, subject to Thomas and Adamson providing an independent view that the original budget was fair, given the design, and that the "Direct Construction Management" would provide savings". "It was also noted for record purposes that both Mr. Mercer and Mr. Clydesdale had intimated and declared interests."

In the close season a "Scottish Super League" was proposed by the top football clubs but failed at the eleventh hour with the withdrawal of Celtic.

On 31 May 1993 Mr.Mercer met his board members in Amsterdam and announced that for tax reasons he had decided to become a resident overseas. It had been decided to consider offers for his 76% stake in the Heart of Midlothian Football Club.

During the close-season there were problems between Hearts and the Scottish Stadia Committee with regard to the lack of progress being made by Hearts in implementing the all-seater rules. The lack of clarity of a final decision by Hearts was most concerning with the fear that government would apply the no standing policy, Compliance by August 1994 would be enforced rigidly.

ALL CHANGE AT TYNECASTLE

Sandy Clark was appointed manager in May 1993 and had his own ideas. In the close-season Derek Ferguson was transferred to Sunderland for £500,000+ and Ian Baird was allowed to leave. John Colquhoun returned from Sunderland and Justin Fashanu – Airdrieonians was brought in. Later Jim Weir – Hamilton Academical and Scott Leitch – Dunfermline Athletic were signed.

From 1993-1994 season each team was permitted to substitute any two from three substitute players, one a goalkeeper, during a match.

Mr.Mercer revealed plans to buy Hearts stadium for £2,000,000, refurbish it then lease it back to Hearts on a 50 year agreement but, under pressure from the Heart of Midlothian Shareholders Association and the Federation of Hearts Supporters Clubs he had a rethink.

Plans were drawn up to develop Tynecastle Park into a fully seated and covered football ground. Phase One would be a new 5,900 seated Wheatfield Stand opposite the Main Stand. Phase Two would be a stand behind each goal for 3,550 seats each, providing a total capacity of 18,500 including 5,500 in the present Main Stand and Enclosure. Phase Three, for much later, would be an improved Mains Stand of 8,000 seats raising the capacity to 21,000.

Sandy Clark led Hearts into the UEFA Cup, who for the first ever time had won a place in European competitions in two consecutive seasons. He had been in charge of Hearts in the UEFA Cup on a previous occasion when they played Dnepr. This time, Hearts were drawn against Atletico Madrid in the First Round, First Leg at home and took a slender 2-1 lead to Spain. Once more an away goal was their downfall and in the Second Leg in Madrid Hearts failed to score and lost 3-0.

The League Cup was not a happy hunting ground despite two home ties. In the Second Round, Stranraer were the visitors and lost 2-0 but in the Third Round the visitors Falkirk won 1-0. They were becoming another Hearts' bogey team. The early exit put pressure on an already delicate financial position.

The League Championship was Hearts chance to show how good they had become but the new manager could not make an impact. Hearts lost the opening match 2-1 against Rangers at Ibrox Park but then had 1-0 victories over both Raith Rovers and Hibernian. With goals at a premium, Hearts slipped into mid-table during September and stuttering form left the club a long way off the pace making it impossible to catch the League leaders. After losing 1-0 to Raith Rovers in Kirkcaldy in mid-October the team was tenth in the table and with three teams to be relegated to revert to a ten club Premier Division the pressure was on the manager.

There was a goal famine and Justin Fashanu was discarded and Mo Johnston – Everton came in and other players were allowed to leave. Having gone out of the Cup in March, the players could concentrate on avoiding relegation from the remaining twelve fixtures, but they only won three and drew seven. On 16 April they lost 2-0 to Dundee at Tynecastle who were already destined for the First Division along with Raith Rovers. The third club to go down would come from Hearts, Kilmarnock, Partick Thistle or St.Johnstone. Hearts drew with St.Johnstone, Aberdeen and Hibernian and with only two matches left, two points separated the relegation rivals.

The outcome was a 2-0 win over Dundee United at Tynecastle, the last home fixture and a 1-0 defeat of Partick Thistle at Firhill Park. The home side were however, spared the drop as St.Johnstone joined the other two. Hearts failed to win a match against Motherwell, Rangers or St.Johnstone but did share all the points with Celtic and continued their unbeaten League record against Hibernian and Partick Thistle. With 20 draws from 44 matches a seventh place finish was not good enough.

On the 11 November 1993 the Hearts 500 Club "Rebuilding Tynecastle" (through which Hearts fans everywhere could contribute to the development of their stadium) was launched. An independent committee was constituted to oversee the raising of the finance but no target was set for the sum to be raised or by what time.

In the Scottish Cup, Third Round, Hearts met Partick Thistle at Firhill Park and won 1-0 in a tense match. In the Fourth Round, Hearts went down to Easter Road for a Sunday televised tie that proved memorable. With the score 1-1 after 87 minutes Wayne Foster scored a dramatic winner to stretch Hearts unbeaten run against their city rivals to 21 matches since January 1989. In the Quarter-Finals, Hearts were drawn away from home for the third time and met Rangers at Ibrox Park, but it was one hurdle too many and they lost 2-0.

On the 17 March 1994 the Directors announced that "Phase One of the Redevelopment of Tynecastle" would proceed, This would involve the building of a new 5,000 seated Wheatfield Stand, with executive boxes and 15,000 square feet of function, conference and meeting facilities in the under croft. Work commenced on 28 March 1994 by removing part of the roof over the covered enclosure opposite the Main Stand, and until the end of the football season, 1993/1994 ground capacity was gradually reduced as the work progressed.

To complete the necessary work for season 1994/1995, the Club applied to have the first two matches played away from home. The Wheatfield Stand, designed by Jim Clydesdale Associates at a cost of £3.3m, with 5,904 seats and new temporary seating for 2,312 away supporters at the Gorgie Road end. The new floodlighting towers were supported by the new stand and the main television platform was suspended from the roof all in place for the first home match of the season on 27 August 1994. Due to the financial position of the Club the executive boxes, function, conference and meeting facilities were not included.

At Board Meetings on 14, 19 & 28 March 1994 Mr.Mercer refused to withdraw his plan for the sale and leaseback of the commercial offices.

On the 17 June 1994 New Hearts Limited (Chris Robinson and Leslie Deans) bought a controlling share of Heart of Midlothian Football Club from Pentland Securities (Holdings) Limited. John Bell's statement in 1981 about one major shareholder, rang true as it was obvious that a major shareholder would only sell to another one and in this case neither gentleman could afford to do it on his own.

The new Board decided to close the 500 Club membership from 1 July1994. The total membership stood at 1171, and it was confirmed that an "Honours Board" listing the names of the Committee and all the Members would be displayed in the concourse of the Wheatfield Stand. Each Member would receive £600 at £100 per season from 1995/96 to 2000/01. Jim Clydesdale, Wallace Mercer, Les Porteous and Pilmar Smith resigned from the Board with Colin Wilson remaining to represent Cosmopolitan Limited and Chris Robinson was appointed Chairman on 17 June 1994.

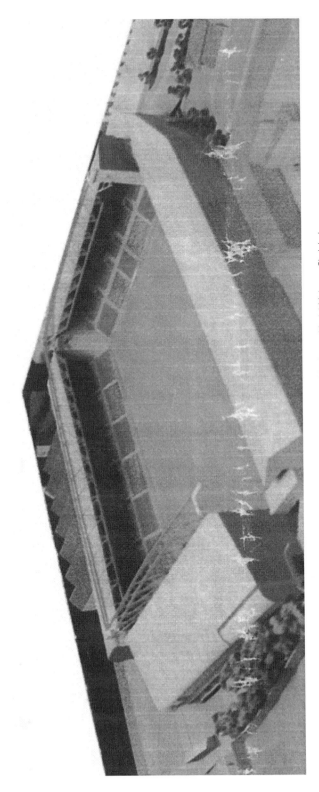

Model of Proposed Development 1994 Model by Angus Model Makers - Clydeholm.

A NEW BOARD – A NEW MANAGER

Sandy Clark was not given a chance to prove his managerial skills as the new directors sacked him on 20 June. Tommy McLean – Motherwell was appointed manager on 1st.July and brought in his own backroom staff.

There were changes in the playing staff – Justin Fashanu and Peter Van de Ven had left and in came Jim Bett-KR Reykjavik and Dave McPherson returned from Rangers in October as Alan McLaren went in the other direction.

Hearts entered the 1994-1995 League Cup competition in the Second Round with an away match against Dunfermline Athletic and won 4-0. The Third Round tie was at Tynecastle and Hearts lost 4-2 to St.Johnstone and losing so easily should have sent a signal to those concerned.

The League Championship stuttered from the beginning, partly due to asking to have the first two matches played away from home. As it happened the first match in the "New Look Tynecastle" was not only a defeat but it meant that as Hibernian won 1-0 they had broken the run of 22 matches without a win. The first victory did not come until 17 September when Dundee United lost 2-1 in Gorgie. It turned into a very average season with only nine home wins and 26 goals. Surprisingly, Celtic were the only team to fail to record a win over Hearts that season. Hearts finished sixth only one better than last season.

A Club Share Prospectus was launched on 6 October 1994 which included the offer to appoint two Club Directors. The Board offered 8,000,000 Club Shares of 10p each at £1.25 per share. The opening date was 6 October 1994 and closed on 15 November 1994. Only 431,200 were subscribed for, giving rise to net proceeds after issue expenses of £147,000. Two Club shareholders were to be appointed at the AGM.

Colin Miller made his first appearance for Canada in a Full International, as a Hearts player, on 24 January 1995 against Denmark in a 1-0 defeat at the Sky Dome, Toronto.

Hearts were out of the League Cup and not in contention for the Title but they made a strong challenge for the Scottish Cup. In the Third Round away to Clydebank a 1-1 draw saw the replay come to Tynecastle and a 2-1 victory. The Fourth Round was played at home against Rangers in an exciting, pulsating and fluctuating match. Hearts went in at the interval 2-0 up but were pulled back to 2-2 within ten minutes of the re-start. With the tremendous vocal backing of the Hearts supporters in the 12,371 crowd the "maroons" scored twice to go into the Quarter-Finals.

Dundee United travelled to Gorgie to face a resurgent Hearts side and lost 2-1 to raise the hopes of the home supporters. The Semi-Final against Airdrieonians at Hampden Park resulted in a disappointing 1-0 defeat. For the third time in five seasons they had put an end to Hearts' Scottish Cup hopes.

Although it had not been a particularly progressive season supporters were surprised when Tommy McLean was relieved of his post as Manager in June.

A FORMER PLAYER AS MANAGER

After much heart searching over four or five days Jim Jefferies eventually accepted an offer to become Hearts manager, and brought his long time assistant, Billy Brown with him. Having signed on 4 August he only had 15 days before the season started in earnest on 19 August.

The 1995-1996 season began with the League Cup and in the Second Round Hearts played Alloa Athletic at Tynecastle and won 3-0. The Third Round was again at home and Dunfermline Athletic lost 2-1. An away match against Dundee was the Fourth Round challenge and Hearts failed. It was 4-4 after extra-time but Hearts lost 5-4 in the penalty shoot-out. Jim Bett and Mo Johnston were released, while Pasquelle Bruno-AC Fiorentina, Steve Fulton-Falkirk, Neil Pointon-Oldham Athletic, Gilles Rousset-Stade Rennais came in. Colin Cameron-Raith Rovers was added in March 1996

The League season started with a home match against Motherwell which ended 1-1 and they were one of the teams not to have a win over Hearts this season along with Raith Rovers. On the down side Celtic won all four encounters with a towering 13-2 goal aggregate. The highlight of the campaign was the 3-0 defeat of Rangers at Ibrox Park on 20 January when Alan Johnston scored all three goals. Alan was only the third Hearts players to score a hat-trick against Rangers in Glasgow, following in the footsteps of Willie Wilson in 1915 and Andy Black in 1937.

With an increase of 12 points over last season Hearts finished in an encouraging fourth place.

In the Scottish Cup Third Round Hearts met Partick Thistle at Tynecastle and won 1-0 in a tight encounter. Kilmarnock awaited them in the Fourth Round at Rugby Park and lost 2-1. The Quarter-Finals took Hearts to McDiarmid Park, Perth and another 2-1 victory this time over St.Johnstone.

The Semi-Finals draw brought up an interesting contest as Hearts were to face Aberdeen. These teams had been drawn against each other seven times in the Scottish Cup and Hearts had never won. On a bright Saturday in April the challenge took place at Hampden Park and at last the "maroons" defeated the "dons" by 2-1.

The Final at Hampden Park on 18 May 1996 was a major disappointment as Rangers defeated Hearts by a resounding 5-1. Gary Locke had to leave the field after six minutes with a knee injury and that affected the game-plan but as the manger said "we were destroyed". Nevertheless, the improvement in one season was encouraging.

The luckless team that day was:- Gillles Rousset, Gary Locke-captain, Paul Ritchie, Alan McManus, Dave McPherson, Pasquale Bruno, Alan Johnston, Gary Mackay, John Colquhoun, Steve Fulton, Neil Pointon. Substitutes Alan Lawrence for Locke and John Robertson for Bruno.

A LONG AWAITED LEAGUE CUP FINAL

The new 500 Club was launched in July 1996 to assist in the third phase of the redevelopment of Tynecastle Stadium - the building of the Gorgie Road Stand. It closed in October 1996 with a membership of 1471 and the names of the Committee and all Members was displayed on an "Honours Board" in the concourse of the Gorgie Stand.

The 1996-1997 season saw the usual comings and goings of players – John Colquhoun went to St.Johnstone and Gary Mackay went to Airdrieonians. The new signings – were Neil McCann-Dundee, Stefano Salvatori-Atlanata and David Weir- Falkirk, turning out to be real successes.

As beaten Scottish Cup finalists Hearts were in Europe once more and in the European Cup Winners Cup competition, for the first time for exactly 20 years. They had to play Red Star Belgrade in the Qualifying Round, First Leg and travelled to Yugoslavia on 8 August and returned home with a creditable 0-0 result.

At home on the 22 August the old bogey of away goals sent them out of the competition after a 1-1 draw.

Hearts entered the League Cup competition in the Second Round against Stenhousemuir at Tynecastle and got the shock of their lives. A 1-1 draw after extra-time saw the tie go to a penalty shoot-out which Hearts survived winning 5-4. The Third Round took Hearts to McDiarmid Park to play St.Johnstone and after a tense struggle a 4-1 victory, after extra-time, saw them progress to the Quarter-Finals.

Celtic were the opposition and must have travelled to Gorgie full of confidence knowing that the home team had four players unavailable after being sent off against Rangers the previous Saturday. Andy Thorn was brought in on loan from Wimbledon and a reshuffle of player resources saw an unusual line-up. Low and behold they played their heart out and won 1-0 in extra time.

The Semi-Finals brought Dundee, at this time playing in the First Division, to face Hearts at Easter Road, but the "maroons" won 3-1. The Final on 24 November against Rangers at Hampden Park ended in a 4-3 win for the Glasgow club but on this occasion they had to struggle for their victory.

The gallant losers were:- Gilles Rousett, David Weir, Neil Pointon, Gary Mackay-captain, Paul Ritchie, Pasquale Bruno, Stephan Paille, Steve Fulton, John Robertson, Colin Cameron, Neil McCann. Darren Beckford came on for Paille.

The League championship was highly competitive and raised many talking points throughout the season. The first nine matchers were average and resulted in three wins, three draws and three defeats. But the match against Rangers on 14 September at Ibrox Park took the biscuit, with a farcical performance from the match officials, which almost led to the away team walking off the pitch. Rangers won 3-0 but their players knew that it was a farce.

Hearts were challenging all the time and over the festive period won four matches on the run against, Dunfermline Athletic, Motherwell, Hibernian and Raith Rovers and sitting in fourth place. Hibernian, Motherwell and Raith Rovers failed to win any matches against Hearts this season.

To some extent Hearts got revenge over Rangers for the September debacle defeating them 3-1 at Tynrecastle in the final match of the Championship. A fourth place finish for the second season in succession identified progress.

Leslie Deans was appointed Chairman on 30 December 1996.

The Scottish Cup competition for this season was a let-down after defeating Cowdenbeath 5-0 at Tynecastle in the Third Round Hearts lost to Dundee United in the Fourth Round. At home Hearts could only draw 1-1 and lost 1-0 at Tannadice Park.

Chris Robinson was appointed Chief Executive on 1 April 1997.

David Weir made his first appearance for Scotland in a Full International on 27 May 1997 against Wales in a 1-0 defeat at Rugby Park, Kilmarnock.

Sadly, Craig Levein, one of Hearts finest ever players, announced on 6 May 1997 that he had been forced into premature retirement due to injury. A player gifted with natural pace and intelligence, he could have gone on to even greater achievements had he not been blighted with serious injury so often.

A SCOTTISH CUP WINNING SEASON

For the first time since October 1962 Hearts supporters were able to celebrate the winning of a major trophy. The Scottish Cup victory was testament to steady improvement over three seasons by a dedicated management team.

Player movements this season were much reduced but Thomas Flogel-FK Austria signed in September and Pasquale Bruno went to Wigan Athletic..

During 1997 the Company changed its name from Heart of Midlothian Football Club plc to Heart of Midlothian plc.

In May 1997 the Directors asked shareholders to approve for the Company to be placed on the London Stock Exchange. When approved the Club Shares converted into Ordinary Shares and a bonus issue of one for one Ordinary Share.

The 1997-1998 League Cup competition started for Hearts on 9 August in the Second Round with a match against Livingston in West Lothian which was won 2-0. The Third Round was against Raith Rovers in Kirkcaldy and Hearts triumphed 2-1. The Quarter-Finals brought Hearts and Dunfermline Athletic together at East End Park, but on this occasion the home team won 1-0 in extra-time.

In the League Hearts huffed and puffed a bit to begin with but had encouraging wins over Aberdeen 4-1 at Tynecastle in August, and 4-1 at Pittodrie in November, and they were one of five teams who failed to defeat Hearts this season. A 1-0 win over Hibernian at Easter Road in August was followed by another win in November by 2-0. The highest scoring match was the 5-3 defeat of Kilmarnock at Tynecastle, another team who failed to defeat Hearts this season.

They finished in third place despite failing to win any matches against Celtic or Rangers but Dundee United, Motherwell and St.Johnstone also failed to defeat Hearts.

The highlight of the season was the Scottish Cup competition. It all began in the Third Round on 24 January 1998 with a home tie against Clydebank in Gorgie, which Hearts won 2-0. The Fourth Round was again played at Tynecastle this time against Albion Rovers who lost 4-0. The luck of the draw saw Hearts drawn at home in the Quarter-Finals and Ayr United were despatched 4-1. So onto the Semi-Finals against Falkirk at Ibrox Park. In a pulsating match with a tense finish Hearts won 3-1 to go into their twelfth Scottish Cup Final.

As fate would have it, this season the Final was to be held at Celtic Park against Rangers on 16 May 1998. On a hot summer-like day a crowd of 48,946 turned up and witnessed an astonishing start with Hearts scoring from a penalty within a minute. As the kick-off took place early they had scored before three o'clock, just as Rangers had against them in 1976. Steve Fulton was the man fouled and Colin Cameron the scorer. In 53 minutes Stephane Adam scored to put Hearts two up but Rangers fought back to 2-1 and in a tense final ten minutes the players held on for a sensational victory.

Those who would be legends were:- Gilles Rousett, Dave McPherson, Gary Naysmith, David Weir, Stefano Salavatori, Paul Ritchie, Neil McCann, Steve Fulton-captain, Stephane Adam, Colin Cameron, Thomas Flogel. Substitute – Jim Hamilton for Adam.

Jim Jefferies and Billy Brown had 'lifted the monkey off the back' of the Hearts supporters. Jim was a man

FIRST TEAM SQUAD 1998/1999 Standing Back Row - D. Murie, G. Naysmith, A. McManus, D. McPherson, M. Hogarth, G. Rousset, R. McKenzie, D. Weir, P. Ritchie, G. Murray, S. Callachan. Standing Middle Row - R. Logan (Coach), S. Fulton, R. McKinnon, S. Salvatori, S. Adam, K. Thomas, S. Pressley, J. Hamilton, T. Flogel, N. Gray (F.it). Seated - P. Houston (Coach), J. Quitongo, L. Makel, J. Jefferies (Manager), G. Locke (Captain), B. Brown (Asst. Manager), N. McCann, C. Cameron, A. Rae (Physio).

born to support Hearts, play for and captain them, and now lead them to a Scottish Cup triumph.

The celebrations after the match in Glasgow, but even more so in Edinburgh, were exhilarating and unbelievable. Crowds lined the streets from the outskirts of the city right through to Gorgie Road.

On the Sunday after a reception at the City Chambers the Cup was paraded through the streets down the Mound along Princes Street, Shandwick Place Dalry Road and Gorgie Road to a gathering of thousands of Hearts supporters in the stadium. The players were introduced one by one and applauded and no one wanted the celebrations to end.

HEARTS GO BACKWARDS

For what ever reason Hearts did not manage to improve in season 1998-1999 they finished sixth in the League and failed to reach the final of the League Cup and Scottish Cup.

Stevie Frail, Neil Pointon and John Robertson left at the end of last season and new signings included Gary McSwegan and Steven Pressley-Dundee United,

As Cup Winners Hearts were back in Europe, and playing in the European Cup Winners Cup competition, for a third time. In the Preliminary Round, First Leg they met FC Lantana in Tallinn, Estonia and before a crowd of about 1,300, won 1-0. In the Second Leg, at Tynecastle Hearts ran out easy victors in a 5-0 win and their best aggregate result in European competitions.

The First Round, First Leg, was played against Real Mallorca in Edinburgh, but again an away goal was lost in a 1-0 defeat. The Second Leg, in Mallorca was a problem from the start with a dispute over the height of one of the goals. Hearts agreed to play under protest but could only draw 1-1. Hearts protested to UEFA but got nowhere and all were convinced they were victims of a miscarriage of justice.

The League Cup saw Hearts meet Raith Rovers in the Third Round at Tynecastle and they forced Hearts into extra-time before losing 4-2. The Fourth Round was again at Tynecastle and Ross County put up stubborn resistance taking Hearts into extra-time again before losing 3-0 on penalties after a 1-1 draw. In the Semi-Final on 27 October, St. Johnstone stunned Hearts by defeating them 3-0 at Easter Road.

Neil McCann made his first appearance for Scotland in a Full International, as a substitute, on 5 September 1998 against Lithuania in a 0-0 draw at Zalgiris Stadionas, Vilnius.

Hearts had a rousing start to the League season defeating Rangers 2-1 at Tynecastle in the first match on 2 August. This was followed by a draw, a win and a defeat and the team never seemed to get a rhythm going. Halfway through the fixtures Hearts were in fifth place with 23 points from 18 matches. Dunfermline Athletic was the only side not to record a win over Hearts. Dundee won all four matches and St.Johnstone drew three and won one of the four matches.

Hearts finished in a flurry winning four out of the five final matches including a sound defeat of Aberdeen by 5-2 at Pittodrie, but this season saw a much poorer all round performance.

Hearts went into the transfer market in the New Year after losing Neil McCann to Rangers in December and signed Darren Jackson-Celtic and Andy Kirk-Glentoran.

The Scottish Cup competition was seen as a relief from the grind of the League but it turned out to be a shocker when Hearts lost 3-1 to Motherwell in the Third Round at Fir Park.

Colin Cameron and Paul Ritchie made their first appearance for Scotland in a Full International, as substitutes, on 28 April 1999 against Germany in a 1-0 win at Weserstadion, Bremen.

SIGNS OF A REVIVAL

In May 1999 the Club offered for sale a Five Year Season Ticket payment for which 500 Club and New 500 Club members could use their vouchers.

Doug Smith was appointed Chairman on 1 June 1999.

There was less movement among personnel before season 1999-2000 started – Dave McPherson, Stefano Salvatori and David Weir were released and Gary Wales-Hamilton Academical was signed. Anti Niemi-Rangers, Gordan Petric- AEK Athens and Robert Tomaschek signed later.

Hearts entered the League Cup competition in the Second Round and defeated Queen of the South 3-1 at Palmerston Park. The Third Round, was again away from home and East Fife lost 2-0 in a match played at Starks Park, Kirkcaldy. Hearts were having no luck with the draw and in the Quarter-Finals had to travel to Rugby Park to play Kilmarnock and lost 1-0.

Hearts held an Extraordinary General Meeting on 30 September 1999 to launch a "Strategic Alliance" with Scottish Media Group (Investments) Limited involving a sum of £8,000,000.

The League Championship started with an away match against St.Johnstone which Hearts won 4-1. After 18 matches Hearts sat in sixth place with five wins, five draws and eight losses. There were no outstanding results but Celtic lost 3-2 in Glasgow and 1-0 in Gorgie in the second half of the campaign. Kilmarnock and St.Johnstone failed to win against the Hearts but they lost all four matches against Rangers.

The final match had a little spice added to it following a comment by a Motherwell player with regard to his team beating Hearts to the UEFA Cup spot. Hearts gained the necessary points needed by defeating Hibernian 2-1 at Tynecastle, to return to European action. Only 47 goals were scored against 40 conceded but a third place was a welcome improvement.

Gary McSwegan made his first appearance for Scotland in a Full International, as a substitute, on 5 October 1999 against Bosnia-Herzegovina in a 1-0 win at Ibrox Stadium, Glasgow.

The Scottish Cup run this term was short and not so sweet. In the Third Round, Stenhousemuir came to Tynecastle and lost 3-2 in a tight tie. Hearts had to travel to meet Clyde and won 2-0 in the Fourth Round. The Quarter-Finals meant Hearts had to face Rangers and lost 4-1 at Ibrox Park.

Steven Pressley made his first appearance for Scotland in a Full International, as a substitute, on 29 March 2000 against France in a 2-0 defeat at Hampden Park, Glasgow.

Thomas Flogel made his first appearance for Austria in a Full International, as a Hearts player, on 29 March 2000 against Sweden, and scored, in a 1-1 draw in Graz.

Robert Tomaschek made his first appearance for Sloavakia in a Full International, as a Hearts player, on 25 April 2000 against Germany 'B' in a 4-1 win at Presov.

Andy Kirk made his first appearance for Northern Ireland in a Full International on 26 April 2000 against Hungary in a 1-0 defeat ar Windsor Park, Belfast.

Anti Niemi made his first appearance for Finland in a Full International, as a Hearts player, on 26 April 2000 against Poland, and had a shut-out, in a 0-0 draw at Lech Poznan Stadium, Poznan.

Gary Naysmith made his first appearance for Scotland in a Full International on 30 May 2000 against Ireland on in a 2-1 win at Landsdowne Road, Dublin.

AN UNEXPECTED DEPARTURE

For season 2000-2001 the Scottish Premier League consisted of twelve clubs who had to play each other three times then split after 33 matches. The two groups of six clubs played to decide the Champions and the relegated club

Giilles Rousset returned to France in May and Gordon Durie-Rangers joined the First Team Squad in September. Darren Jackson left for Livingston and Gordan Petric returned home. Austin McCann-Airdrieonians, Kevinn McKenna-Energie Cottbus and Andy Webster-Arbroath were added to the squad in the New Year.

Fitzroy Simpson made his first appearance for Jamaica in a Full International, as a Hearts player, on 2 July 2000 against Cuba in 1-1 draw in Kingston.

Hearts had an early start to their UEFA Cup competition having to play after only two League matches. In the Qualifying Round, 1st.Leg on 10 August in Iceland, IBV Vestmannyjar lost 2-0. The 2nd.Leg at Tynecastle on 24 August saw Hearts win 3-0 with a comfortable display. The First Round, 1st.Leg meant a trip to Germany in September, and the team produced an accomplished performance to hold VfB Stuttgart to 1-0 win.

At Tynecastle on 28 September Hearts were ravaged by injuries but they rose to the challenge to score early and level the aggregate. Stuttgart then scored twice but the makeshift line-up scored twice – 'game on'. The players were somewhat unfortunate to win 3-2 but become victims, yet again, to the away goals rule.

Hearts did not have to enter the League Cup competition until the Third Round due to playing in a European competition and defeated Livingston 2-0 in Midlothian. In the Quarter-Finals, Celtic won 5-2 at Tynecastle in a tense tussle, but the final score did not reflect the closeness of the match.

The aim in the League championship was to improve on last season's third place. Hibernian drew 0-0 at Tynecastle then there were two more draws – St.Johnstone and Aberdeen. A 4-2 defeat by Celtic followed, then another draw this time to Dundee and at last a win – 2-0 against Dunfermline Athletic. It was turning out to be that sort of campaign but no one foresaw the departure of Jim Jefferies.

Although Hearts were sitting in seventh place in the table, the team had been plagued with injuries. In view of the five seasons of real progress the supporters still had faith in Jim Jefferies and Billy Brown – but not the Board.

Results were not all that much better but with the appointment of Craig Levein as the Head Coach – all was forgiven! The highlight of the season had to be the 7-1 thrashing of Dunfermline Athletic at Tynecastle on 24 February. Dundee United and St.Mirren failed to defeat Hearts in the three encounters and Dundee did not win any of their four matches. For the first time since 1976/1977 the "maroons" failed to defeat Hibernian in any of the four League matches. Celtic once again won all four matches and Hearts finished in fifth place.

The Scottish Cup was Craig Levein's first real chance to win a trophy. In the Third Round, Hearts travelled to meet Berwick Rangers but could only draw in a tight match. The Replay at Tynecastle was before a small crowd of 7,368 but the team made sure they got through to the next round with a 2-1 win.

The Fourth Round was ten days later against Dundee at Tynecastle which resulted in a nerve wracking 1-1 draw. The Replay was just as tense but Hearts travelled home happy despite a scrappy 1-0 victory. The Quarter-Finals meant the "maroons" had to visit Glasgow to face Celtic and in another very tight match lost 1-0.

Kevin McKenna made his first appearance for Canada in a Full International, as a Hearts player, on 26 April 2001 against Iran in 1-0 win the National Stadium, Cairo.

CRAIG LEVEIN'S FIRST FULL SEASON

On 31 July 2001 Hearts announced ambitious plans for a new stadium at Braehead – The Pentland Stadium. The timing of the announcement was made to coincide with the submission requirements of the SFA relative to the national bid to host the Euro 2008 Championship. From a club aspect there were meetings with supporters groups.

The aim was to improve performances in all competitions and to finish high enough in the League table to qualify again for a European competition. Gordon Durie had left in May and Colin Cameron went to Wolverhampton Wanderers in August. Stephane Mahe-Celtic and Alan Maybury-Leeds United added to the Squad.

The 2001-2002 League Cup competition saw Hearts travel to Dingwall on 25 September and suffer an embarrassing defeat by Ross County. There was no scoring before Full-Time nor in extra-time but the visitors lost 5-4 on penalties.

Hearts start to the Championship caused some concern, in particular the defeat by Livingston by 2-1 in Midlothian as they were new to the Premier League. Unbelievably, Hearts lost all four matches to the newcomers which didn't help their cause. Most matches were quite close without any particular highlight. Dunfermline Athletic failed to defeat Hearts in any of the four matches and Dundee lost two and drew one of theirs. When Hearts defeated Hibernian 2-1 at Easter Road on 16 March the "greens" were out of the top six. Celtic won all four matches against Hearts who finished in fifth place again.

Scott Severin made his first appearance for Scotland in a Full International, as a substitute, on 6 October 2001 against Latvia in a 2-1 win at Hampen Park, Glasgow.

In the Scottish Cup, we witnessed the quirks of Scottish football, when Hearts were drawn to play Ross County in the Third Round at Tynecastle. The players were much more aware in this match and won 2-1. The Fourth Round meant another Highland club came to Tynecastle and to the surprise, bordering on disgust, the Hearts supporters cringed as they watched Inverness Caledonian Thistle win 3-1. The last remaining chance of a trophy this season was lost.

Tommi Gronland made his first appearance for Finland in a Full International, as a Hearts player, as a substitute on 27 March 2002 against Portugal in a 4-1 win at the Estadio do Bessa, Porto.

A LOCAL DERBY STORY

Thomas Flogel, Gary McSwegan and Robert Tomaschek were released and Stevie Fulton and Anti Niemi were transferred. Craig Levein freshened up the Squad and signed – Mark De Vries-FC Dordrecht 90, Neil MacFarlane-Airdrieonians, Phil Stamp- Middlesbrough and Jean-Lois Valois-Luton Town.

Without a European competition to play in during 2002-2003 the manager could use all his resources to win a domestic trophy.

The League Cup Second Round, saw Hearts travel to play Stirling Albion on 25 September and they recorded a 3-2 victory. Fate played its part again, and in the Third Round, Hearts returned to Dingwall to play Ross County but there were to be no hiccups this time in a 3-0 win. The Quarter-Finals draw meant Hearts had to travel once more and in a tight match defeated Aberdeen 1-0. The "maroons" were in the Semi-Finals of the League Cup for the first time in four years and before a 31,600 they pushed Rangers all the way but lost 1-0. This was another step forward on the learning curve.

The League campaign this season was almost all about Hearts v Hibernian. After only drawing 1-1 against Dundee at Dens Park on the opening day the first home match was to be against Hibernian and there were questions to be answered. On Sunday 11 August the Edinburgh derby turned out to be an outstanding advert for Scottish football live on TV. Hearts were two up at the interval then the "greens" scored but to no avail as the "maroons" scored three more for a 5-1 drubbing. New signing Mark DeVries scored four goals in his 'derby' debut.

The return match on Sunday 3 November at Easter Road produced a much closer result of 2-1. The score did not tell the real story as the home side appeared to be cruising to a 1-0 win with only five minutes to play but Hearts scored twice for a surprise victory. The match on Thursday 3 January was not expected to be as exciting as the first two but that proved to be wrong. Hibernian were determined to make up for the previous two results and it turned out to be a rollicking goal spree over 90 minutes and added-time. Hibernian opened the scoring and were two up before Hearts pulled one back with a penalty. In 63 minutes it was all-square then the "greens" scored twice to lead 4-2 with a minute to go plus added-time. Quite unbelievably the "maroons" scored twice through Graeme Weir for a 4-4 draw.

There was no fourth match as Hibernian failed to stay in the top six. Other teams who failed to win against Hearts were Dundee United who lost all three matches, Livingston and Partick Thistle. Rangers won all four matches and Hearts finished in third place.

The Third Round of the Scottish Cup was the first match to be played after the 'winter' break. Whether that was the reason, the team failed to perform on the day, and lost 4-0 to Falkirk at Brockville Park is open to speculation..

Andy Webster made his first appearance for Scotland in a Full International on 30 April 2003 against Austria in a 2-0 defeat at Hampden Park, Glasgow.

EUROPE HERE WE COME

Paul Hartley - St.Johnstone, Patrick Kisnorbo - South Melbourne and Dennis Wyness - Inverness Caledonian Thistle were signed in time for pre-season training.

The 2003-2004 Season saw yet another improvement in performances under Craig Levein's ever improving coaching style.

In the UEFA Cup, First Round, First Leg Hearts faced FK Zelijeznivar at Tynecastle on 24 September and produced a competent 2-0 win. The Second Leg on 15 October in Bosnia was a tight tense affair but resulted in a 0-0 draw. In the Second Round, First Leg, Hearts travelled to France to play FC Girondins de Bordeaux and came home after a creditable 1-0 victory. Sadly, the Second Leg at Tynecastle on 27 November was a disappointment as the French side won 2-0.

Teuve Moilanen made his first appearance for Finland in a Full International, as a Hearts player, on 17 November 2003 in a 2-1 win over Honduras, at the Robertson Stadium, Houston, Texas.

In the League Cup, Hearts entered in Round Three and defeated Falkirk 2-1 at Tynecastle. The Quarter-Finals took them to Dens Park where they lost 1-0 after extra-time.

The League campaign witnessed an early shock on 17 August when Hibernian won 1-0 at Easter Road in time added-on. Crowd trouble marred the match during the first half and at full-time. At Tynecastle on 23 November Hearts won 2-0 to even things up. Once again there were only three matches as Hibernian were not in the top six even though they drew 1-1 at Easter Road on 15 February. Because of TV most local derby matches were now on a Sunday.

On the downside there was an embarrassing 5-0 defeat by Celtic in Glasgow in October. Hearts record against Celtic since the twelve club League began was:- 1 win, 2 draws and 13 losses. However, Aberdeen, Dundee, Kilmarnock, Livingston and Motherwell failed to win a match against Hearts who finished in a very encouraging third place.

Andy Kirk scored Hearts 7,000th. League goal in their 3,797th. match, on 20 December 2003 in a 2-1 defeat by Rangers at Ibrox Park, Glasgow.

There was no extended run in the Scottish Cup because after defeating Berwick Rangers 2-0 in the Third Round, Celtic ran out clear 3-0 winners in the Fourth Round. Both ties were played at Tynecastle so home advantage did not work.

Jean-Lois Valois left in January and Mark DeVries, Andy Kirk, Austin McCann and Gary Wales were released. Jamie McAllister - Livingston and Michael Stewart - Manchester United - loan were signed in the close-season.

THE COACH CALLS IT A DAY

Alan Maybury made his first appearance for Ireland in a Full International, as a Hearts player, on 31 March 2004 against the Czech Republic in a 2-1 win at Landsdowne Road, Dublin.

George Foulkes was appointed Chairman on 6 April 2004.

Craig Gordon made his first appearance for Scotland in a Full International on 30 May 2004 against Trinidad & Tobago in a 4-1 win at Easter Road, Edinburgh.

Patrick Kisnorbo made his first appearance for Australia in Full International, as a Hearts player, as a substitute, on 31 May 2004 against Tahiti in a 9-0 win in the Hindmarsh Stadium, Adelaide.

Season 2004-2005 saw Hearts play in a European competition in two successive seasons, for the first time in eleven years,

The question posed was how well would Hearts do in their ninth entry into the UEFA Cup competition and because of the co-efficient avoided the Qualifying Rounds.

The First Round, First Leg, was on 16 September at Tynecastle where SC Braga lost 3-1. The Second Leg, in Portugal saw Hearts draw 2-2 and progress into Group Secton A. The First match was against Feyenoord in Holland and Hearts were soundly beaten 3-0. The Second match was played at Murrayfield before a crowd of 27,272 against Schalke 04 who won 1-0. DF Basel were the Third match opponents on 25 November in Switzerland, which Hearts won 2-1 with a last minute goal.

Back at Murrayfield on 16 December John Robertson saw his side lose narrowly by 1-0 to Ferencvaros of Hungary. But this had been a successful competition with several players serving their European apprenticeship.

A NEW HEAD COACH

The League Cup, Third Round, against Kilmarnock at Tynecastle was won 2-1 before John was appointed but he was in charge for the Fourth Round. Hearts travelled to East End Park and defeated Dunfermline Athletic 3-1. The Semi-Final tie was played at Easter Road on Tuesday 1 February and Motherwell triumphed 3-2 after extra-time. It was 1-0 at half-time then 2-0 for Motherwell then Hearts scored and just before the final whistle equalised. In extra-time there were chances for both sets of players but it was Motherwell who scored the winner with a penalty shoot-out beckoning.

The League was going to be a major challenge after the team had finished third in the past two seasons. The team had a very mixed start to the campaign and after playing each team once they were in fourth place on 16 points. Although disappointed not to have more points on board there were valid reasons which had been well documented.

One of the four wins at that stage was against Hibernian who had upset the manager and players by some comments in the media. One ahead at half-time the "maroons" had survived some roughhouse tactics. Another goal after the interval put the "greens" on their heels but they rallied and scored a late consolation goal.

Hibernian managed to get into the top six this season, sharing the results equally with Hearts, and capped it by finishing third in the Table. Dundee, Kilmarnock and Livingston were the teams who failed to record a win against Hearts but the "maroons" failed to win against Rangers and finished in fifth place.

On 13 September 2004 an Extraordinary General Meeting approved a resolution for the "Proposed Disposal of Tynecastle Including Proposed Indemnity to Cala Management Limited in respect of the Disposal".

This led to a lot of unpleasantness, with supporters having differing views over the rights and wrongs of such a move. A massive campaign 'Save Our Hearts' took place with efforts being made to buy a majority shareholding in the Company. Regretfully, as in 1903, 1905, 1979 and 1981 supporters and shareholders were unable to raise enough money to achieve their aim. John Bell's statement in 1981 that with one majority shareholder Hearts would lose out, came back to haunt everyone again.

At the same time Vladimir Romanov came on the scene and over a period of several months began buying the shares from people and groups with large shareholdings and eventually gaining control of the Company through UAB Ukio Banko Investicine Grupe and Heart of Midlothian 2005 Limited.

In December 2004 the Stadium Working Group submitted their Report with regard to the options for a suitable stadium for the club and to make recommendations to the Board of Heart of Midlothian plc. The three options researched were:-
To stay at the present stadium
To build a new stadium on a green field site
To sell the existing stadium and rent an alternative ground.

A 'disclaimer' was part of the submission pointing out that should the Club elect to implement any of the recommendations contained in the report they are advised to take independent advice from professional advisers.

In essence the conclusion was stay at Tyencastle, make improvements and resolve the UEFA pitch dimensions size.

Lee Miller-loan-Bristol City, Devidas Cesnauskis and Saulius Mikoliumas-loan-FBK Kaunas arrived in January

The Scottish Cup was a bit more exciting this season, commencing with an away tie against Partick Thistle in the Third Round and a 0-0 draw. The Replay at Tynecastle resulted in a 2-1 victory and so on to the Fourth Round. Kilmarnock came to Gorgie and forced a 2-2 draw but in the Replay at Rugby Park they lost 3-1. The Quarter-Finals brought Livingston to Tynecastle and Hearts eventually won 2-1. The Semi-Finals were played at Hampden Park where Hearts met Celtic. The "maroons" went behind early on but held out until half-time. Celtic scored again shortly after the interval and Hearts goal, late on, was only a consolation.

Devidas Cesnauskis made his first appearance for Lithuania in a Full International, as a Hearts player, on 9 February 2005 against Georgia in a 1-0 defeat in the Lokomotiv Stadium, Tbilisi.

Paul Hartley made his first appearance for Scotland in a Full International on 26 March 2005 against Italy in a 2-0 defeat at the Stadio Giuseppe Meazza, Milan.

Saulius Mikoliunas made his first appearance for Lithuania in a Full International, as a Hearts player, on 30 March 2005 as a substitute, against Bosnia & Herzegovina in a 1-1 draw at Kosevo Stadium, Sarajevo.

A 'LUCKY THIRTEENTH' SCOTTISH CUP FINAL

George Burley was a surprise appointment as Head Coach on 1 July 2005 and with little time to recruit and organise before the first competition match on 30 July. He was not the only one to have doubts.

There was a lot of movement on the player front, with Patrick Kisnorbo, Kevin McKenna, Alan Maybury, Lee Miller, Phil Stamp, Michael Stewart and Dennis Wyness all leaving. Roman Bednar, Juilien Brellier, Takis Fyssas, Edgras Jankauskas, Michal Pospisil, Rudolf Skacel and Ibrahim Tall came in.

The League Cup for 2005-2006 was a disaster for the new manager. Hearts met Queen's Park at Hampden Park in the Second Round and won 2-0 with a 'fringe' team. The same experiment in the Third Round, against Livingston in Midlothian, led to a humiliating 1-0 defeat.

Panagiotis [Takis] Fyssas made his first appearance for Greece in a Full International, as a Hearts player, on 17 August 2005 against Belgium in a 2-0 defeat at the King Baudouin Stadium, Brussels.

Edgaras Jankauskas made his first appearance for Lithuania in a Full International, as a Hearts player, on 17 August 2005 against Belarus in a 1-0 win at the Vetra Stadium, Vilnius.

Rudi Skacel made his first appearance for the Czech Republic in a Full International, as a Hearts player, on 17 August 2005 against Sweden, as a substitute, in a 2-1 defeat in the Ullevi Stadium, Olomouc.

The League campaign was a different story all together with an opening win over Kilmarnock at Rugby Park by 4-2. The first home match followed with a 4-0 thrashing of Hibernian at Tynecastle. This heralded an amazing run of eight wins in a row. The last time that happened was in 1914/1915 although in 1894/1895 they won their first eleven matches. The next two matches were drawn and astonishingly George Burley was dismissed the day before the match on 22 October against Dunfermline Athletic which Hearts won 2-0.

Graham Rix was appointed Head Coach on 7 November and inherited a team on-a-roll. This was a campaign of highs without any lows. Dundee United, Dunfermline Athletic, Falkirk, Inverness Caledonian Thistle, Livingston and Motherwell all failed to win a single match against a rampant Hearts side. Hearts for the first time in many seasons defeated every team at least once.

Four was a favourite number, as in addition, to the match in August they defeated Hibernian 4-1 on their return to Tynecastle in January. Livingston lost 4-1 in September and Dunfermline Athletic lost 4-1 in Fife in January and 4-0 in Edinburgh in April. At Tynecastle the "maroons" skelped the "bairns" 5-0 on Boxing Day and finished the season in second place and Hearts would be playing in the Champions League next season. For the second season in a row Hearts used 33 players.

Roman Romanov was appointed Chairman and Acting Chief Executive on 31 October 2005.

In November 2005 a 'Recommended Cash Offer' by British Linen Advisers Limited on behalf of Heart of Midlothian 2005 Limited to acquire the whole of the issued and to be issued share capital of Heart of Midlothian plc not already owned or controlled by UAB Ukio Banko Investicine Grupe. The offer was 35p in cash for each ordinary share of Hearts. The outcome was that Hearts became a subsidiary of UBIG – they holding 81.13% and HoM 2005 13.94% of the total Issued Shares.

Ibrahim Tall made his first appearance for Senegal in a Full International, as a Hearts player, on 12

November 2005 against South Africa, as a substitute, in a 3-2 win in the Eastern Province Rugby Stadium, Port Elizabeth.

In January Bruno Aguiar-loan FBK Kaunas and Jose Goncalves were signed.

Juho Makela made his first appearance for Finland in a Full International, as a Hearts player, on 21 January 2006 against Saudi Arabia, as a substitute, in a 1-1 draw in Riyhad.

Mirsad Beslija made his first appearance for Bosnia & Herzegovina in a Full International, as a Hearts player, on 28 February 2006 against Japan in a 2-2 draw at Westfalenstadion, Dortmund.

Graham Rix left in March and Valdas Ivanauskas became temporary Head Coach.

The League position was not to be the icing on the cake as the Scottish Cup competition was an electrifying experience. Kilmarnock came to Tynecastle in the Third Round and lost 2-1. In the Fourth Round, Aberdeen an erstwhile bogey team in the Scottish Cup also lost in Gorgie to the tune of 3-0 – that really was sweet. The Quarter-Finals draw was kind and gave Hearts a third home tie but Partick Thistle lost 2-1. The Semi-Finals brought the two Capital City clubs face to face, but many would have preferred it was in a final at Murrayfield.

On the day it was all about Hearts who had sold their allocation of tickets whereas there were large spaces in the Hibernian area. It was a disaster for the "greens" as the "maroons" dominated the match from start to finish with Paul Hartley scoring a hat-trick. His was possibly the finest performance of a Hearts player over the entire 90 minutes plus of any match far less a Hearts v Hibernian Scottish Cup Semi-Final. It was difficult for the supporters to contain themselves after savouring the magnitude of the victory.

The Final at Hampden Park on 13 May 2006 was against lowly Gretna who had defeated Preston Athletic, Cove Rangers, St.Johnstone, Clyde, St.Mirren and Dundee in an unbelievable run for such a young club. Once again the Hearts supporters outnumbered their opponents but not their loyalty. But the players appeared to be apprehensive and it turned in to a very tense affair. Hearts went ahead in the first half but Gretna equalised with a penalty and the score remained at 1-1 at full-time and after extra-time. In the penalty shoot-out Hearts scored four out of four, Gretna had one saved and missed one, to lose 4-2.

Steven Pressley accepted the Cup after the players and was joined on the pitch by Valdas Ivanauskas who had steered Hearts to second place in the League and to a Scottish Cup victory.

The new century legends were:- Craig Gordon, Robbie Neilson, Takis Fyssas, Steven Pressley-captain, Rudi Skacel, Edgaras Jankauskas, Paul Hartley, Roman Bednar, Devidas Cesnauskis, Ibrahim Tall, Bruno Aguiar. Substitutes:- Michal Pospisil for Bednar, Juilen Brellier for Aguiar, Sauliunas Mikoliunas for Cesnauskis.

Although the celebrations may not have been as extensive as 1998 nevertheless the players in the open topped bus were cheered all the way from the outskirts to the team celebration at Murrayfield Stadium. On the Sunday the same route from the City Chambers reception, as in 1998, to Tynecastle was as crowded and joyous as ever – the futures was maroon.

SCOTTISH CUP WINNERS 2005/2006 Standing Back Row – G. Paterson (Kit), J. Brellier, I. Tall, S. Banks, C. Gordon, E. Jankauskas, C. Berra, D. Valentine (Masseur).
Standing Middle Row – A. Robson (Masseur), A. Caldwell (Physio), T. Ritchie (Coach), S. Mikolounas, R. Bednar, R. Neilson, M. Pospisil, D. Cesnauskis, S. Frail (Youth Coach), J. Stewart (Coach), Dr. Melvin.
Seated – B. Aguiar, T. Fyssas, V. Ivanauskas (Head Coach), V. Romanov, S. Pressley (Captain), R. Romanov (Chairman), J. McGlynn (Asst. Head Coach), P. Hartley, R. Skacel.

ROTATION – ROTATION

Neil MacFarlane left in January, Jamie McAllister left in March and Rudi Skacel did not want to stay with Hearts and left for Southampton. Andy Webster resigned in July under a little known UEFA rule and Hristos Karipidis–PAOK Salonika, Andrius Velicka and Marius Zaliukas both–loan FBK Kaunas came in.

Roman Bednar made his first appearance for the Czech Republic in a Full International as a Hearts player, on 16 August 2006 against Serbia, as a substitute, in a 3-1 defeat in the Stadion Crvena Zvezda, Belgrade..

Season 2006-2007 was going to be a major test for the owners, staff and players if they were to maintain or improve on the previous season.

The Champions League was the pinnacle of achievement from the Premier League and Hearts had to prove their metal. The Second Qualifying Round, First Leg, brought NK Siroki Brijeg to Edinburgh for a match played at Murrayfield on 26 July before a new record for that venue of 28,486 and Hearts won 3-0. The Second Leg, in Bosnia on 2 August was a nervous match but ended in a 0-0 draw. Hearts were now amongst the 'big boys' and in the Third Qualifying Round, First Leg, played AEK Athens at Murrayfield on 9 August to yet another record crowd of 32,459 but lost 2-1. The Second Leg in Greece was spoilt by the referee sending off two Hearts players – the 3-0 defeat was irrelevant.

Having progressed from the Third Qualifying Round, Hearts were able to enter the UEFA Cup at the First Round. In the First Leg, Sparta Prague came to Murrayfield on 14 September and went away with a 2-0 win. In the Second Leg, in the Czech Republic Hearts performed well and came home proud after a 0-0 draw. Murrayfield had not proved to be the ideal venue either for crowd numbers or atmosphere and probably financially.

Because they were in a European competition Hearts did not enter the League Cup until the Third Round and defeated Alloa Athletic 4-0 at Recreation Park. In the Quarter-Finals it was Hibernian at Easter Road and the home side won 1-0 as Hearts tumbled tamely out of a second competition.

Maurico Pinilla made his first appearance for Chile in a Full International, as a Hearts player, on 7 October 2006 against Peru in a 3-2 win at Estado Nacional, Lima.

Robbie Neilson made his first appearance for Scotland in a Full International on 11 October 2006 against Ukraine in a 2-0 defeat in the Olympic Stadium, Kiev.

Marius Zaliukas made his first appearance for Lithuania in a Full International, as a Hearts player, on 11 October 2006 against Kuwait in 1-0 defeat in Kuwait.

Nerijus Barasa made his first appearance for Lithuania in a Full International, as a Hearts player, on 15 November 2006 against Malta in a 4-1 win at the Hibernian Football Grounds, Malta.

The League campaign was going to be more difficult after Hearts had been runners-up last season, as other teams would see them as a worthy scalp. An early sign that the players were ready for the challenge saw Celtic lose 2-1 in Gorgie but the frailty manifested itself when they could only draw 0-0 with Falkirk the following Saturday. Inverness C T were the first team to feel the full brunt of a revived team when they lost 4-1 at Tynecastlle in August. Then Dundee United lost to Hearts favourite score of 4-0 at Tynecastle in October.

Results were mixed and team changes regular but the third team to lose four goals was Motherwell in a 4-1 defeat at Tynecastle in December. There were the usual teams that failed to gain a win against Hearts including Dunfermline Athletic, Falkirk, Hibernian, Inverness Caledonian Thistle and Motherwell. Sadly, St.Mirren managed to prevent Hearts winning a match as did Rangers but the team finished in fourth place.

Steven Pressley played his last game for Hearts on 25 November 2006 in a 0-0 draw in Inverness and left in December. He was followed by Paul Hartley who signed for Celtic in January. While Laryea Kingston came in.

The Scottish Cup competition did not last long and in the Third Round Hearts defeated Stranraer with another 4-0 at Stair Park. The team did not deserve to lose 1-0 at Dunfermline Athletic at East End Park, in the Fourth Round. as they started well but the 90th.minute goal was a killer.

Laryea Kingston mad his first appearance for Ghana as a Full International, as a Hearts player, on 6 February 2007 against Nigeria and scored ina 4-1 win at Griffin Park, Brentford, London.

Andrius Velicka made his first appearance for Lithuania as a Full International, as a Hearts player, on 6 February 2007 against Mali in a 3-1 defeat in Marville a la Courneuve, Saint Denis.

Valdas Ivanauskas was absent though ill-health and Sport Director Anatoly Korobochka became Interim Head Coach on 17 March 2007.

HEARTS MISS OUT ON TOP SIX

On 20 August 2007 Hearts announced their £51 million plan for a major development of the site including a new 10,000 seat main stand, a hotel with Skyline Restaurant, gymnasium, an office block and residential apartments.

Jose Goncalves went on loan to FC Nurenberg for the season on 7 July. Michael Stewart returned from Hibernian in July and a raft of new signings including – Christain Nade-Sheffield United and Ruben Palazuelos-Gimnastica came in.

Kestutis Ivaskevicius and Audrius Ksanavicius made their first appearance for Lithuania in a Full International, as Hearts players, on 22 August 2007 against Turkmenistan ina 2-1 win at the Darius ir Girenas Stadium, Kaunas.

Season 2007-2008 proved to be a step backwards for Hearts who, for the first time, failed to gain a place in the 'top six'. The only two with a perfect record are Celtic and Rangers.

Anatoly Korobochka as Sport Director was responsible for team matters with Steven Frail as Assistant Head Coach when football started in earnest.

The League Cup competition saw Hearts face Second Division, Stirling Albion in the Second Round, at Forthbank Stadium and win 2-0. In the Third Round, at Tynecastle, First Division, Dunfermline Athletic gave the home side an uncomfortable time. After going ahead the team scorned several opportunities to win the tie and lost a goal in the 84th.minute to force extra-time. Here they did what they should have done all evening ended up winning 4-1.

Model of Proposed Development 2007 Model by Omega Models Ltd - Kirkintilloch.

The Quarter-Finals brought Celtic and Hearts together in Glasgow on 31 October and after a quite sensational 90 minutes the "maroons" defeated "celts" 2-0 with two late strikes. The Semi-Finals were played at Hampden Park and on 30 January it was Rangers v Hearts turn and each side gave as good as they got but two goals in the second half saw the "gers" reach the final

Eggert Jonsson made his first appearance for Iceland in a Full International on 21 November 2007 against Denmark in a 3-0 defeat at the Parken Stadion, Kobenhavn.

The League campaign could not have got off to a worst start when Hibernian defeated Hearts at Tynecastle by 1-0, in the opening match. As had happened when Livingston and Inverness Caledonian Thistle came into the Premier League, Hearts could not raise their game against the 'new boys'. In August Gretna drew 1-1 in Gorgie drew 1-1 again in January and although Hearts won at home in February they lost the final match of the season.

The team provided the home supporters with some cheer with a 4-2 win over Rangers-15 September, 4-2 victory over Falkirk-6 October and a 4-1 victory over Aberdeen-11 November. As it was Remembrance Sunday a special shirt was worn by the players showing the names of the seven players who died in WW1. The team failed to win a match from that day until they defeated Hibernian on 19 January – nine matches. The only team not to win against Hearts were Aberdeen and Celtic and Kilmarnock were the teams not to lose to the "maroons". A very lowly eighth place was unacceptable.

Michal Pospisil and Andrius Velicka were transferred and Stevie Frail was asked to act as Caretaker Manager from 5 January 2008.

The Scottish Cup competition lasted for only one round. On 12 January Hearts met Motherwell in the Fourth Round at Tynecastle and although the "maroons" led by 2-0 early in the second-half the "well" managed a 2-2 draw. In the Replay at Fir Park a penalty in the first-half saw Motherwell through.

Christophe Berra made his first appearance for Scotland in a Full International on 30 May 2008 against the Czech Republic in a 3-1 defeat in the Toyota Arena, Praha.

Ibrahim Tall left for Nantes and Roman Bednar for West Bromwich in May and Jose Goncalves went out on a season long loan to FC Nurinberg in July.

An Extraordinary General meeting was held on 31 July 2008 to consider a Proposed Debt for Equity Conversion from UAB Ukio Banko Investicine Grupe. All three resolutions were passed.

THE LOQUACIOUS AND PERSONABLE CSABA LAZLO

Despite the usual media speculation during the close season, they were wrong again, and were taken by surprise when Csaba Lazlo was announced as Hearts new Manager on 11 July 2008. He so impressed at his interview on the Friday that his appointment was released then, instead of on the Monday as forecast.

New players were quickly brought in including Janos Balogh-loan Debrecan VSC, Marian Kello-loan FBK Kaunas, David Obua-Kaizer Chiefs and Mike Tullberg-loan Regina,

The whole 2008-2009 campaign from the League Cup, through the League Championship and onto the Scottish Cup would have to be vastly improved. There was to be a rapidly increasing learning process not only for the players but just as much for supporters and the media. Although sarcastically referred to as motor mouth, and criticised for his longwinded answers to questions, Csaba Lazlo won over the majority with his 'Together' slogan and the supporters and the media watched with admiration, as he brought virtually the same squad of players, from eighth place ignominy in 2007/2008, to the top six and finally to third by the end of the season.

Michael Stewart made his first appearance for Scotland in a Full International, as a Hearts player, on 20 August 2008 against Northern Ireland in a 0-0 draw at Hampden Park, Glasgow.

In the League Cup, Second Round Hearts met Airdrie United at Tynecastle and with no goals after 90 minutes and after extra-time the home side lost 4-3 on penalties. This time there was no disrespect for the competition and it was a recognised first team that played and lost.

David Obua made his first appearance for Uganda in a Full International, as a Hearts player, on 7 September 2008 against Niger and scored, in a 3-1 win in the Stade Genersal Seyni Kountche. Niamey.

The League Championship was very much a see-saw affair with tight results and some alarming incidents but progress was seen to be made. Surprisingly, Hearts failed to score in 14 matches but there were twelve in which they did not concede a goal, leading to five 0-0 results. .

The highlights before 'the split' came in March and April, when Hearts drew with Rangers [2-2] defeated Kilmarnock [3-1] and drew [1-1] with Celtic after being a goal down, in each match, this ensured their place in the 'top six'. The piece de resistance, however, was the defeat of Dundee United on 16 May, which was to ensure third place in the League

Two of the worst nights in the season occurred firstly, on 7 January, when Hearts were away from home and overwhelmed by a very poor Motherwell side losing 1-0 in a dire performance. Secondly, on 7 May, when Hearts allowed Hibernian to defeat them in a vital match for third place in the League. Questions were asked of the manager and his selection, then of the players, none of whom deserved pass marks.

Team selection was much more regular and for the first time since 2003-2004 the number of players used fell to 30. The defence conceded only 37 goals but a lack of a natural striker meant Hearts only scored 40 goals. Inverness Caledonian Thistle lost all three matches and were relegated while St.Mirren failed to win against Hearts, and just avoided relegation. The Tynecastle side failed to defeat Celtic [3 draws & 1 defeat] and Hibernian [2 draws & 2 defeats].

The Scottish Cup, was not to be the shining beacon, although in the Fourth Round against Hibernian, it was encouraging to get a straightforward 2-0 victory at Easter Road. To then receive a home tie in the Fifth Round was all that could be asked for. Sadly, Falkirk came to Edinburgh and won 1-0. Hopes had been high after defeating their city rivals and the supporters were very angry at the defeat. Although Hearts did not play well, it was a decision by an assistant referee to convince the referee to reverse a late penalty decision, that caused the damage.

This was a season when the Hearts supporters were confident of being in the 'top six', with the previous season's eighth place, being an unnecessary blip by Scotland's third biggest club. They hoped for third place in the Championship and when it came it was after, possibly, the best performance of the campaign, in the final match at home on 13 May with a 3-0 win, and coasting. As fate decreed, the only time Hearts scored more than two goals in a match was in the first and last home fixtures against Motherwell and Dundee United respectively.

Casba Lazlo rightfully was voted the Scottish Football Writers Association, Manager of the Year, and the Clydesdale Bank Premier League Manager of the Year. How he failed to be voted the SPFA Manager of the Year, will remain the secret of the other SPL managers.

A season with many plus points, leading to a rejuvenated fan base, and a justified entry into the first ever Europa League competition.

ROSEBERY CHARITY CUP

"Presented to the EFA by the Right Hon. The Earl of Rosebery" engraved "Rosebery Charity Challenge Cup 1882". It is in the form of a Monteith, sterling silver rose bowl which stands on a tapered black wood plinth with silver mounts bearing winners names.

It was played for from 1882-1883 season to 1944-1945 season – on 63 occasions. Hearts winners 32 times; Hibernian 22 times; Leith Athletic and St. Bernards 4 times; Mossend Swifts once.

In accordance with the wishes of the Earl of Rosebery, Hearts hold the trophy in perpetuity.

SEASON	DATE	RESULT
1882-1883	21 Apr' 1883	Hearts 2 v St. Bernards 0.
1883-1884	14 May' 1884	Hibernian 1 v St. Bernards 0. *
1884-1885	25 Apr' 1885	Hibernian 3 v Hearts 0.
1885-1886	24 Jun' 1886	Hearts 1 v Hibernian 0.
1886-1887	16 May' 1887	Hibernian 7 v Hearts 1.
1887-1888	12 May' 1888	Hibernian 1 v Mossend Swifts 0.
1888-1889	22 May' 1889	Mossend Swifts 4 v St. Bernards 3. *
1889-1890	10 May' 1890	Hearts 4 v Leith Athletic 2.
1890-1891	27 Jun' 1891	Leith Athletic 3 v Hearts 2.
1891-1892	28 May' 1892	Hearts 2 v Leith Athletic 1.
1892-1893	27 May' 1893	Hearts 3 v St. Bernards 3. (St. Bernards Withdrew) *
1893-1894	31 May' 1894	Hibernian 4 v Hearts 2.
1894-1895	29 May' 1895	Hearts 3 v Leith Athletic 1.
1895-1896	25 May' 1896	Hearts 8 v Leith Athletic 2.
1896-1897	11 May' 1897	Hibernian 3 v Hearts 0.
1897-1898	21 May' 1898	Hearts 6 v Hibernian 1.
1898-1899	27 May' 1899	Leith Athletic 1 v Hearts 0.
1899-1900	23 May' 1900	Hearts 3 v Hibernian 0. **
1900-1901	31 May' 1901	Hibernian 4 v Hearts 0.
1901-1902	24 May' 1902	Hibernian 1 v Hearts 0.
1902-1903	30 May' 1903	Hibernian 3 v Leith Athletic 1.
1903-1904	30 May' 1904	Hearts 3 v Hibernian 0.
1904-1905	27 May' 1905	Hearts 5 v Leith Athletic 0.
1905-1906	30 May' 1906	Hibernian 2 v Hearts 0.
1906-1907	1 Jun' 1907	Hearts 4 v Leith Athletic 1.
1907-1908	16 May' 1908	St. Bernards 3 v Hearts 2.
1908-1909	15 May' 1909	Hibernian 3 v Leith Athletic 0.
1909-1910	14 May' 1910	Hibernian 2 v Leith Athletic 0.
1910-1911	13 May' 1911	Hibernian 5 v St. Bernards 0.
1911-1912	11 May' 1912	Hibernian 0 v Edinburgh X1 0. *
1912-1913	10 May' 1913	Hibernian 2 v Hearts 0.
1913-1914	9 May' 1914	Hearts 3 v Hibernian 2.
1914-1915	8 May' 1915	St. Bernards 4 v Hibernian 3.
1915-1916	13 May' 1916	Hearts 4 v Hibernian 0.
1916-1917	12 May' 1917	Hearts 5 v Armadale 3.
1917-1918	18 May' 1918	Hibernian 2 v Hearts 0.
1918-1919	17 May' 1919	Hearts 2 v Hibernian 1.
1919-1920	15 May' 1920	Hearts 2 v Hibernian 0.
1920-1921	14 May' 1921	Hearts 1 v St. Bernards 0.
1921-1922	13 May' 1922	Hibernian 3 v Leith Athletic 0.
1922-1923	12 May' 1923	Hearts 2 v Hibernian 1.
1923-1924	10 May' 1924	Hibernian 2 v Hearts 0.
1924-1925	16 May' 1925	Hibernian 1 v Hearts 0.
1925-1926	15 May' 1926	Hearts 9 v Leith Athletic 0.
1926-1927	14 May' 1927	Hearts 1 v Hibernian 0.
1927-1928	12 May' 1928	Hearts 2 v Leith Athletic 0.
1928-1929	11 May' 1929	Hearts 5 v Hibernian 1.
1929-1930	10 May' 1930	Hearts 2 v Leith Athletic 1.
1930-1931	9 May' 1931	St. Bernards 2 v Hearts 1.
1931-1932	14 May' 1932	Leith Athletic 2 v Hearts 1.
1932-1933	13 May' 1933	Hearts 3 v Motherwell 1.
1933-1934	12 May' 1934	Hearts 2 v Hibernian 1.
1934-1935	15 May' 1935	Hearts 2 v Leith Athletic 1.
1935-1936	15 May' 1936	Hearts 2 v St. Bernards 0.
1936-1937	15 May' 1937	Hearts 2 v Hibernian 0.
1937-1938	14 May' 1938	St. Bernards 4 v Leith Athletic 0.
1938-1939	13 May' 1939	Leith Athletic 2 v Hearts 0.
1939-1940	1 Jun' 1940	Hibernian 5 v Hearts 2.
1940-1941	31 May' 1941	Hearts 2 v Hibernian 0.
1941-1942	23 May' 1942	Hearts 1 v Hibernian 1. ***
1942-1943	22 May' 1943	Hearts 1 v Hibernian 1. ***
1943-1944	27 May' 1944	Hibernian 4 v Hearts 1.
1944-1945	9 May' 1945	Hibernian 2 v Hearts 2 ****

* won on corners; ** Replay after 3-3 draw; *** Won after toss of a coin; **** lost on corners.

THE DUNEDIN CUP

In December 1908 – Mr. Wm. Sharp and Mr. Wm. Sharp Junior formally handed over to the custody of the Club the Wm. Sharp Cup engraved "Presented by Wm.Sharp Esq". "The Sharp Cup". "For annual competition among East of Scotland Clubs". The trophy a handsome sterling silver baluster plus plinth stand 36" high.

"At a meeting held for the purpose of considering a new football competition for a Cup presented by Wm. Sharp Esq. Leith". Representatives were present from Heart of Midlothian, Hibernians, Falkirk, Leith Athletic, Raith Rovers & St. Bernards".

As it was not in accordance with the Rules of the S.F.A. to name a cup competition after a person. It was decided to change the name of the competition to 'The Dunedin Cup".

In May 1914 – the number of membership clubs was changed from six to four. It was agreed that Heart of Midlothian, Hibernian, Falkirk, and Raith Rovers, be the four clubs to compete for the cup in future.

It was played for from 1909-1910 season to 1932-1933 season – on 20 occasions. Hearts winners 13 times; Falkirk 3 times; Hibernian twice; St. Bernards and Raith Rovers once.

When the competition was discontinued, the trophy was returned to Wm. Sharp who in turn handed it over to the "custody" of the Heart of Midlothian Football Club.

SEASON	DATE	RESULT
1909-1910	1 Sep'1909	St. Bernards 1 v Raith Rovers 0.
1910-1911	29 Aug'1910	Hearts 5 v Falkirk 1.
1911-1912	11 Sep'1911	Hearts 1 v Raith Rovers 0.
1912-1913	28 Aug'1912	Hearts 1 v Hibernian 0.
1913-1914	24 Sep'1913	Falkirk 4 v Hibernian 1.
1914-1915	26 Aug'1914	Hearts 6 v Hibernian 0.
1915-1916		In Abeyance.
1916-1917		In Abeyance.
1917-1918	27 Apr'1918	Falkirk 5 v Hibernian 3.
1918-1919		In Abeyance.
1919-1920		In Abeyance.
1920-1921	20 Apr'1921	Hearts 2 v Hibernian 0.
1921-1922	12 Apr'1922	Hibernian 1 v Falkirk 0.
1922-1923	18 Apr'1923	Falkirk 1 v Raith Rovers 0.
1923-1924	30 Apr'1924	Raith Rovers 1 v Hibernian 0.
1924-1925	22 Apr'1925	Hearts 2 v Falkirk 1.
1925-1926	22 Apr'1926	Hearts 2 v Hibernian 1.
1926-1927	13 Apr'1927	Hearts 3 v Falkirk 1.
1927-1928	18 Apr'1928	Hearts 2 v Raith Rovers 2. *
1928-1929	17 Apr'1929	Hearts 8 v Hibernian 2.
1929-1930	16 Apr'1930	Hibernian 0 v Hearts 0. *
1930-1931	22 Apr'1931	Hearts 3 v Hibernian 0.
1931-1932	19 Sep'1932	Hearts 9 v Falkirk 3.
1932-1933	26 Apr'1933	Hearts 1 v Hibernian 0.

* won on corners.

FULL INTERNATIONALS – ORDER OF APPEARANCE

N=NATIONALITY – A=TOTAL APPEARANCES

No.	DEBUT	N	A	NAME
1	19/02/1887	S	1	Tom Jenkinson
2	24/03/1888	S	1	Tom Brackenridge
3	09/03/1889	S	3	Jimmy Adams
4	29/03/1890	S	3	Davie Baird
	29/03/1890	S	4	Isaac Begbie
6	04/04/1891	S	1	Johnny Hill
	04/04/1891	S	1	John McPherson
8	02/04/1892	S	1	Willie Taylor
9	24/03/1894	S	1	Tom Chambers
10	30/03/1895	S	2	Davie Russell
	30/03/1895	S	3	John Walker
12	21/03/1896	S	2	Alex King
13	28/03/1896	S	2	Geordie Hogg
14	26/03/1898	S	1	Tom Robertson
15	03/03/1900	S	2	Harry Rennie
	03/03/1900	S	29	Bobby Walker
17	02/03/1901	S	1	Markie Bell
18	01/03/1902	S	2	Albert Buick
	01/03/1902	S	1	George Key
20	15/03/1902	S	1	Henry Allan
21	21/03/1903	S	1	Bill Porteous
22	12/03/1904	S	4	George Wilson
23	26/03/1904	S	12	Charlie Thomson
24	07/04/1906	S	1	Alex Menzies
	01/03/1909	S	1	Tom Collins
26	19/03/1910	S	3	George Sinclair
27	02/03/1912	S	2	Bob Mercer
28	15/03/1913	S	2	Peter Nellies
29	03/03/1923	S	1	Jock White
30	27/10/1928	S	9	Jack Harkness
31	26/10/1929	S	3	John Johnston
32	20/10/1930	S	1	Willie Reid
33	25/10/1930	S	1	Barney Battles
34	01/04/1933	S	11	Alex Massie
35	20/10/1934	S	23	Andy Anderson
36	21/11/1934	S	1	Andy Herd
37	21/11/1934	S	1	Dave McCulloch
	31/10/1936	S	20	Tommy Walker
39	17/10/1937	S	2	Alex Munro
40	08/12/1937	S	3	Freddie Warren
41	08/12/1937	S	3	Andy Black
	21/05/1938	S	1	Willie Waugh
43	09/11/1938	S	2	Jimmy Dykes
44	24/05/1947	S	1	Archie Miller
45	15/04/1950	S	3	Willie MacFarlane
46	26/04/1950	S	1	Willie Bauld
47	08/12/1954	S	3	Bobby Dougan
48	08/12/1954	S	9	John Cumming
	02/05/1956	S	2	Jimmy Wardhaugh
50	02/05/1956	S	1	Alfie Conn

No.	DEBUT	N	A	NAME
51	26/05/1957	S	4	Dave Mackay
52	19/04/1958	S	5	Jimmy Murray
53	09/04/1960	S	6	Alex Young
54	08/05/1963	S	5	Davie Holt
55	12/05/1964	S	6	Jim Cruickshank
56	25/11/1964	S	3	Willie Wallace
57	08/05/1969	N	3	Roald Jensen
58	17/11/1973	S	3	Donald Ford
59	11/11/1987	S	4	Gary Mackay
60	17/02/1988	S	2	John Colquhoun
	17/02/1988	S	3	Henry Smith
62	26/04/1989	S	20	Dave McPherson
63	06/09/1989	Ni	4	Dave McCreery
64	28/03/1990	S	16	Craig Levein
65	12/09/1990	S	16	John Robertson
66	17/05/1992	S	14	Alan McLaren
67	24/03/1993	S	1	Nicky Walker
68	24/01/1995	C	5	Colin Miller
69	27/05/1997	S	9	David Weir
70	05/09/1998	S	1	Neil McCann
71	28/04/1999	S	11	Colin Cameron
	28/04/1999	S	4	Paul Ritchie
73	05/10/1999	S	2	Gary McSwegan
74	29/03/2000	S	32	Steven Pressley
	29/03/2000	A	15	Thomas Flogel
76	25/04/2000	Sl	9	Robert Tomaschek
77	26/04/2000	Ni	5	Andy Kirk
	26/04/2000	F	15	Anti Niemi
79	30/05/2000	S	4	Gary Naysmith
80	02/07/2000	J	4	Fitzroy Simpson
81	26/04/2001	C	24	Kevin McKenna
82	06/10/2001	S	8	Scott Severin
83	27/03/2002	F	2	Tommi Gronlund
	30/04/2003	S	22	Andy Webster
85	17/11/2003	F	7	Teuvo Moilanen
86	31/03/2004	R	7	Alan Maybury
87	30/05/2004	S	23	Craig Gordon
	31/05/2005	Aa	3	Patrick Kisnorbo
89	09/02/2005	L	21	Deividas Cesnauskis
90	26/03/2005	S	11	Paul Hartley
91	30/03/2005	L	27	Saulius Mikoliunas
92	17/08/2005	G	13	Panagiotis Fyssas
	17/08/2005	L	5	Edgaras Jankauskas
	17/08/2005	Cz	2	Rudolf Skacel
95	21/01/2006	Se	1	Ibrahim Tall
96	28/02/2006	F	3	Juho Makela
97	16/08/2006	B	3	Mirsad Beslija
98	07/10/2006	Cz	1	Roman Bednar
	07/10/2006	Ch	3	Maurico Pinilla
100	11/10/2006	S	1	Robbie Neilson

No.	DEBUT	N	A	NAME
	11/10/2006	L	6	Marius Zaliukas
	15/11/2006	L	1	Nerijus Barasa
102	06/02/2007	Gh	20	Larvea Kingston
103	06/02/2007	L	7	Andrius Velicka
	22/08/2007	L	2	Kestutis Ivaskevicius
105	22/08/2007	L	11	Audrius Ksanavicius
107	21/11/2007	I	3	Eggert Jonsson
108	30/05/2008	S	3	Christophe Berra
109	20/08/2008	S	1	Michael Stewart
110	07/09/2008	U	1	David Obua

NATIONS

S	Scotland
Ni	Northern Ireland
W	Wales
N	Norway
C	Canada
A	Austria
Sl	Slovakia
F	Finland
J	Jamaica
R	Republic of Ireland
Aa	Australia
L	Lithuania
G	Greece
Cz	Czech Republic
Se	Senegal
B	Bosnia & Hertz
Ch	Chile
Gh	Ghana
I	Iceland
U	Uganda

as at 31 May 2009

LEAGUE INTERNATIONALS – ORDER OF APPEARANCE
A=TOTAL APPEARANCES

	DEBUT	NAME	A		DEBUT	NAME	A
1	08/04/1893	Jimmy Adams	2	51	27/09/1950	Bobby Dougan	3
		Isaac Begbie	3	52	17/01/1951	Jimmy Wardhaugh	9
3	29/04/1893	Davie Baird	2	53	17/03/1952	Davie Laing	3
		Jock Fairbairn	1	54	15/09/1954	John Urquhart	1
5	11/04/1896	George Hogg	1	55	18/11/1954	Willie Duff	1
		Alex King	1	56	16/03/1955	John Cumming	7
		John Walker	2	57	13/03/1957	Dave Mackay	3
8	29/01/1898	Bob McCartney	1	58	26/03/1958	Alex Young	2
		Harry Marshall	2	59	08/10/1958	Johnny Hamilton	1
10	11/02/1899	Harry Allan	2	60	14/10/1959	George Thomson	2
		Albert Buick	2	61	23/03/1960	Bobby Blackwood	1
		Willie Michael	1	62	05/02/1962	Billy Higgins	1
		Bobby Walker	14	63	14/11/1962	Willie Hamilton	1
14	31/03/1900	Harry Rennie	1	64	24/02/1964	Jim Cruickshank	4
15	08/03/1902	George McWattie	1			Chris Shevlane	2
16	27/02/1904	Charlie Thomson	5			Tommy White	1
17	24/03/1906	George Wilson	1	67	23/09/1964	Davie Holt	1
18	27/02/1909	Tom Collins	2	68	08/09/1965	Willie Wallace	2
19	04/03/1911	Roderick Walker	1	69	19/11/1969	Dave Clunie	1
20	30/10/1911	Tom Allan	1			Eddie Thomson	1
		Peter Nellies	9	71	17/03/1971	Donald Ford	3
22	17/02/1912	Bob Mercer	5	72	20/03/1974	Jimmy Brown	1
23	14/10/1912	George Sinclair	2			Bobby Prentice	1
24	12/10/1914	Paddy Crossan	1	74	01/11/1978	Eamonn Bannon	1
		Harry Graham	1				
		Jimmy Low	2				
27	18/11/1914	Tom Gracie	1				
28	20/03/1915	Willie Wilson	1				
29	26/10/1921	Bob Birrell	1				
30	17/02/1923	John White	4				
31	31/10/1923	Willie White	4				
32	29/10/1924	Jimmy Smith	3				
33	27/10/1926	Peter Kerr	1				
		Tommy Reid	1				
35	31/10/1928	Barney Battles	5				
		John Johnston	3				
37	07/11/1928	Bob Bennie	1				
38	19/10/1932	Alex Massie	6				
39	10/02/1934	Andy Anderson	4				
40	31/10/1934	Andy Herd	1				
		Dave McCulloch	1				
42	30/10/1935	Tommy Walker	5				
43	01/09/1937	Andy Black	2				
44	22/09/1937	Jimmy Dykes	3				
45	07/09/1938	Archie Miller	1				
46	17/03/1939	Tommy Brown	1				
47	30/04/1947	Willie Macfarlane	1				
48	24/04/1948	George Hamilton	1				
49	08/11/1948	Alfie Conn	3				
50	07/09/1949	Willie Bauld	13				

THE CAPITAL CITY CHAMPIONS

Competition	HOME P	W	D	L	F	A	AWAY P	W	D	L	F	A	NEUTRAL P	W	D	L	F	A	TOTAL P	W	D	L	F	A
League	71	35	17	19	135	103	71	32	17	22	128	99							142	67	34	41	263	202
%		49.3		26.8				45.1		31.0										47.2		28.9		
Premier/SPL	54	25	20	9	77	48	54	16	22	16	66	65							108	41	42	25	143	113
%		46.3		16.7				29.6		29.6										38.0		23.1		
League Matches	125	60	37	28	212	151	125	48	39	38	194	164							250	108	76	66	406	315
%		48.0		22.4				38.4		30.4										43.2		26.4		
Scottish Cup	12	4	4	4	22	18	12	6	2	4	19	17	5	3	1	1	11	4	29	13	7	9	52	39
%		33.3		33.3				50.0		33.3				60.0		20.0				44.8		31.1		
League Cup	2	2			8	2	3	2		1	4	3							5	4		1	12	5
%		100.0						66.7		33.3										80.0		20.0		
TOTAL	139	66	41	32	242	171	140	56	41	43	217	184	5	3	1	1	11	4	284	125	83	76	470	359
%		47.5		23.0				40.0		30.7				60.0		20.0				44.0		26.8		

Competition	HOME P	W	D	L	F	A	AWAY P	W	D	L	F	A	NEUTRAL P	W	D	L	F	A	TOTAL P	W	D	L	F	A
League	71	35	17	19	135	103	71	32	17	22	128	99							142	67	34	41	263	202
%		49.3		26.8				45.1		31.0										47.2		28.9		
Premier/SPL	54	25	20	9	77	49	54	16	22	16	66	65							108	41	42	25	143	113
%		46.3		16.7				29.6		29.6										38.0		23.1		
League Matches	125	60	37	28	212	151	125	48	39	38	194	164							250	108	76	66	406	315
%		48.0		22.4				38.4		30.4										43.2		26.4		
1939–40/1945–46	7	2		5	13	16	7	2	2	3	13	15							14	4	2	8	26	31
New Total	132	62	37	33	225	167	132	50	41	41	207	179							264	112	78	74	432	346
%		47.0		25.0				37.9		31.1										42.4		28.0		
Scottish Cup	12	4	4	4	22	18	12	6	2	4	19	17	5	3	1	1	11	4	29	13	7	9	52	39
%		33.3		33.3				50.0		33.3				60.0		20.0				44.8		31.1		
League Cup	2	2			8	2	3	2		1	4	3							5	4		1	12	5
%		100.0						66.7		33.3										80.0		20.0		
Grand Total	146	68	41	37	255	187	147	58	43	46	230	199	5	3	1	1	11	4	298	129	85	84	496	390
%		46.6		25.3				39.5		31.3				60.0		20.0				43.3		28.2		

FINAL TABLES & FINISHING POSITION

SEASON	HOME Played	W	D	L	F	A	Pts	AWAY Played	W	D	L	F	A	Pts	TOTAL Played	W	D	L	F	A	Pts	Pos'n.	
1890-91	9	4	2	3	20	15	10	9	2	0	7	11	22	4	18	6	2	10	31	37	14	6	
1891-92	11	10	1	0	32	11	21	11	5	3	3	33	24	13	22	15	4	3	65	35	34	3	
1892-93	9	4	2	3	21	15	10	9	4	0	5	18	26	8	18	8	2	8	39	41	18	5	
1893-94	9	4	2	3	21	17	10	9	7	2	0	25	15	16	18	11	4	3	46	32	26	2	
1894-95	9	7	1	1	27	12	15	9	8	0	1	23	6	16	18	15	1	2	50	18	31	1	
1895-96	9	7	0	2	38	11	14	9	4	0	5	30	25	8	18	11	0	7	68	36	22	4	
1896-97	9	7	2	0	24	8	16	9	6	0	3	23	14	12	18	13	2	3	47	22	28	1	
1897-98	9	5	2	2	30	15	12	9	3	2	4	24	18	8	18	8	4	6	54	33	20	4	
1898-99	9	7	1	1	32	13	15	9	5	1	3	24	17	11	18	12	2	4	56	30	26	2	
1899-00	9	7	1	1	24	8	15	9	3	2	4	17	16	8	18	10	3	5	41	24	23	4	
sub-total	92	62	14	16	269	125	138	92	47	10	35	228	183	104	184	109	24	51	497	308	242		
1900-01	10	1	3	6	10	14	5	10	4	1	5	12	16	9	20	5	4	11	22	30	14	10	
1901-02	9	6	2	1	21	8	14	9	4	0	5	11	13	8	18	10	2	6	32	21	22	3	
1902-03	11	6	2	3	23	14	14	11	5	4	2	23	13	14	22	11	6	5	46	27	28	4	
1903-04	13	13	0	0	41	9	26	13	5	3	5	22	26	13	26	18	3	5	63	35	39	2	
1904-05	13	10	0	3	33	13	20	13	1	3	9	13	31	5	26	11	3	12	46	44	25	7 =	
1905-06	15	12	3	0	35	8	27	15	6	4	5	29	19	16	30	18	7	5	64	27	43	2	
1906-07	17	7	7	3	27	16	21	17	4	6	7	19	27	14	34	11	13	10	46	43	35	9	
1907-08	17	9	1	7	33	24	19	17	2	5	10	17	38	9	34	11	6	17	50	62	28	11 =	
1908-09	17	8	5	4	26	17	21	17	4	3	10	28	32	11	34	12	8	14	54	49	32	11 =	
1909-10	17	9	3	5	37	19	21	17	3	4	10	22	31	10	34	12	7	15	59	50	31	12 =	
sub-total	231	143	40	48	555	267	326	231	85	43	103	424	429	213	462	228	83	151	979	696	539		
1910-11	17	7	6	4	27	18	20	17	1	2	14	15	41	4	34	8	8	18	42	59	24	14 =	

1000th. League goal scored on 19th.November,1910 – Hearts 2 v Airdrieonians 2; scored by Bobby Walker. 477 matches @ 2.10 goals per match.

	Played	W	D	L	F	A	Pts.	Played	W	D	L	F	A	Pts.	Played	W	D	L	F	A	Pts.	Pos'n.	
1911-12	17	11	2	4	28	16	24	17	5	6	6	26	24	16	34	16	8	10	54	40	40	4 =	
1912-13	17	10	4	3	42	18	24	17	7	3	7	29	25	17	34	17	7	10	71	43	41	3 =	
1913-14	19	17	1	1	43	7	35	19	6	7	6	27	22	19	38	23	8	7	70	29	54	3 =	
1914-15	19	17	1	1	50	13	35	19	10	6	3	33	19	26	38	27	7	4	83	32	61	2	
1915-16	19	12	1	6	35	23	25	18	8	5	5	31	22	21	37	20	6	11	66	45	46	5 =	
1916-17	19	9	1	9	25	30	19	19	5	3	11	19	29	13	38	14	4	20	44	59	32	14	
1917-18	17	11	1	5	24	15	23	17	3	3	11	17	43	9	34	14	4	16	41	58	32	10	
1918-19	17	8	5	4	31	20	21	17	6	4	7	28	32	16	34	14	9	11	59	52	37	7	
1919-20	21	8	5	8	31	28	21	21	6	4	11	26	44	16	42	14	9	19	57	72	37	15 =	
sub-total	413	253	67	93	891	455	573	412	142	86	184	675	730	370	825	395	153	277	1566	1185	943		
1920-21	21	15	2	4	48	16	32	21	5	8	8	26	33	18	42	20	10	12	74	49	50	3	
1921-22	21	9	6	6	34	21	24	21	2	4	15	16	39	8	42	11	10	21	50	60	32	19	0.833
1922-23	19	6	10	3	29	20	22	19	5	5	9	22	30	15	38	11	15	12	51	50	37	12	1.020
1923-24	19	12	4	3	43	17	28	19	2	6	11	18	33	10	38	14	10	14	61	50	38	9	1.220
1924-25	19	10	6	3	44	28	26	19	2	5	12	20	40	9	38	12	11	15	64	68	35	10	0.941
1925-26	19	14	2	3	52	21	30	19	7	6	6	35	35	20	38	21	8	9	87	56	50	3	1.554
1926-27	19	7	7	5	34	25	21	19	5	4	10	31	39	14	38	12	11	15	65	64	35	13	1.016

2000th. League goal scored on 5th.February,1927 – Hearts 1 v Motherwell 3; scored by Dave Edgar. 1087 matches @ 1.84 goals per match (610 matches @ 1.64 goals per match)

	Played	W	D	L	F	A	Pts.	Played	W	D	L	F	A	Pts.	Played	W	D	L	F	A	Pts.	Pos'n.	
1927-28	19	10	5	4	47	20	25	19	10	2	7	42	30	22	38	20	7	11	89	50	47	4	1.780
1928-29	19	13	4	2	56	23	30	19	6	5	8	35	34	17	38	19	9	10	91	57	47	4	1.596
1929-30	19	8	6	5	35	22	22	19	6	3	10	34	43	15	38	14	9	15	69	69	37	10	=
sub-total	607	357	119	131	1313	672	833	606	192	134	280	954	1086	518	1213	549	253	411	2267	1758	1351		
1930-31	19	12	2	5	58	33	26	19	7	4	8	32	30	18	38	19	6	13	90	63	44	5	1.429
1931-32	19	10	5	4	35	18	25	19	7	0	12	28	43	14	38	17	5	16	63	61	39	8	1.033
1932-33	19	15	3	1	49	16	33	19	6	5	8	35	35	17	38	21	8	9	84	51	50	6	1.647
1933-34	19	11	5	3	52	23	27	19	6	5	8	34	36	17	38	17	10	11	86	59	44	6	1.458
1934-35	19	11	5	3	42	19	27	19	9	5	5	45	32	23	38	20	10	8	87	51	50	3	1.706
1935-36	19	14	4	1	56	20	32	19	6	3	10	32	35	15	38	20	7	11	88	55	47	5	1.600
1936-37	19	17	0	2	67	22	34	19	7	3	9	32	38	17	38	24	3	11	99	60	51	5	1.650
1937-38	19	16	2	1	48	16	34	19	10	4	5	42	34	24	38	26	6	6	90	50	58	2	1.800
1938-39	19	13	1	5	61	30	27	19	7	4	8	37	40	18	38	20	5	13	98	70	45	4	1.400

3000th. League goal scored on 26th.November,1938 – Raith Rovers 1 v Hearts 2; scored by Tommy Brown. 1535 matches @ 1.95 goals per match (448 mathes @ 2.23 goals per match)

	Played	W	D	L	F	A	Pts.	Played	W	D	L	F	A	Pts.	Played	W	D	L	F	A	Pts.	Pos'n.	
1939-40	14	11	1	2	66	26	23	15	7	3	5	38	40	17	29	18	4	7	104	66	40	2	1.576
sub-total	792	487	147	158	1847	895	1121	792	264	170	358	1309	1449	698	1584	751	317	516	3156	2344	1819		
1940-41	15	8	3	4	38	29	19	15	4	2	9	26	42	10	30	12	5	13	64	71	29	10	0.901
1941-42	15	10	1	4	52	28	21	15	4	3	8	33	44	11	30	14	4	12	85	72	32	5	1.181
1942-43	15	9	1	5	41	33	19	15	3	6	6	27	31	12	30	12	7	11	68	64	31	7	1.063
1943-44	15	6	5	4	40	24	17	15	8	2	5	27	26	18	30	14	7	9	67	50	35	6	1.340
1944-45	15	11	3	1	47	19	25	15	3	4	8	28	41	10	30	14	7	9	75	60	35	6	1.250
1945-46	15	6	5	4	32	23	17	15	5	3	7	31	34	13	30	11	8	11	63	57	30	7	1.105
1946-47	15	8	3	4	30	24	19	15	8	3	4	22	19	19	30	16	6	8	52	43	38	4	1.209
1947-48	15	7	3	5	21	18	17	15	3	5	7	16	24	11	30	10	8	12	37	42	28	9	0.881
1948-49	15	8	2	5	37	22	18	15	4	4	7	27	32	12	30	12	6	12	64	54	30	8	1.185
1949-50	15	12	1	2	55	16	25	15	8	2	5	31	24	18	30	20	3	7	86	40	43	3	2.150
sub-total	942	572	174	196	2240	1131	1318	942	314	204	424	1577	1766	832	1884	886	378	620	3817	2897	2150		

SEASON	HOME Played	W	D	L	F	A	Pts.	AWAY Played	W	D	L	F	A	Pts.	TOTAL Played	W	D	L	F	A	Pts.		Pos'n.
1950-51	15	10	3	2	46	17	23	15	6	2	7	26	28	14	30	16	5	9	72	45	37	4	1.600
1951-52	15	9	5	1	44	25	23	15	5	2	8	25	28	12	30	14	7	9	69	53	35	4	1.302
1952-53	15	8	3	4	36	18	19	15	4	3	8	23	32	11	30	12	6	12	59	50	30	4	1.180

4000th. League goal scored on 7th.March,1953 – Hearts 3 v Aberdeen 1; scored by Jimmy Wardhaugh. 1969 matches @ 2.03 goals per match (434 matches @ 2.30 goals per match)

SEASON	HOME Played	W	D	L	F	A	Pts.	AWAY Played	W	D	L	F	A	Pts.	TOTAL Played	W	D	L	F	A	Pts.		Pos'n.
1953-54	15	9	3	3	42	24	21	15	7	3	5	28	21	17	30	16	6	8	70	45	38	2	1.556
1954-55	15	10	2	3	40	25	22	15	6	5	4	34	20	17	30	16	7	7	74	45	39	4	1.644
1955-56	17	13	2	2	65	17	28	17	6	5	6	34	30	17	34	19	7	8	99	47	45	3	2.106
1956-57	17	11	3	3	40	23	25	17	13	2	2	41	25	28	34	24	5	5	81	48	53	2	1.688
1957-58	17	15	2	0	79	17	32	17	14	2	1	53	12	30	34	29	4	1	132	29	62	1	4.552
1958-59	17	12	2	3	49	25	26	17	9	4	4	43	26	22	34	21	6	7	92	51	48	2	1.804
1959-60	17	14	2	1	56	22	30	17	9	6	2	46	29	24	34	23	8	3	102	51	54	1	2.000
sub-total	1102	683	201	218	2737	1344	1567	1102	393	238	471	1930	2017	1024	2204	1076	439	689	4667	3361	2591		
1960-61	17	8	3	6	26	25	19	17	5	5	7	25	28	15	34	13	8	13	51	53	34	7	0.962
1961-62	17	7	5	5	30	28	19	17	9	1	7	24	21	19	34	16	6	12	54	49	38	6	1.102
1962-63	17	10	4	3	45	26	24	17	7	5	5	40	33	19	34	17	9	8	85	59	43	5	1.441
1963-64	17	8	5	4	39	23	21	17	11	4	2	35	17	26	34	19	9	6	74	40	47	4	1.850
1964-65	17	11	3	3	46	24	25	17	11	3	3	44	25	25	34	22	6	6	90	49	50	2	1.837

5000TH. League goal scored on 10th.March,1965 – Greenock Morton 2 v Hearts 3; Danny Ferguson. 2367 matches @ 2.11 goals per match (398 matches @ 2.51 goals per match)

SEASON	HOME Played	W	D	L	F	A	Pts.	AWAY Played	W	D	L	F	A	Pts.	TOTAL Played	W	D	L	F	A	Pts.		Pos'n.
1965-66	17	7	5	5	28	21	19	17	6	7	4	28	27	19	34	13	12	9	56	48	38	7	1.167
1966-67	17	7	6	4	22	16	20	17	4	2	11	17	32	10	34	11	8	15	39	48	30	11	0.813
1967-68	17	9	1	7	24	23	19	17	4	3	10	32	38	11	34	13	4	17	56	61	30	12	0.918
1968-69	17	7	7	3	26	20	21	17	7	1	9	26	34	15	34	14	8	12	52	54	36	8	0.963
1969-70	17	6	7	4	28	19	19	17	7	5	5	22	17	19	34	13	12	9	50	36	38	4	1.389
sub-total	1272	763	247	262	3051	1569	1773	1272	464	274	534	2223	2289	1202	2544	1227	521	796	5274	3858	2975		
1970-71	17	8	5	4	24	16	21	17	5	2	10	17	24	12	34	13	7	14	41	40	33	11	1.020
1971-72	17	10	5	2	29	17	25	17	3	8	6	24	32	14	34	13	13	8	53	49	39	6	GD 4
1972-73	17	7	4	6	15	17	18	17	5	2	10	24	33	12	34	12	6	16	39	50	30	10	-11
1973-74	17	6	6	5	26	20	18	17	8	4	5	28	23	20	34	14	10	10	54	43	38	6	11
1974-75	17	8	6	3	24	16	22	17	3	7	7	23	36	13	34	11	13	10	47	52	35	8	-5
1975-76	18	7	5	6	23	20	19	18	6	4	8	16	25	16	36	13	9	14	39	45	35	5	-6
1976-77	18	5	6	7	26	28	16	18	2	7	9	23	38	11	36	7	13	16	49	66	27	9	-17
1977-78	19	13	4	2	37	18	30	20	11	6	3	40	24	28	39	24	10	5	77	42	58	2*	35
1978-79	18	5	5	8	19	25	15	18	2	3	13	20	46	8	36	8	7	21	39	71	23	9	-32
1979-80	20	13	6	1	33	18	32	19	7	7	5	25	21	21	39	20	13	6	58	39	53	1*	19
sub-total	1450	845	299	306	3307	1764	1989	1450	517	323	610	2463	2591	1357	2900	1362	622	916	5770	4355	3346		
1980-81	18	3	4	11	10	27	10	18	3	2	13	17	44	8	36	6	6	24	27	71	18	10	-44
1981-82	19	12	2	5	33	19	26	20	9	6	5	32	18	24	39	21	8	10	65	37	50	3*	28
1982-83	20	13	4	3	46	20	30	19	9	6	4	33	18	24	39	22	10	7	79	38	54	2*	41
1983-84	18	5	9	4	23	23	19	18	5	7	6	15	24	17	36	10	16	10	38	47	36	5	-9
1984-85	18	6	3	9	21	26	15	18	7	2	9	26	38	16	36	13	5	18	47	64	31	7	-17

6000th. League goal scored on 15th. December,1984 – Dundee United 5 v Hearts 2; scored by Jimmy Bone. 3069 matches @ 1.96 goals per match (702 matches @ 1.42 goals per match)

SEASON	HOME Played	W	D	L	F	A	Pts.	AWAY Played	W	D	L	F	A	Pts.	TOTAL Played	W	D	L	F	A	Pts.		Pos'n.
1985-86	18	13	5	0	38	10	31	18	7	5	6	21	23	19	36	20	10	6	59	33	50	2	26
1986-87	22	13	7	2	42	19	33	22	8	7	7	22	24	23	44	21	14	9	64	43	56	5	21
1987-88	22	13	8	1	37	17	34	22	10	8	4	37	15	28	44	23	16	5	74	32	62	2	42
1988-89	18	7	6	5	22	17	20	18	2	7	9	13	25	11	36	9	13	14	35	42	31	6	-1
1989-90	18	8	6	4	28	17	22	18	8	6	4	26	18	22	36	16	12	8	54	35	44	3	19
sub-total	1641	938	353	350	3607	1959	2229	1641	585	379	677	2705	2838	1549	3282	1523	732	1027	6312	4797	3778		
1990-91	18	10	3	5	28	22	23	18	4	4	10	20	33	12	36	14	7	15	48	55	35	5	-7
1991-92	22	12	7	3	26	15	31	22	15	2	5	34	22	32	44	27	9	8	60	37	63	2	23
1992-93	22	12	6	4	26	15	30	22	3	8	11	20	36	14	44	15	14	15	46	51	44	5	-5
1993-94	22	6	9	7	22	24	21	22	5	11	6	15	19	21	44	11	20	13	37	43	42	7	-6
1994-95	18	9	4	5	26	14	31	18	3	3	12	18	37	12	36	12	7	17	44	51	43	6	-7
1995-96	18	10	2	6	33	26	32	18	6	5	7	22	27	23	36	16	7	13	55	53	55	4	2
1996-97	18	8	6	4	27	20	30	18	6	4	8	19	23	22	36	14	10	12	46	43	52	4	3
1997-98	18	10	5	3	36	24	35	18	9	5	4	34	22	32	36	19	10	7	70	46	67	3	24
1998-99	18	8	2	8	27	26	26	18	3	7	8	17	24	16	36	11	9	16	44	50	42	6	-6
1999-00	18	7	4	6	25	18	25	18	3	7	8	22	22	22	36	10	11	12	47	40	54	5	7
sub-total	1833	1030	403	400	3883	2163	2515	1833	647	431	755	2926	3103	1760	3666	1677	834	1155	6809	5266	4275		
2000-01	19	11	2	6	36	21	35	19	3	8	8	20	29	17	38	14	10	14	56	50	52	5	6
2001-02	19	8	3	8	30	27	27	19	6	3	10	22	30	21	38	14	6	18	52	57	48	5	-5
2002-03	19	12	3	4	36	24	39	19	6	6	7	21	27	24	38	18	9	11	57	51	63	3	6
2003-04	19	12	5	2	32	17	41	19	7	6	6	24	23	27	38	19	11	8	56	40	68	3	16

7000th. League goal scored on 20th.December,2003 – Rangers 2 v Hearts 1; scored by Andy Kirk. 3797 matches @ 1.84 goals per match (728 matches @ 1.37 goals per match)

SEASON	HOME Played	W	D	L	F	A	Pts.	AWAY Played	W	D	L	F	A	Pts.	TOTAL Played	W	D	L	F	A	Pts.		Pos'n.
2004-05	19	9	4	6	25	15	31	19	4	7	8	18	26	19	38	13	11	14	43	41	50	5	2
2005-06	19	15	2	2	43	9	47	19	7	6	6	28	22	27	38	22	8	8	71	31	74	2	40
2006-07	19	9	4	6	26	19	31	19	8	6	5	21	16	30	38	17	10	11	47	35	61	4	12
2007-08	19	8	4	7	27	26	28	19	5	5	9	20	29	20	38	13	9	16	47	55	48	8	- 8
2008-09	19	11	5	3	28	18	38	19	5	6	8	12	19	21	38	16	11	11	40	37	59	3	3

1915-16 = Incomplete programme – war time shortage of players. 1939-40 = Scottish Regional League – war time restrictions on travel. 1940-41 to 1945-46 Scottish Southern League – war time revised Leagues.

Scottish League Championship
Division One 1890-1891

Sat 16 Aug	Rangers	2-5
Sat 23 Aug	CELTIC	0-5
Sat 30 Aug	Dumbarton	1-3
Sat 13 Sep	COWLAIRS	4-0
Sat 25 Oct	V' OF LEVEN	8-1
Sat 24 Jan	RANGERS	0-1
Sat 14 Feb	CAMBUSL'G	2-2
Sat 21 Feb	St.MIRREN	1-0
Sat 28 Feb	Celtic	0-1
Sat 7 Mar	Cowlairs	2-1
Sat 21 Mar	3rd.LANARK	4-1
Sat 28 Mar	ABERCORN	1-1
Sat 11 Apr	St.Mirren	2-3
Sat 18 Apr	Third Lanark	0-4
Mon 20 Apr	DUMBARTON	0-4
Sat 25 Apr	Abercorn	0-1
Sat 2 May	Cambuslang	0-2
Sat 9 May	Vale of Leven	4-2

Played 18	W6; D2; L10;	
Pts.14	F31; A37;	6th.

Scottish League Championship
Division One 1891-1892

Sat 15 Aug	CELTIC	3-1
Sat 22 Aug	St.Mirren	5-2
Sat 29 Aug	DUMBARTON	3-1
Sat 5 Sep	Cambuslang	3-3
Sat 12 Sep	RENTON	4-2
Sat 19 Sep	Dumbarton	1-5
Mon 21 Sep	ABERCORN	2-1
Sat 26 Sep	3rd.LANARK	2-0
Sat 3 Oct	Clyde	10-3
Sat 10 Oct	St.MIRREN	2-2
Sat 17 Oct	Celtic	1-3
Sat 24 Oct	LEITH ATH.	3-1
Sat 31 Oct	Vale of Leven	2-2
Sat 21 Nov	Rangers	1-0
Sat 26 Dec	CAMBUSL'G	1-0
Sat 12 Mar	Abercorn	3-1
Sat 19 Mar	V' OF LEVEN	7-0
Sat 9 Apr	Renton	3-0
Sat 16 Apr	CLYDE	2-1
Sat 23 Apr	RANGERS	3-2
Sat 30 Apr	Leith Athletic	2-2
Sat 7 May	Third Lanark	2-3

Played 22	W15; D4; L3;	
Pts.34	F65; A35;	3rd.

Scottish League Championship
Division One 1892-1893

Sat 20 Aug	Third.Lanark	4-1
Sat 27 Aug	CELTIC	3-1
Sat 3 Sep	Abercorn	4-3
Sat 10 Sep	RENTON	2-2
Sat 17 Sep	Leith Athletic	3-1
Sat 24 Sep	St.MIRREN	4-0
Sat 1 Oct	Renton	1-4
Sat 8 Oct	DUMBARTON	1-3
Sat 15 Oct	Clyde	3-2
Sat 5 Nov	Celtic	0-5
Sat 18 Feb	St.Mirren	1-3
Sat 4 Mar	3rd.LANARK	2-2
Sat 11 Mar	ABERCORN	3-1
Sat 18 Mar	RANGERS	1-2
Sat 1 Apr	Dumbarton	1-5
Sat 15 Apr	LEITH ATH.	3-1
Sat 29 Apr	CLYDE	2-3
Sat 6 May	Rangers	1-2

Played 18	W8; D2; L8;	
Pts.18	F39; A41;	5th.

Scottish League Championship
Division One 1893-1894

Sat 19 Aug	LEITH ATH.	0-2
Sat 26 Aug	St.Mirren	3-2
Sat 2 Sep	Third Lanark	3-1
Sat 9 Sep	CELTIC	2-4
Sat 23 Sep	3rd.LANARK	2-2
Sat 30 Sep	Dumbarton	2-2
Sat 7 Oct	St.Bernards	2-1
Sat 14 Oct	RANGERS	4-2
Sat 21 Oct	Dundee	5-2
Sat 4 Nov	Renton	3-2
Sat 18 Nov	St.MIRREN	1-1
Sat 2 Dec	Leith Athletic	2-2
Sat 16 Dec	DUNDEE	3-0
Sat 3 Mar	RENTON	5-1
Sat 10 Mar	Celtic	3-2
Sat 7 Apr	St.BERNARDS	2-4
Sat 14 Apr	Rangers	2-1
Sat 28 Apr	DUMBARTON	2-1

Played 18	W11; D4; L3;	
Pts.26	F46; A32;	2nd.

Scottish League Championship
Division One 1894–1895

Sat 18 Aug	3rd.LANARK	6-3
Sat 1 Sep	St.MIRREN	1-0
Sat 8 Sep	Third Lanark	3-0
Sat 15 Sep	LEITH ATH	3-1
Sat 29 Sep	Dumbarton	4-1
Sat 6 Oct	St.BERNARDS	4-3
Sat 13 Oct	St.Mirren	2-1
Sat 20 Oct	Rangers	1-0
Sat 27 Oct	DUMBARTON	3-1
Sat 3 Nov	Celtic	2-0
Sat 17 Nov	Leith Athletic	4-1
Sat 1 Dec	CLYDE	2-4
Sat 22 Dec	Dundee	2-0
Sat 19 Jan	RANGERS	0-0
Sat 16 Feb	CELTIC	4-0
Sat 23 Mar	Clyde	2-3
Sat 30 Mar	DUNDEE	4-0
Sat 6 Apr	St.Bernards	3-0

Played 18	W15; D1; L2;	
Pts.31	F50; A18;	1st.

Scottish League Championship
Division One 1895–1896

Sat 17 Aug	St.Mirren	1-2
Sat 24 Aug	Clyde	2-1
Sat 31 Aug	RANGERS	1-2
Sat 7 Sep	3rd.LANARK	3-0
Sat 14 Sep	Celtic	5-0
Sat 21 Sep	St.Bernards	5-0
Sat 28 Sep	HIBERNIAN	4-3
Sat 5 Oct	CLYDE	9-1
Sat 12 Oct	Dundee	0-5
Sat 19 Oct	Dumbarton	9-2
Sat 26 Oct	St.MIRREN	5-1
Sat 2 Nov	DUNDEE	2-0
Sat 23 Nov	CELTIC	1-4
Sat 30 Nov	Third Lanark	4-5
Sat 7 Dec	Rangers	2-7
Sat 14 Dec	St.BERNARDS	6-0
Sat 21 Dec	Hibernian	2-3
Sat 15 Feb	DUMBARTON	7-0

Played 18	W11; D0; L7;	
Pts.22	F68; A36;	4th.

Scottish League Championship
Division One 1896–1897

Sat 15 Aug	Dundee	5-0
Sat 22 Aug	ABERCORN	6-1
Sat 29 Aug	St.MIRREN	2-1
Sat 5 Sep	Celtic	0-3
Sat 12 Sep	Rangers	0-5
Sat 19 Sep	DUNDEE	2-2
Mon 21 Sep	RANGERS	2-1
Sat 26 Sep	Hibernian	0-2
Sat 3 Oct	St.Bernards	5-2
Sat 17 Oct	St.Mirren	2-0
Sat 24 Oct	CELTIC	1-1
Sat 31 Oct	Abercorn	1-0
Sat 7 Nov	St.BERNARDS	3-1
Sat 21 Nov	3rd.LANARK	2-1
Sat 5 Dec	HIBERNIAN	1-0
Sat 12 Dec	Third Lanark	5-1
Sat 13 Feb	Clyde	5-1
Sat 20 Feb	CLYDE	5-0

Played 18	W13; D2; L3;	
Pts.28	F47; A22;	1st.

Scottish League Championship
Division One 1897–1898

Sat 4 Sep	Partick Thistle	2-3
Sat 11 Sep	CELTIC	0-0
Sat 18 Sep	Hibernian	1-1
Mon 20 Sep	RANGERS	2-2
Sat 25 Sep	St.MIRREN	2-4
Sat 2 Oct	Rangers	0-2
Sat 9 Oct	St.BERNARDS	5-1
Sat 16 Oct	Dundee	6-1
Sat 23 Oct	Celtic	2-3
Sat 30 Oct	DUNDEE	2-0
Sat 6 Nov	Clyde	2-2
Sat 13 Nov	3rd.LANARK	2-3
Sat 20 Nov	St.Bernards	5-1
Sat 27 Nov	St.Mirren	1-3
Sat 4 Dec	CLYDE	8-1
Sat 11 Dec	Third Lanark	5-2
Sat 18 Dec	H1BERNIAN	3-2
Sat 25 Dec	PARTICK TH.	6-2

Played 18	W8; D4; L6;	
Pts.20	F54; A33;	4th.

Scottish League Championship
Division One 1898–1899

Sat 3 Sep	RANGERS	2-3
Sat 10 Sep	St.Mirren	3-2
Sat 17 Sep	St.Bernards	3-1
Mon 19 Sep	CELTIC	2-2
Sat 24 Sep	CLYDE	4-0
Sat 1 Oct	Rangers	1-3
Sat 8 Oct	HIBERNIAN	4-0
Sat 15 Oct	PARTICK TH.	5-1
Sat 22 Oct	Clyde	3-3
Sat 29 Oct	Hibernian	5-1
Sat 5 Nov	St.BERNARDS	3-1
Sat 12 Nov	3rd.LANARK	2-1
Sat 26 Nov	DUNDEE	6-3
Sat 3 Dec	Dundee	5-2
Sat 10 Dec	Third Lanark	1-2
Sat 17 Dec	Celtic	2-3
Sat 24 Dec	St.MIRREN	4-2
Sat 7 Jan	Partick Thistle	1-0

Played 18	W12; D2; L4;	
Pts.26	F56; A30;	2nd.

Scottish League Championship
Division One 1899–1900

Sat 2 Sep	Rangers	3-4
Sat 9 Sep	St.Bernards	4-2
Sat 16 Sep	St.MIRREN	3-0
Mon 18 Sep	RANGERS	1-1
Sat 23 Sep	KILMARN'K	1-0
Sat 30 Sep	Celtic	2-0
Sat 7 Oct	3rd.LANARK	2-0
Sat 14 Oct	St.BERNARDS	5-0
Sat 21 Oct	Clyde	2-1
Sat 28 Oct	Hibernian	0-1
Sat 4 Nov	CELTIC	3-2
Sat 11 Nov	DUNDEE	4-1
Sat 18 Nov	St.Mirren	2-2
Sat 25 Nov	HIBERNIAN	1-3
Sat 9 Dec	CLYDE	4-1
Sat 16 Dec	Dundee	1-1
Sat 23 Dec	Third Lanark	2-3
Sat 17 Mar	Kilmarnock	1-2

Played 18	W10; D3; L5;	
Pts.23	F41; A24;	4th.

Scottish League Championship
Division One 1900–1901

Sat 25 Aug	RANGERS	0-1
Sat 1 Sep	Hibernian	0-3
Sat 8 Sep	DUNDEE	0-4
Sat 15 Sep	Morton	2-2
Mon 17 Sep	CELTIC	0-2
Sat 22 Sep	QUEEN'S P'K	1-2
Mon 24 Sep	Rangers	0-1
Sat 29 Sep	Dundee	2-1
Sat 6 Oct	PARTICK TH.	1-3
Sat 13 Oct	HIBERNIAN	0-0
Sat 20 Oct	St.Mirren	1-2
Sat 27 Oct	MORTON	1-2
Sat 3 Nov	3rd.LANARK	0-0
Sat 10 Nov	Kilmarnock	3-1
Sat 17 Nov	Celtic	3-1
Sat 1 Dec	St.MIRREN	0-0
Sat 8 Dec	KILMARN'K	7-0
Sat 15 Dec	Partick Thistle	1-0
Sat 22 Dec	Third Lanark	0-1
Sat 19 Jan	Queen's Park	0-4

Played 20	W5; D4; L11;	
Pts.14	F22; A30;	10th.

Scottish League Championship
Division One 1901–1902

Sat 17 Aug	HIBERNIAN	2-1
Sat 24 Aug	Rangers	1-2
Sat 31 Aug	MORTON	3-1
Sat 7 Sep	Third Lanark	0-2
Sat 14 Sep	Hibernian	2-1
Mon 16 Sep	RANGERS	0-2
Sat 21 Sep	KILMARN'K	3-0
Sat 28 Sep	QUEEN'S P'K	1-1
Sat 5 Oct	St.Mirren	2-1
Sat 12 Oct	DUNDEE	4-0
Sat 19 Oct	Kilmarnock	0-1
Sat 26 Oct	Queen's Park	1-2
Sat 2 Nov	CELTIC	2-2
Sat 9 Nov	3rd.LANARK	4-1
Sat 16 Nov	Morton	3-1
Sat 23 Nov	St.MIRREN	2-0
Sat 30 Nov	Celtic	2-1
Sat 7 Dec	Dundee	0-2

Played 18	W10; D2; L6;	
Pts.22	F32; A21;	3rd.

Scottish League Championship
Division One 1902–1903

Sat 16 Aug	Morton	2-3
Sat 23 Aug	DUNDEE	0-2
Sat 30 Aug	St.Mirren	1-1
Sat 6 Sep	RANGERS	2-1
Sat 13 Sep	Hibernian	0-0
Mon 15 Sep	CELTIC	1-2
Sat 20 Sep	QUEEN'S P'K	4-0
Sat 27 Sep	Partick Thistle	2-2
Mon 29 Sep	Celtic	2-2
Sat 4 Oct	Rangers	1-2
Sat 11 Oct	HIBERNIAN	1-1
Sat 18 Oct	Dundee	1-0
Sat 25 Oct	PORT GLA'W	3-1
Sat 1 Nov	Queen's Park	5-2
Sat 8 Nov	St.MIRREN	1-3
Sat 15 Nov	Third Lanark	3-0
Sat 22 Nov	Kilmarnock	3-1
Sat 29 Nov	PARTICK TH.	4-2
Sat 6 Dec	KILMARN'K	1-1
Sat 20 Dec	Port Glasgow	3-0
Sat 27 Dec	MORTON	3-0
Sat 3 Jan	3rd.LANARK	3-1

Played 22	W11; D6; L5;	
Pts.28	F46; A27;	4th.

Scottish League Championship
Division One 1903–1904

Sat 15 Aug	St.MIRREN	5-1
Sat 22 Aug	Third Lanark	1-2
Sat 29 Aug	DUNDEE	4-2
Sat 5 Sep	Partick Thistle	1-1
Sat 12 Sep	MOTHERW'L	5-0
Sat 19 Sep	Rangers	1-5
Sat 26 Sep	KILMARN'K	2-1
Sat 10 Oct	HIBERNIAN	2-0
Sat 17 Oct	Dundee	1-2
Sat 24 Oct	Celtic	0-4
Sat 31 Oct	PARTICK TH.	4-1
Sat 14 Nov	PORT GLA'W	2-0
Sat 21 Nov	Port Glasgow	1-1
Sat 28 Nov	Motherwell	4-0
Sat 19 Dec	MORTON	1-0
Sat 26 Dec	Airdrieonians	2-1
Sat 2 Jan	QUEEN'S P'K	3-1
Sat 9 Jan	Morton	2-1
Sat 16 Jan	St.Mirren	0-3
Sat 30 Jan	RANGERS	2-1
Sat 6 Feb	Queen's Park	2-2
Sat 13 Feb	3rd.LANARK	4-1
Sat 20 Feb	Hibernian	4-2
Sat 27 Feb	AIRDRIE	5-0
Sat 5 Mar	Kilmarnock	3-2
Sat 2 Apr	CELTIC	2-1

Played 26	W18; D3; L5;	
Pts.39	F63; A35;	2nd.

Scottish League Championship
Division One 1904–1905

Sat 20 Aug	Kilmarnock	2-3
Sat 27 Aug	3rd.LANARK	4-1
Sat 3 Sep	Celtic	1-1
Sat 17 Sep	Motherwell	4-2
Mon 19 Sep	CELTIC	2-0
Sat 24 Sep	Airdrieonians	2-3
Mon 26 Sep	Rangers	1-1
Sat 1 Oct	PARTICK TH.	0-1
Sat 15 Oct	Partick Thistle	1-2
Sat 22 Oct	St.MIRREN	3-1
Sat 29 Oct	Hibernian	0-3
Sat 5 Nov	RANGERS	0-5
Sat 12 Nov	Dundee	0-2
Sat 19 Nov	PORT GLA'W	5-0
Sat 26 Nov	Third Lanark	1-7
Sat 3 Dec	AIRDRIE	6-0
Sat 10 Dec	St.Mirren	1-1
Sat 24 Dec	Port Glasgow	0-3
Sat 31 Dec	MOTHERW'L	4-1
Mon 2 Jan	HIBERNIAN	1-0
Sat 7 Jan	KILMARN'K	1-3
Sat 4 Feb	Queen's Park	0-2
Sat 18 Feb	Morton	0-1
Sat 25 Feb	DUNDEE	3-1
Sat 4 Mar	MORTON	2-0
Sat 11 Mar	QUEEN'S P'K	2-0

Played 26	W11; D3; L12;	
Pts.25	F46; A44;	7th.=

Scottish League Championship
Division One 1905–1906

Sat 19 Aug	3rd.LANARK	3-2
Sat 26 Aug	St.Mirren	1-0
Sat 2 Sep	MOTHERW'L	4-0
Sat 9 Sep	Port Glasgow	5-2
Mon 11 Sep	CELTIC	1-1
Sat 16 Sep	KILMARN'K	3-0
Mon 18 Sep	Hibernian	3-0
Mon 25 Sep	Rangers	5-0
Sat 30 Sep	Queen's Park	3-0
Sat 14 Oct	PARTICK TH.	2-0
Sat 21 Oct	Dundee	1-1
Sat 28 Oct	ABERDEEN	1-1
Sat 4 Nov	HIBERNIAN	1-0
Sat 11 Nov	AIRDRIE	2-1
Sat 18 Nov	Kilmarnock	1-1
Sat 25 Nov	FALKIRK	1-0
Sat 2 Dec	Aberdeen	1-2
Sat 9 Dec	PORT GLA'W	4-0
Sat 16 Dec	Morton	1-2
Sat 23 Dec	St.MIRREN	1-0
Sat 30 Dec	Motherwell	1-2
Tue 2 Jan	Third Lanark	3-1
Sat 6 Jan	Airdrieonians	1-1
Sat 13 Jan	DUNDEE	4-0
Sat 20 Jan	Falkirk	2-2
Sat 3 Feb	Partick Thistle	1-4
Sat 17 Feb	QUEEN'S P'K	4-1
Sat 10 Mar	MORTON	2-0
Sat 7 Apr	RANGERS	2-2
Sat 21 Apr	Celtic	0-1

Played 30	W18; D7; L5;	
Pts.43	F64; A27;	2nd.

Scottish League Championship Division One 1906–1907

Sat 18 Aug	Clyde	3-1		Sat 15 Dec	3rd.LANARK	1-1
Sat 25 Aug	St.MIRREN	1-1		Sat 22 Dec	St.Mirren	2-0
Sat 1 Sep	Third Lanark	2-2		Tue 1 Jan	Hibernian	0-0
Sat 8 Sep	DUNDEE	0-0		Sat 12 Jan	AIRDRIE	0-1
Sat 15 Sep	Celtic	0-3		Sat 19 Jan	Port Glasgow	0-0
Sat 22 Sep	HIBERNIAN	4-1		Sat 2 Mar	Morton	0-0
Mon 24 Sep	Rangers	1-1		Sat 16 Mar	KILMARN'K	1-0
Sat 29 Sep	Falkirk	1-2		Sat 6 Apr	MOTHERW'L	1-1
Sat 13 Oct	HAMILTON	3-1		Mon 8 Apr	Dundee	0-2
Sat 20 Oct	Airdrieonians	2-3		Sat 13 Apr	RANGERS	0-1
Sat 27 Oct	QUEENS P'K	2-2		Mon 15 Apr	ABERDEEN	1-1
Sat 3 Nov	Aberdeen	3-2		Wed 24 Apr	Queen's Park	2-1
Sat 10 Nov	PORT GLA'W	2-0		Sat 27 Apr	PARTICK TH.	5-1
Sat 17 Nov	Kilmarnock	2-2		Wed 1 May	FALKIRK	2-1
Sat 24 Nov	Partick Thistle	0-1		Sat 4 May	CLYDE	0-1
Sat 1 Dec	MORTON	1-0		Mon 6 May	Hamilton Aca'l	1-5
Sat 8 Dec	Motherwell	0-2		Sat 11 May	CELTIC	3-3

Played 34   W11; D13; L10;
F46; A43;   Pts.35..   9th.

Scottish League Championship Division One 1907–1908

Sat 17 Aug	KILMARN'K	1-0		Sat 21 Dec	Aberdeen	0-1
Sat 24 Aug	Clyde	1-1		Sat 28 Dec	PARTICK TH.	1-3
Sat 31 Aug	QUEENS' P'K	7-2		Thu 2 Jan	PORT GLA'W	5-0
Sat 7 Sep	Morton	1-1		Sat 4 Jan	Dundee	0-0
Sat 14 Sep	DUNDEE	1-0		Sat 11 Jan	St.MIRREN	0-1
Sat 21 Sep	St.Mirren	1-3		Sat 18 Jan	Port Glasgow	1-1
Sat 28 Sep	HAMILTON	4-3		Sat 1 Feb	Kilmarnock	0-2
Sat 5 Oct	Third Lanark	1-2		Sat 15 Feb	MORTON	2-2
Sat 19 Oct	Falkirk	0-3		Sat 29 Feb	Rangers	1-2
Sat 26 Oct	ABERDEEN	3-1		Sat 7 Mar	3rd.LANARK	1-2
Sat 2 Nov	Partick Thistle	1-1		Sat 14 Mar	MOTHERW'L	0-3
Sat 9 Nov	Airdrieonians	3-2		Sat 28 Mar	Hamilton Aca'l	1-2
Sat 16 Nov	Hibernian	3-2		Sat 4 Apr	HIBERNIAN	1-2
Sat 23 Nov	CELTIC	1-0		Sat 11 Apr	AIRDRIE	2-0
Sat 30 Nov	Motherwell	0-3		Sat 18 Apr	CLYDE	1-0
Sat 7 Dec	RANGERS	1-2		Mon 20 Apr	Celtic	0-6
Sat 14 Dec	FALKIRK	2-3		Tue 28 Apr	Queen's Park	3-6

Played 34   W11; D6; L17;
F50; A62;   Pts.28.   11th.=

Scottish League Championship Division One 1908–1909

Sat 15 Aug	Dundee	1-2		Sat 19 Dec	Third Lanark	3-1
Sat 22 Aug	CLYDE	1-1		Sat 26 Dec	HAMILTON	1-0
Sat 29 Aug	St.Mirren	0-2		Sat 2 Jan	3rd.LANARK	1-2
Sat 5 Sep	QUEEN'S P'K	3-0		Sat 9 Jan	Celtic	1-1
Sat 12 Sep	Motherwell	6-1		Sat 16 Jan	MOTHERW'L	3-2
Sat 19 Sep	HIBERNIAN	1-1		Sat 30 Jan	Morton	1-4
Sat 26 Sep	AIRDRIE	2-6		Sat 13 Feb	Aberdeen	0-1
Sat 10 Oct	KILMARN'K	0-0		Sat 20 Feb	Kilmarnock	5-2
Sat 17 Oct	PORT GLA'W	3-0		Sat 13 Mar	Clyde	0-1
Sat 24 Oct	Partick Thistle	2-3		Sat 20 Mar	DUNDEE	1-0
Sat 31 Oct	ABERDEEN	1-1		Sat 27 Mar	Queen's Park	2-2
Sat 7 Nov	Hibernian	1-0		Sat 3 Apr	RANGERS	0-0
Sat 14 Nov	Hamilton Aca'l	1-1		Sat 10 Apr	Airdrieonians	1-2
Sat 21 Nov	St.MIRREN	1-2		Sat 17 Apr	FALKIRK	1-0
Sat 28 Nov	Rangers	3-4		Mon 19 Apr	CELTIC	1-2
Sat 5 Dec	MORTON	5-0		Sat 24 Apr	Falkirk	1-4
Sat 12 Dec	Port Glasgow	0-1		Wed 28 Apr	PARTICK TH.	1-0

Played 34   W12; D8; L14;
F54; A49;   Pts.32.   11th.=

Scottish League Championship Division One 1909–1910

Sat 21 Aug	CLYDE	2-0		Sat 1 Jan	HIBERNIAN	1-0
Sat 28 Aug	Queen's Park	2-2		Mon 3 Jan	DUNDEE	1-0
Sat 4 Sep	ABERDEEN	0-0		Sat 8 Jan	Rangers	0-1
Sat 18 Sep	Port Glasgow	2-0		Sat 15 Jan	AIRDRIE	0-1
Mon 20 Sep	CELTIC	1-2		Sat 29 Jan	Falkirk	1-2
Sat 2 Oct	KILMARN'K	3-0		Sat 5 Mar	Partick Thistle	3-1
Sat 9 Oct	St.Mirren	0-1		Sat 12 Mar	Aberdeen	0-3
Sat 16 Oct	MORTON	5-1		Sat 19 Mar	PORT GLA'W	6-0
Sat 23 Oct	Hibernian	4-1		Sat 26 Mar	Airdrieonians	1-3
Sat 30 Oct	PARTICK TH.	2-2		Sat 2 Apr	3rd.LANARK	2-2
Sat 6 Nov	Celtic	0-1		Sat 9 Apr	Motherwell	0-1
Sat 13 Nov	Dundee	1-4		Wed 13 Apr	Clyde	2-2
Sat 20 Nov	HAMILTON	1-2		Sat 16 Apr	FALKIRK	4-2
Sat 27 Nov	St.MIRREN	0-1		Mon 18 Apr	RANGERS	1-3
Sat 11 Dec	MOTHERW'L	5-1		Wed 20 Apr	Third Lanark	1-3
Sat 18 Dec	Morton	3-3		Sat 23 Apr	Hamilton Aca'l	1-2
Sat 25 Dec	QUEEN'S P'K	3-2		Sat 30 Apr	Kilmarnock	1-1

Played 34 — W12; D7; L15;
F59; A50; Pts.31. 12th.=

Scottish League Championship Division One 1910–1911

Sat 20 Aug	Clyde	0-4		Sat 10 Dec	Dundee	1-4
Sat 27 Aug	QUEEN'S P'K	4-1		Sat 17 Dec	ABERDEEN	0-3
Sat 3 Sep	Motherwell	2-3		Sat 24 Dec	Rangers	0-2
Sat 17 Sep	Kilmarnock	1-3		Sat 31 Dec	3rd.LANARK	0-1
Mon 19 Sep	RANGERS	1-4		Mon 2 Jan	Hibernian	0-1
Sat 24 Sep	MORTON	2-0		Sat 7 Jan	MOTHERW'L	1-0
Mon 26 Sep	Third Lanark	0-1		Sat 14 Jan	PARTICK TH.	3-1
Sat 1 Oct	Partick Thistle	1-2		Sat 21 Jan	St.MIRREN	0-0
Sat 8 Oct	RAITH ROV'S	0-0		Sat 11 Feb	KILMARN'K	5-0
Sat 15 Oct	Celtic	0-0		Sat 18 Feb	Raith Rovers	2-3
Sat 22 Oct	HIBERNIAN	2-0		Sat 25 Feb	Morton	2-2
Sat 29 Oct	DUNDEE	2-3		Sat 4 Mar	Falkirk	1-3
Sat 5 Nov	Aberdeen	2-3		Sat 11 Mar	Airdrieonians	1-4
Sat 12 Nov	Hamilton Aca'l	2-1		Sat 18 Mar	HAMILTON	2-0
Sat 19 Nov	AIRDRIE	2-2		Sat 25 Mar	FALKIRK	1-1
Sat 26 Nov	St.Mirren	0-3		Sat 1 Apr	CELTIC	1-1
Sat 3 Dec	CLYDE	1-1		Sat 29 Apr	Queen's Park	0-2

Played 34 — W8; D8; L18;
F 42; A59; Pts.24. 14th.=

Scottish League Championship Division One 1911–1912

Sat 19 Aug	CLYDE	1-0		Sat 23 Dec	Motherwell	3-0
Sat 26 Aug	Queen's Park	3-0		Sat 30 Dec	3rd.LANARK	4-0
Sat 2 Sep	AIRDRIE	2-1		Mon 1 Jan	HIBERNIAN	3-0
Sat 16 Sep	KILMARN'K	1-1		Sat 6 Jan	Celtic	1-1
Sat 23 Sep	Morton	2-2		Sat 13 Jan	St.MIRREN	1-2
Sat 30 Sep	CELTIC	2-1		Sat 20 Jan	MORTON	2-0
Sat 7 Oct	Dundee	1-1		Sat 17 Feb	Raith Rovers	1-3
Sat 14 Oct	FALKIRK	0-2		Sat 2 Mar	Hamilton Aca'l	1-1
Sat 21 Oct	Third Lanark	0-3		Sat 16 Mar	Aberdeen	0-1
Sat 28 Oct	DUNDEE	1-4		Sat 23 Mar	QUEEN'S P'K	0-0
Sat 4 Nov	RAITH ROV'S	2-0		Sat 6 Apr	Airdrieonians	0-2
Sat 11 Nov	Partick Thistle	2-2		Sat 13 Apr	Clyde	2-1
Sat 18 Nov	Kilmarnock	3-1		Mon 15 Apr	RANGERS	2-1
Sat 25 Nov	ABERDEEN	1-2		Sat 20 Apr	St.Mirren	0-2
Sat 2 Dec	Falkirk	2-2		Mon 22 Apr	MOTHERW'L	2-1
Sat 9 Dec	Hibernian	4-0		Wed 24 Apr	HAMILTON	2-0
Sat 16 Dec	Rangers	1-2		Sat 27 Apr	PARTICK TH.	2-1

Played 34 — W16; D8; L10;
F54; A40; Pts.40. 4th.=

Scottish League Championship Division One 1912–1913

Date	Opponent	Score		Date	Opponent	Score
Sat 17 Aug	Clyde	0-0		Sat 21 Dec	HAMILTON	0-0
Sat 24 Aug	QUEEN'S P'K	10-3		Sat 28 Dec	Kilmarnock	2-2
Sat 31 Aug	Motherwell	2-1		Sat 4 Jan	CLYDE	3-2
Sat 7 Sep	AIRDRIE	1-1		Sat 11 Jan	Hamilton Aca'l	2-4
Sat 21 Sep	Rangers	4-2		Sat 18 Jan	Raith Rovers	3-3
Sat 28 Sep	HIBERNIAN	1-0		Sat 25 Jan	St.Mirren	1-2
Sat 5 Oct	Falkirk	0-2		Sat 1 Feb	ABERDEEN	4-1
Sat 12 Oct	3rd.LANARK	1-2		Sat 15 Feb	Queen's Park	6-1
Sat 19 Oct	Aberdeen	1-0		Sat 1 Mar	Morton	2-1
Sat 26 Oct	KILMARN'K	5-0		Sat 15 Mar	RANGERS	1-1
Sat 2 Nov	PARTICK TH.	4-0		Sat 22 Mar	DUNDEE	4-3
Sat 9 Nov	Celtic	0-1		Sat 5 Apr	Third Lanark	0-1
Sat 16 Nov	St.MIRREN	2-0		Sat 12 Apr	MORTON	4-2
Sat 23 Nov	Airdrieonians	0-1		Wed 16 Apr	Hibernian	3-0
Sat 30 Nov	RAITH ROV'S	2-0		Mon 21 Apr	CELTIC	0-0
Sat 7 Dec	Partick Thistle	3-1		Wed 23 Apr	FALKIRK	0-2
Sat 14 Dec	Dundee	0-3		Sat 26 Apr	MOTHERW'L	0-1

Played 34 W17; D7; L10;
F71; A43; Pts.41.   3rd.=

Scottish League Championship Division One 1913–1914

Date	Opponent	Score		Date	Opponent	Score
Sat 16 Aug	AIRDRIE	3-1		Sat 20 Dec	CLYDE	1-0
Sat 23 Aug	Ayr United	4-0		Sat 27 Dec	Airdrieonians	2-2
Sat 30 Aug	QUEEN'S P'K	1-0		Sat 3 Jan	AYR UNITED	2-1
Sat 6 Sep	Falkirk	0-0		Sat 10 Jan	Aberdeen	1-0
Sat 13 Sep	RANGERS	2-1		Sat 17 Jan	Dumbarton	1-2
Mon 15 Sep	CELTIC	2-0		Sat 24 Jan	DUNDEE	3-0
Sat 20 Sep	Clyde	2-2		Sat 31 Jan	Queen's Park	1-1
Sat 27 Sep	MORTON	4-0		Sat 14 Feb	HIBERNIAN	3-1
Sat 4 Oct	Raith Rovers	0-0		Sat 21 Feb	Morton	0-3
Sat 11 Oct	PARTICK TH.	1-0		Sat 28 Feb	HAMILTON	1-0
Sat 18 Oct	Hamilton Aca'l	3-1		Sat 7 Mar	KILMARN'K	0-1
Sat 25 Oct	3rd.LANARK	0-0		Sat 21 Mar	FALKIRK	1-0
Sat 1 Nov	St.Mirren	0-1		Tue 24 Mar	Celtic	0-0
Sat 8 Nov	Hibernian	2-1		Sat 28 Mar	Partick Thistle	1-2
Sat 15 Nov	St.MIRREN	6-0		Wed 1 Apr	Motherwell	2-0
Sat 22 Nov	Dundee	?-?		Sat 4 Apr	DUMBARTON	5-1
Sat 29 Nov	ABERDEEN	4-0		Sat 11 Apr	Third Lanark	1-2
Sat 6 Dec	MOTHERW'L	2-1		Sat 18 Apr	RAITH ROV'S(N)	2-0
Sat 13 Dec	Kilmarnock	3-0		Sat 25 Apr	Rangers	2-3

Played 38 W23; D8; L7;
F70; A29; Pts.54.   3rd.=

Scottish League Championship Division One 1914–1915

Date	Opponent	Score		Date	Opponent	Score
Sat 15 Aug	CELTIC	2-0		Sat 19 Dec	Queen's Park	4-0
Sat 22 Aug	Raith Rovers	3-1		Sat 26 Dec	RAITH ROV'S	4-0
Sat 29 Aug	3rd.LANARK	2-0		Sat 2 Jan	Falkirk	1-1
Sat 5 Sep	Kilmarnock	2-0		Mon 4 Jan	HAMILTON	3-0
Sat 12 Sep	St.MIRREN	5-0		Sat 9 Jan	MORTON	1-0
Sat 19 Sep	Rangers	2-1		Sat 16 Jan	DUNDEE	3-2
Mon 21 Sep	AYR UNITED	1-0		Sat 23 Jan	Third Lanark	2-2
Sat 26 Sep	ABERDEEN	2-0		Sat 30 Jan	Celtic	1-1
Sat 3 Oct	Dumbarton	2-3		Sat 6 Feb	KILMARN'K	3-1
Sat 10 Oct	MOTHERW'L	2-0		Sat 13 Feb	Motherwell	1-0
Sat 17 Oct	Dundee	2-1		Sat 20 Feb	RANGERS	3-4
Sat 24 Oct	QUEEN'S P'K	2-2		Sat 27 Feb	Hibernian	2-2
Sat 31 Oct	Ayr United	2-0		Sat 6 Mar	DUMBARTON	4-1
Sat 7 Nov	Clyde	2-1		Sat 13 Mar	Airdrieonians	2-2
Sat 14 Nov	FALKIRK	2-0		Sat 20 Mar	PARTICK TH.	3-1
Sat 21 Nov	Partick Thistle	2-0		Sat 27 Mar	CLYDE	2-0
Sat 28 Nov	Hamilton Aca'l	3-1		Sat 3 Apr	Aberdeen	0-0
Sat 5 Dec	HIBERNIAN	3-1		Sat 10 Apr	Morton	0-2
Sat 12 Dec	AIRDRIE	3-1		Sat 17 Apr	St.Mirren	0-1

Played 38 W27; D7; L4;
F83; A32; Pts.61.   2nd.

Scottish League Championship Division One 1915–1916

Sat 21 Aug	St.Mirren	1-4		Sat 25 Dec	Third Lanark	3-1
Sat 28 Aug	HAMILTON	3-0		Sat 8 Jan	Ayr United	1-3
Sat 4 Sep	Partick Thistle	2-0		Sat 15 Jan	St.MIRREN	3-1
Sat 11 Sep	KILMARN'K	0-1		Sat 22 Jan	Hamilton Aca'l	2-3
Sat 18 Sep	Clyde	4-1		Sat 29 Jan	RAITH ROV'S	2-1
Mon 20 Sep	Hibernian	2-1		Sat 5 Feb	Dumbarton	1-1
Sat 25 Sep	AIRDRIE	1-1		Sat 12 Feb	RANGERS	1-2
Sat 2 Oct	Falkirk	1-1		Sat 19 Feb	3rd.LANARK	2-0
Sat 9 Oct	AYR UNITED	0-5		Sat 26 Feb	Airdrieonians	0-0
Sat 16 Oct	Rangers	4-0		Sat 4 Mar	PARTICK TH.	1-0
Sat 23 Oct	MORTON	2-0		Sat 11 Mar	Aberdeen	1-1
Sat 30 Oct	Motherwell	3-1		Sat 18 Mar	FALKIRK	0-2
Sat 6 Nov	Dundee	0-1		Sat 1 Apr	CLYDE	3-1
Sat 13 Nov	CELTIC	2-0		Sat 8 Apr	QUEEN'S P'K	5-3
Sat 20 Nov	Queen's Park	3-0		Sat 15 Apr	Kilmarnock	1-3
Sat 27 Nov	DUMBARTON	3-1		Mon 17 Apr	HIBERNIAN	1-3
Sat 4 Dec	ABERDEEN	1-2		Sat 22 Apr	Celtic	0-0
Sat 11 Dec	Raith Rovers	2-1		Sat 29 Apr	DUNDEE	1-0
Sat 18 Dec	MOTHERW'L	4-0				

Played 37   W20; D6; L11;
F66; A45;   Pts.46.   5th.=

Scottish League Championship Division One 1916–1917

Sat 19 Aug	Morton	2-3		Sat 23 Dec	AYR UNITED	1-2
Sat 26 Aug	RANGERS	1-3		Sat 30 Dec	Third Lanark	1-1
Sat 2 Sep	Airdrieonians	2-3		Tue 2 Jan	HAMILTON	3-1
Sat 9 Sep	3rd.LANARK	2-1		Sat 6 Jan	Rangers	0-1
Sat 16 Sep	Ayr United	0-2		Sat 13 Jan	CELTIC	0-1
Mon 18 Sep	HIBERNIAN	2-1		Sat 20 Jan	Raith Rovers	4-1
Sat 23 Sep	FALKIRK	1-6		Sat 27 Jan	Dundee	3-2
Sat 30 Sep	Celtic	0-1		Sat 3 Feb	Dumbarton	1-4
Sat 7 Oct	RAITH ROV'S	2-1		Sat 10 Feb	ABERDEEN	2-0
Sat 14 Oct	Kilmarnock	0-3		Sat 17 Feb	Partick Thistle	0-0
Sat 21 Oct	CLYDE	0-3		Sat 24 Feb	MOTHERW'L	1-3
Sat 28 Oct	Hamilton Aca'l	0-1		Sat 3 Mar	St.MIRREN	1-2
Sat 4 Nov	PARTICK TH'	1-0		Sat 10 Mar	AIRDRIE	1-4
Sat 11 Nov	St.Mirren	1-0		Sat 17 Mar	Clyde	1-0
Sat 18 Nov	Aberdeen	0-2		Sat 24 Mar	Falkirk	1-2
Sat 25 Nov	QUEEN'S P'K	2-0		Sat 31 Mar	MORTON	4-1
Sat 2 Dec	DUMBARTON	0-1		Sat 7 Apr	KILMARN'K	0-0
Sat 9 Dec	Motherwell	0-2		Mon 16 Apr	Hibernian	2-0
Sat 16 Dec	DUNDEE	1-0		Sat 28 Apr	Queen's Park	1-1

Played 38   W14; D4; L20;
F44; A59;   Pts.32.   14th.

Scottish League Championship Division One 1917–1918

Sat 18 Aug	St.MIRREN	2-1		Sat 15 Dec	Morton	1-1
Sat 25 Aug	Queen's Park	0-4		Sar 22 Dec	MOTHERW'L	0-1
Sat 1 Sep	HIBERNIAN	1-0		Sat 29 Dec	Dumbarton	1-1
Sat 8 Sep	Motherwell	0-4		Sat 5 Jan	QUEEN'S P'K	2-1
Sat 15 Sep	MORTON	1-0		Sat 12 Jan	Rangers	0-2
Sat 22 Sep	Falkirk	0-4		Satr 26 Jan	HAMILTON	3-2
Sat 29 Sep	CELTIC	0-1		Sat 2 Feb	Hibernian	3-1
Sat 6 Oct	Kilmarnock	3-4		Sat 9 Feb	Celtic	0-3
Sat 13 Oct	Partick Thistle	1-4		Sat 16 Feb	CLYDEBANK	1-0
Sat 20 Oct	AYR UNITED	2-0		Sat 23 Feb	3rd.LANARK	3-1
Sat 27 Oct	AIRDRIE	1-0		Sat 9 Mar	Airdrieonians	1-0
Sat 3 Nov	Clydebank	1-3		Sat 16 Mar	CLYDE	3-0
Sat 10 Nov	RANGERS	0-3		Sat 23 Mar	Ayr United	1-1
Sat 17 Nov	Hamilton Aca'l	0-3		Sat 30 Mar	PARTICK TH.	1-1
Sat 24 Nov	FALKIRK	0-2		Sat 6 Apr	Third Lanark	3-2
Sat 1 Dec	Clyde	0-3		Sat 13 Apr	DUMBARTON	1-2
Sat 8 Dec	KILMARN'K	3-0		Sat 20 Apr	St.Mirren	2-3

Played 34   W14; D4; L16;
F41; A58;   Pts.32.   10th.

Scottish League Championship Division One 1918-1919

Date	Opponent	Score		Date	Opponent	Score
Sat 17 Aug	Morton	0-2		Sat 21 Dec	Falkirk	0-0
Sat 24 Aug	RANGERS	1-4		Sat 28 Dec	AIRDRIE	0-0
Sat 31 Aug	Airdrieonians	0-1		Sat 4 Jan	Ayr United	2-1
Sat 7 Sep	MOTHERW'L	0-0		Sat 11 Jan	HIBERNIAN	3-1
Sat 14 Sep	St.MIRREN	0-0		Sat 18 Jan	Third Lanark	1-3
Sat 21 Sep	Dumbarton	2-1		Sat 25 Jan	Queen's Park	0-4
Sat 28 Sep	PARTICK TH.	1-0		Sat 1 Feb	HAMILTON	4-1
Sat 5 Oct	Hamilton Aca'l	4-1		Sat 8 Feb	Clydebank	3-1
Sat 12 Oct	AYR UNITED	2-3		Sat 15 Feb	QUEEN'S P'K	2-2
Sat 19 Oct	Hibernian	3-1		Sat 22 Feb	Kilmarnock	2-2
Sat 26 Oct	Clyde	2-4		Sat 1 Mar	Rangers	2-3
Sat 2 Nov	KILMARN'K	1-4		Sat 8 Mar	Motherwell	2-1
Sat 9 Nov	Celtic	1-1		Sat 22 Mar	CLYDE	3-0
Sat 16 Nov	FALKIRK	5-0		Sat 5 Apr	MORTON	1-1
Sat 23 Nov	3rd.LANARK	2-0		Mon 28 Apr	CELTIC	2-3
Sat 7 Dec	CLYDEBANK	2-1		Sat 3 May	DUMBARTON	2-0
Sat 14 Dec	Partick Thistle	1-3		Sat 10 May	St.Mirren	3-3

Played 34   W14; D9; L11;
F59; A52;   Pts.37.   7th.

Scottish League Championship Division One 1919-1920

Date	Opponent	Score		Date	Opponent	Score
Sat 16 Aug	QUEEN'S P'K	3-1		Sat 27 Dec	MORTON	3-6
Sat 23 Aug	Ayr United	2-1		Thu 1 Jan	HIBERNIAN	1-3
Sat 30 Aug	HAMILTON	2-0		Sat 3 Jan	Motherwell	1-4
Sat 6 Sep	Raith Rovers	1-0		Mon 5 Jan	AYR UNITED	0-1
Sat 13 Sep	CELTIC	0-1		Sat 10 Jan	3rd.LANARK	1-1
Mon 15 Sep	Hibernian	4-2		Sat 17 Jan	Aberdeen	1-1
Sat 20 Sep	Dundee	0-1		Sat 31 Jan	Partick Thistle	2-0
Sat 27 Sep	CLYDEBANK	4-2		Sat 14 Feb	DUNDEE	2-1
Mon 29 Sep	Rangers	0-3		Sat 28 Feb	RAITH ROV'S	1-1
Sat 4 Oct	Morton	0-2		Sat 6 Mar	Queen's Park	2-2
Sat 11 Oct	ALBION R.	0-0		Sat 13 Mar	Hamilton Aca'l	2-2
Sat 18 Oct	Clyde	1-0		Sat 20 Mar	CLYDE	0-3
Sat 25 Oct	ABERDEEN	1-1		Sat 27 Mar	Clydebank	1-0
Sat 1 Nov	MOTHERW'L	2-0		Sat 3 Apr	Albion Rovers	2-6
Sat 8 Nov	St.Mirren	1-4		Sat 10 Apr	RANGERS	0-0
Sar 15 Nov	AIRDRIE	3-1		Sat 17 Apr	DUMBARTON	1-2
Sat 22 Nov	Kilmarnock	1-2		Mon 19 Apr	FALKIRK	3-0
Sat 29 Nov	Dumbarton	0-2		Wed 21 Apr	Airdrieonians	1-4
Sat 6 Dec	PARTICK TH.	3-1		Sat 24 Apr	Third Lanark	1-2
Sat 13 Dec	Falkirk	3-3		Wed 28 Apr	KILMARN'K	0-1
Sat 20 Dec	St.MIRREN	1-2		Sat 1 May	Celtic	0-3

Played 42   W14; D9; L19;
F57; A72;   Pts.37.   15th.=

Scottish League Championship Division One 1920-1921

Date	Opponent	Score		Date	Opponent	Score
Sat 21 Aug	Clyde	1-2		Sat 11 Dec	Third Lanark	0-3
Mon 23 Aug	Albion Rovers	1-1		Sat 18 Dec	St.MIRREN	1-0
Sat 28 Aug	HIBERNIAN	5-1		Sat 25 Dec	DUMBARTON	6-2
Sat 4 Sep	Morton	1-1		Sat 1 Jan	Hibernian	0-3
Wed 8 Sep	AYR UNITED	4-1		Mon 3 Jan	FALKIRK	0-2
Sat 11 Sep	CLYDEBANK	2-0		Sat 8 Jan	PARTICK TH.	1-0
Tue 14 Sep	Clydebank	2-1		Sat 15 Jan	Kilmarnock	2-1
Sat 18 Sep	Ayr United	0-0		Sat 22 Jan	Partick Thistle	0-0
Mon 20 Sep	RANGERS	0-4		Sat 29 Jan	MORTON	0-1
Sat 25 Sep	RAITH ROV'S	2-0		Sat 12 Feb	MOTHERW'L	1-0
Sat 2 Oct	Hamilton Aca'l	1-3		Wed 23 Feb	Raith Rovers	1-2
Mon 4 Oct	Dundee	0-3		Sat 26 Feb	3rd.LANARK	3-0
Sat 9 Oct	ALBION R.	1-1		Sat 12 Mar	AIRDRIE	2-1
Sat 16 Oct	Queen's Park	1-1		Sat 19 Mar	Celtic	2-3
Sat 23 Oct	DUNDEE	3-1		Sat 2 Apr	CLYDE	6-0
Sat 30 Oct	CELTIC	0-1		Sat 9 Apr	Aberdeen	2-5
Sat 6 Nov	Airdrieonians	1-0		Mon 11 Apr	Dumbarton	3-0
Sat 13 Nov	ABERDEEN	0-0		Fri 15 Apr	St.Mirren(East.Rd)	4-0
Sat 20 Nov	Falkirk	2-2		Sat 23 Apr	QUEEN'S P'K	4-0
Sat 27 Nov	KILMARN'K	4-1		Wed 27 Apr	Rangers	0-0
Sat 4 Dec	Motherwell	2-2		Sat 30 Apr	HAMILTON	3-0

Played 42   W20; D10; L12
F74; A49;   Pts.50.   3rd.

Scottish League Championship Division One 1921–1922

Wed 17 Aug	Hamilton Aca'l	0-1		Sat 24 Dec	Third Lanark	0-2
Sat 20 Aug	ALBION R.	2-2		Mon 26 Dec	KILMARN'K	1-0
Tue 23 Aug	Clyde	2-3		Sat 31 Dec	Kilmarnock	0-3
Sat 27 Aug	Morton	1-1		Mon 2 Jan	HIBERNIAN	0-2
Sat 3 Sep	HAMILTON	0-0		Tue 3 Jan	St.MIRREN	3-2
Sat 10 Sep	Hibernian	1-2		Sat 7 Jan	Raith Rovers	1-3
Sat 17 Sep	CLYDE	0-1		Sat 14 Jan	QUEEN'S P'K	0-1
Mon 19 Sep	RANGERS	1-2		Sat 21 Jan	3rd.LANARK	3-1
Sat 24 Sep	Partick Thistle	1-1		Sat 4 Feb	Falkirk	0-1
Sat 1 Oct	FALKIRK	4-1		Sat 18 Feb	Airdrieonians	0-3
Sat 8 Oct	Rangers	2-0		Wed 1 Mar	Albion Rovers	0-2
Sat 15 Oct	DUNDEE	0-0		Sat 4 Mar	AYR UNITED	6-2
Sat 22 Oct	Ayr United	1-2		Sat 11 Mar	CLYDEBANK	3-0
Sat 29 Oct	DUMBARTON	2-0		Sat 18 Mar	Dundee	0-2
Sat 5 Nov	Celtic	0-3		Sat 25 Mar	CELTIC	1-2
Sat 12 Nov	Motherwell	1-3		Wed 29 Mar	MOTHERW'L	0-0
Sat 19 Nov	RAITH ROV'S	1-1		Sat 1 Apr	PARTICK TH.	1-3
Sat 26 Nov	Clydebank	1-1		Sat 8 Apr	MORTON	0-0
Sat 3 Dec	ABERDEEN	2-1		Sat 15Apr	St.Mirren	1-2
Sat 10 Dec	Queen's Park	1-1		Sat 22 Apr	Dumbarton	2-3
Sat 17 Dec	AIRDRIE	4-0		Sat 29 Apr	Aberdeen	1-0

Played 42 **W11; D10; L21**
F50; A60; **Pts.32.** 19th.

Scottish League Championship Division One 1922–1923

Sat 19 Aug	Clyde	1-1		Sat 23 Dec	Albion Rovers	2-1
Sat 26 Aug	DUNDEE	2-1		Sat 30 Dec	HAMILTON	1-2
Sat 2 Sep	Hamilton Aca'l	1-3		Mon 1 Jan	Hibernian	1-2
Sat 9 Sep	ALBION R.	2-2		Tue 2 Jan	St.Mirren	1-2
Sat 16 Sep	Ayr United	1-1		Sat 6 Jan	3rd.LANARK	2-0
Mon 18 Sep	RANGERS	0-0		Sat 20 Jan	Dundee	0-0
Sat 23 Sep	HIBERNIAN	2-2		Sat 3 Feb	Raith Rovers	1-2
Sat 30 Sep	Alloa Athletic	3-0		Wed 7 Feb	CLYDE	2-1
Sat 7 Oct	RAITH ROV'S	0-0		Sat 10 Feb	KILMARN'K	5-0
Sat 14 Oct	Partick Thistle	2-2		Sat 17 Feb	Third Lanark	1-3
Sat 21 Oct	Kilmarnock	2-1		Sat 24 Feb	AIRDRIE	1-1
Sat 28 Oct	FALKIRK	1-1		Sat 3 Mar	Falkirk	0-1
Sat 4 Nov	St.MIRREN	2-2		Wed 14 Mar	MOTHERW'L	1-2
Sat 11 Nov	Aberdeen	1-0		Sat 17 Mar	Morton	1-0
Sat 18 Nov	MORTON	3-1		Sat 24 Mar	ALLOA ATH.	1-1
Sat 25 Nov	Airdrieonians	2-2		Sat 31 Mar	ABERDEEN	0-0
Sat 2 Dec	PARTICK TH.	3-0		Sat 7 Apr	Celtic	1-2
Sat 9 Dec	Motherwell	1-4		Sat 21 Apr	AYR UNITED	1-1
Sat 16 Dec	CELTIC	0-3		Sat 28 Apr	Rangers	0-3

Played 38 **W11; D15; L12;**
F51; A50; **Pts.37.** 12th.

Scottish League Championship Division One 1923–1924

Sat 18 Aug	CLYDE	6-0		Sat 22 Dec	Kilmarnock	1-2
Sat 25 Aug	Dundee	1-5		Sat 29 Dec	DUNDEE	1-0
Sat 1 Sep	HAMILTON	4-0		Tue 1 Jan	HIBERNIAN	1-1
Sat 8 Sep	Hibernian	1-1		Wed 2 Jan	St.MIRREN	0-0
Sat 15 Sep	CLYDEBANK	2-0		Sat 5 Jan	Aberdeen	1-2
Mon 17 Sep	RANGERS	0-0		Sat 12 Jan	QUEEN'S P'K	5-2
Sat 22 Sep	Morton	0-1		Sat 19 Jan	Clydebank	1-2
Sat 29 Sep	AYR UNITED	2-3		Sat 2 Feb	Queen's Park	1-1
Sat 6 Oct	Third Lanark	1-2		Wed 13 Feb	AIRDRIE	4-2
Sat 13 Oct	CELTIC	0-0		Sat 16 Feb	Hamilton Aca'l	3-1
Sat 20 Oct	Falkirk	0-0		Tue 26 Feb	Celtic	1-4
Sat 27 Oct	PARTICK TH.	2-1		Sat 1 Mar	RAITH ROV'S	1-2
Sat 3 Nov	Motherwell	2-3		Tue 11 Mar	Rangers	0-1
Sat 10 Nov	KILMARN'K	4-1		Sat 15 Mar	3rd.LANARK	3-1
Sat 17 Nov	Airdrieonians	0-3		Sat 22 Mar	Ayr United	1-2
Sat 24 Nov	Raith Rovers	1-1		Sat 29 Mar	MOTHERW'L	2-1
Sat 1 Dec	MORTON	3-1		Sat 5 Apr	FALKIRK	3-1
Sat 8 Dec	ABERDEEN	0-1		Sat 19 Apr	Partick Thistle	1-0
Sat 15 Dec	St.Mirren	0-0		Mon 21 Apr	Clyde	2-2

Played 38 **W14; D10; L14;**
F61; A50; **Pts.38.** 9th.

Scottish League Championship Division One 1924–1925

Sat 16 Aug	Cowdenbeath	2-1		Sat 6 Dec	Queen's Park	0-2
Wed 20 Aug	COWDEN'TH	3-3		Sat 13 Dec	CELTIC	3-1
Sat 23 Aug	AYR UNITED	2-3		Sat 20 Dec	Motherwell	0-0
Sat 30 Aug	Dundee	0-6		Sat 27 Dec	St.MIRREN	5-2
Sat 6 Sep	MORTON	5-1		Thu 1 Jan	Hibernian	1-2
Sat 13 Sep	Falkirk	1-2		Sat 3 Jan	Ayr United	1-2
Mon 15 Sep	RANGERS	1-2		Sat 10 Jan	RAITH ROV'S	2-2
Sat 20 Sep	AIRDRIE	2-0		Sat 17 Jan	St.Mirren	1-3
Sat 27 Sep	Hamilton Aca'l	2-0		Sat 31 Jan	St.JOHNST'E	1-1
Mon 29 Sep	Rangers	1-4		Wed 11 Feb	PARTICK TH.	2-1
Sat 4 Oct	MOTHERW'L	2-2		Sat 14 Feb	Morton	0-2
Sat 11 Oct	Celtic	0-1		Sat 21 Feb	Third Lanark	2-2
Sat 18 Oct	HIBERNIAN	2-0		Sat 28 Feb	HAMILTON	3-2
Sat 25 Oct	Partick Thistle	3-3		Sat 7 Mar	Airdrieonians	2-2
Sat 1 Nov	Raith Rovers	0-2		Sat 14 Mar	KILMARN'K	1-1
Sat 8 Nov	ABERDEEN	1-1		Sat 28 Mar	QUEEN'S P'K	3-1
Sat 15 Nov	3rd.LANARK	2-3		Sat 4 Apr	Aberdeen	0-0
Sat 22 Nov	Kilmarnock	1-2		Sat 11 Apr	St.Johnstone	3-4
Sat 29 Nov	FALKIRK	3-2		Sat 18 Apr	DUNDEE	1-0

Played 38 W12; D11; L15;
F64; A68; Pts.35. 10th.

Scottish League Championship Division One 1925–1926

Sat 15 Aug	FALKIRK	1-1		Sat 19 Dec	Motherwell	1-3
Sat 22 Aug	Hamilton Aca'l	0-3		Sat 26 Dec	St.MIRREN	1-0
Sat 29 Aug	AIRDRIE	0-2		Fri 1 Jan	HIBERNIAN	1-4
Sat 5 Sep	Morton	1-1		Sat 2 Jan	Cowdenbeath	2-1
Sat 12 Sep	CLYDEBANK	7-0		Mon 4 Jan	Raith Rovers	3-1
Sat 19 Sep	Queen's Park	4-3		Sat 9 Jan	QUEEN'S P'K	4-2
Mon 21 Sep	ABERDEEN	1-0		Sat 16 Jan	Rangers	2-2
Sat 26 Sep	RANGERS	3-0		Sat 30 Jan	Falkirk	3-3
Sat 3 Oct	Dundee	0-1		Wed 10 Feb	HAMILTON	4-0
Sat 10 Oct	COWDEN'TH	4-3		Sat 13 Feb	Airdrieonians	2-2
Sat 17 Oct	Hibernian	0-0		Wed 24 Feb	Dundee United	3-2
Sat 24 Oct	PARTICK TH.	3-0		Wed 3 Mar	CELTIC	1-2
Sat 31 Oct	St.Mirren	1-2		Sat 6 Mar	St.Johnstone	1-1
Sat 7 Nov	D/D UNITED	1-0		Sat 13 Mar	MORTON	6-1
Sat 14 Nov	MOTHERW'L	3-1		Sat 20 Mar	Kilmarnock	1-5
Wed 25 Nov	Celtic	0-3		Sat 27 Mar	DUNDEE	2-2
Sat 28 Nov	KILMARN'K	1-0		Sat 3 Apr	RAITH ROV'S	5-1
Sat 5 Dec	Aberdeen	2-0		Sat 17 Apr	Clydebank	5-1
Sat 12 Dec	St.JOHNST'E	4-2		Sat 24 Apr	Partick Thistle	4-1

Played 38 W21; D8; L9;
F87; A56; Pts.50. 3rd.

Scottish League Championship Division One 1926–1927

Sat 14 Aug	Dundee	1-4		Sat 25 Dec	DUNDEE	0-0
Sat 21 Aug	QUEEN'S P'K	4-1		Sat 1 Jan	Hibernian	2-2
Sat 28 Aug	Cowdenbeath	1-2		Mon 3 Jan	COWDEN'TH	4-3
Sat 4 Sep	HAMILTON	1-1		Sat 8 Jan	Hamilton Aca'l	1-2
Sat 11 Sep	Morton	3-1		Sat 15 Jan	MORTON	3-0
Sat 18 Sep	RANGERS	0-2		Sat 29 Jan	Rangers	0-1
Sat 25 Sep	Kilmarnock	4-1		Sat 5 Feb	MOTHERW'L	1-3
Sat 2 Oct	FALKIRK	0-0		Sat 12 Feb	Falkirk	1-2
Sat 9 Oct	Clyde	3-2		Sat 19 Feb	KILMARN'K	1-1
Sat 16 Oct	PARTICK TH.	1-0		Wed 23 Feb	CLYDE	5-0
Sat 23 Oct	Motherwell	1-5		Sat 26 Feb	Partick Thistle	2-2
Sat 30 Oct	HIBERNIAN	2-2		Sat 12 Mar	Queens Park	0-2
Sat 6 Nov	St.MIRREN	4-3		Sat 19 Mar	St.Mirren	1-0
Sat 13 Nov	Celtic	0-1		Wed 30 Mar	CELTIC	3-0
Sat 20 Nov	Aberdeen	5-6		Sat 2 Apr	ABERDEEN	2-2
Sat 27 Nov	St.JOHNST'E	0-0		Sat 9 Apr	St.Johnstone	1-1
Sat 4 Dec	Dundee United	3-5		Sat 16 Apr	D/D UNITED	1-2
Sat 11 Dec	AIRDRIE	1-3		Sat 23 Apr	Airdrieonians	0-0
Sat 18 Dec	Dunfermline	2-0		Sat 30 Apr	DUNF/LINE	1-2

Played 38 W12; D11; L15;
F65; A64; Pts.35. 13th.

Scottish League Championship Division One 1927–1928

Sat 13 Aug	KILMARN'K	0-1	Sat 24 Dec	Kilmarnock	0-5
Sat 20 Aug	Rangers	1-4	Sat 31 Dec	HAMILTON	2-1
Sat 27 Aug	CLYDE	5-0	Mon 2 Jan	HIBERNIAN	2-2
Sat 3 Sep	Hamilton Aca'l	6-1	Tue 3 Jan	Dunfermline	2-0
Sat 10 Sep	DUNF/LINE	6-0	Sat 7 Jan	Clyde	2-2
Sat 17 Sep	Queen's Park	2-0	Sat 14 Jan	QUEEN'S P'K	4-2
Sat 24 Sep	RAITH ROV'S	2-0	Sat 28 Jan	Dundee	7-2
Sat 1 Oct	Falkirk	3-1	Wed 8 Feb	FALKIRK	9-3
Sat 8 Oct	DUNDEE	1-0	Sat 11 Feb	Raith Rovers	5-0
Sat 15 Oct	Hibernian	1-2	Wed 22 Feb	PARTICK TH.	1-2
Sat 22 Oct	MOTHERW'L	0-0	Sat 26 Feb	Motherwell	3-0
Sat 29 Oct	Partick Thistle	3-1	Wed 7 Mar	RANGERS	0-0
Sat 5 Nov	St.Mirren	0-2	Sat 10 Mar	St.MIRREN	2-1
Sat 12 Nov	CELTIC	2-2	Sat 17 Mar	Celtic	1-2
Sat 19 Nov	ABERDEEN	3-0	Sat 24 Mar	Aberdeen	0-2
Sat 26 Nov	St.Johnstone	3-2	Sat 31 Mar	St.JOHNST'E	0-2
Sat 3 Dec	BO'NESS	5-0	Sat 7 Apr	Boness	2-2
Sat 10 Dec	Airdrieonians	0-2	Sat 14 Apr	AIRDRIE	1-1
Sat 17 Dec	COWDEN'TH	2-3	Sat 21 Apr	Cowdenbeath	1-0

Played 38 **W20; D7; L11;**
F89; A50; **Pts.47.** **4th.**

Scottish League Championship Division One 1928–1929

Sat 11 Aug	Queen's Park	3-1	Sat 22Dec	Hamilton Aca'l	2-3
Sat 18 Aug	HAMILTON	5-0	Tue 25 Dec	St.MIRREN	1-0
Sat 25 Aug	Clyde	1-1	Sat 29 Dec	QUEEN'S P'K	4-1
Sat 1 Sep	AYR UNITED	7-3	Tue 1 Jan	Hibernian	0-1
Sat 8 Sep	Raith Rovers	2-0	Wed 2 Jan	ABERDEEN	3-2
Sat 15 Sep	RANGERS	0-1	Sat 5 Jan	CLYDE	4-0
Sat 22 Sep	Airdrieonians	1-1	Sat 12 Jan	Ayr United	4-2
Sat 29 Sep	Dundee	3-5	Sat 26 Jan	CELTIC	2-1
Sat 6 Oct	FALKIRK	6-2	Sat 9 Feb	AIRDRIE	3-0
Sat 13 Oct	COWDEN'TH	4-1	Sat 23 Feb	Falkirk	3-3
Sat 20 Oct	HIBERNIAN	1-1	Sat 2 Mar	Cowdenbeath	2-1
Sat 27 Oct	Aberdeen	3-1	Wed 6 Mar	DUNDEE	1-1
Sat 3 Nov	St.Johnstone	3-0	Sat 9 Mar	St.JOHNST'E	0-3
Sat 10 Nov	MOTHERW'L	5-1	Tue 12 Mar	Rangers	0-2
Sat 17 Nov	St.Mirren	2-2	Sat 16 Mar	Motherwell	2-3
Sat 24 Nov	Kilmarnock	2-3	Sat 30 Mar	KILMARN'K	3-3
Sat 1 Dec	3rd.LANARK	4-1	Mon 1 Apr	Third Lanark	2-2
Sat 8 Dec	PARTICK TH.	2-1	Sat 20 Apr	Partick Thistle	0-2
Sat 15 Dec	Celtic	0-1	Sat 27 Apr	RAITH ROV'S	1-1

Played 38 **W19; D9; L10;**
F91; A57; **Pts.47.** **4th.**

Scottish League Championship Division One 1928–1930

Sat 10 Aug	Celtic	1-2	Sat 21 Dec	CELTIC	1-3
Sat 17 Aug	KILMARN'K	1-1	Sat 28 Dec	Kilmarnock	1-2
Sat 24 Aug	Cowdenbeath	1-0	Wed 1 Jan	HIBERNIAN	1-1
Sat 31 Aug	St.MIRREN	5-0	Thu 2 Jan	Aberdeen	2-2
Sat 7 Sep	Motherwell	2-0	Sat 4 Jan	COWDEN'TH	2-2
Sat 14 Sep	D/D UNITED	3-1	Sat 11 Jan	St.Mirren	2-6
Sat 21 Sep	Partick Thistle	1-2	Sat 25 Jan	MOTHERW'L	3-2
Sat 28 Sep	St.JOHNST'E	2-2	Sat 8 Feb	PARTICK TH.	0-0
Sat 5 Oct	RANGERS	2-0	Wed 19 Feb	St.Johnstone	3-0
Sat 12 Oct	Falkirk	3-2	Sat 22 Feb	Rangers	3-1
Sat 19 Oct	ABERDEEN	2-2	Sat 8 Mar	Hamilton Aca'l	1-2
Sat 26 Oct	Hibernian	1-1	Wed 12 Mar	FALKIRK	0-2
Sat 2 Nov	HAMILTON	6-4	Sat 15 Mar	AYR UNITED	1-2
Sat 9 Nov	Ayr United	1-3	Wed 26 Mar	Morton	2-3
Sat 16 Nov	MORTON	4-0	Sat 29 Mar	QUEEN'S P'K	0-3
Sat 23 Nov	Queen's Park	2-6	Tue 1 Apr	Dundee United	3-2
Sat 30 Nov	Clyde	3-3	Sat 5 Apr	CLYDE	0-1
Sat 7 Dec	AIRDRIE	1-0	Sat 12 Apr	Airdrieonians	2-3
Sat 14 Dec	Dundee	0-3	Sat 19 Apr	DUNDEE	1-0

Played 38 **W14; D9; L15;**
F69; A69; **Pts.37.** **10th.**

Scottish League Championship Division One 1930-1931

Sat 9 Aug	HAMILTON	0-4	Sat 20 Dec	Hamilton Aca'l	2-3
Sat 16 Aug	Rangers	1-4	Sat 27 Dec	RANGERS	3-0
Sat 23 Aug	EAST FIFE	6-1	Thu 1 Jan	Hibernian	2-2
Sat 30 Aug	Kilmarnock	1-0	Sat 3 Jan	East Fife	0-1
Sat 6 Sep	MORTON	2-4	Mon 5 Jan	ABERDEEN	3-2
Sat 13 Sep	Clyde	2-1	Sat 10 Jan	KILMARN'K	1-4
Sat 20 Sep	HIBERNIAN	4-1	Sat 24 Jan	Morton	4-2
Sat 27 Sep	Aberdeen	1-2	Wed 11 Feb	Queen's Park	2-1
Sat 4 Oct	QU'N'S PARK	2-1	Wed 18 Feb	FALKIRK	4-2
Sat 11 Oct	Falkirk	3-0	Sat 21 Feb	Leith Athletic	1-2
Sat 18 Oct	LEITH ATH.	5-2	Sat 28 Feb	AYR UNITED	9-0
Sat 25 Oct	Ayr United	1-1	Sat 7 Mar	Cowdenbeath	2-2
Sat 1 Nov	COWDEN'TH	1-1	Wed 18 Mar	CELTIC	1-1
Sat 8 Nov	Celtic	1-2	Sat 21 Mar	Motherwell	0-2
Sat 15 Nov	MOTHERW'L	5-1	Sat 28 Mar	CLYDE	0-3
Sat 22 Nov	Dundee	3-1	Sat 4 Apr	DUNDEE	2-0
Sat 29 Nov	St.MIRREN	3-1	Sat 11 Apr	St.Mirren	3-0
Sat 6 Dec	Partick Thistle	1-2	Sat 18 Apr	PARTICK TH.	1-2
Sat 13 Dec	AIRDRIE	6-3	Sat 25 Apr	Airdrieonians	2-2

Played 38	W19; D6; L13;		
F90; A63;	Pts.44.	5th.	

Scottish League Championship Division One 1931-1932

Sat 8 Aug	Dundee United	2-0	Sat 21 Nov	CELTIC	2-1
Sat 15 Aug	KILMARN'K	3-0	Sat 28 Nov	Partick Thistle	0-1
Wed 19 Aug	Celtic	0-3	Sat 5 Dec	Airdrieonians	1-3
Sat 22 Aug	Morton	2-1	Sat 12 Dec	COWDEN'TH	3-2
Tue 25 Aug	PARTICK TH.	0-1	Sat 19 Dec	D/D UNITED	5-0
Sat 29 Aug	CLYDE	2-0	Sat 26 Dec	Kilmarnock	1-2
Tue 1 Sep	AIRDRIE	0-2	Fri 1 Jan	LEITH. ATH	4-2
Sat 5 Sep	Leith Athletic	0-2	Sat 2 Jan	Aberdeen	2-1
Wed 9 Sep	Cowdenbeath	1-2	Sat 9 Jan	MORTON	0-0
Sat 12 Sep	ABERDEEN	0-0	Sat 23 Jan	Clyde	2-6
Sat 19 Sep	Queen's Park	2-5	Sat 6 Feb	Rangers	2-4
Sat 26 Sep	RANGERS	0-0	Sat 20 Feb	Falkirk	2-0
Sat 3 Oct	Hamilton Aca'l	4-1	Sat 27 Feb	MOTHERW'L	0-1
Sat 10 Oct	FALKIRK	2-0	Sat 5 Mar	Dundee	0-1
Sat 17 Oct	Motherwell	0-2	Sat 12 Mar	St.MIRREN	2-2
Sat 24 Oct	DUNDEE	3-1	Sat 19 Mar	Third Lanark	4-3
Sat 31 Oct	St.Mirren	1-5	Sat 26 Mar	AYR UNITED	1-1
Sat 7 Nov	3rd.LANARK	2-3	Sat 9 Apr	HAMILTON	4-2
Sat 14 Nov	Ayr United	2-1	Sat 16 Apr	QUEEN'S P'K	2-0

Played 38	W17;D5;L16;		
F63; A61	Pts.39.	8th.	

Scottish League Championship Division One 1932-1933

Sat 13 Aug	Partick Thistle	2-1	Sat 3 Dec	KILMARN'K	1-0
Sat 20 Aug	AIRDRIE	4-0	Sat 10 Dec	ABERDEEN	3-1
Wed 24 Aug	Hamilton Aca'l	2-3	Sat 17 Dec	St.Johnstone	1-2
Sat 27 Aug	St.Mirren	1-0	Sat 24 Dec	PARTICK TH.	1-2
Sat 3 Sep	AYR UNITED	4-2	Sat 31 Dec	Airdrieonians	7-2
Sat 10 Sep	Cowdenbeath	0-0	Mon 2 Jan	COWDEN'TH	3-1
Tue 13 Sep	QUEEN'S P'K	5-0	Tue 3 Jan	Dundee	2-2
Sat 17 Sep	DUNDEE	1-0	Sat 7 Jan	St.MIRREN	0-0
Sat 24 Sep	Third Lanark	1-2	Sat 14 Jan	Ayr United	1-1
Mon 26 Sep	Aberdeen	0-3	Sat 28 Jan	3rd.LANARK	3-1
Sat 1 Oct	CELTIC	1-1	Sat 11 Feb	Celtic	2-3
Sat 8 Oct	East Stirling're	3-1	Sat 25 Feb	EAST STIR'G	3-1
Sat 15 Oct	MOTHERW'L	2-0	Sat 11 Mar	Rangers	4-4
Sat 22 Oct	RANGERS	1-0	Sat 25 Mar	MORTON	5-2
Sat 29 Oct	Falkirk	1-3	Wed 29 Mar	Motherwell	1-5
Sat 5 Nov	HAMILION	6-1	Sat 1 Apr	FALKIRK	3-2
Sat 12 Nov	Queen's Park	1-2	Sat 8 Apr	CLYDE	1-1
Sat 19 Nov	Morton	5-1	Wed 12 Apr	Kilmarnock	0-0
Sat 26 Nov	Clyde	1-0	Sat 29 Apr	St.JOHNST'E	2-1

Played 38	W21; D8; L9;		
F84; A51;	Pts.50.	3rd.	

Scottish League Championship Division One 1933–1934

Sat 12 Aug	St.MIRREN	6-0		Sat 16 Dec	St.Johnstone	1-3
Sat 19 Aug	Ayr United	3-4		Sat 23 Dec	St.Mirren	1-1
Tue 22 Aug	HAMILTON	4-2		Mon 25 Dec	AIRDRIE	8-1
Sat 26 Aug	3rd.LANARK	5-1		Sat 30 Dec	AYR UNITED	1-1
Sat 2 Sep	Celtic	0-0		Mon 1 Jan	Hibernian	4-1
Sat 9 Sep	HIBERNIAN	0-0		Tue 2 Jan	DUNDEE	0-1
Tue 12 Sep	Queen's Park	1-1		Sat 6 Jan	Third Lanark	1-1
Sat 23 Sep	COWDEN'TH	5-4		Sat 13 Jan	CELTIC	2-1
Sat 30 Sep	Dundee	1-0		Sat 27 Jan	Cowdenebath	5-1
Sat 7 Oct	PARTICK TH.	1-0		Sat 24 Feb	Partick Thistle	2-7
Sat 14 Oct	Motherwell	1-2		Sat 10 Mar	RANGERS	1-2
Sat 21 Oct	Rangers	1-3		Sat 17 Mar	Falkirk	1-2
Sat 28 Oct	FALKIRK	3-1		Sat 24 Mar	Queen of the S	1-3
Sat 4 Nov	Hamilton Aca'l	1-1		Tue 27 Mar	Clyde	2-1
Sat 11 Nov	QUEEN'S P'K	4-0		Sat 7 Apr	KILMARN'K	1-1
Sat 18 Nov	QUEEN O.T.S	1-3		Sat 14 Apr	Airdrieonians	2-3
Sat 25 Nov	CLYDE	1-1		Mon 16 Apr	MOTHERW'L	1-3
Sat 2 Dec	Kilmarnock	5-2		Sat 21 Apr	Aberdeen	1-0
Sat 9 Dec	ABERDEEN	0-0		Sat 28 Apr	St.JOHNST'E	2-1

Played 38   **W17; D10; L11;**
F86; A59;   **Pts.44.**   **6th.**

Scottish League Championship Division One 1934–1935

Sat 11 Aug	Falkirk	2-0		Sat 8 Dec	RANGERS	4-1
Sat 18 Aug	CELTIC	0-0		Sat 15 Dec	Albion Rovers	2-2
Wed 22 Aug	Rangers	1-2		Sat 22 Dec	FALKIRK	4-1
Sat 25 Aug	Dunfermline	2-1		Sat 29 Dec	Celtic	2-4
Sat 1 Sep	DUNDEE	1-1		Tue 1 Jan	HIBERNIAN	5-2
Sat 8 Sep	Hibernian	0-1		Wed 2 Jan	Dundee	5-1
Wed 12 Sep	ALBION R.	4-0		Sat 5 Jan	DUN/LINE	0-1
Sat 15 Sep	AIRDRIE	1-0		Sat 12 Jan	Airdrieonians	7-4
Sat 22 Sep	Partick Thistle	3-1		Sat 19 Jan	PARTICK TH.	1-2
Sat 29 Sep	AYR UNITED	5-0		Sat 2 Feb	Ayr United	3-0
Sat 6 Oct	St.Mirren	4-2		Sat 16 Feb	St.MIRREN	0-1
Sat 13 Oct	MOTHERW'L	2-1		Sat 2 Mar	Motherwell	2-2
Wed 24 Oct	HAMILTON	1-1		Sat 16 Mar	QUEEN'S P'K	2-1
Sat 27 Oct	Queen's Park	3-3		Sat 23 Mar	QUEEN O.T.S.	4-2
Sat 3 Nov	Queen of the So.	3-1		Fri 5 Apr	Hamilton Aca'l	0-2
Sat 10 Nov	Clyde	1-0		Sat 13 Apr	Kilmarnock	3-3
Sat 17 Nov	KILMARN'K	2-2		Mon 15 Apr	CLYDE	2-0
Sat 24 Nov	Aberdeen	0-1		Sat 20 Apr	ABERDEEN	2-1
Sat 1 Dec	St.JOHNST'E	2-2		Sat 27 Apr	St.Johnstone	2-2

Played 38   **W20; D10; L8;**
F87; A51;   **Pts.50.**   **3rd.**

Scottish League Championship Division One 1935–1936

Sat 10 Aug	PARTICK TH.	2-0		Sat 7 Dec	QUEEN'S P'K	4-1
Sat 17 Aug	Airdrieonians	1-3		Sat 14 Dec	QUEEN O.T.S.	2-0
Sat 24 Aug	DUN/LINE	1-1		Sat 28 Dec	AIRDRIE	3-0
Tue 27 Aug	Queen's Park	2-2		Wed 1 Jan	Hibernian	1-1
Sat 31 Aug	Dundee	5-2		Thu 2 Jan	DUNDEE	3-0
Sat 7 Sep	ARBROATH	2-1		Sat 4 Jan	Dunfermline	0-2
Sat 14 Sep	Ayr United	3-1		Sat 11 Jan	Arbroath	3-1
Wed 18 Sep	Queen of the So.	0-2		Sat 18 Jan	AYR UNITED	3-0
Sat 21 Sep	HIBERNIAN	8-3		Sat 1 Feb	CELTIC	1-0
Sat 28 Sep	Celtic	1-2		Sat 8 Feb	Partick Thistle	0-1
Sat 5 Oct	3rd.LANARK	2-0		Sat 15 Feb	Third Lanark	5-1
Sat 12 Oct	Motherwell	2-4		Sat 22 Feb	HAMILTON	4-1
Sat 19 Oct	Rangers	1-1		Sat 29 Feb	MOTHERW'L	2-2
Sat 26 Oct	ALBION R.	4-2		Sat 14 Mar	Albion Rovers	2-1
Sat 2 Nov	St.JOHNST'E	6-1		Sat 21 Mar	St.Johnstone	1-3
Sat 9 Nov	Kilmarnock	0-2		Wed 1 Apr	KILMARN'K	4-2
Sat 16 Nov	CLYDE	3-3		Sat 11 Apr	Clyde	0-1
Sat 23 Nov	Hamilton Aca'l	4-3		Wed 22 Apr	RANGERS	1-1
Sat 30 Nov	Aberdeen	1-2		Sat 25 Apr	ABERDEEN	1-2

Played 38   **W20; D7; L11;**
F88; A55;   **Pts.47.**   **5th.**

Scottish League Championship Division One 1936–1937

Sat 8 Aug	Dunfermline	5-2		Sat 12 Dec	Albion Rovers	3-1
Sat 15 Aug	MOTHERW'L	3-4		Sat 19 Dec	ARBROATH	4-1
Wed 19 Aug	DUN/LINE	3-2		Sat 26 Dec	St.Mirren	2-2
Sat 22 Aug	Arbroath	3-0		Fri 1 Jan	HIBERNIAN	3-2
Sat 29 Aug	St.MIRREN	2-1		Sat 2 Jan	Dundee	0-1
Sat 5 Sep	Third Lanark	0-3		Mon 4 Jan	Rangers	1-0
Wed 9 Sep	Motherwell	3-1		Sat 9 Jan	3rd.LANARK	5-2
Sat 12 Sep	FALKIRK	3-1		Sat 16 Jan	Falkirk	0-3
Sat 19 Sep	Hibernian	3-3		Sat 23 Jan	PARTICK TH.	5-1
Sat 26 Sep	CELTIC	0-1		Sat 6 Feb	Celtic	2-3
Sat 3 Oct	Partick Thistle	2-2		Sat 20 Feb	St.JOHNST'E	3-1
Sat 10 Oct	DUNDEE	4-0		Sat 6 Mar	Kilmarnock	0-3
Sat 17 Oct	St.Johnstone	0-3		Sat 20 Mar	Hamilton Aca'l	1-5
Sat 24 Oct	KILMARN'K	5-0		Tue 23 Mar	Clyde	1-2
Sat 7 Nov	HAMILTON	6-0		Sat 27 Mar	Aberdeen	0-4
Sat 14 Nov	ABERDEEN	2-0		Sat 3 Apr	QUEEN'S P'K	3-1
Sat 21 Nov	Queen's Park	2-0		Sat 10 Apr	QUEEN O.T.S.	4-2
Sat 28 Nov	Queen of the So.	4-0		Mon 19 Apr	CLYDE	2-1
Sat 5 Dec	RANGERS	5-2		Sat 24 Apr	ALBION R.	5-0

Played 38 W24; D3; L11;
F99; A60; Pts.51.   5th.

Scottish League Championship Division One 1937–1938

Sat 14 Aug	St.JOHNST'E	2-1		Sat 11 Dec	ARBROATH	4-1
Sat 21 Aug	St.Mirren	1-1		Sat 25 Dec	Third Lanark	0-3
Wed 25 Aug	St.Johnstone	2-1		Sat 1 Jan	Hibernian	2-2
Sat 28 Aug	3RDLANARK	2-1		Mon 3 Jan	DUNDEE	2-1
Sat 4 Sep	Falkirk	2-4		Tue 4 Jan	FALKIRK	1-0
Sat 11 Sep	HIBERNIAN	3-2		Sat 8 Jan	CELTIC	2-4
Wed 15 Sep	St.MIRREN	4-0		Sat 15 Jan	Partick Thistle	1-3
Sat 18 Sep	Celtic	1-2		Sat 29 Jan	MOTHERW'L	2-0
Sat 25 Sep	PARTICK TH.	3-0		Sat 5 Feb	Ayr United	4-2
Sat 2 Oct	Motherwell	3-3		Sat 12 Feb	Kilmarnock	1-3
Sat 9 Oct	AYR UNITED	7-0		Sat 19 Feb	Clyde	3-1
Sat 16 Oct	Dundee	2-0		Sat 26 Feb	HAMILTON	2-1
Sat 23 Oct	CLYDE	0-0		Sat 12 Mar	ABERDEEN	2-1
Sat 30 Oct	Hamilton Aca'l	3-2		Sat 19 Mar	Queen's Park	4-1
Sat 6 Nov	Aberdeen	0-0		Sat 26 Mar	Queen of the So.	3-2
Sat 13 Nov	QUEEN'S P'K	2-0		Wed 13 Apr	Morton	2-1
Sat 20 Nov	QUEEN O.T.S,	0-0		Sat 16 Apr	Arbroath	5-3
Sat 27 Nov	Rangers	3-0		Sat 23 Apr	RANGERS	3-2
Sat 4 Dec	MORTON	2-1		Sat 30 Apr	KILMARN'K	5-1

Played 38 W26; D6; L6;
F90; A50; Pts.58.   2nd.

Scottish League Championship Division One 1938–1939

Sat 13 Aug	Third Lanark	4-1		Sat 10 Dec	Clyde	6-2
Sat 20 Aug	FALKIRK	6-2		Sat 17 Dec	HAMILTON	2-3
Wed 24 Aug	3rd.LANARK	4-2		Sat 24 Dec	PARTICK TH.	5-0
Sat 27 Aug	Partick Thistle	1-3		Sat 31 Dec	Celtic	2-2
Sat 3 Sep	CELTIC	1-5		Mon 2 Jan	HIBERNIAN	0-1
Sat 10 Sep	Hibernian	0-4		Tue 3 Jan	Arbroath	1-1
Tue 13 Sep	Falkirk	1-0		Wed 11 Jan	AYR UNITED	2-0
Sat 17 Sep	MOTHERW'L	4-0		Tue 24 Jan	St.Mirren	1-1
Sat 24 Sep	Ayr United	1-3		Sat 28 Jan	St.JOHNST'E	8-2
Sat 1 Oct	St.MIRREN	5-2		Sat 11 Feb	Motherwell	2-4
Sat 8 Oct	St.Johnstone	7-1		Sat 25 Feb	Aberdeen	3-4
Sat 15 Oct	ARBROATH	1-1		Sat 4 Mar	QEEN'S P'K	8-3
Sat 22 Oct	ABERDEEN	5-2		Sat 11 Mar	QUEEN O.T.S.	1-2
Sat 29 Oct	Queen's Park	1-4		Sat 18 Mar	Rangers	1-1
Sat 5 Nov	Queen of the So.	1-0		Wed 29 Mar	ALBION R.	2-0
Sat 12 Nov	RANGERS	1-3		Sat 1 Apr	RAITH ROV'S	2-1
Sat 19 Nov	Albion Rovers	1-0		Sat 8 Apr	Kilmarnock	1-4
Sat 26 Nov	Raith Rovers	2-1		Wed 26 Apr	CLYDE	2-0
Sat 3 Dec	KILMARN'K	2-1		Sat 29 Apr	Hamilton Aca'l	1-4

Played 38 W20; D5; L13;
F98; A70; Pts.45.   4th.

Scottish League East & North Division 1939–1940

Sat 21 Oct	FALKIRK	2-3		Sat 10 Feb	ALLOA ATH.	7-2
Sat 28 Oct	Raith Rovers	5-1		Sat 17 Feb	Dundee United	2-3
Sat 4 Nov	St.BERNARDS	2-2		Sat 16 Mar	Aberdeen	0-3
Sat 11 Nov	Alloa Athletic	3-2		Sat 30 Mar	Stenhousemuir	0-1
Sat 18 Nov	D/D UNITED	9-2		Wed 3 Apr	Falkirk	1-7
Sat 25 Nov	Dunfermline	2 6		Sat 6 Apr	HIBERNIAN	4-0
Sat 2 Dec	EAST FIFE	6-3		Wed 10 Apr	RAITH ROV'S	4-3
Sat 9 Dec	Dundee	6-4		Sat 13 Apr	Arbroath	2-2
Sat 16 Dec	ABERDEEN	3-2		Mon 15 Apr	St.Bernards	2-0
Sar 23 Dec	Cowdenbeath	3-2		Sat 20 Apr	KING'S PARK	7-2
Sat 30 Dec	STENH'MUIR	8-2		Sat 27 Apr	St.Johnstone	2-2
Mon 1 Jan	Hibernian	6-5		Sat 4 May	East Fife	2-1
Tue 2 Jan	ARBROATH	7-2		Sat 11 May	DUNDEE	2-3
Sat 6 Jan	King's Park	2-2		Sat 25 May	DUN/LINE	2-0
Sat 13 Jan	St.JOHNST'E	3-0				

Played 29	W18; D4; L7;	
F104;A66;	Pts.40.	2nd.

Scottish Southern League 1940–1941

Sat 10 Aug	Motherwell	3-2		Sat 23 Nov	MOTHERW'L	1-1
Sat 17 Aug	FALKIRK	2-3		Sat 30 Nov	Falkirk	3-3
Sat 24 Aug	Celtic	1-2		Sat 7 Dec	CELTIC	2-1
Sat 31 Aug	AIRDRIE	0-2		Sat 14 Dec	Airdrieonians	1-3
Sat 7 Sep	Hibernian	1-2		Sat 21 Dec	PARTICK TH.	2-1
Sat 14 Sep	3rd.LANARK	4-2		Sat 28 Dec	Third Lanark	0-2
Sat 21 Sep	Partick Thistle	2-4		Sat 4 Jan	St.Mirren	1-0
Sat 28 Sep	St.MIRREN	5-1		Sat 18 Jan	Rangers	0-3
Sat 5 Oct	Queen's Park	1-3		Sat 25 Jan	CLYDE	3-5
Sat 12 Oct	RANGERS	1-1		Sat 1 Feb	Morton	1-1
Sat 19 Oct	Clyde	3-10		Sat 8 Feb	HAMILTON	5-2
Sat 26 Oct	MORTON	3-3		Sat 15 Feb	DUMBARTON	3-1
Sat 2 Nov	Hamilton Aca'l	2-6		Sat 12 Apr	Albion Rovers	3-0
Sat 9 Nov	Dumbarton	4-1		Mon 28 Apr	HIBERNIAN	3-5
Sat 16 Nov	ALBION R.	3-1		Sat 3 May	QUEEN'S P'K	1-0

Played 30	W12; D5; L13;	
F64; A71;	Pts.29.	10th.

Scottish Southern League 1941–1942

Sat 9 Aug	CELTIC	3-0		Sat 22 Nov	Celtic	4-4
Sat 16 Aug	Airdrieonians	2-1		Sat 29 Nov	AIRDRIE	2-1
Sat 23 Aug	PARTICK TH.	4-1		Sat 6 Dec	Partick Thistle	1-2
Sat 30 Aug	Third Lanark	4-6		Sat 13 Dec	3rd.LANARK	1-5
Sat 6 Sep	HIBERNIAN	2-4		Sat 20 Dec	Motherwell	2-6
Sat 13 Sep	St.Mirren	3-0		Sat 27 Dec	FALKIRK	7-0
Sat 20 Sep	MOTHERW'L	2-1		Thu 1 Jan	Hibernian	2-2
Sat 27 Sep	Falkirk	6-2		Sat 3 Jan	St.MIRREN	8-2
Sat 4 Oct	CLYDE	4-1		Sat 17 Jan	MORTON	1-2
Sat 11 Oct	Morton	0-4		Sat 31 Jan	Dumbarton	3-3
Sat 18 Oct	HAMILTON	6-2		Sat 14 Feb	Queen's Park	1-4
Sat 25 Oct	DUMBARTON	7-4		Sat 21 Feb	RANGERS	0-1
Sat 1 Nov	Albion Rovers	2-1		Sat 18 Apr	ALBION R.	2-2
Sat 8 Nov	QUEEN'S P'K	3-2		Tue 28 Apr	Clyde	0-2
Sat 15 Nov	Rangers	2-5		Sat 2 May	Hamilton Aca'l	1-2

Played 30	W14; D4; L12;	
F85; A72;	Pts.32.	5th.

Scottish Southern League 1942–1943

Sat 8 Aug	Partick Thistle	2-2		Sat 21 Nov	PARTICK	3-3
Sat 15 Aug	3rd.LANARK	3-1		Sat 28 Nov	Third Lanark	2-1
Sat 22 Aug	Motherwell	2-3		Sat 5 Dec	MOTHERW'L	1-6
Sat 29 Aug	St.MIRREN	4-2		Sat 12 Dec	St.Mirren	1-2
Sat 5 Sep	Hibernian	2-2		Sat 19 Dec	CLYDE	1-3
Sat 12 Sep	FALKIRK	3-2		Sat 26 Dec	Falkirk	2-2
Sat 19 Sep	Clyde	2-2		Fri 1 Jan	HIBERNIAN	1-4
Sat 26 Sep	MORTON	5-2		Sat 9 Jan	Morton	0-2
Sat 3 Oct	Hamilton Aca'l	2-3		Sat 16 Jan	DUMBARTON	0-1
Sat 10 Oct	Dumbarton	2-2		Sat 23 Jan	Albion Rovers	3-1
Sat 17 Oct	ALBION R.	5-1		Sat 30 Jan	QUEEN'S P'K	1-0
Sat 24 Oct	Queen's Park	2-3		Sat 6 Feb	Rangers	1-1
Sat 31 Oct	RANGERS	0-3		Sat 13 Feb	CELTIC	5-3
Sat 7 Nov	Celtic	0-3		Sat 20 Feb	Airdrieonians	4-2
Sat 14 Nov	AIRDRIE	5-2		Sat 10 Apr	HAMILTON	4-0

Played 30 **W12; D7; L11;**
F68; A64; **Pts.31** **7th.**

Scottish Southern League 1943–1944

Sat 14 Aug	PARTICK TH.	2-3		Sat 27 Nov	Pertick Thistle	1-0
Sat 21 Aug	Falkirk	3-2		Sat 4 Dec	FALKIRK	1-1
Sat 28 Aug	MOTHERW'L	3-1		Sat 11 Dec	Motherwell	2-2
Sat 4 Sep	Third Lanark	2-1		Sat 18 Dec	3rd.LANARK	6-3
Sat 11 Sep	HIBERNIAN	0-1		Sat 25 Dec	St.MIRREN	5-2
Sat 18 Sep	St.Mirren	3-5		Sat 1 Jan	Hibernian	1-0
Sat 25 Sep	CELTIC	0-0		Mon 3 Jan	Hamilton Aca'l	1-2
Sat 2 Oct	Airdrieonians	3-1		Sat 8 Jan	Celtic	0-4
Sat 9 Oct	MORTON	1-1		Sat 15 Jan	AIRDRIE	1-1
Sat 16 Oct	Rangers	3-1		Sat 22 Jan	Morton	3-1
Sat 23 Oct	QUEEN'S P'K	9-0		Sat 29 Jan	RANGERS	1-3
Sat 30 Oct	Clyde	0-2		Sat 5 Feb	Queen's Park	2-2
Sat 6 Nov	DUMBARTON	3-0		Sat 12 Feb	CLYDE	2-2
Sat 13 Nov	Albion Rovers	2-1		Sat 19 Feb	Dumbarton	1-2
Sat 20 Nov	HAMILTON	5-6		Sat 26 Feb	ALBION R.	1-0

Played 30 **W14; D7; L9;**
F67; A50; **Pts.35.** **4th.**

Scottish Southern League 1944–1945

Sat 12 Aug	Celtic	1-4		Sat 25 Nov	CELTIC	2-0
Sat 19 Aug	AIRDRIE	3-2		Sat 2 Dec	Airdrieonians	1-1
Sat 26 Aug	Motherwell	1-4		Sat 9 Dec	MOTHERW'L	3-3
Sat 2 Sep	St.MIRREN	7-0		Sat 16 Dec	St.Mirren	2-1
Sat 9 Sep	Hibernian	1-3		Sat 23 Dec	PARTICK TH.	3-3
Sat 16 Sep	3rd.LANARK	4-1		Sat 30 Dec	Third Lanark	2-1
Sat 23 Sep	Partick Thistle	1-2		Mon 1 Jan	HIBERNIAN	3-0
Sat 30 Sep	FALKIRK	1-2		Tue 2 Jan	HAMILTON	4-2
Sat 7 Oct	MORTON	2-1		Sat 6 Jan	Falkirk	2-2
Sat 14 Oct	DUMBARTON	4-0		Sat 13 Jan	Morton	1-5
Sat 21 Oct	Queen's Park	1-1		Sat 3 Feb	Rangers	0-4
Sat 28 Oct	RANGERS	1-1		Sat 10 Feb	CLYDE	6-2
Sat 4 Nov	Clyde	1-5		Sat 17 Feb	ALBION R.	2-1
Sat 11 Nov	Albion Rovers	10-3		Sat 7 Apr	QUEEN'S P'K	2-1
Sat 18 Nov	Hamilton Aca'l	2-2		Sat 21 Apr	Dumbarton	2-3

Played 30 **W14; D7; L9;**
F75; A60; **Pts.35.** **6th.**

Scottish League Championship 'A' Division 1945–1946

Sat 11 Aug	FALKIRK	4-1	Sat 24 Nov	Falkirk	5-3
Sat 18 Aug	Partick Thistle	3-1	Sat 1 Dec	PARTICK TH.	4-1
Sat 25 Aug	MOTHERW'L	0-0	Sat 8 Dec	Motherwell	4-5
Sat 1 Sep	Third Lanark	2-1	Sat 15 Dec	3rd.LANARK	2-1
Sat 8 Sep	HIBERNIAN	0-2	Sat 22 Dec	St.MIRREN	2-2
Sat 15 Sep	St.Mirren	1-3	Sat 29 Dec	Celtic	5-3
Sat 22 Sep	CELTIC	2-2	Tue 1 Jan	Hibernian	0-1
Sat 29 Sep	Kilmarnock	2-2	Wed 2 Jan	KILMARN'K	1-4
Sat 6 Oct	MORTON	6-0	Sat 5 Jan	Morton	2-4
Sat 13 Oct	HAMILTON	4-1	Sat 12 Jan	Hamilton Aca'l	0-2
Sat 20 Oct	Queen of the So.	3-3	Sat 26 Jan	Queen's Park	1-0
Sat 27 Oct	QUEEN'S P'K	3-3	Sat 2 Feb	CLYDE	1-1
Sat 3 Nov	Clyde	1-3	Sat 9 Feb	Aberdeen	1-2
Sat 10 Nov	ABERDEEN	1-2	Sat 16 Feb	RANGERS	2-0
Sat 17 Nov	Rangers	1-1	Mon 15 Apr	QUEEN O.T.S.	0-3

Played 30   W11; D8; L11;
F63; A57;   Pts.30.   7th.

Scottish League Championship 'A' Division 1946–1947

Sat 10 Aug	Falkirk	3-3	Sat 7 Dec	FALKIRK	1-1
Wed 14 Aug	PARTICK TH.	1-4	Sat 14 Dec	Partick Thistle	2-1
Sat 17 Aug	3rd.LANARK	4-1	Sat 21 Dec	CELTIC	2-1
Wed 21 Aug	Celtic	3-2	Sat 28 Dec	St.Mirren	0-1
Sat 24 Aug	Motherwell	2-0	Wed 1 Jan	HIBERNIAN	2-3
Wed 28 Aug	St.MIRREN	2-2	Thu 2 Jan	Third Lanark	1-4
Sat 31 Aug	QUEEN O.T.S.	1-1	Sat 4 Jan	Kilmarnock	0-0
Wed 4 Sep	Hamilton Aca'l	1-3	Sat 11 Jan	MOTHERW'L	2-1
Sat 7 Sep	Hibernian	1-0	Sat 18 Jan	HAMILTON	4-3
Sat 14 Sep	KILMARN'K	2-0	Sat 1 Feb	Queen of the So.	1-0
Sat 2 Nov	Queen's Park	2-2	Sat 8 Feb	Clyde	2-0
Sat 9 Nov	CLYDE	2-1	Sat 29 Mar	QUEEN'S P'K	1-3
Sat 16 Nov	Morton	1-0	Sat 5 Apr	MORTON	2-0
Sat 23 Nov	Aberdeen	1-2	Mon 7 Apr	Rangers	2-1
Sat 30 Nov	RANGERS	0-3	Sat 17 May	ABERDEEN	4-0

Played 30   W16; D6; L8;
F52; A43;   Pts.38.   4th.

Scottish League Championship 'A' Division 1947–1948

Wed 13 Aug	St.MIRREN	3-2	Sat 27 Dec	MOTHERW'L	0-1
Wed 27 Aug	Motherwell	1-3	Thu 1 Jan	Hibernian	1-3
Sat 20 Sep	HIBERNIAN	2-1	Sat 3 Jan	CELTIC	1-0
Sat 4 Oct	3rd.LANARK	1-3	Sat 10 Jan	Third Lanark	1-4
Mon 6 Oct	Dundee	1-2	Sat 17 Jan	DUNDEE	0-1
Sat 18 Oct	PARTICK TH.	1-2	Sat 31 Jan	Partick Thistle	1-1
Sat 1 Nov	QUEEN'S P'K	1-0	Sat 14 Feb	FALKIRK	3-2
Sat 8 Nov	Morton	1-1	Sat 28 Feb	MORTON	3-0
Sat 15 Nov	Aberdeen	1-1	Sat 6 Mar	ABERDEEN	1-1
Sat 22 Nov	QUEEN O.T.S.	1-0	Sat 13 Mar	Queen of the So.	1-0
Sat 29 Nov	Airdrieonians	1-1	Sat 20 Mar	AIRDRIE	2-2
Sat 6 Dec	RANGERS	1-2	Sat 3 Apr	CLYDE	1-1
Sat 13 Dec	Clyde	1-2	Sat 17 Apr	Falkirk	2-0
Sat 20 Dec	St.Mirren	0-1	Sat 24 Apr	Queen's Park	0-0
Thu 25 Dec	Celtic	2-4	Mon 3 May	Rangers	2-1

Played 30   W10; D8; L12;
F37; A42;   Pts.28.   9th.

Scottish League Championship 'A' Division 1948–1949

Sat 14 Aug	Dundee	1-2	Sat 25 Dec	Third Lanark	1-1
Wed 18 Aug	3rd.LANARK	3-2	Sat 1 Jan	HIBERNIAN	3-2
Sat 21 Aug	Hibernian	1-3	Mon 3 Jan	Celtic	0-2
Sat 28 Aug	CELTIC	1-2	Sat 8 Jan	DUNDEE	0-1
Wed 1 Sep	Motherwell	0-3	Sat 15 Jan	St.Mirren	2-1
Sat 4 Sep	St.MIRREN	1-3	Sat 29 Jan	MOTHERW'L	5-1
Sat 23 Oct	RANGERS	2-0	Sat 12 Feb	CLYDE	3-0
Sat 30 Oct	Clyde	3-3	Sat 26 Feb	FALKIRK	3-1
Sat 6 Nov	PARTICK TH.	1-3	Sat 12 Mar	MORTON	2-4
Sat 13 Nov	Falkirk	3-5	Sat 19 Mar	ABERDEEN	1-1
Sat 20 Nov	QUEEN O.T.S.	1-1	Sat 2 Apr	ALBION R.	7-1
Sat 27 Nov	Morton	2-0	Tue 5 Apr	Rangers	1-2
Sat 4 Dec	Aberdeen	2-2	Wed 20 Apr	Partick Thistle	1-1
Sat 11 Dec	EAST FIFE	4-0	Sat 23 Apr	Queen of the So.	4-1
Sat 18 Dec	Albion Rovers	5-1	Fri 29 Apr	East Fife	1-5

Played 30   W12; D6; L12;
F64; A54;   Pts.30.   8th.

Scottish League Championship 'A' Division 1949–1950

Sat 10 Sep	EAST FIFE	0-1	Sat 31 Dec	CELTIC	4-2
Sat 17 Sep	Celtic	2-3	Mon 2 Jan	Hibernian	2-1
Sat 24 Sep	HIBERNIAN	5-2	Tue 3 Jan	St.MIRREN	5-0
Sat 1 Oct	St.Mirren	3-3	Sat 7 Jan	Dundee	1-3
Sat 15 Oct	Third Lanark	0-3	Sat 14 Jan	3rd.LANARK	1-0
Sat 22 Oct	Rangers	0-1	Sat 21 Jan	RANGERS	0-1
Sat 29 Oct	CLYDE	6-2	Sat 4 Feb	Clyde	4-3
Sat 5 Nov	Partick Thistle	1-0	Sat 18 Feb	Falkirk	1-1
Sat 12 Nov	FALKIRK	9-0	Sat 25 Feb	QUEEN O.T.S.	3-0
Sat 19 Nov	Queen of the So.	4-0	Sat 4 Mar	Motherwell	3-2
Sat 26 Nov	MOTHERW'L	2-0	Sat 18 Mar	STIRLING AL.	5-2
Sat 3 Dec	ABERDEEN	4-1	Sat 25 Mar	Raith Rovers	0-2
Sat 10 Dec	Stirling Albion	4-2	Sat 8 Apr	Aberdeen	5-0
Sat 17 Dec	RAITH RO'RS	2-0	Mon 17 Apr	PARTICK TH.	3-3
Sat 24 Dec	East Fife	1-0	Sat 22 Apr	DUNDEE	6-2

Played 30   W20; D3; L7;
F86; A40;   Pts.43.   3rd.

Scottish League Championship 'A' Division 1950–1951

Sat 9 Sep	Dundee	0-1	Sat 23 Dec	DUNDEE	1-1
Sat 16 Sep	EAST FIFE	5-1	Sat 30 Dec	Celtic	2-2
Sat 23 Sep	Hibernian	1-0	Mon 1 Jan	HIBERNIAN	2-1
Sat 30 Sep	St.MIRREN	1-0	Tue 2 Jan	St.Mirren	0-1
Sat 7 Oct	East Fife	4-1	Sat 20 Jan	Rangers	1-2
Sat 14 Oct	AIRDRIE	2-0	Sat 3 Feb	CLYDE	4-0
Sat 21 Oct	Partick Thistle	2-5	Sat 17 Feb	3rd.LANARK	4-0
Sat 28 Oct	Clyde	2-2	Sat 3 Mar	MORTON	8-0
Sat 4 Nov	PARTICK TH.	4-5	Sat 17 Mar	Falkirk	4-5
Sat 11 Nov	Third Lanark	2-1	Sat 24 Mar	RAITH ROV'S	3-1
Sat 18 Nov	MOTHERW'L	3-3	Sat 7 Apr	CELTIC	1-1
Sat 25 Nov	Morton	1-0	Sat 14 Apr	Airdrieonians	3-2
Sat 2 Dec	Aberdeen	0-2	Wed 18 Apr	ABERDEEN	4-1
Sat 9 Dec	FALKIRK	4-2	Sat 21 Apr	RANGERS	0-1
Sat 16 Dec	Raith Rovers	0-2	Sat 5 May	Motherwell	4-2

Played 30   W16; D5; L9;
F72; A45;   Pts.37.   4th.

Scottish League Championship 'A' Division 1951–1952

Sat 8 Sep	EAST FIFE	3-1		Sat 22 Dec	East Fife	4-2
Sat 15 Sep	Airdrieonians	0-2		Sat 29 Dec	AIRDRIE	6-1
Sat 22 Sep	HIBERNIAN	1-1		Tue 1 Jan	Hibernian	3-2
Sat 29 Sep	Celtic	3-1		Wed 2 Jan	CELTIC	2-1
Sat 6 Oct	DUNDEE	4-2		Sat 5 Jan	Dundee	3-3
Sat 13 Oct	St Mirren	0-1		Sat 12 Jan	St.MIRREN	2-1
Sat 20 Oct	Rangers	0-2		Sat 19 Jan	RANGERS	2-2
Sat 27 Oct	3rd.LANARK	2-2		Sat 26 Jan	Aberdeen	0-3
Sat 3 Nov	Partick Thistle	0-2		Wed 13 Feb	PARTICK TH.	1-2
Sat 10 Nov	QUEEN O.T.S.	4-3		Sat 16 Feb	Queen of the So.	1-1
Sat 17 Nov	Motherwell	5-0		Sat 1 Mar	Morton	1-3
Sat 24 Nov	MORTON	4-1		Sat 15 Mar	STIRLING AL.	5-2
Sat 1 Dec	ABERDEEN	2-2		Sat 22 Mar	Raith Rovers	1-2
Sat 8 Dec	Stirling Albion	4-0		Mon 14 Apr	Third Lanark	0-4
Sat 15 Dec	RAITH ROV'S	4-2		Wed 30 Apr	MOTHERW'L	2-2

Played 30   W14; D7; L9;
F69; A53;   Pts.35.   4th.

Scottish League Championship 'A' Division 1952–1953

Sat 6 Sep	Third Lanark	3-2		Sat 20 Dec	3rd.LANARK	3-3
Sat 13 Sep	St.MIRREN	1-2		Sat 27 Dec	St.Mirren	0-1
Sat 20 Sep	Hibernian	1-3		Thu 1 Jan	HIBERNIAN	1-2
Sat 27 Sep	AIRDRIE	4-0		Sat 3 Jan	Airdrieonians	2-1
Sat 4 Oct	East Fife	1-3		Sat 17 Jan	Partick Thistle	2-2
Sat 11 Oct	PARTICK TH.	2-1		Sat 24 Jan	Motherwell	3-1
Sat 18 Oct	Dundee	1-2		Sat 31 Jan	DUNDEE	1-1
Sat 25 Oct	CELTIC	1-0		Sat 14 Feb	Celtic	1-1
Sat 1 Nov	FALKIRK	0-1		Sat 28 Feb	QUEEN O.T.S.	3-0
Sat 8 Nov	Queen of the So.	2-4		Sat 7 Mar	ABERDEEN	3-1
Sat 15 Nov	Aberdeen	0-3		Sat 21 Mar	RAITH ROV'S	1-2
Sat 22 Nov	MOTHERW'L	3-1		Sat 28 Mar	CLYDE	7-0
Sat 29 Nov	Raith Rovers	1-1		Mon 6 Apr	Rangers	0-3
Sat 6 Dec	Clyde	2-3		Sat 18 Apr	Falkirk	4-2
Sat 13 Dec	RANGERS	2-2		Tue 28 Apr	EAST FIFE	4-2

Played 30   W12; D6; L12;
F59; A50;   Pts.30.   4th.

Scottish League Championship 'A' Division 1953–1954

Sat 5 Sep	EAST FIFE	2-2		Sat 19 Dec	East Fife	2-2
Sat 12 Sep	QUEEN O.T.S.	1-4		Sat 26 Dec	PARTICK TH.	0-2
Sat 19 Sep	HIBERNIAN	4-0		Fri 1 Jan	Hibernian	2-1
Sat 26 Sep	Airdrieonians	1-2		Sar 2 Jan	AIRDRIE	4-3
Sat 3 Oct	STIRLING AL.	6-1		Sat 9 Jan	Stirling Albion	3-0
Sat 10 Oct	St.Mirren	1-1		Sat 16 Jan	St.MIRREN	5-1
Sat 17 Oct	DUNDEE	2-1		Sat 23 Jan	Dundee	4-2
Sat 24 Oct	Celtic	0-2		Sat 30 Jan	FALKIRK	0-0
Sat 31 Oct	Rangers	1-0		Sat 6 Feb	CELTIC	3-2
Sat 7 Nov	CLYDE	1-2		Sat 20 Feb	RANGERS	3-3
Sat 14 Nov	RAITH ROV'S	5-1		Sat 6 Mar	Raith Rovers	2-4
Sat 21 Nov	Hamilton Aca'l	5-1		Wed 17 Mar	HAMILTON	3-0
Sat 28 Nov	ABERDEEN	3-2		Sat 20 Mar	Aberdeen	0-1
Sat 5 Dec	Queen of the So.	2-2		Sat 17 Apr	Clyde	1-0
Sat 12 Dec	Falkirk	3-1		Mon 19 Apr	Partick Thistle	1-2

Played 30   W16; D6; L8;
F70; A45;   Pts.38.   2nd.

Scottish League |Championship 'A' Division 1954–1955

Date	Opponent	Score		Date	Opponent	Score
Sat 11 Sep	PARTICK TH.	5-4		Sat 8 Jan	DUNDEE	2-1
Sat 18 Sep	Hibernian	3-2		Sat 29 Jan	Celtic	0-2
Sat 2 Oct	Dundee	2-3		Sat 12 Feb	STIRLING AL.	3-0
Sat 16 Oct	East Fife	2-0		Sat 26 Feb	Falkirk	2-2
Sat 30 Oct	Stirling Albion	5-0		Sat 12 Mar	ABERDEEN	2-0
Sat 6 Nov	FALKIRK	5-3		Sat 19 Mar	Queen of the So.	1-1
Sat 20 Nov	Aberdeen	0-1		Sat 26 Mar	RAITH ROV'S	2-0
Wed 24 Nov	Kilmarnock	3-1		Sat 2 Apr	CLYDE	3-0
Sat 27 Nov	QUEEN O.T.S.	3-1		Wed 6 Apr	KILMARN'K	2-2
Sat 4 Dec	Raith Rovers	6-0		Sat 9 Apr	Rangers	1-2
Sat 11 Dec	Clyde	3-0		Wed 13 Apr	EAST FIFE	1-3
Sat 18 Dec	RANGERS	3-4		Sat 16 Apr	Motherwell	1-1
Sat 25 Dec	Partick Thistle	4-4		Mon 18 Apr	MOTHERW'L	3-2
Sat 1 Jan	HIBERNIAN	5-1		Fri 22 Apr	St.Mirren	1-1
Mon 3 Jan	St.Mirren	1-1		Sat 30 Apr	CELTIC	0-3

Played 30   W16; D7; L7;
F74; A45;   Pts.39.   4th.

Scottish League Championship 'A' Division 1955–1956

Date	Opponent	Score		Date	Opponent	Score
Sat 10 Sep	DUNDEE	4-0		Sat 7 Jan	PARTICK TH.	5-0
Sat 24 Sep	HIBERNIAN	0-1		Sat 14 Jan	Dundee	2-0
Sat 1 Oct	Airdrieonians	4-1		Sat 21 Jan	AIRDRIE	4-1
Sat 8 Oct	CELTIC	2-1		Sat 28 Jan	Celtic	1-1
Sat 15 Oct	Queen of the So.	3-4		Sat 11 Feb	QUEEN O.T.S.	2-2
Sat 22 Oct	EAST FIFE	3-1		Sat 25 Feb	East Fife	4-1
Sat 29 Oct	St.Mirren	1-3		Wed 7 Mar	St.MIRREN	4-1
Sat 5 Nov	STIRLING AL.	5-0		Sat 10 Mar	Stirling Albion	2-0
Sat 12 Nov	Rangers	1-4		Sat 17 Mar	RANGERS	1-1
Sat 19 Nov	CLYDE	5-1		Sat 31 Mar	DUNF/LINE	5-0
Sat 26 Nov	Dunfermline	5-1		Mon 2 Apr	Partick Thistle	0-2
Sat 3 Dec	ABERDEEN	3-0		Sat 7 Apr	Aberdeen	1-4
Sat 10 Dec	Falkirk	1-1		Wed 11 Apr	Clyde	2-2
Sat 17 Dec	MOTHERW'L	7-1		Mon 16 Apr	FALKIRK	8-3
Sat 24 Dec	Kilmarnock	4-2		Mon 23 Apr	Motherwell	0-1
Sat 31 Dec	Raith Rovers	1-1		Wed 25 Apr	KILMARN'K	0-2
Mon 2 Jan	Hibernian	2-2		Sat 28 Apr	RAITH ROV'S	7-2

Played 34   W19; D7; L8;
F99; A 47;   Pts.45.   3rd.

Scottish League Championship 'A' Division 1956–1957

Date	Opponent	Score		Date	Opponent	Score
Sat 8 Sep	Dunfermline	3-2		Tue 1 Jan	HIBERNIAN	0-2
Sat 15 Sep	St.MIRREN	2-2		Wed 2 Jan	St.Mirren	2-0
Sat 22 Sep	Hibernian	3-2		Sat 5 Jan	DUNF/LINE	5-1
Sat 29 Sep	DUNDEE	2-1		Sat 12 Jan	Dundee	3-0
Sat 6 Oct	Ayr United	2-0		Sat 19 Jan	AYR UNITED	2-2
Sat 13 Oct	EAST FIFE	2-5		Sat 26 Jan	East Fife	3-1
Sat 20 Oct	Airdrieonians	4-3		Sat 9 Feb	AIRDRIE	2-0
Sat 27 Oct	Falkirk	2-0		Sat 23 Feb	FALKIRK	1-1
Sat 3 Nov	PARTICK TH.	1-0		Sat 2 Mar	Partick Thistle	2-2
Sat 10 Nov	Raith Rovers	3-2		Sat 9 Mar	RAITH ROV'S	2-1
Sat 17 Nov	KILMARN'K	3-2		Sat 16 Mar	Kilmarnock	1-4
Sat 24 Nov	QUEEN'S P'K	6-1		Mon 25 Mar	Queen's Park	1-0
Sat 1 Dec	Celtic	1-1		Sat 30 Mar	CELTIC	3-1
Sat 8 Dec	MOTHERW'L	3-2		Say 6 Apr	Motherwell	3-1
Sat 15 Dec	Rangers	3-5		Sat 13 Apr	RANGERS	0-1
Sat 22 Dec	QUEEN O.T.S.	3-1		Sat 20 Apr	Queen of the So.	2-0
Sat 29 Dec	Aberdeen	3-2		Sat 27 Apr	ABERDEEN	3-0

Played 34   W24; D5; L5;
F81; A48;   Pts.53.   2nd.

Scottish League Championship 'A' Division 1957–1958

Sat 7 Sep	DUNDEE	6-0		Wed 1 Jan	Hibernian	2-0
Sat 14 Sep	Airdrieonians	7-2		Thu 2 Jan	AIRDRIE	4-0
Sat 21 Sep	HIBERNIAN	3-1		Sat 4 Jan	Dundee	5-0
Sat 5 Oct	EAST FIFE	9-0		Sat 11 Jan	PARTICK TH.	4-1
Sat 12 Oct	Third Lanark	0-0		Sat 18 Jan	East Fife	3-0
Sat 19 Oct	ABERDEEN	1-0		Sat 25 Jan	3rd.LANARK	7-2
Sat 26 Oct	Rangers	3-2		Sat 22 Feb	Motherwell	4-0
Sat 2 Nov	MOTHERW'L	2-2		Sat 8 Mar	Queen's Park	4-1
Sat 9 Nov	Queen of the So.	4-1		Mon 10 Mar	QUEEN O.T.S.	3-1
Mon 11 Nov	Partick Thistle	3-1		Fri 14 Mar	CELTIC	5-3
Sat 16 Nov	QUEEN'S P'K	8-0		Wed 19 Mar	CLYDE	2-2
Sat 23 Nov	Clyde	1-2		Sat 22 Mar	Falkirk	4-0
Sat 30 Nov	FALKIRK	9-1		Sat 29 Mar	RAITH ROV'S	4-1
Sat 7 Dec	Raith Rovers	3-0		Sat 5 Apr	Kilmarnock	1-1
Sat 14 Dec	KILMARN'K	2-1		Sat 12 Apr	St.Mirren	3-2
Sat 21 Dec	St.MIRREN	5-1		Wed 16 Apr	Aberdeen	4-0
Sat 28 Dec	Celtic	2-0		Sat 30 Apr	RANGERS	2-1

Played 34   W29; D4; L1;
F132; A29;   Pts.62.   1st.

Scottish League Championship 'A' Division 1958–1959

Wed 20 Aug	DUNF/LINE	6-2		Sat 27 Dec	Dunfermline	3-3
Sat 6 Sep	Hibernian	4-0		Thu 1 Jan	HIBERNIAN	1-3
Sat 13 Sep	AIRDRIE	4-3		Sat 3 Jan	Airdrieonians	3-2
Sat 20 Sep	St.Mirren	1-1		Say 24 Jan	STIRLING AL.	1-4
Sat 27 Sep	3rd.LANARK	8-3		Sat 7 Feb	DUNDEE	1-0
Sat 4 Oct	Stirling Albion	2-1		Wed 18 Feb	Partick Thistle	1-2
Sat 11 Oct	Dundee	3-3		Sat 21 Feb	RAITH ROV'S	2-1
Sat 18 Oct	PARTICK TH.	2-0		Wed 25 Feb	Third Lanark	4-0
Wed 29 Oct	Raith Rovers	5-0		Wed 4 Mar	Motherwell	1-0
Sat 1 Nov	MOTHERW'L	0-2		Sat 7 Mar	QUEEN O.T.S.	2-1
Sat 8 Nov	Queen of the So.	5-0		Mon 9 Mar	St.MIRREN	4-0
Sat 15 Nov	CLYDE	2-2		Sat 14 Mar	Clyde	2-2
Sat 22 Nov	FALKIRK	5-1		Sat 21 Mar	Falkirk	2-0
Sat 29 Nov	Kilmarnock	2-3		Sat 28 Mar	KILMARN'K	3-1
Sat 6 Dec	ABERDEEN	5-1		Sat 11 Apr	RANGERS	2-0
Sat 13 Dec	Rangers	0-5		Wed 15 Apr	Aberdeen	4-2
Sat 20 Dec	CELTIC	1-1		Sat 18 Apr	Celtic	1-2

Played 34   W21; D6; L7
F92; A51;   Pts.48.   2nd.

Scottish League Championship 'A' Division 1959–1960

Wed 19 Aug	Dundee	3-1		Sat 26 Dec	DUNDEE	3-0
Sat 5 Sep	HIBERNIAN	2-2		Fri 1 Jan	Hibernian	5-1
Sat 12 Sep	Celtic	4-3		Sat 2 Jan	CELTIC	3-1
Sat 19 Sep	DUNF/LINE	3-1		Sat 9 Jan	Dunfermline	2-2
Sat 26 Sep	Stirling Albion	2-2		Sat 16 Jan	STIRLING AL.	4-0
Sat 3 Oct	AYR UNITED	5-3		Sat 23 Jan	Ayr United	1-1
Sat 10 Oct	Airdrieonians	5-2		Sat 30 Jan	MOTHERW'L	1-1
Sat 17 Oct	Arbroath	4-1		Sat 6 Feb	AIRDRIE	3-2
Wed 28 Oct	3rd.LANARK	6-2		Sat 27 Feb	Third Lanark	4-1
Sat 31 Oct	Rangers	2-0		Sat 5 Mar	RANGERS	2-0
Sat 7 Nov	PARTICK TH.	5-3		Wed 9 Mar	ARBROATH	4-1
Sat 14 Nov	KILMARN'K	3-1		Tue 15 Mar	Partick Thistle	2-1
Sat 21 Nov	Aberdeen	3-1		Sat 19 Mar	Kilmarnock	1-2
Sat 28 Nov	Clyde	2-2		Sat 26 Mar	ABERDEEN	3-0
Sat 5 Dec	St.MIRREN	0-2		Tue 5 Apr	CLYDE	5-2
Sat 12 Dec	Motherwell	0-3		Sat 16 Apr	St,Mirren	4-4
Sat 19 Dec	RAITH ROV'S	4-1		Sat 30 Apr	Raith Rovers	2-2

Played 34   W23; D8; L3;
F102; A51;   Pts.54.   1st.

Scottish League Championship 'A' Division 1960–1961

Wed 24 Aug	ST.JOHNST'E	3-1	Sat 31 Dec	St.Johnstone	3-2
Sat 10 Sep	Hibernian	4-1	Mon 2 Jan	HIBERNIAN	1-2
Sat 17 Sep	DUNF/LINE	1-1	Sat 7 Jan	Dumfermline	1-2
Sat 24 Sep	Airdrieonians	2-2	Sat 14 Jan	AIRDRIE	3-1
Sat 1 Oct	D/D UNITED	1-1	Sat 21 Jan	Dundee United	0-3
Sat 8 Oct	PARTICK TH.	0-1	Sat 4 Feb	Partick Thistle	1-4
Sat 15 Oct	Ayr United	0-1	Sat 18 Feb	AYR UNITED	2-1
Wed 26 Oct	RANGERS	1-3	Sat 4 Mar	MOTHERW'L	1-5
Sat 29 Oct	Motherwell	1-1	Wed 8 Mar	Rangers	0-3
Sat 5 Nov	ABERDEEN	3-4	Tue 14 Mar	Aberdeen	2-0
Sat 12 Nov	Kilmarnock	1-2	Sat 18 Mar	KILMARN'K	0-1
Sat 19 Nov	Clyde	1-1	Sat 25 Mar	CLYDE	4-2
Sat 26 Nov	RAITH ROV'S	1-0	Sat 1 Apr	Raith Rovers	1-1
Sat 3 Dec	Third Lanark	3-0	Sat 8 Apr	3rd.LANARK	1-0
Sat 10 Dec	St.Mirren	0-2	Sat 15 Apr	St.MIRREN	0-0
Sat 17 Dec	CELTIC	2-1	Sat 29 Apr	DUNDEE	2-1
Sat 24 Dec	Dundee	2-2	Tue 2 May	Celtic	3-1

Played 34   W13; D8; L13;
F51; A53;   Pts.34.   7th.

Scottish League Championship 'A' Division 1961–1962

Wed 23 Aug	St.MIRREN	2-2	Wed 17 Jan	Hibernian	4-1
Sat 9 Sep	Dunfermline	1-2	Sat 20 Jan	Airdrieonians	3-2
Sat 16 Sep	HIBERNIAN	4-2	Wed 24 Jan	D/D UNITED	2-1
Sat 23 Sep	Dundee	0-2	Wed 31 Jan	DUNF/LINE	3-2
Sat 30 Sep	AIRDRIE	4-1	Sat 3 Feb	STIRLING AL.	0-0
Sat 7 Oct	Stirling Albion	1-3	Wed 7 Feb	3rd.LANARK	2-1
Sat 14 Oct	Aberdeen	2-0	Sat 10 Feb	ABERDEEN	1-1
Sat 21 Oct	CELTIC	2-1	Wed 21 Feb	Celtic	2-2
Sat 4 Nov	St.Johnstone	2-0	Sat 24 Feb	RANGERS	0-1
Sat 11 Nov	PARTICK TH.	2-0	Sat 3 Mar	ST.JOHNST'E	1-1
Sat 25 Nov	Raith Rovers	1-0	Sat 10 Mar	Partick Thistle	1-3
Sat 2 Dec	MOTHERW'L	2-6	Sat 17 Mar	Third Lanark	0-1
Sat 16 Dec	KILMARN'K	3-3	Sat 24 Mar	RAITH ROV'S	0-1
Sat 23 Dec	Falkirk	2-0	Mon 2 Apr	Motherwell	2-1
Sat 6 Jan	St.Mirren	1-0	Sat 7 Apr	Kilmarnock	0-2
Wed 10 Jan	Rangers	1-2	Sat 21 Apr	FALKIRK	2-3
Sat 13 Jan	DUNDEE	0-2	Sat 28 Apr	Dundee United	1-0

Played 34   W16; D6; L12;
F54; A49;   Pts.38.   6th.

Scottish League Championship 'A' Division 1962–1963

Wed 22 Aug	DUNDEE	3-1	Wed 13 Mar	FALKIRK	5-0
Sat 8 Sep	Hibernian	4-0	Sat 16 Mar	Clyde	6-0
Sat 15 Sep	AIRDRIE	6-1	Mon 18 Mar	KILMARN'K	2-3
Sat 22 Sep	Partick Thistle	4-3	Sat 23 Mar	3rd.LANARK	2-0
Sat 29 Sep	QUEEN O.T.S.	3-0	Wed 27 Mar	RANGERS	0-5
Sat 6 Oct	Dunfermline	2-2	Tue 2 Apr	St.Mirren	3-7
Sat 13 Oct	Kilmarnock	2-2	Sat 6 Apr	RAITH ROV'S	2-1
Sat 20 Oct	MOTHERW'L	2-1	Wed 10 Apr	PARTICK TH.	2-4
Tue 30 Oct	Falkirk	0-2	Sat 20 Apr	Dundee United	0-0
Sat 3 Nov	ABERDEEN	1-1	Wed 24 Apr	Queen of the So.	3-0
Sat 10 Nov	CLYDE	1-1	Sat 27 Apr	Rangers	1-5
Sat 17 Nov	Third Lanark	2-1	Mon 29 Apr	CELTIC	4-3
Sat 24 Nov	St.MIRREN	5-0	Sat 4 May	HIBERNIAN	3-3
Sat 1 Dec	Raith Rovers	3-0	Mon 6 May	Dundee	2-2
Sat 8 Dec	Celtic	2-2	Sat 11 May	Motherwell	3-1
Sat 15 Dec	D/D UNITED	2-2	Mon 13 May	Airdrieonians	2-4
Sat 9 Mar	Aberdeen	1-2	Sat 18 May	DUNF/LINE	2-0

Played 34   W17; D9; L8;
F85; A59;   Pts.43.   5th.

Scottish League Championship Division One 1963–1964

Wed 21 Aug	Airdrieonians	2-0		Sat 28 Dec	AIRDRIE	4-0
Sat 7 Sep	HIBERNIAN	4-2		Wed 1 Jan	Hibernian	1-1
Sat 14 Sep	Dunfermline	2-2		Thu 2 Jan	DUNF/LINE	2-1
Sat 21 Sep	PARTICK TH.	4-1		Sat 4 Jan	Partick Thistle	1-2
Sat 28 Sep	Falkirk	2-1		Sat 11 Jan	EAST STIR'G	4-0
Sat 5 Oct	ST.JOHNST'E	3-3		Fri 17 Jan	FALKIRK	4-1
Sat 12 Oct	QUEEN O.T.S.	0-1		Sat 1 Feb	St.Johnstone	4-1
Sat 19 Oct	Third Lanark	2-0		Sat 8 Feb	Queen of the So.	4-1
Sat 26 Oct	Kilmarnock	1-3		Sat 22 Feb	KILMARN'K	1-1
Sat 2 Nov	ABERDEEN	0-0		Sat 29 Feb	Aberdeen	2-1
Sat 9 Nov	St.MIRREN	5-1		Wed 4 Mar	3rd.LANARK	4-1
Sat 16 Nov	Dundee United	0-0		Sat 7 Mar	St.Mirren	2-0
Sat 23 Nov	DUNDEE	1-3		Sat 14 Mar	D/D UNITED	0-4
Sat 30 Nov	Rangers	3-0		Sat 21 Mar	Dundee	4-2
Sat 7 Dec	MOTHERW'L	1-1		Wed 1 Apr	RANGERS	1-2
Sat 14 Dec	CELTIC	1-1		Sat 4 Apr	Motherwell	1-0
Sat 21 Dec	East Striling're	3-2		Sat 18 Apr	Celtic	1-1

Played 34 W19; D9; L6
F74; A40; Pts.47.   4th.

Scottish League Championship Division One 1964–1965

Wed 19 Aug	AIRDRIE	8-1		Sat 26 Dec	Airdrieonians	2-1
Sat 5 Sep	Hibernian	5-3		Fri 1 Jan	HIBERNIAN	0-1
Sat 12 Sep	DUNF/LINE	1-1		Sat 2 Jan	Dunfermline	2-3
Sat 19 Sep	Third Lanark	5-1		Sat 9 Jan	3rd.LANARK	3-1
Sat 26 Sep	CELTIC	4-2		Sat 16 Jan	Celtic	2-1
Sat 3 Oct	Partick Thistle	3-1		Sat 23 Jan	PARTICK TH.	1-0
Sat 10 Oct	St.MIRREN	0-0		Sat 30 Jan	St.Mirren	1-2
Sat 17 Oct	RANGERS	1-1		Sat 13 Feb	Rangers	1-1
Sat 24 Oct	Dundee	2-1		Sat 27 Feb	DUNDEE	1-7
Sat 31 Oct	MORTON	4-1		Wed 10 Mar	Morton	3-2
Sat 7 Nov	Falkirk	2-2		Sat 13 Mar	FALKIRK	5-2
Sat 14 Nov	Motherwell	3-1		Sat 20 Mar	MOTHERW'L	2-0
Sat 21 Nov	CLYDE	3-0		Sat 27 Mar	Clyde	5-2
Sat 28 Nov	St.Johnstone	3-0		Sat 3 Apr	St.JOHNST'E	4-1
Sat 5 Dec	D/D UNITED	3-1		Sat 10 Apr	Dundee United	1-1
Sat 12 Dec	ABERDEEN	6-3		Sat 17 Apr	Abedeen	3-0
Sat 19 Dec	Kilmarnock	1-3		Sat 24 Apr	KILMARN'K	0-2

Played 34 W22; D6; L6;
F90; A 49; Pts.50.   2nd.

Scottish League Championship Division One 1965–1966

Wed 25 Aug	HAMILTON	2-0		Mon 3 Jan	DUNF/LINE	0-0
Sat 11 Sep	Dunfermline	1-1		Sat 8 Jan	Hamilton Aca'l	1-0
Sat 18 Sep	HIBERNIAN	0-4		Sat 15 Jan	St.JOHNST'E	0-0
Sat 25 Sep	St.Johnstone	2-3		Sat 29 Jan	CELTIC	3-2
Sat 2 Oct	DUNDEE	0-0		Sat 12 Feb	PARTICK TH.	3-1
Sat 9 Oct	Celtic	2-5		Sat 26 Feb	Aberdeen	1-0
Sat 16 Oct	Partick Thistle	3-3		Sat 12 Mar	Rangers	1-1
Sat 23 Oct	MOTHERW'L	5-2		Wed 16 Mar	D/D UNITED	0-1
Sat 30 Oct	ABERDEEN	1-1		Sat 19 Mar	Morton	3-0
Sat 6 Nov	Dundee United	2-2		Wed 23 Mar	Motherwell	2-4
Sat 13 Nov	RANGERS	0-2		Sat 26 Mar	FALKIRK	1-2
Sat 20 Nov	MORTON	2-1		Mon 4 Apr	Kilmarnock	2-2
Sat 27 Nov	Falkirk	1-0		Sat 9 Apr	KILMANR'K	2-3
Sat 11 Dec	CLYDE	4-1		Wed 13 Apr	Dundee	0-1
Sat 18 Dec	Stirling Albion	2-2		Sat 16 Apr	Clyde	1-0
Sat 25 Dec	St.MIRREN	4-0		Sat 23 Apr	STIRLING AL.	1-1
Sat 1 Jan	Hibernian	3-2		Sat 30 Apr	St.Mirren	1-1

Played 34 W13; D12; L9;
F56; A48; Pts.38.   7th.

Scottish League Championship Division One 1966–1967

Sat 10 Sep	Hibernian	1-3	Mon 2 Jan	HIBERNIAN	0-0
Sat 17 Sep	AIRDRIE	1-1	Sat 14 Jan	Dundee	1-1
Sat 24 Sep	Stirling Albion	3-0	Sat 21 Jan	AYR UNITED	1-0
Sat 1 Oct	DUNDEE	3-1	Sat 4 Feb	Rangers	1-5
Sat 8 Oct	Ayr United	1-0	Sat 11 Feb	St.JOHNST'E	1-0
Sat 15 Oct	RANGERS	1-1	Sat 25 Feb	Clyde	1-2
Sat 22 Oct	St.Johnstone	2-3	Sat 4 Mar	ABERDEEN	0-3
Sat 29 Oct	CLYDE	0-1	Sat 18 Mar	St.Mirren	0-3
Sat 5 Nov	Aberdeen	1-3	Wed 22 Mar	Dunfermline	0-1
Sat 12 Nov	DUNF/LINE	1-1	Sat 25 Mar	CELTIC	0-3
Sat 19 Nov	St.MIRREN	4-0	Sat 1 Apr	PARTICK TH.	0-0
Sat 26 Nov	Celtic	0-3	Sat 8 Apr	Dundee United	0-2
Sat 3 Dec	Partick Thistle	1-1	Wed 12 Apr	Falkirk	1-2
Sat 10 Dec	D/D UNITED	2-1	Wed 19 Apr	STIRLING AL.	5-1
Sat 17 Dec	FALKIRK	1-1	Sat 22 Apr	KILMARN'K	1-0
Sat 24 Dec	Kilmarnock	2-1	Wed 26 Apr	Airdrieonians	2-1
Sat 31 Dec	MOTHERW'L	1-2	Sat 29 Apr	Motherwell	0-1

Played 34   W11; D8; L15;   **F39; A48;**   Pts.30.   11th.

Scottish League Championship Division One 1967–1968

Sat 9 Sep	HIBERNIAN	1-4	Mon 1 Jan	Hibernian	0-1
Sat 16 Sep	Dunfermline	3-1	Tue 2 Jan	DUNF/LINE	1-2
Sat 23 Sep	DUNDEE	1-0	Sat 13 Jan	RANGERS	2-3
Sat 30 Sep	Rangers	1-1	Sat 20 Jan	Clyde	3-6
Sat 7 Oct	CLYDE	2-3	Sat 10 Feb	Aberdeen	0-2
Sat 14 Oct	Raith Rovers	4-2	Wed 28 Feb	MOTHERW'L	3-2
Sat 21 Oct	ABERDEEN	2-1	Sat 2 Mar	Falkirk	1-4
Sat 28 Oct	Motherwell	5-2	Mon 4 Mar	RAITH ROV'S	0-2
Sat 4 Nov	FALKIRK	1-0	Sat 16 Mar	PARTICK TH.	0-1
Sat 11 Nov	D/D UNITED	1-0	Wed 20 Mar	Dundee United	1-2
Sat 18 Nov	Partick Thistle	3-3	Sat 23 Mar	St.Johnstone	2-3
Sat 25 Nov	St.JOHNST'E	1-1	Sat 6 Apr	CELTIC	0-2
Sat 2 Dec	Kilmarnock	2-3	Wed 10 Apr	KILMARN'K	1-0
Sat 9 Dec	Celtic	1-3	Sat 13 Apr	Airdrieonians	2-2
Sat 16 Dec	AIRDRIE	3-1	Wed 17 Apr	Dundee	0-1
Sat 23 Dec	Stirling Albion	4-1	Sat 20 Apr	STIRLING AL.	2-1
Sat 30 Dec	MORTON	3-0	Mon 29 Apr	Morton	0-1

Played P34   W13; D4; L17;   **F56; A61;**   Pts.30.   12th.

Scottish League Championship Division One 1968–1969

Sat 7 Sep	Hibernian	3-1	Wed 1 Jan	HIBERNIAN	0-0
Sat 14 Sep	DUNF/LINE	3-1	Thu 2 Jan	Dunfermline	2-4
Sat 21 Sep	Airdrieonians	1-2	Sat 4 Jan	AIRDRIE	1-1
Sat 28 Sep	RANGERS	1-1	Sat 11 Jan	Rangers	0-2
Sat 5 Oct	Aberdeen	2-1	Sat 18 Jan	ABERDEEN	3-2
Sat 12 Oct	CELTIC	0-1	Sat 1 Feb	Celtic	0-5
Sat 19 Oct	Falkirk	3-1	Sat 22 Feb	Kilmarnock	0-1
Sat 26 Oct	Dundee	1-3	Sat 1 Mar	Partick Thistle	1-5
Sat 2 Nov	KILMARN'K	0-1	Sat 8 Mar	D/D UNITED	1-0
Sat 9 Nov	PARTICK TH.	2-0	Wed 12 Mar	DUNDEE	2-2
Sat 16 Nov	Dundee United	2-4	Sat 15 Mar	St.Johnstone	1-2
Sat 23 Nov	St.JOHNST'E	2-2	Mon 24 Mar	MORTON	2-2
Sat 30 Nov	Morton	2-0	Sat 29 Mar	Clyde	1-0
Sat 7 Dec	CLYDE	2-3	Wed 2 Apr	FALKIRK	2-1
Sat 14 Dec	RAITH ROV'S	1-0	Sat 5 Apr	Raith Rovers	3-0
Sat 21 Dec	Arbroath	3-2	Sat 12 Apr	ARBROATH	2-2
Sat 28 Dec	St.Mirren	1-1	Sat 19 Apr	St.MIRREN	2-1

Played 34   W14; D8; L12;   **F52; A54;**   Pts.36.   8th.

Scottish League Championship Division One 1969–1970

Sat 30 Aug	MORTON	0-1	Sat 20 Dec	AIRDRIE	5-0	
Wed 3 Sep	Airdrieonians	2-1	Sat 27 Dec	D/D UNITED	2-2	
Sat 6 Sep	St.Johnstone	3-3	Thu 1 Jan	Hibernian	0-0	
Sat 13 Sep	KILMARN'K	4-1	Sat 3 Jan	DUNF/LINE	2-0	
Sat 20 Sep	Dunfermline	0-1	Sat 10 Jan	Dundee United	3-2	
Sat 27 Sep	HIBERNIAN	0-2	Sat 17 Jan	Kilmarnock	0-0	
Sat 4 Oct	St.Mirren	0-0	Sat 31 Jan	St.JOHNST'E	0-0	
Sat 11 Oct	MOTHERW'L	2-2	Sat 21 Feb	St.MIRREN	1-0	
Sat 18 Oct	Ayr United	0-0	Sat 28 Feb	Motherwell	2-0	
Sat 25 Oct	PARTICK TH.	1-1	Sat 7 Mar	AYR UNITED	3-0	
Sat 1 Nov	RAITH ROV'S	3-2	Sat 14 Mar	Partick Thistle	0-1	
Sat 8 Nov	Celtic	2-0	Sat 21 Mar	Raith Rovers	3-0	
Sat 15 Nov	ABERDEEN	2-2	Wed 25 Mar	Rangers	2-3	
Sat 22 Nov	Dundee	0-2	Sat 28 Mar	CELTIC	0-0	
Sat 6 Dec	RANGERS	1-2	Sat 4 Apr	Aberdeen	1-0	
Sat 13 Dec	Morton	3-2	Sat 11 Apr	CLYDE	1-1	
Tue 16 Dec	Clyde	1-2	Sat 18 Apr	DUNDEE	1-3	

Played 34   W13; D12; L9;
F50; A36;   **Pts.38.**   4th.

Scottish League Championship Division One 1970–1971

Sat 29 Aug	St.JOHNST'E	1-3	Sat 26 Dec	St.Johnstone	1-2
Sat 5 Sep	Hibernian	0-0	Fri 1 Jan	HIBERNIAN	0-0
Sat 12 Sep	DUNF/LINE	3-0	Sat 9 Jan	CLYDE	3-1
Sat 19 Sep	Clyde	0-1	Sat 16 Jan	Airdrieonians	0-0
Sat 26 Sep	AIRDRIE	5-2	Sat 30 Jan	KILMARN'K	2-0
Sat 3 Oct	Kilmarnock	0-3	Sat 6 Feb	Rangers	0-1
Sat 10 Oct	RANGERS	0-1	Sat 20 Feb	DUNDEE	0-0
Sat 17 Oct	Dundee	0-1	Sat 27 Feb	CELTIC	1-1
Wed 28 Oct	Celtic	2-3	Sat 6 Mar	Falkirk	4-2
Sat 7 Nov	St.Mirren	1-0	Sat 13 Mar	St.MIRREN	1-0
Wed 11 Nov	FALKIRK	1-1	Sat 20 Mar	Dundee United	1-4
Sat 14 Nov	D/D UNITED	1-0	Wed 24 Mar	Dunfermline	2-1
Sat 21 Nov	Aberdeen	0-1	Sat 27 Mar	ABERDEEN	1-3
Sat 28 Nov	AYR UNITED	2-1	Sat 3 Apr	Ayr United	0-1
Sat 5 Dec	MORTON	2-2	Sat 10 Apr	Morton	0-3
Sat 12 Dec	Motherwell	2-1	Sat 17 Apr	MOTHERW'L	0-1
Sat 19 Dec	COWDEN'TH	1-0	Sat 24 Apr	Cowdenbeath	4-0

Played 34   W13; D7; L14;
F41; A40;   **Pts.33.**   11th.

Scottish League Championship Division One 1971–1972

Sat 4 Sep	HIBERNIAN	0-2	Sat 1 Jan	Hibernian	0-0
Sat 11 Sep	Dunfermline	4-1	Mon 3 Jan	DUNF/LINE	1-1
Sat 18 Sep	St.JOHNST'E	2-1	Sat 8 Jan	St.Johnstone	1-1
Sat 25 Sep	Dundee	0-0	Sat 15 Jan	DUNDEE	2-5
Sat 2 Oct	RANGERS	2-1	Sat 22 Jan	Rangers	0-6
Sat 9 Oct	Clyde	1-0	Sat 29 Jan	CLYDE	2-0
Sat 16 Oct	AIRDRIE	1-1	Sat 12 Feb	Airdrieonians	1-1
Sat 23 Oct	Kilmarnock	2-2	Sat 19 Feb	KILMARN'K	2-1
Sat 30 Oct	EAST FIFE	1-1	Sat 4 Mar	East Fife	2-2
Sat 6 Nov	Motherwell	3-5	Sat 11 Mar	MOTHERW'L	0-0
Sat 13 Nov	MORTON	6-1	Tue 21 Mar	Morton	1-1
Sat 20 Nov	AYR UNITED	1-0	Sat 25 Mar	Ayr United	0-1
Sat 27 Nov	Aberdeen	3-2	Sat 1 Apr	ABERDEEN	1-0
Sat 4 Dec	D/D UNITED	3-2	Sat 8 Apr	Dundee United	2-3
Sat 11 Dec	Falkirk	0-2	Sat 15 Apr	FALKIRK	1-0
Sat 18 Dec	PARTICK TH.	0-0	Sat 22 Apr	Partick Thistle	2-2
Sat 25 Dec	Celtic	2-3	Sat 29 Apr	CELTIC	4-1

Played 34   W13; D13; L8;
F53; A49;   **Pts.39.**   6th.

Scottish League Championship Division One 1972–1973

Sat 2 Sep	St.JOHNST'E	1-0		Sat 30 Dec	St.Johnstone	2-3
Sat 9 Sep	Hibernian	0-2		Mon 1 Jan	HIBERNIAN	0-7
Sat 16 Sep	DUMBARTON	1-0		Sat 6 Jan	Dumbarton	2-0
Sat 23 Sep	Morton	4-2		Sat 20 Jan	EAST FIFE	1-1
Sat 30 Sep	East Fife	0-1		Sat 27 Jan	Aberdeen	1-3
Sat 7 Oct	ABERDEEN	2-1		Sat 10 Feb	D/D UNITED	0-2
Sat 14 Oct	Dundee United	2-3		Mon 19 Feb	Motherwell	2-2
Sat 21 Oct	MOTHERW'L	0-0		Sat 3 Mar	Arbroath	0-3
Sat 28 Oct	ARBROATH	3-0		Sat 10 Mar	FALKIRK	1-0
Sat 4 Nov	Falkirk	3-1		Mon 12 Mar	MORTON	0-0
Sat 11 Nov	AYR UNITED	3-0		Wed 21 Mar	Ayr United	0-2
Sat 18 Nov	Celtic	2-4		Sat 24 Mar	CELTIC	0-2
Sat 25 Nov	PARTICK TH.	2-0		Sat 31 Mar	Partick Thistle	0-3
Sat 2 Dec	Rangers	1-0		Sat 7 Apr	RANGERS	0-1
Sat 9 Dec	KILMARN'K	0-0		Sat 14 Apr	Kilmarnock	1-2
Sat 16 Dec	Airdrieonians	2-0		Sat 21 Apr	AIRDRIE	0-1
Sat 23 Dec	DUNDEE	1-2		Sat 28 Apr	Dundee	2-2

Played 34   W12; D6; L16;
F39; A50;   Pts.30.   **10th.**

Scottish League Championship Division One 1973–1974

Sat 1 Sep	Morton	3-2		Tue 1 Jan	Hibernian	1-3
Sat 8 Sep	HIBERNIAN	4-1		Sat 5 Jan	MOTHERWELL	2-0
Sat 15 Sep	Motherwell	2-2		Sat 19 Jan	RANGERS	2-4
Sat 22 Sep	DUNDEE	2-2		Sat 9 Feb	St.JOHNST'E	0-2
Sat 29 Sep	Rangers	3-0		Sat 23 Feb	Dumbarton	1-0
Sat 6 Oct	DUNF/LINE	3-0		Sat 2 Mar	Celtic	0-1
Sat 13 Oct	St.Johnstone	2-0		Sat 16 Mar	Dundee United	3-3
Sat 20 Oct	DUMBARTON	0-0		Sat 23 Mar	ABERDEEN	0-0
Sat 27 Oct	CELTIC	1-3		Sat 30 Mar	Falkirk	2-0
Sat 3 Nov	Arbroath	3-2		Tue 2 Apr	ARBROATH	4-0
Sat 10 Nov	D/D UNITED	1-1		Sat 13 Apr	EAST FIFE	2-2
Sat 17 Nov	Aberdeen	1-3		Wed 17 Apr	Dunfermline	3-2
Sat 24 Nov	FALKIRK	2-1		Sat 20 Apr	Ayr United	1-2
Sat 8 Dec	East Fife	0-0		Wed 24 Apr	Clyde	0-2
Sat 15 Dec	AYR UNITED	0-1		Sat 27 Apr	PARTICK TH.	3-1
Sat 22 Dec	Partick Thistle	3-1		Sat 4 May	CLYDE	0-0
Sat 29 Dec	MORTON	0-2		Mon 6 May	Dundee	0-0

Played 34   W14; D10; L10;
F54; A43;   Pts.38.   **6th.**

Scottish League Championship Division One 1974–1975

Sat 31 Aug	St.JOHNST'E	1-2		Sat 28 Dec	St.Johnstone	3-2
Sat 7 Sep	Hibernian	1-2		Wed 1 Jan	HIBERNIAN	0-0
Sat 14 Sep	KILMARN'K	1-1		Sat 4 Jan	Kilmarnock	1-1
Sat 21 Sep	Dunfermline	2-2		Sat 11 Jan	DUNF/LINE	1-0
Sat 28 Sep	Partick Thistle	1-4		Sat 18 Jan	PARTICK TH.	3-1
Sat 5 Oct	ABERDEEN	1-4		Sat 1 Feb	Aberdeen	2-2
Sat 12 Oct	Dundee United	0-5		Sat 8 Feb	D/D UNITED	3-1
Sat 19 Oct	AIRDRIE	2-1		Sat 22 Feb	Airdrieonians	1-1
Sat 26 Oct	RANGERS	1-1		Sat 1 Mar	Rangers	1-2
Sat 2 Nov	Ayr United	3-3		Sat 15 Mar	Dumbarton	1-0
Sat 9 Nov	DUMBARTON	2-1		Wed 19 Mar	AYR UNITED	1-0
Sat 16 Nov	Arbroath	1-3		Sat 22 Mar	ARBROATH	0-0
Sat 23 Nov	CELTIC	1-1		Sat 29 Mar	Celtic	1-4
Sat 30 Nov	Clyde	2-2		Sat 5 Apr	CLYDE	0-1
Sat 7 Dec	MORTON	3-1		Sat 12 Apr	Morton	0-0
Sat 14 Dec	Motherwell	3-1		Sat 19 Apr	MOTHERW'L	4-1
Sat 21 Dec	DUNDEE	0-0		Wed 23 Apr	Dundee	0-2

Played 34   W11; D13; L10;
F47; A52;   Pts.35.   **8th.**

Scottish League Championship Premier Division 1975–1976

Sat 30 Aug	Hibernian	0-1		Thu 1 Jan	Hibernian	0-3
Sat 6 Sep	RANGERS	0-2		Sat 3 Jan	RANGERS	1-2
Sat 13 Sep	Dundee	3-2		Sat 10 Jan	Dundee	1-4
Sat 20 Sep	ABERDEEN	2-2		Sat 17 Jan	ABERDEEN	3-3
Sat 27 Sep	Motherwell	1-1		Sat 31 Jan	Motherwell	0-2
Sat 4 Oct	Celtic	1-3		Sat 7 Feb	Celtic	0-2
Sat 11 Oct	D/D UNITED	1-0		Sat 21 Feb	D/D UNITED	0-1
Sat 18 Oct	AYR UNITED	2-1		Sat 28 Feb	AYR UNITED	1-0
Sat 25 Oct	St.Johnstone	1-0		Sat 13 Mar	HIBERNIAN	0-1
Sat 1 Nov	HIBERNIAN	1-1		Sat 20 Mar	Rangers	1-3
Sat 8 Nov	Rangers	2-1		Sat 27 Mar	DUNDEE	3-0
Sat 15 Nov	DUNDEE	1-1		Wed 7 Apr	Aberdeen	3-0
Sat 22 Nov	Aberdeen	0-0		Sat 10 Apr	MOTHERW'L	1-2
Sat 29 Nov	MOTHERW'L	3-3		Sat 17 Apr	Dundee United	0-2
Sat 6 Dec	CELTIC	0-1		Wed 21 Apr	Ayr United	1-0
Sat 13 Dec	Dundee United	1-0		Sat 24 Apr	St.JOHNST'E	1-0
Sat 20 Dec	Ayr United	1-1		Mon 26 Apr	St.Johnstone	0-0
Sat 27 Dec	St.JOHNST'E	2-0		Mon 3 May	CELTIC	1-0

Played 36	W13; D9; L14;		
F39; A45;	Pts.35.	5th.	

Scottish League Championship Premier Division 1976–1977

Sat 4 Sep	Aberdeen	2-2		Sat 22 Jan	Rangers	2-3
Sat 11 Sep	PARTICK TH.	0-0		Wed 26 Jan	HIBERNIAN	0-1
Sat 18 Sep	Celtic	2-2		Sat 5 Feb	KILMARN'K	4-0
Sat 25 Sep	Rangers	2-4		Mon 7 Feb	Celtic	1-5
Sat 2 Oct	KILMARN'K	2-2		Tue 15 Feb	Kilmarnock	1-2
Sat 9 Oct	AYR UNITED	2-2		Sat 19 Feb	Motherwell	1-2
Sat 16 Oct	Motherwell	1-1		Sat 5 Mar	D/D UNITED	1-1
Sat 23 Oct	D/D UNITED	1-2		Sat 19 Mar	ABERDEEN	1-1
Sat 30 Oct	Hibernian	1-1		Wed 23 Mar	Hibernian	1-3
Wed 10 Nov	ABERDEEN	2-1		Sat 26 Mar	Partick Thistle	0-2
Sat 20 Nov	CELTIC	3-4		Sat 2 Apr	CELTIC	0-3
Sat 27 Nov	RANGERS	0-1		Wed 6 Apr	AYR UNITED	1-2
Tue 30 Nov	Partick Thistle	1-2		Sat 9 Apr	RANGERS	1-3
Sat 11 Dec	Ayr United	1-0		Wed 13 Apr	HIBERNIAN	2-2
Sat 18 Dec	MOTHERW'L	2-1		Sat 16 Apr	Kilmarnock	2-2
Mon 27 Dec	Dundee United	1-1		Wed 20 Apr	Dundee United	2-1
Mon 3 Jan	Aberdeen	1-4		Sat 23 Apr	Ayr United	1-1
Sat 8 Jan	PARTICK TH.	1-0		Sat 30 Apr	MOTHERW'L	3-2

Played 36	W7; D13; L16;		
F49; A66;	Pts.27.	9th.	

Scottish League Championship First Division 1977–1978

Sat 13 Aug	Dumbarton	2-2		Sat 24 Dec	Arbroath	7-0
Sat 20 Aug	DUNDEE	2-1		Sat 31 Dec	KILMARN'K	3-0
Sat 27 Aug	Kilmarnock	1-1		Mon 2 Jan	East Fife	2-1
Sat 10 Sep	EAST FIFE	4-1		Sat 7 Jan	DUNDEE	2-2
Wed 14 Sep	Queen O.T.S.	3-3		Sat 14 Jan	QUEEN O.T.S.	1-0
Sat 17 Sep	St.JOHNST'E	3-0		Sat 4 Feb	HAMILTON	1-0
Sat 24 Sep	Stirling Albion	4-2		Sat 25 Feb	AIRDRIE	3-0
Wed 28 Sep	ALLOA ATH.	1-0		Sat 4 Mar	DUMBARTON	1-1
Sat 1 Oct	HAMILTON	0-2		Wed 8 Mar	Morton	1-0
Sat 8 Oct	Morton	3-5		Sat 11 Mar	Alloa Athletic	2-0
Sat 15 Oct	AIRDRIE	3-2		Wed 15 Mar	StirlingAlbion	2-1
Wed 19 Oct	Montrose	1-3		Sat 18 Mar	MONTROSE	2-2
Sat 22 Oct	DUMBARTON	2-1		Sat 25 Mar	Montrose	0-0
Sat 29 Oct	Dundee	1-1		Sun 2 Apr	Hamilton Aca'l	2-0
Sat 5 Nov	KILMARN'K	1-2		Sat 8 Apr	ARBROATH	3-2
Sat 12 Nov	East Fife	0-2		Wed 12 Apr	St.Johnstone	2-0
Sat 19 Nov	St.Johnstone	1-0		Sat 15 Apr	Queen of the So.	1-1
Sat 26 Nov	STIRLING AL.	2-0		Sat 22 Apr	ALLOA ATH.	2-1
Sat 10 Dec	MORTON	1-1		Sat 29 Apr	Arbroath	1-0
Sat 17 Dec	Airdrieonians	4-2				

Played 39	W24; D10; L5;		
F77; A42;	Pts.58.	2nd.	

Scottish League Championship Premier Division 1978–1979

Sat 12 Aug	ABERDEEN	1-4	Sat 20 Jan	Motherwell	2-3
Sat 19 Aug	Celtic	0-4	Sat 10 Feb	St.MIRREN	1-2
Sat 26 Aug	HIBERNIAN	1-1	Sat 24 Feb	RANGERS	3-2
Sat 9 Sep	Partick Thistle	2-3	Sat 17 Mar	Hibernian	1-1
Sat 16 Sep	MORTON	1-1	Wed 28 Mar	HIBERNIAN	1-2
Sat 23 Sep	Motherwell	1-0	Sat 31 Mar	Morton	2-2
Sat 30 Sep	Dundee United	1-3	Wed 4 Apr	D/D UNITED	2-0
Sat 7 Oct	St.MIRREN	1-1	Sat 7 Apr	MOTHERW'L	3-0
Sat 14 Oct	RANGERS	0-0	Wed 11 Apr	PARTICK TH.	0-2
Sat 21 Oct	Aberdeen	2-1	Sat 14 Apr	D/D UNITED	0-3
Sat 28 Oct	CELTIC	2-0	Wed 18 Apr	CELTIC	0-3
Sat 4 Nov	Hibernian	2-1	Sat 21 Apr	St.Mirren	1-2
Sat 11 Nov	PARTICK TH.	0-1	Wed 25 Apr	Dundee United	1-2
Sat 18 Nov	Morton	2-3	Sat 28 Apr	Rangers	0-4
Sat 25 Nov	MOTHERW'L	3-2	Wed 2 May	Aberdeen	0-5
Sat 9 Dec	St.Mirren	0-4	Sat 5 May	Partick Thistle	0-2
Sat 16 Dec	Rangers	3-5	Mon 7 May	MORTON	0-1
Sat 23 Dec	ABERDEEN	0-0	Mon 14 May	Celtic	0-1

Played 36   W8; D7; L21;
F39; A71;   **Pts.23.**   9th.

Scottish League Championship First Division 1979–1980

Sat 11 Aug	Arbroath	2-1	Sat 15 Dec	HAMILTON	0-0
Sat 18 Aug	AYR UNITED	4-2	Sat 5 Jan	CLYDEBANK	3-3
Sat 25 Aug	Berwick Rangers	3-1	Sat 12 Jan	Stirling Albion	1-0
Wed 5 Sep	St.JOHNST'E	2-1	Sat 19 Jan	Motherwell	0-0
Sat 8 Sep	CLYDEBANK	2-1	Sat 9 Feb	Dumbarton	1-1
Tue 11 Sep	Raith Rovers	2-3	Sat 23 Feb	HAMILTON	1-0
Sat 15 Sep	STIRLING AL.	2-1	Sat 1 Mar	ARBROATH	2-1
Wed 19 Sep	Motherwell	2-4	Sat 15 Mar	Raith Rovers	0-0
Sat 22 Sep	AIRDRIE	2-2	Tue 25 Mar	Dunfermline	3-0
Sat 29 Sep	CLYDE	4-1	Sat 29 Mar	ARBROATH	1-0
Sat 6 Oct	Dumbarton	1-1	Tue 1 Apr	AYR UNITED	0-1
Sat 13 Oct	Hamilton Aca'l	1-3	Sat 5 Apr	Airdrieonians	1-0
Sat 20 Oct	DUNF/LINE	2-1	Wed 9 Apr	RAITH ROV'S	2-2
Sat 27 Oct	Ayr United	0-2	Sun 13 Apr	Clyde	1-2
Sat 3 Nov	Berwick Rangers	0-0	Wed 16 Apr	St.Johnstone	1-0
Sat 10 Nov	Clydebank	1-1	Sat 19 Apr	DUNF/LINE	0-0
Sat 17 Nov	STIRLING AL.	1-0	Wed 23 Apr	BERWICK R.	1-1
Sat 24 Nov	MOTHERW'L	2-1	Sat 26 Apr	St.Johnstone	3-0
Sat 1 Dec	Clyde	2-2	Wed 30 Apr	AIRDRIE	1-0
Sat 8 Dec	DUMBARTON	1-0			

Played 39   W20; D13; L6;
F58; A39;   **Pts.53.**   1st.

Scottish League Championship Premier Division 1980–1981

Sat 9 Aug	Partick Thistle	2-3	Sat 27 Dec	Dundee United	1-4
Sat 16 Aug	AIRDRIE	0-2	Thu 1 Jan	AIRDRIE	2-3
Sat 23 Aug	St.Mirren	3-1	Sat 3 Jan	Partick Thistle	0-1
Sat 6 Sep	Kilmarnock	1-0	Sat 10 Jan	ABERDEEN	0-2
Sat 13 Sep	CELTIC	0-2	Sat 31 Jan	CELTIC	0-3
Sat 20 Sep	MORTON	0-1	Sat 21 Feb	St.Mirren	1-2
Sat 27 Sep	Dundee United	1-1	Sat 28 Feb	PARTICK TH.	1-1
Sat 4 Oct	ABERDEEN	0-1	Sat 7 Mar	Aberdeen	1-4
Sat 11 Oct	Rangers	1-3	Sat 14 Mar	RANGERS	2-1
Sat 18 Oct	PARTICK TH.	0-1	Sat 21 Mar	Morton	0-3
Sat 25 Oct	Airdrieonians	0-3	Tue 24 Mar	Kilmarnock	0-2
Sat 1 Nov	St.MIRREN	1-1	Sat 28 Mar	D/D UNITED	0-4
Sat 8 Nov	D/D UNITED	0-3	Wed 1 Apr	Celtic	0-6
Sat 15 Nov	Morton	2-2	Sat 4 Apr	KILMARN'K	1-0
Sat 22 Nov	RANGERS	0-0	Sat 11 Apr	Aberdeen	0-1
Sat 6 Dec	KILMARN'K	2-0	Sat 18 Apr	St.MIRREN	1-2
Sat 13 Dec	Celtic	2-3	Sat 25 Apr	Airdrieonains	2-1
Sat 20 Dec	MORTON	0-0	Sat 2 May	Rangers	0-4

Played 36   W6; D6; L24;
F27; A71;   **Pts.18.**   10th.

Scottish League Championship First Division 1981-1982

Sat 29 Aug	Dunfermline	1-1		Tue 9 Feb	FALKIRK	3-0
Sat 5 Sep	KILMARN'K	0-1		Wed 17 Feb	QUEEN O.T.S.	4-1
Sat 12 Sep	Falkirk	0-0		Sat 20 Feb	Ayr United	3-0
Wed 16 Sep	HAMILTON	2-1		Tue 23 Feb	St.Johnstone	1-2
Sat 19 Sep	CLYDEBANK	1-0		Sat 27 Feb	RAITH ROV'S	4-0
Wed 23 Sep	Ayr United	0-0		Sat 6 Mar	Falkirk	1-3
Sat 26 Sep	DUMBARTON	2-1		Sat 13 Mar	Queen of the So.	5-1
Sat 3 Oct	Queen's Park	0-1		Sat 20 Mar	QUEEN'S P'K	1-0
Wed 7 Oct	St.JOHNST'E	3-1		Sat 27 Mar	Clydebank	1-2
Sat 10 Oct	Queen of the So.	2-1		Wed 31 Mar	Raith Rovers	3-0
Sat 17 Oct	RAITH ROV'S	2-1		Sat 3 Apr	St.JOHNST'E	3-0
Sat 24 Oct	Motherwell	2-2		Sat 10 Apr	Hamilton Aca'l	2-0
Sat 31 Oct	EAST STIR'G	0-1		Wed 14 Apr	Clydebank	5-1
Sat 7 Nov	Kilmarnock	0-0		Wed 21 Apr	AYR UNITED	2-1
Sat 14 Nov	DUNF/LINE	1-1		Sat 24 Apr	Dunfermline	2-1
Sat 21 Nov	Hamilton Aca'l	2-0		Tue 27 Apr	EAST STIR'G	2-0
Sat 28 Nov	Dumbarton	1-3		Sat 1 May	DUMBARTON	2-5
Sat 5 Dec	QUEEN'S P'K	1-1		Sat 8 May	Kilmarnock	0-0
Sat 30 Jan	MOTHERW'L	0-3		Sat 15 May	MOTHERW'L	0-1
Sat 6 Feb	East Stirling're	1-0				

Played 39 **W21; D8; L10;**
F65; A37; **Pts.50.** **3rd.**

Scottish League Championship First Division 1982-1983

Sat 4 Sep	Queen's Park	2-1		Mon 3 Jan	Airdrieonians	1-0
Sat 11 Sep	AYR UNITED	1-1		Sat 8 Jan	HAMILTON	2-1
Wed 15 Sep	St.Johnstone	1-1		Sat 15 Jan	Alloa Athletic	0-0
Sat 18 Sep	Falkirk	1-1		Sat 22 Jan	PARTICK TH.	0-1
Sat 25 Sep	CLYDE	1-0		Wed 9 Feb	Dunfermline	1-2
Wed 29 Sep	CLYDEBANK	4-1		Sat 12 Feb	AYR UNITED	5-1
Sat 2 Oct	Raith Rovers	0-1		Sat 26 Feb	Queen's Park	3-0
Wed 6 Oct	DUMBARTON	1-1		Sat 5 Mar	FALKIRK	1-2
Sat 9 Oct	ALLOA ATH.	3-0		Sat 19 Mar	PARTICK TH.	4-0
Sat 16 Oct	Hamilton Aca'l	3-1		Sat 26 Mar	CLYDE	3-1
Sat 23 Oct	DUNF/LINE	4-1		Tue 29 Mar	Raith Rovers	2-4
Sat 30 Oct	Partick Thistle	1-1		Sat 2 Apr	Airdrieonians	2-0
Sat 6 Nov	AIRDRIE	2-4		Wed 6 Apr	QUEEN'S P'K	2-0
Sat 13 Nov	Clydebank	3-0		Sat 9 Apr	St.Johnstone	1-2
Sat 20 Nov	FALKIRK	3-1		Sat 16 Apr	CLYDEBANK	2-2
Sat 27 Nov	Dumbarton	1-1		Sat 23 Apr	Alloa Athletic	1-1
Sat 4 Dec	RAITH ROV'S	2-0		Sat 30 Apr	DUNF/LINE	3-3
Sat 11 Dec	Clyde	3-2		Sat 7 May	Dumbarton	4-0
Mon 27 Dec	Ayr United	3-0		Sat 14 May	HAMILTON	2-0
Sat 1 Jan	St.JOHNST'E	1-0				

Played 39 **W22; D10; L7;**
F79; A38; **Pts.54.** **2nd.**

Scottish League Championship Premier Division 1983-1984

Sat 20 Aug	St.Johnstone	1-0		Sat 31 Dec	St.Johnstone	2-1
Sat 3 Sep	HIBERNIAN	3-2		Mon 2 Jan	HIBERNIAN	1-1
Sat 10 Sep	RANGERS	3-1		Sat 7 Jan	Dundee	1-4
Sat 17 Sep	Dundee	2-1		Sat 11 Feb	RANGERS	2-2
Sat 24 Sep	St.Mirren	1-0		Sat 25 Feb	Celtic	1-4
Sat 1 Oct	ABERDEEN	0-2		Sat 3 Mar	MOTHERW'L	2-1
Sat 8 Oct	MOTHERW'L	0-0		Sun 11 Mar	Dundee United	1-3
Sat 15 Oct	Celtic	1-1		Sat 17 Mar	St.Mirren	1-1
Sat 22 Oct	Dundee United	0-1		Sat 24 Mar	St.MIRREN	2-1
Sat 29 Oct	St.JOHNST'E	2-0		Sat 31 Mar	D/D UNITED	0-0
Sat 5 Nov	Hibernian	1-1		Mon 2 Apr	Aberdeen	1-1
Sun 13 Nov	DUNDEE	1-3		Sat 7 Apr	Rangers	0-0
Sat 19 Nov	Aberdeen	0-2		Sat 21 Apr	Hibernian	0-0
Sat 26 Nov	St.MIRREN	2-2		Sat 28 Apr	St.JOHNST'E	2-2
Sat 3 Dec	Rangers	0-3		Wed 2 May	ABERDEEN	0-1
Sat 10 Dec	D/D UNITED	0-0		Sat 5 May	CELTIC	1-1
Sat 17 Dec	CELTIC	1-3		Wed 9 May	DUNDEE	1-1
Mon 26 Dec	Motherwell	1-1		Sat 12 May	Motherwell	1-0

Played 36 **W10; D16; L10;**
F38; A47; **Pts.36.** **5th.**

Scottish League Championship Premier Division 1984–1985

Sat 11 Aug	Dundee United	0-2		Sat 15 Dec	Dundee United	2-5
Sat 18 Aug	MORTON	1-2		Sat 29 Dec	MORTON	1-0
Sat 25 Aug	Hibernian	2-1		Tue 1 Jan	Hibernian	2-1
Sat 1 Sep	DUMBARTON	1-0		Sat 5 Jan	DUMBARTON	5-1
Sat 8 Sep	St.MIRREN	1-2		Sat 12 Jan	St.MIRREN	0-1
Sat 15 Sep	Celtic	0-1		Sun 3 Feb	DUNDEE	3-3
Sat 22 Sep	DUNDEE	0-2		Sat 9 Feb	Aberedeen	2-2
Sat 29 Sep	Aberdeen	0-4		Sat 23 Feb	RANGERS	2-0
Sat 6 Oct	RANGERS	1-0		Sat 2 Mar	Morton	1-0
Sat 13 Oct	D/D UNITED	2-0		Sat 16 Mar	D/D UNITED	0-1
Sat 20 Oct	Morton	3-2		Wed 20 Mar	Celtic	2-3
Sat 27 Oct	HIBERNIAN	0-0		Sat 23 Mar	Dumbarton	3-1
Sat 3 Nov	Dumbarton	1-0		Tue 2 Apr	HIBERNIAN	2-2
Sat 10 Nov	St.Mirren	3-2		Sat 6 Apr	CELTIC	0-2
Sat 17 Nov	CELTIC	1-5		Sat 20 Apr	Dundee	0-3
Sat 24 Nov	Dundee	1-2		Sat 27 Apr	Rangers	1-3
Sat 1 Dec	ABERDEEN	1-2		Sat 4 May	ABERDEEN	0-3
Sat 8 Dec	Rangers	1-1		Sat 11 May	St.Mirren	2-5

Played 36 W13; D5; L18;
F47; A64; Pts.31.   7th.

Scottish League Championship Premier Division 1985–1986

Sat 10 Aug	CELTIC	1-1		Sat 14 Dec	CELTIC	1-1
Sat 17 Aug	St.Mirren	2-6		Sat 21 Dec	St.Mirren	1-0
Sat 24 Aug	Rangers	1-3		Sat 28 Dec	Rangers	2-0
Sat 31 Aug	HIBERNIAN	2-1		Wed 1 Jan	HIBERNIAN	3-1
Sat 7 Sep	Aberdeen	0-3		Sat 4 Jan	Motherwell	3-1
Sat 14 Sep	D/D UNITED	2-0		Sat 11 Jan	D/D UNITED	1-1
Sat 21 Sep	Motherwell	1-2		Sat 18 Jan	Aberdeen	1-0
Sat 28 Sep	Clydebank	0-1		Sat 1 Feb	Clydebank	1-1
Sat 5 Oct	DUNDEE	1-1		Sat 8 Feb	DUNDEE	3-1
Sat 12 Oct	Celtic	1-0		Sat 22 Feb	Celtic	1-1
Sat 19 Oct	St.MIRREN	3-0		Sat 15 Mar	MOTHERW'L	2-0
Wed 30 Oct	ABERDEEN	1-0		Sat 22 Mar	Hibernian	2-1
Sat 2 Nov	Dundee United	1-1		Tue 25 Mar	St.MIRREN	3-0
Sat 9 Nov	Hibernian	0-0		Sat 29 Mar	RANGERS	3-1
Sat 16 Nov	RANGERS	3-0		Sat 12 Apr	Dundee United	3-0
Sat 23 Nov	MOTHERW'L	3-0		Sun 20 Apr	ABERDEEN	1-1
Sat 30 Nov	CLYDEBANK	4-1		Sat 26 Apr	CLYDEBANK	1-0
Sat 7 Dec	Dundee	1-1		Sat 3 May	Dundee	0-2

Played 36 W20; D10; L6;
F59; A33; Pts.50.   2nd.

Scottish League Championship Premier Division 1986–1987

Sat 9 Aug	St.Mirren	0-0		Sat 6 Dec	St.Mirren	0-0
Wed 13 Aug	HAMILTON	1-0		Sat 13 Dec	HAMILTON	7-0
Sat 16 Aug	FALKIRK	1-0		Sat 20 Dec	Dundee United	1-3
Sat 23 Aug	Dundee United	0-1		Sat 27 Dec	FALKIRK	4-0
Sat 30 Aug	Hibernian	3-1		Sat 3 Jan	CLYDEBANK	3-0
Sat 6 Sep	CLYDEBANK	2-1		Tue 6 Jan	Hibernian	2-2
Sat 13 Sep	Aberdeen	1-0		Wed 21 Jan	Aberdeen	1-2
Sat 20 Sep	MOTHERW'L	4-0		Sat 24 Jan	Dundee	1-0
Sat 27 Sep	Dundee	0-0		Sat 7 Feb	RANGERS	2-5
Sat 4 Oct	RANGERS	1-1		Sat 14 Feb	Celtic	1-1
Wed 8 Oct	Celtic	0-2		Wed 25 Feb	MOTHERW'L	1-1
Sat 11 Oct	St.MIRREN	0-0		Sat 28 Feb	St.MIRREN	1-0
Sat 18 Oct	Hamilton Aca'l	3-1		Sat 7 Mar	Hamilton Aca'l	1-0
Sat 25 Oct	D/D UNITED	2-2		Sat 21 Mar	Falkirk	0-0
Wed 29 Oct	Falkirk	0-2		Sat 28 Mar	Clydebank	1-1
Sat 1 Nov	HIBERNIAN	1-1		Sat 4 Apr	HIBERNIAN	2-1
Sat 8 Nov	Clydebank	3-0		Wed 15 Apr	Motherwell	1-0
Sat 15 Nov	ABERDEEN	2-1		Sat 18 Apr	ABERDEEN	1-1
Wed 19 Nov	Motherwell	3-2		Sat 25 Apr	Rangers	0-3
Sat 22 Nov	DUNDEE	3-1		Sat 2 May	DUNDEE	1-3
Sat 29 Nov	Rangers	0-3		Sat 9 May	CELTIC	1-0
Wed 3 Dec	CELTIC	1-0		Mon 11 May	D/D UNITED	1-1

Played 44 W21; D14; L9;
F64; A43; Pts.56.   5th.

Scottish League Championship Premier Division 1987–1988

Date	Opponent	Score		Date	Opponent	Score
Sat 8 Aug	FALKIRK	4-2		Sat 5 Dec	FALKIRK	1-0
Wed 12 Aug	Celtic	0-1		Sat 12 Dec	Celtic	2-2
Sat 15 Aug	St.Mirren	1-1		Wed 16 Dec	MOTHERW'L	1-1
Sat 22 Aug	D/D UNITED	4-1		Sat 19 Dec	Dundee	0-0
Sat 29 Aug	HIBERNIAN	1-0		Sat 26 Dec	Morton	0-0
Sat 5 Sep	Morton	2-1		Sat 2 Jan	HIBERNIAN	0-0
Sat 12 Sep	MOTHERW'L	1-0		Sat 5 Jan	Dunfermline	4-0
Sat 19 Sep	Dundee	3-1		Sat 16 Jan	RANGERS	1-1
Sat 26 Sep	Dunfermline	1-0		Wed 3 Feb	D/D UNITED	1-1
Sat 3 Oct	RANGERS	0-0		Sat 6 Feb	St.Mirren	6-0
Wed 7 Oct	ABERDEEN	2-1		Sat 13 Feb	ABERDEEN	2-2
Sat 10 Oct	Falkirk	5-1		Sat 27 Feb	Falkirk	0-2
Sat 17 Oct	Hibernian	1-2		Tue 8 Mar	Motherwell	2-0
Sat 24 Oct	MORTON	3-0		Sat 19 Mar	Hibernian	0-0
Tue 27 Oct	Motherwell	3-0		Sat 26 Mar	MORTON	2-0
Sat 31 Oct	DUNDEE	4-2		Wed 30 Mar	DUNDEE	2-0
Sat 7 Nov	CELTIC	1-1		Sat 2 Apr	Rangers	2-1
Sat 14 Nov	Aberdeen	0-0		Wed 13 Apr	DUNF/LINE	2-1
Wed 18 Nov	Dundee United	3-0		Sat 16 Apr	CELTIC	2-1
Sat 21 Nov	St.MIRREN	0-0		Sat 23 Apr	Aberdeen	0-0
Tue 24 Nov	DUNF/LINE	3-2		Sat 30 Apr	St.MIRREN	0-1
Sat 28 Nov	Rangers	2-3		Sat 7 May	Dundee United	0-0

Played 44 W23; D16; L5;
F74; A32; Pts.62. 2nd.

Scottish League Championship Premier Division 1988–1989

Date	Opponent	Score		Date	Opponent	Score
Sat 13 Aug	Celtic	0-1		Sat 10 Dec	RANGERS	2-0
Sat 20 Aug	HAMILTON	3-2		Sat 17 Dec	HAMILTON	2-0
Sat 27 Aug	Hibernian	0-0		Sat 31 Dec	Celtic	2-4
Sat 3 Sep	St.MIRREN	1-2		Wed 4 Jan	Hibernian	0-1
Sat 17 Sep	RANGERS	1-2		Sat 7 Jan	St.MIRREN	2-0
Sat 24 Sep	Aberdeen	0-1		Sat 14 Jan	MOTHERW'L	0-0
Wed 28 Sep	DUNDEE	1-1		Sat 21 Jan	Dundee United	0-0
Sat 1 Oct	Dundee United	0-0		Sat 11 Feb	DUNDEE	3-1
Sat 8 Oct	MOTHERW'L	2-2		Sat 25 Feb	Aberdeen	0-3
Tue 11 Oct	Hamilton Aca'l	4-0		Sat 11 Mar	CELTIC	0-1
Sat 22 Oct	CELTIC	0-2		Sat 25 Mar	Hamilton Aca'l	2-0
Sat 29 Oct	ABERDEEN	1-1		Sat 1 Apr	HIBERNIAN	2-1
Tue 1 Nov	Rangers	0-3		Sat 8 Apr	St.Mirren	1-1
Sat 5 Nov	St.Mirren	1-1		Sat 15 Apr	Dundee	1-2
Sat 12 Nov	HIBERNIAN	1-2		Sat 22 Apr	ABERDEEN	1-0
Sat 19 Nov	D/D UNITED	0-0		Sat 29 Apr	Rangers	0-4
Sat 26 Nov	Motherwell	0-2		Sat 6 May	D/D UNITED	0-0
Sat 3 Dec	Dundee	1-1		Sat 13 May	Motherwell	1-1

Played 36 W9; D13; L14;
F35; A42; Pts.31. 6th.

Scottish League Championship Premier Division 1989–1990

Date	Opponent	Score		Date	Opponent	Score
Sat 12 Aug	CELTIC	1-3		Tue 26 Dec	CELTIC	0-0
Sat 19 Aug	St.Mirren	2-1		Sat 30 Dec	St.Mirren	0-2
Sat 26 Aug	HIBERNIAN	1-0		Mon 1 Jan	HIBERNIAN	2-0
Sat 9 Sep	Dundee	2-2		Sat 6 Jan	Dundee	1-0
Sat 16 Sep	Motherwell	3-1		Sat 13 Jan	Motherwell	3-0
Sat 23 Sep	D/D UNITED	1-1		Sat 27 Jan	D/D UNITED	3-2
Sat 30 Sep	Rangers	0-1		Sat 3 Feb	Aberdeen	2-2
Wed 4 Oct	DUNF/LINE	1-2		Sat 10 Feb	DUNF/LINE	0-2
Sat 14 Oct	Aberdeen	3-1		Sat 17 Feb	Rangers	0-0
Sat 21 Oct	Celtic	1-2		Sat 3 Mar	MOTHERW'L	2-0
Sat 28 Oct	St.MIRREN	4-0		Sat 10 Mar	Celtic	1-1
Sat 4 Nov	Hibernian	1-1		Sat 24 Mar	St.MIRREN	0-0
Sat 11 Nov	DUNDEE	6-3		Sat 31 Mar	Hibernian	2-1
Sat 18 Nov	MOTHERW'L	3-0		Wed 4 Apr	DUNDEE	0-0
Sat 25 Nov	Dundee United	1-2		Sat 14 Apr	Dunfermline	1-0
Sat 2 Dec	RANGERS	1-2		Sat 21 Apr	ABERDEEN	1-0
Sat 9 Dec	Dunfermline	2-0		Sat 28 Apr	Dundee United	1-1
Wed 20 Dec	ABERDEEN	1-1		Sat 5 May	RANGERS	1-1

Played 36 W16; D12; L8;
F54; A35; Pts.44. 3rd.

Scottish League Championship Premier Division 1990–1991

Sat 25 Aug	St.MIRREN	1-1		Sat 29 Dec	Celtic	1-1
Sat 1 Sep	Dunfermline	0-2		Wed 2 Jan	Hibernian	4-1
Sat 8 Sep	RANGERS	1-3		Sat 5 Jan	RANGERS	0-1
Sat 15 Sep	Hibernian	3-0		Sat 12 Jan	St.MIRREN	2-0
Sat 22 Sep	Celtic	0-3		Sat 2 Feb	Aberdeen	0-5
Sat 29 Sep	D/D UNITED	1-0		Sat 16 Feb	D/D UNITED	2-1
Sat 6 Oct	Motherwell	1-1		Sat 23 Feb	Dunfermline	1-3
Sat 13 Oct	St.JOHNST'E	2-3		Sat 2 Mar	Motherwell	3-1
Sat 20 Oct	Aberdeen	0-3		Wed 6 Mar	St.JOHNST'E	2-1
Sat 27 Oct	St.Mirren	1-2		Sat 9 Mar	Rangers	1-2
Sat 3 Nov	DUNF/LINE	1-1		Sat 23 Mar	HIBERNIAN	3-1
Sat 10 Nov	CELTIC	1-0		Sat 30 Mar	St.Mirren	0-0
Sat 17 Nov	Dundee United	1-1		Sat 6 Apr	DUNF/LINE	4-1
Sat 24 Nov	HIBERNIAN	1-1		Sat 13 Apr	ABERDEEN	1-4
Sat 1 Dec	Rangers	0-4		Sat 20 Apr	St.Johnstone	2-0
Sat 8 Dec	ABERDEEN	1-0		Sat 27 Apr	CELTIC	0-1
Sat 15 Dec	St.Johnstone	1-2		Sat 4 May	Dundee United	1-2
Sat 22 Dec	MOTHERW'L	3-2		Sat 11 May	MOTHERW'L	2-1

Played 36 **W14; D7; L15;**
F48; A55; **Pts.35.** **5th.**

Scottish League Championship Premier Division 1991–1992

Sat 10 Aug	Dunfermline	2-1		Sat 7 Dec	Dunfermline	2-0
Tue 13 Aug	Airdrieonians	3-2		Sat 14 Dec	MOTHERW'L	3-1
Sat 17 Aug	RANGERS	1-0		Sat 21 Dec	St.Mirren	1-0
Sat 24 Aug	St.Johnstone	1-0		Sat 28 Dec	St.Johnstone	5-0
Sat 31 Aug	HIBERNIAN	0-0		Wed 1 Jan	HIBERNIAN	1-1
Sat 7 Sep	MOTHERW'L	2-0		Sat 4 Jan	Celtic	2-1
Sat 14 Sep	St.Mirren	3-2		Sat 11 Jan	ABERDEEN	0-4
Sat 21 Sep	D/D UNITED	1-1		Sat 18 Jan	Airdrieonians	1-2
Sat 28 Sep	Falkirk	2-1		Sat 1 Feb	RANGERS	0-1
Sat 5 Oct	Celtic	1-3		Sat 8 Feb	D/D UNITED	1-0
Wed 9 Oct	ABERDEEN	1-0		Sat 29 Feb	CELTIC	1-2
Sat 12 Oct	DUNF/LINE	1-0		Wed 4 Mar	Falkirk	2-1
Sat 19 Oct	Rangers	0-2		Sat 14 Mar	St.JOHNST'E	2-0
Sat 26 Oct	Motherwell	1-0		Wed 18 Mar	Aberdeen	0-2
Wed 30 Oct	St.MIRREN	0-0		Sat 21 Mar	Hibernian	2-1
Sat 2 Nov	Hibernian	1-1		Sat 28 Mar	DUNF/LINE	1-0
Sat 9 Nov	St.JOHNST'E	2-1		Tue 7 Apr	Motherwell	1-0
Sat 16 Nov	CELTIC	3-1		Sat 11 Apr	St.MIRREN	0-0
Wed 20 Nov	Aberdeen	2-0		Sat 18 Apr	Dundee United	0-2
Sat 23 Nov	Dundee United	1-0		Sat 25 Apr	AIRDRIE	2-2
Sat 30 Nov	AIRDRIE	1-0		Tue 28 Apr	Rangers	1-1
Wed 4 Dec	FALKIRK	1-1		Sat 2 May	FALKIRK	2-0

Played 44 **W27; D9; L8;**
F60; A37; **Pts.63.** **2nd.**

Scottish League Championship Premier Division 1992–1993

Sat 1 Aug	CELTIC	0-1		Sat 19 Dec	CELTIC	1-0
Wed 5 Aug	FALKIRK	3-0		Sat 26 Dec	PARTICK TH.	1-1
Sat 8 Aug	Dundee United	1-1		Sat 2 Jan	Hibernian	0-0
Sat 15 Aug	PARTICK TH.	2-1		Wed 20 Jan	St.JOHNST'E	2-0
Sat 22 Aug	Hibernian	0-0		Sat 23 Jan	MOTHERW'L	0-0
Sat 29 Aug	MOTHERW'L	1-0		Sat 30 Jan	Dundee United	1-0
Tue 1 Sep	Dundee	3-1		Wed 3 Feb	Dundee	0-1
Sat 12 Sep	ABERDEEN	1-0		Sat 13 Feb	FALKIRK	3-1
Sat 19 Sep	Rangers	0-2		Sat 20 Feb	Airdrieonians	0-0
Sat 26 Sep	Airdrieonians	0-1		Sat 27 Feb	Rangers	1-2
Sat 3 Oct	St.JOHNST'E	1-1		Wed 10 Mar	Celtic	0-1
Wed 7 Oct	Celtic	1-1		Sat 13 Mar	D/D UNITED	1-0
Sat 17 Oct	D/D UNITED	1-0		Sat 20 Mar	HIBERNIAN	1-0
Sat 24 Oct	Motherwell	3-1		Sat 27 Mar	Partick Thistle	1-1
Sat 31 Oct	DUNDEE	1-0		Sat 10 Apr	DUNDEE	0-0
Sat 7 Nov	HIBERNIAN	1-0		Wed 14 Apr	RANGERS	2-3
Tue 10 Nov	Partick Thistle	1-1		Sat 17 Apr	Aberdeen	2-3
Sat 21 Nov	RANGERS	1-1		Tue 20 Apr	Motherwell	1-2
Sat 28 Nov	Aberdeen	2-6		Sat 1 May	Falkirk	0-6
Wed 2 Dec	Falkirk	1-2		Wed 5 May	ABERDEEN	1-2
Sat 5 Dec	AIRDRIE	1-3		Sat 8 May	AIRDRIE	1-1
Sat 12 Dec	St.Johnstone	1-1		Sat 15 May	St.Johnstone	1-3

Played 44 **W15; D14; L15;**
F46; A51; **Pts.44.** **5th.**

Scottish League Championship Premier Division 1993–1994

Sat 7 Aug	Rangers	1-2		Sat 18 Dec	RAITH ROV'S	0-1
Sat 14 Aug	RAITH ROV'S	1-0		Mon 27 Dec	Rangers	2-2
Sat 21 Aug	HIBERNIAN	1-0		Sat 8 Jan	Dundee United	0-3
Sat 28 Aug	Dundee United	0-0		Wed 12 Jan	HIBERNIAN	1-1
Sat 4 Sep	PARTICK TH.	2-1		Sat 15 Jan	PARTICK TH.	1-0
Sat 11 Sep	Motherwell	0-2		Sat 22 Jan	KILMARN'K	1-1
Sat 18 Sep	KILMARN'K	0-1		Sat 6 Feb	Motherwell	1-1
Sat 25 Sep	CELTIC	1-0		Sat 12 Feb	CELTIC	0-2
Sat 2 Oct	Dundee	0-2		Tue 1 Mar	Dundee	2-0
Tue 5 Oct	Aberdeen	0-0		Sat 5 Mar	Aberdeen	1-0
Sat 9 Oct	St.JOHNST'E	1-1		Sat 19 Mar	Raith Rovers	2-2
Sat 16 Oct	Raith Rovers	0-1		Sat 26 Mar	RANGERS	1-2
Sat 23 Oct	Partick Thistle	0-0		Wed 30 Mar	MOTHERW'L	0-0
Sat 30 Oct	Hibernian	2-0		Sat 2 Apr	Kilmarnock	1-0
Wed 3 Nov	RANGERS	2-2		Wed 6 Apr	St.JOHNST'E	2-2
Sat 6 Nov	D/D UNITED	1-1		Sat 9 Apr	Celtic	2-2
Sat 13 Nov	DUNDEE	1-2		Sat 16 Apr	DUNDEE	0-2
Sat 20 Nov	Celtic	0-0		Sat 23 Apr	St.Johnstone	0-0
Tue 30 Nov	Kilmarnock	0-0		Wed 27 Apr	ABERDEEN	1-1
Sat 4 Dec	ABERDEEN	1-1		Sat 30 Apr	Hibernian	0-0
Sat 11 Dec	St.Johnstone	0-2		Sat 7 May	D/D UNITED	2-0
Wed 15 Dec	MOTHERW'L	2-3		Sat 14 May	Partick Thistle	1-0

Played 44   W11; D20; L13;
F37; A43;   Pts.42.   7th.

Scottish League Championship Premier Division 1994–1995

Sat 13 Aug	Aberdeen	1-3		Sun 8 Jan	Motherwell	2-1
Sat 20 Aug	Motherwell	1-1		Wed 11 Jan	Celtic	1-1
Sat 27 Aug	HIBERNIAN	0-1		Sat 14 Jan	D/D UNITED	2-0
Sun 11 Sep	Rangers	0-3		Wed 18 Jan	HIBERNIAN	2-0
Sat 17 Sep	D/D UNITED	2-1		Sat 21 Jan	Rangers	0-1
Sat 24 Sep	KILMARN'K	3-0		Sat 4 Feb	Falkirk	0-2
Sat 1 Oct	Falkirk	1-2		Sat 11 Feb	KILMARN'K	2-2
Sat 8 Oct	Partick Thistle	1-0		Sat 25 Feb	CELTIC	1-1
Sat 15 Oct	CELTIC	1-0		Sat 18 Mar	RANGERS	2-1
Sat 22 Oct	ABERDEEN	2-0		Tue 21 Mar	Dundee United	1-1
Sat 29 Oct	Hibernian	1-2		Sat 1 Apr	FALKIRK	0-1
Sat 5 Nov	MOTHERW'L	1-2		Tue 4 Apr	Partick Thistle	1-3
Wed 9 Nov	RANGERS	1-1		Wed 12 Apr	Kilmarnock	2-3
Sat 19 Nov	Dundee United	2-5		Sat 15 Apr	PARTICK TH.	0-1
Sat 26 Nov	Kilmarnock	1-3		Wed 19 Apr	Celtic	1-0
Sat 3 Dec	FALKIRK	1-1		Sat 29 Apr	ABERDEEN	1-2
Mon 26 Dec	PARTICK TH.	3-0		Sat 6 May	Hibernian	1-3
Sat 31 Dec	Aberdeen	1-3		Sat 13 May	MOTHERW'L	2-0

Played 36   W12; D7; L17;
F44; A51;   Pts.43.   6th.

Scottish League Championship Premier Division 1995–1996

Sat 26 Aug	MOTHERW'L	1-1		Mon 1 Jan	Hibernian	1-2
Sat 9 Sep	FALKIRK	4-1		Sat 6 Jan	Partick Thistle	1-0
Sat 16 Sep	Partick Thistle	0-2		Wed 10 Jan	MOTHERW'L	4-0
Sat 23 Sep	CELTIC	0-4		Sat 13 Jan	FALKIRK	2-1
Sun 1 Oct	Hibernian	2-2		Wed 17 Jan	CELTIC	1-2
Wed 4 Oct	ABERDEEN	1-2		Sat 20 Jan	Rangers	3-0
Sat 7 Oct	Kilmarnock	1-3		Sat 3 Feb	RAITH ROV'S	2-0
Sat 14 Oct	RAITH ROV'S	4-2		Sat 10 Feb	ABERDEEN	1-3
Sat 21 Oct	Rangers	1-4		Sat 24 Feb	Kilmarnock	2-0
Sat 28 Oct	Falkirk	0-2		Sat 2 Mar	Celtic	0-4
Sat 4 Nov	PARTICK TH.	3-0		Sat 16 Mar	HIBERNIAN	1-1
Tue 7 Nov	Motherwell	0-0		Sat 23 Mar	PARTICK TH.	2-5
Sat 11 Nov	KILMARN'K	2-1		Sat 30 Mar	Falkirk	2-0
Sun 19 Nov	HIBERNIAN	2-1		Wed 10 Apr	RANGERS	2-0
Sat 25 Nov	Celtic	1-3		Sat 13 Apr	Raith Rovers	3-1
Sat 2 Dec	RANGERS	0-2		Sat 20 Apr	Aberdeen	1-1
Sat 9 Dec	Raith Rovers	1-1		Sat 27 Apr	KILMARN'K	1-0
Sat 16 Dec	Aberdeen	2-1		Sat 4 May	Motherwell	1-1

Played 36   W16; D7; L13;
F55; A53'   Pts.55.   4th.

Scottish League Championship Premier Division 1996–1997

Sat 17 Aug	KILMARN'K	3-2		Thu 26 Dec	Dunfermline	3-2
Sun 25 Aug	Aberdeen	0-4		Sat 28 Dec	MOTHERW'L	4-1
Sat 7 Sep	D/D UNITED	1-0		Wed 1 Jan	Hibernian	4-0
Tue 10 Sep	Dunfermline	1-2		Sat 4 Jan	Raith Rovers	2-1
Sat 14 Sep	Rangers	0-3		Sat 11 Jan	CELTIC	1-2
Sat 21 Sep	MOTHERW'L	1-1		Sat 18 Jan	D/D UNITED	1-2
Sat 28 Sep	Hibernian	3-1		Sat 1 Feb	Rangers	0-0
Sat 12 Oct	Raith Rovers	1-1		Sat 8 Feb	KILMARN'K	2-0
Sun 20 Oct	CELTIC	2-2		Mon 10 Feb	Aberdeen	0-0
Sat 26 Oct	Dundee United	0-1		Sat 22 Feb	RAITH ROV'S	3-2
Sat 2 Nov	DUNF/LINE	2-0		Sat 1 Mar	Celtic	0-2
Mon 11 Nov	Motherwell	2-0		Sat 15 Mar	HIBERNIAN	1-0
Sat 16 Nov	HIBERNIAN	0-0		Sat 22 Mar	Motherwell	1-0
Sat 30 Nov	Celtic	2-2		Sat 5 Apr	Kilmarnock	0-1
Sat 7 Dec	RAITH ROV'S	0-0		Sat 12 Apr	ABERDEEN	0-0
Wed 11 Dec	ABERDEEN	1-2		Sat 19 Apr	DUNF/LINE	1-1
Sat 14 Dec	Kilmarnock	0-2		Sat 3 May	Dundee United	0-1
Sat 21 Dec	RANGERS	1-4		Sat 10 May	RANGERS	3-1

Played 36　　W14; D10; L12;
D46; A43;　　Pts.52.　　　　　　　　　　4th.

Scottish League Championship Premier Division 1997–1998

Mon 4 Aug	Rangers	1-3		Sat 27 Dec	Dunfermline	3-1
Sat 16 Aug	ABERDEEN	4-1		Thu 1 Jan	HIBERNIAN	2-2
Sat 23 Aug	Dunfermline	1-2		Mon 12 Jan	St.Johnstone	3-2
Sat 30 Aug	Hibernian	1-0		Sat 17 Jan	Kilmarnock	2-2
Sat 13 Sep	St.Johnstone	2-1		Sat 31 Jan	D/D UNITED	2-0
Sat 20 Sep	D/D UNITED	2-1		Sun 8 Feb	CELTIC	1-1
Sat 27 Sep	Kilmarnock	3-0		Sat 21 Feb	Motherwell	4-2
Sat 4 Oct	Motherwell	4-1		Wed 25 Feb	ABERDEEN	3-1
Sat 18 Oct	CELTIC	1-2		Sat 28 Feb	Rangers	2-2
Tue 29 Oct	DUNF/LINE	3-1		Sat 14 Mar	KILMARN'K	1-1
Sat 1 Nov	Aberdeen	4-1		Sat 21 Mar	Dundee United	1-0
Sat 8 Nov	HIBERNIAN	2-0		Sat 28 Mar	Celtic	0-0
Sat 15 Nov	St.JOHNST'E	2-1		Wed 8 Apr	MOTHERW'L	1-1
Sun 23 Nov	KILMARN'K	5-3		Sat 11 Apr	Hibernian	1-2
Sat 6 Dec	MOTHERW'L	2-0		Sat 18 Apr	St.JOHNST'E	1-1
Tue 9 Dec	Dundee United	0-0		Sat 25 Apr	RANGERS	0-3
Sat 13 Dec	Celtic	0-1		Sat 2 May	Aberdeen	2-2
Sat 20 Dec	RANGERS	2-5		Sat 9 May	DUNF/LINE	2-0

Played 36　　W19; D10; L7;
F70; A46;　　Pts.67.　　　　　　　　　　3rd.

Scottish League Championship Premier Division 1998–1999

Sun 2 Aug	RANGERS	2-1		Sat 19 Dec	RANGERS	2-3
San 16 Aug	Dundee United	0-0		Sat 26 Dec	Kilmarnock	0-1
Sat 22 Aug	ABERDEEN	2-0		Wed 30 Dec	DUNDEE	1-2
Sun 30 Aug	Kilmarnock	0-3		Sat 2 Jan	Dunfermline	0-0
Sat 12 Sep	DUNDEE	0-2		Sat 30 Jan	MOTHERW'L	0-2
Sun 20 Sep	Dunfermline	1-1		Sat 6 Feb	Celtic	0-3
Wed 23 Sep	MOTHERW'L	3-0		Sat 20 Feb	St.JOHNST'E	0-2
Sat 26 Sep	Celtic	1-1		Sat 27 Feb	ABERDEEN	0-2
Sun 4 Oct	St.JOHNST'E	1-1		Sat 20 Mar	Dundee	0-2
Sat 17 Oct	Rangers	0-3		Sat 3 Apr	KILMARN'K	2-2
Sat 24 Oct	D/D UNITED	0-1		Tue 6 Apr	Dundee United	3-1
Sat 31 Oct	Dundee	0-1		Wed 14 Apr	CELTIC	2-4
Sat 7 Nov	KILMARN'K	2-1		Sat 17 Apr	St.Johnstone	0-0
Sat 14 Nov	Motherwell	2-3		Sat 24 Apr	Motherwell	4-0
Sat 21 Nov	DUNF/LINE	2-1		Mon 3 May	DUNF/LINE	2-0
Sat 6 Dec	CELTIC	2-1		Sun 9 May	Rangers	0-0
Wed 9 Dec	St.Johnstone	1-1		Sat 15 May	D/D UNITED	4-1
Sat 12 Dec	Aberdeen	0-2		Sun 23 May	Aberdeen	5-2

Played 36　　W11; D9; L16;
F44; A50;　　Pts.42.　　　　　　　　　　6th.

Scottish League Championship Premier Division 1999-2000

Sat 31 Jul	St.Johnstone	4-1		Sat 22 Jan	DUNDEE	2-0
Sat 7 Aug	RANGERS	0-4		Sat 5 Feb	Celtic	3-2
Sat 14 Aug	Hibernian	1-1		Sat 26 Feb	KILMARN'K	0-0
Sun 22 Aug	ABERDEEN	3-0		Wed 1 Mar	Motherwell	2-0
Sun 29 Aug	Celtic	0-4		Sat 4 Mar	Dundee United	1-0
Sat 11 Sep	DUNDEE	4-0		Wed 15 Mar	St.Johnstone	1-0
Sat 25 Sep	Dundee United	2-0		Sat 18 Mar	Hibernian	1-3
Sat 16 Oct	St.JOHNST'E	1-1		Wed 22 Mar	ABERDEEN	3-0
Wed 27 Oct	KILMARN'K	2-2		Sat 25 Mar	MOTHERW'L	0-0
Sat 30 Oct	Dundee	0-1		Sat 1 Apr	Dundee	0-0
Sat 6 Nov	MOTHERW'L	1-1		Sat 8 Apr	CELTIC	1-0
Sat 20 Nov	CELTIC	1-2		Wed 12 Apr	RANGERS	1-2
Tue 23 Nov	Motherwell	1-2		Sat 15 Apr	Aberdeen	2-1
Sat 27 Nov	Kilmarnock	2-2		Sat 22 Apr	D/D UNITED	1-2
Sun 5 Dec	D/D UNITED	3-0		Sat 29 Apr	Kilmarnock	1-0
Wed 8 Dec	Aberdeen	1-3		Sat 6 May	St.JOHNST'E	0-0
Sun 19 Dec	HIBERNIAN	0-3		Sat 13 May	Rangers	0-1
Wed 22 Dec	Rangers	0-1		Sun 21 May	HIBERNIAN	2-1

Played 36 W15; D9; L12;
F47; A40; Pts.54. 3rd.

Scottish Premier League Championship 2000-2001

Sun 30 Jul	HIBERNIAN	0-0		Sat 9 Dec	Kilmarnock	3-0
Sun 6 Aug	St.Johnstone	2-2		Sat 16 Dec	Motherwell	0-2
Sun 13 Aug	Aberdeen	1-1		Sat 23 Dec	D/D UNITED	3-1
Sat 19 Aug	CELTIC	2-4		Tue 26 Dec	HIBERNIAN	1-1
Sun 27 Aug	Dundee	1-1		Sat 30 Dec	St.Johnstone	2-2
Sat 9 Sep	DUNF/LINE	2-0		Tue 2 Jan	Aberdeen	0-1
Sun 17 Sep	Rangers	0-1		Wed 31 Jan	St.MIRREN	1-0
Wed 20 Sep	St.MIRREN	2-0		Sun 4 Feb	CELTIC	0-3
Sun 24 Sep	KILMARN'K	0-2		Sat 24 Feb	DUNF/LINE	7-1
Sun 1 Oct	MOTHERW'L	3-0		Sat 3 Mar	Rangers	0-2
Sat 14 Oct	Dundee United	4-0		Wed 14 Mar	KILMARN'K	3-0
Sun 22 Oct	Hibernian	2-6		Sun 18 Mar	Dundee	0-0
Sat 28 Oct	St.JOHNST'E	0-3		Sat 31 Mar	MOTHERW'L	3-0
Sat 4 Nov	ABERDEEN	3-0		Sat 7 Apr	Dundee United	1-1
Sat 11 Nov	St.Mirren	2-1		Sun 22 Apr	Celtic	0-1
Sat 18 Nov	Celtic	1-6		Fri 27 Apr	Kilmarnock	1-1
Sat 25 Nov	DUNDEE	3-1		Sat 5 May	RANGERS	1-4
Wed 29 Nov	Dunfermline	0-1		Sun 13 May	Hibernian	0-0
Sun 3 Dec	RANGERS	0-1		Sun 20 May	DUNDEE	2-0

Played 38 W14; D10; L14;
F56; A50; Pts.52. 5th.

Scottish Premier League Championship 2001-2002

Sat 28 Jul	Livingston	1-2		Sat 22 Dec	MOTHERW'L	3-1
Sat 4 Aug	ABERDEEN	1-0		Wed 26 Dec	Dundee United	2-0
Sat 11 Aug	Celtic	0-2		Sat 29 Dec	HIBERNIAN	1-1
Sat 18 Aug	DUNDEE	3-1		Wed 2 Jan	St.Johnstone	2-0
Sat 25 Aug	Dunfermline	1-0		Sat 12 Jan	ABERDEEN	3-1
Sat 8 Sep	RANGERS	2-2		Sat 19 Jan	Livingston	0-2
Sun 16 Sep	Kilmarnock	0-1		Wed 23 Jan	Celtic	0-2
Sat 22 Sep	Motherwell	0-2		Sat 2 Feb	Dunfermline	1-1
Sat 29 Sep	D/D UNITED	1-2		Sat 9 Feb	RANGERS	0-2
Sat 13 Oct	St.JOHNST'E	3-0		Sat 16 Feb	Kilmarnock	3-3
Sun 21 Oct	Hibernian	1-2		Sat 2 Mar	Motherwell	2-1
Sat 27 Oct	Aberdeen	2-3		Sat 9 Mar	D/D UNITED	1-2
Sat 3 Nov	LIVINGSTON	1-3		Sat 16 Mar	Hibernian	2-1
Sat 10 Nov	DUNDEE	2-0		Sat 23 Mar	St.JOHNST'E	1-3
Sat 17 Nov	CELTIC	0-1		Sun 7 Apr	Rangers	0-2
Sat 24 Nov	Dundee	1-1		Sat 13 Apr	Aberdeen	3-2
Sat 1 Dec	DUNF/LINE	1-1		Sat 20 Apr	DUNF/LINE	2-0
Sun 9 Dec	Rangers	1-3		Sun 28 Apr	CELTIC	1-4
Sat 15 Dec	KILMARN'K	2-0		Sun 12 May	LIVINGSTON	2-3

Played 38 W14; D6; L18;
F52; A57; Pts.48;. 5th.

Scottish Premier League Championship 2002–2003

Sat 3 Aug	Dundee	1-1		Sat 14 Dec	PARTICK TH.	1-0
Sun 11 Aug	HIBERNIAN	5-1		Sat 21 Dec	Dundee United	3-0
Sun 18 Aug	Aberdeen	1-1		Thu 26 Dec	Celtic	2-4
Sat 24 Aug	DUNF/LINE	2-0		Sun 29 Dec	Dundee	2-1
Sat 31 Aug	KILMARN'K	1-1		Thu 2 Jan	HIBERNIAN	4-4
Wed 11 Sep	Rangers	0-2		Tue 28 Jan	Aberdeen	1-0
Sun 15 Sep	MOTHERW'L	4-2		Sat 1 Feb	DUNF/LINE	3-0
Sat 21 Sep	D/D UNITED	2-0		Sat 8 Feb	KILMARN'K	3-0
Sat 28 Sep	Partick Thistle	2-2		Sat 15 Feb	Rangers	0-1
Sun 6 Oct	Livingston	1-1		Sat 1 Mar	MOTHERW'L	2-1
Sun 20 Oct	CELTIC	1-4		Sat 8 Mar	Livingston	1-1
Sat 26 Oct	DUNDEE	1-2		Sat 5 Apr	D/D UNITED	2-1
Sun 3 Nov	Hibernian	2-1		Sat 12 Apr	Partick Thistle	1-1
Sat 9 Nov	ABERDEEN	0-0		Sat 19 Apr	CELTIC	2-1
Sun 17 Nov	Dunfermline	1-3		Sat 26 Apr	Dunfermline	1-0
Sat 23 Nov	Kilmarnock	1-0		Sat 3 May	Kilmarnock	0-1
Sun 1 Dec	RANGERS	0-4		Sat 10 May	Celtic	0-1
Wed 4 Dec	Motherwell	1-6		Sun 18 May	RANGERS	0-2
Sat 7 Dec	LIVINGSTON	2-1		Sun 25 May	DUNDEE	1-0

Played 38	W18; D9; L11;	
F57; A51;	Pts.63.	3rd.

Scottish Premier League Championship 2003–2004

Sat 9 Aug	ABERDEEN	2-0		Sun 18 Jan	CELTIC	0-1
Sun 17 Aug	Hibernian	0-1		Sat 24 Jan	PARTICK TH.	2-0
Sat 23 Aug	D/D UNITED	3-0		Wed 11 Feb	ABERDEEN	1-0
Sun 31 Aug	DUNF/LINE	1-0		Sun 15 Feb	Hibernian	1-1
Sat 13 Sep	Kilmarnock	2-0		Sat 21 Feb	D/D UNITED	3-1
Sun 21 Sep	RANGERS	0-4		Tue 24 Feb	Livingston	3-2
Sat 27 Sep	Motherwell	1-1		Sat 28 Feb	Dunfermline	0-0
Sat 4 Oct	DUNDEE	2-2		Sun 7 Mar	Kilmarnock	1-1
Sat 18 Oct	Celtic	0-5		Sat 13 Mar	RANGERS	1-1
Sat 25 Oct	Partick Thistle	4-1		Sat 27 Mar	DUNDEE	3-1
Sat 1 Nov	LIVINGSTON	3-1		Sat 3 Apr	Celtic	2-2
Sun 9 Nov	Aberdeen	1-0		Wed 7 Apr	Motherwell	1-1
Sun 23 Nov	HIBERNIAN	2-0		Sat 10 Apr	Partick Thistle	0-1
Sun 30 Nov	Dundee United	1-2		Sat 17 Apr	LIVINGSTON	1-1
Sat 6 Dec	Dunfermline	1-2		Sun 25 Apr	CELTIC	1-1
Sat 13 Dec	KILMARN'K	2-1		Sat 1 May	Dundee United	2-0
Sat 20 Dec	Rangers	1-2		Sat 8 May	DUNF'LINE	2-1
Sat 27 Dec	MOTHERW'L	0-0		Wed 12 May	Rangers	1-0
Tue 6 Jan	Dundee	2-1		Sun 16 May	MOTHERW'L	3-2

Played 38	W19; D11; L8;	
F56; A40;	Pts.68.	3rd.

Scottish Premier League Championship 2004–2005

Sat 7 Aug	Dundee	1-0		Sun 2 Jan	Hibernian	1-1
Sat 14 Aug	ABERDEEN	0-0		Sat 15 Jan	D/D UNITED	3-2
Sat 21 Aug	KILMARN'K	3-0		Sat 22 Jan	Dundee	1-1
Sat 28 Aug	Motherwell	0-2		Tue 25 Jan	Livingston	2-1
Sun 12 Sep	RANGERS	0-0		Sat 29 Jan	ABERDEEN	1-0
Sun 19 Sep	Dunfermline	0-1		Sat 12 Feb	KILMARN'K	3-0
Sat 25 Sep	INV'NESS CT	1-0		Sat 19 Feb	Motherwell	0-2
Sun 3 Oct	LIVINGSTON	0-0		Wed 2 Mar	RANGERS	1-2
Sat 16 Oct	Celtic	0-3		Sat 5 Mar	Dunfermline	1-1
Sun 24 Oct	HIBERNIAN	2-1		Sat 12 Mar	INV'NESS CT	0-2
Wed 27 Oct	Dundee United	1-1		Sat 19 Mar	LIVINGSTON	3-1
Sat 30 Oct	DUNDEE	3-0		Sat 2 Apr	Celtic	2-0
Sun 7 Nov	Aberdeen	1-0		Wed 13 Apr	HIBERNIAN	1-2
Sat 13 Nov	Kilmarnock	1-1		Sat 16 Apr	Dundee United	1-2
Sat 20 Nov	MOTHERW'L	0-1		Sat 23 Apr	Hibernian	2-2
Sun 28 Nov	Rangers	2-3		Sat 30 Apr	MOTHERW'L	0-0
Sat 4 Dec	DUNF'LINE	3-0		Sat 7 May	Rangers	1-2
Sat 11 Dec	Inverness C T	1-1		Sun 15 May	CELTIC	1-2
Sun 26 Dec	CELTIC	0-2		Sun 22 May	Aberdeen	0-2

Played 38	W13; D11; L14;	
F43; A41;	Pts.50.	5th.

Scottish Premier League Championship 2005–2006

Sat 30 Jul	Kilmarnock	4-2		Mon 26 Dec	FALKIRK	5-0
Sun 7 Aug	HIBERNIAN	4-0		Sun 1 Jan	CELTIC	2 3
Sun 14 Aug	Dundee United	3-0		Sat 14 Jan	Dunfermline	4-1
Sat 20 Aug	ABERDEEN	2-0		Sat 21 Jan	Kilmarnock	0-1
Sat 27 Aug	MOTHERW'L	2-1		Sat 28 Jan	HIBERNIAN	4-1
Sun 11 Sep	Livingston	4 1		Tue 7 Feb	Dundee United	1-1
Sat 17 Sep	Inverness C T	1-0		Sat 11 Feb	ABERDEEN	1-2
Sat 24 Sep	RANGERS	1-0		Sat 18 Feb	MOTHEREW'L	3-0
Sun 2 Oct	Falkirk	2-2		Sun 5 Mar	Livingston	3-2
Sat 15 Oct	Celtic	1-1		Sat 11 Mar	Inverness C T	0-0
Sat 22 Oct	DUNF'LINE	2-0		Sun 19 Mar	RANGERS	1-1
Wed 26 Oct	KILMARN'K	1-0		Sat 25 Mar	Falkirk	2-1
Sat 29 Oct	Hibernian	0-2		Wed 5 Apr	Celtic	0-1
Sat 5 Nov	D/D UNITED	3-0		Sat 8 Apr	DUNF'LINE	4-0
Sun 20 Nov	Aberdeen	1-1		Sat 15 Apr	KILMARN'K	2-0
Sat 26 Nov	Motherwell	1-1		Sat 22 Apr	Hibernian	1-2
Sat 3 Dec	LIVINGSTON	2-1		Sun 30 Apr	CELTIC	3-0
Sat 10 Dec	INV'NESS CT	0-0		Wed 3 May	ABERDEEN	1-0
Sat 17 Dec	Rangers	0-1		Sun 7 May	Rangers	0-2

Played 38   W22; D8; L8;
F71; A31;   Pts.74.   2nd.

Scottish Premier League Championship 2006–2007

Sat 29 Jul	Dunfermline	2-1		Sat 23 Dec	Dundee United	1-0
Sun 6 Aug	CELTIC	2-1		Tue 26 Dec	HIBERNIAN	3-2
Sat 12 Aug	FALKIRK	0-0		Sat 30 Dec	Kilmarnock	0-0
Sat 19 Aug	Rangers	0-2		Tue 2 Jan	Dunfermline	1-0
Sat 26 Aug	INV'NESS CT	4-1		Sun 14 Jan	CELTIC	1-2
Sat 9 Sep	ST.MIRREN	0-1		Sat 20 Jan	FALKIRK	1-0
Sun 17 Sep	Motherwell	1-0		Sat 27 Jan	Rangers	0-0
Sun 24 Sep	Aberdeen	3-1		Sat 10 Feb	INV'NESS CT	1-0
Sun 1 Oct	D/D UNITED	4-0		Sat 17 Feb	ST.MIRREN	1-1
Sun 15 Oct	Hibernian	2-2		Mon 5 Mar	Motherwell	2-0
Sat 21 Oct	KILMARN'K	0-2		Sat 10 Mar	Aberdeen	0-1
Sat 28 Oct	DUNF'LINE	1-1		Sat 17 Mar	D/D UNITED	0-4
Sat 4 Nov	Celtic	1-2		Sun 1 Apr	Hibernian	1-0
Mon 13 Nov	Falkirk	1-1		Sat 7 Apr	KILMARN'K	1-0
Sun19 Nov	RANGERS	0-1		Sat 21 Apr	Rangers	1-2
Sat 25 Nov	Inverness CT	0-0		Sun 29 Apr	Celtic	3-1
Sat 2 Dec	St.Mirren	2-2		Sun 6 May	ABERDEEN	1-1
Sat 9 Dec	MOTHERW'L	4-1		Sat 12 May	HIBERNIAN	2-0
Sat 16 Dec	ABERDEEN	0-1		Sun 20 May	Kilmarnock	0-1

Played 38   W17; D10; L11;
F47; A35;   Pts.61.   4th.

Scottish Premier League Championship 2007–2008

Mon 6 Aug	HIBERNIAN	0-1		Sat 29 Dec	Falkirk	1-2
Sun 12 Aug	Aberdeen	1-1		Wed 2 Jan	Dundee United	1-4
Sat 18 Aug	GRETNA	1-1		Sat 5 Jan	KILMARN'K	1-1
Sat 25 Aug	Celtic	0-5		Sat 19 Jan	HIBERANIAN	1-0
Mon 3 Sep	Motherwell	2-0		Sat 26 Jan	Aberdeen	1-0
Sat 15 Sep	RANGERS	4-2		Sat 9 Feb	GRETNA	2-0
Sat 22 Sep	Inverness C T	1-2		Sat 16 Feb	Celtic	0-3
Sun 30 Sep	St.Mirren	3-1		Sat 23 Feb	Motherwell	1-0
Sat 6 Oct	FALKIRK	4-2		Wed 27 Feb	RANGERS	0-4
Sat 20 Oct	D/D UNITED	1-3		Sat 1 Mar	Inverness C T	3-0
Sat 27 Oct	Kilmarnock	1-3		Sat 15 Mar	St.Mirren	1-1
Sun 4 Nov	Hibernian	1-1		Sat 22 Mar	FALKIRK	0-0
Sun 11 Nov	ABERDEEN	4-1		Sat 29 Mar	D/D UNITED	1-0
Sun 25 Nov	Gretna	1-1		Sat 5 Apr	Kilmarnock	0-0
Sat 1 Dec	CELTIC	1-1		Sat 19 Apr	ST.MIRREN	3-2
Sat 8 Dec	MOTHERW'L	1-2		Sat 26 Apr	INV'NESS CT	1-0
Sat 15 Dec	Rangers	1-2		Mon 5 May	Falkirk	1-2
Sat 22 Dec	IN'NESS CT	2-3		Sat 10 May	KILMARN'K	0-2
Wed 26 Dec	ST.MIRREN	0-1		Tue 13 May	Gretna	0-1

Played 38   W13,D9,L16
F47;A55;   Pts.48.   8th.

Scottish Premier League Championship 2008–2009

Sat 9 Aug	MOTHERW'L	3-2	Sat 3 Jan	HIBERNIAN	0-0	
Sat 16 Aug	Rangers	0-2	Wed 7 Jan	Motherwell	0-1	
Sat 23 Aug	ST.MIRREN	2-1	Sat 17 Jan	Kilmarnock	2-0	
Sat 30 Aug	Hamilton	2-1	Sat 24 Jan	IN'NESS CT	3-2	
Sat 13 Sep	Falkirk	1-2	Sat 31 Jan	Hamilton	0-2	
Sat 20 Sep	IN'NESS CT	1-0	Sat 14 Feb	ABERDEEN	2-1	
Sat 27 Sep	Dundee United	0-3	Sat 21 Feb	ST.MIRREN	1-1	
Sat 4 Oct	KILMARN'K	1-2	Sat 28 Feb	Dundee United	1-0	
Sun 10 Oct	Hibernian	1-1	Wed 4 Mar	MOTHERW'L	2-1	
Sat 25 Oct	ABERDEEN	1-1	Sat 14 Mar	Hibernian	0-1	
Sun 2 Nov	CELTIC	0-2	Sat 21 Mar	Rangers	2-2	
Sat 8 Nov	St.Mirren	1-0	Sat 4 Apr	KILMARN'K	3-1	
Wed 12 Nov	HAMILTON	1-0	Sat 11 Apr	CELTIC	1-1	
Sat 15 Nov	Inverness CT	1-0	Sat 18 Apr	Falkirk	0-0	
Sat 22 Nov	FALKIRK	2-1	Sun 3 May	Rangers	0-2	
Sat 29 Nov	RANGERS	2-1	Thu 7 May	HIBERNIAN	0-1	
Sat 13 Dec	Celtic	1-1	Tue 12 May	Aberdeen	0-0	
Sat 20 Dec	D/D UNITED	0-0	Sat 16 May	D/D United	3-0	
Sat 27Dec	Aberdeen	0-1	Sun 24 May	Celtic	0-0	

Played 38	W16,D11,L11		
F40;A37;	Pts.59.	3rd.	